AFFIRMATIVE ACTION
AND RACIAL PREFERENCE

POINT/COUNTERPOINT SERIES

Series Editor

James P. Sterba, University of Notre Dame

GOD? A DEBATE BETWEEN A CHRISTIAN AND AN ATHEIST

William Lane Craig & Walter Sinnott-Armstrong

AFFIRMATIVE ACTION AND RACIAL PREFERENCE

Carl Cohen & James P. Sterba

AFFIRMATIVE ACTION AND RACIAL PREFERENCE

A DEBATE

Carl Cohen
James P. Sterba

OXFORD
UNIVERSITY PRESS
2003

OXFORD
UNIVERSITY PRESS

Oxford   New York
Auckland   Bangkok   Buenos Aires
Cape Town   Chennai   Dar es Salaam   Delhi   Hong Kong   Istanbul
Karachi   Kolkata   Kuala Lumpur   Madrid   Melbourne   Mexico City   Mumbai
Nairobi   São Paulo   Shanghai   Taipei   Tokyo   Toronto

Published by Oxford University Press, Inc.
198 Madison Avenue, New York, New York 10016

www.oup.com

Oxford is a registered trademark of Oxford University Press.

Library of Congress Cataloging-in-Publication Data
Cohen, Carl, 1931–
Affirmative action and racial preference : a debate / Carl Cohen, James P. Sterba.
p. cm.—(Point/counterpoint series)
Includes bibliographical references.
ISBN 0–19–514894–0 (cloth) ISBN 0–19–514895–9 (pbk.)
1. Affirmative action programs—Law and legislation—United States.
I. Sterba, James P.
II. Title.
III. Point/counterpoint series (Oxford, England).

KF4755.5.A95 2003
342.73'087—dc21   2003051868

9 8 7 6 5 4 3 2 1

Printed in the United States of America
on acid-free paper

CONTENTS

SECTION ONE: WHY RACE PREFERENCE IS WRONG AND BAD

Carl Cohen

SECTION TWO: DEFENDING AFFIRMATIVE ACTION, DEFENDING PREFERENCES

James P. Sterba

SECTION THREE: REPLY TO JAMES P. STERBA

Carl Cohen

SECTION FOUR: REPLY TO CARL COHEN

James P. Sterba

SECTION FIVE: COMMENTS ON THE SUPREME COURT DECISION

Carl Cohen and James P. Sterba

PREFACE ONE

Rejected by the Harvard law school some years ago, Stephen Carter (now a distinguished professor of law at Yale) was later called by a succession of Harvard officials who told him that his rejection had been a mistake. Said one: "We assumed from your record that you were white." Carter had been managing editor of the *Stanford Daily* as an undergraduate; Harvard, having acquired "additional information" about his skin color, now wanted him badly. "I was good enough for a top law school," Carter later wrote, "only because I happened to be black."

Race preference, ugly and unfair, is standard practice in American colleges and universities; it is enforced by rule in state and local governments, and in the federal government also; it plays a critical role in hiring and promotions in much of the private sector. Well-meaning racism is unhappily but widely ensconced. My essay, with which this book begins, presents the case for a great and wholesome change: the elimination of all preference by race.

The book continues with an essay in defense of race preference by my friend and colleague, James Sterba. He calls what he defends "affirmative action," and he defines affirmative action so that it will encompass both unobjectionable, non-preferential efforts to be fair *and* outright race preference. He is at liberty to define and defend as he pleases, of course. But clumping the just with the unjust obscures what is truly at issue. Many good policies are appropriately called affirmative action, but outright race preference is not made good by giving it that name.

The appropriate *order* of the pieces in this book was a source of intense disagreement between Professor Sterba and me. He very much wanted to present a defense of "affirmative action" first, to be followed by my critical essay. This was unacceptable to me because affirmative action (some of which is entirely honorable) is not the object of my critique, and I certainly do not wish to be understood as opposing all affirmative action. What I oppose are those forms of affirmative action giving preference to the members of some ethnic groups over the members of others.

Race preference is the heart of the matter now before the courts and the nation, and before us as well. How Professor Sterba defines affirmative action is not a matter of general interest, nor is it my concern in this book. The central question is this: shall persons of some races (and national origins) be preferred over persons of other races (and origins) *because of their race (or origin)*? Ought some be favored, and others disfavored, because of the color of their skin? I contend that preferential practices, whatever they may be called, are *morally wrong*. Invidious classifications by race are also *unlawful* in my view, and *unconstitutional*. In the highest courts of the land the uses of racial classifications were under attack even as we wrote, but the expression "affirmative action" is rarely encountered in those proceedings.

Beyond its wrongfulness, race preference is also unwise. It is counterproductive for the minorities preferred, and it does serious damage to relations among the races, on university campuses and in our society at large. Its consequences, on balance, are dreadful. And so we open with an essay condemning (*not* all affirmative action but) all preference by race. This essay I entitle: "Why Race Preference Is Wrong and Bad."

Carl Cohen
Ann Arbor, November 2002

PREFACE TWO

Work on this volume began in friendship and almost ended in a lawsuit. I invited Carl Cohen to coauthor this volume right after getting approval for the Point/Counterpoint Series from Oxford University Press. Professor Cohen and I signed a contract with Oxford, and after considerable discussion, agreed in writing that the order of our essays would be my defense followed by Professor Cohen's critique of affirmative action/racial preference. We subsequently publicly debated our topic at the University of Notre Dame using that same order for our presentations. However, later, when it was time for us to exchange our initial essays, Professor Cohen wanted the order of essays reversed. Rather than delay the timely publication of this volume with a lawsuit and destroy our friendship, I have agreed to reverse the order of our essays.

Professor Cohen's basic argument for the present order of our essays is that an attack should precede a defense. But while attack-preceding-defense is the usual pattern found in warfare, it is not the pattern that is standardly found in public debate, where defense precedes attack or critique. Of course, if the audience for this volume were well aware of the arguments in favor of affirmative action/racial preference, it might be appropriate to reverse the standard order and start with a critique followed by a defense. But with respect to affirmative action/racial preference, especially in the present political climate, the general public, and particularly our students, seem to be far more aware of the arguments against affirmative action/racial preference than they are of the arguments in favor of it—all the more reason, then, to retain the standard debate format with respect to our topic.

Professor Cohen also did not want his critique to follow my defense of affirmative action because he does not see himself as a critic of all forms of affirmative action, but only of those forms that involve racial preference. But this is no reason to oppose the originally agreed-upon ordering of our essays because the affirmative action that I defend in my essay is essentially identified with racial preference. So if Professor Cohen really opposes racial preference, as he says he does, he should have had no problem presenting himself as a critic of what I defend in my essay using a standard debate format.

Accordingly, it falls to you, our readers, to evaluate our disagreement over the order in which our essays should be presented, and then to read the essays in the order you deem appropriate.

I am pleased to acknowledge that earlier versions of my initial essay were presented at the University of Notre Dame, the University of Missouri, the Research Triangle Ethics Discussion Circle, the Mary Lou Williams Center for Black Culture at Duke University, and the University of California at Irvine. Comments on earlier versions of the essay were received from a number of people. I would especially like to thank Terry Pell of the Center of Individual Rights, Roger Pilon of the Cato Institute, John Robinson at the University of Notre Dame Law School, and my fellow academics, Tista Bagchi, Bernard Boxill, Jan Boxill, Allen Buchanan, Leon Dunkley, Gerald Early, Don Garrett, Bernard Gert, Thomas Hill Jr., Aaron James, Lynn Joy, Bonnie Kent, Janet Kourany, Douglas MacLean, Terry McConnell, Charles Mills, Albert Mosley, Alan Nelson, James Nickel, Louis Pojman, Gerald Postema, Philip Quinn, James Radowski, David Reeve, Geoffrey Sayre-McCord, George Sher, David Solomon, Cynthia Stark, and David Wong. I also wish to thank Robert Miller, Executive Editor at Oxford University Press, for persevering with this project through difficult times; the Institute for Scholarship in the Liberal Arts at the University of Notre Dame; and the National Humanities Center in North Carolina for financial support to complete the project, and in the case of the center, an ideal environment in which to do it.

James P. Sterba
Notre Dame, December 2002

CASES

CONSTITUTIONAL AUTHORITIES

Constitution of the United States
    Amendment XIII
    Amendment XIV
    Amendment XV
Constitution of the State of California
    Article 1, Section 31

FEDERAL STATUTES

Civil Rights Act of 1866
Civil Rights Act of 1875
Civil Rights Act of 1964
Civil Rights Act of 1991

STATE STATUTES

Revised Code of Washington, RCW 49.60.400

EXECUTIVE ORDERS

Executive Order 10925 (Pres. J.F. Kennedy, 1961)
Executive Order 11246 (Pres. L.B. Johnson, 1965)
Executive Order 11375 (Pres. L.B. Johnson, 1967)

SECTION ONE

Why Race Preference Is Wrong and Bad

Carl Cohen

PROLOGUE

Wrongness and Badness

There is a great and important difference between the rightness of an action and the goodness of its results. Some acts that are right have very unfortunate consequences; some acts that are wrong produce very satisfying outcomes. Some policies we condemn because they are *wrong*, that is, unjust or unfair. Others we reject because they are *bad*, that is, hurtful or counterproductive.

Race preference—the policy of giving special advantages to the members of certain minorities simply on the ground that they are members of those ethnic groups—is unjust to both minority and majority, *and* damaging to both minority and majority. Race preference is to be condemned, I argue in this book, because it is both wrong and bad.

To prefer whites because they are white, or blacks because they are black—or the members of any ethnic group because they are members of that group—is *wrong*. Such preference is forbidden by the guarantee of the Fourteenth Amendment of the U.S. Constitution that no person may be denied the equal protection of the laws. It is forbidden also, very explicitly, by an act of Congress, the Civil Rights Act of 1964. But above all, race preference is morally wrong because it violates the most fundamental principles of fair treatment.

Supporters of race preference commonly suppose that it gives justified redress for injury. It does not, as I will show. Naked race preference does not even address the injuries of those earlier damaged by prejudice. But it does penalize persons because of their skin color, persons who are themselves innocent of the wrongs for which redress had been sought. The wrongness of preference, in morals and in law, is explained in Part II of this essay.

Supporters of race preference commonly suppose that, although preference may be somewhat unfair, its very important objectives render it beneficial on balance. The preferential pill may be bitter, it is said, but we must swallow it because it is good for us. But preference by race is *not* good for us. It is deeply divisive, hindering the quest for a society in which racial segregation has been overcome and racial hostilities healed. It damages and corrupts the institutions in which it is practiced, especially the universities. And worst of all, it undermines, seriously and cruelly, the minorities it purports to assist. These unhappy consequences for all of us are explained in Part III.

Part I presents an overview of the tension between the American ideal of equality and our historical failures to realize that ideal. The major steps in our painfully slow progress toward a society that is racially just—and the origin and transformation of affirmative action—are there briefly traced.

Race preference, old and new, has been a moral catastrophe in our country from its beginnings. Its unfairness is matched only by its hurtfulness. What is unjust may sometimes be useful. But that cannot be said of preference by race which (as I aim to show) is as bad as it is wrong.

PART I

Equality and Race Preference

1

Equality as a Moral Ideal

The principle of human equality has guided the American republic since its founding. Of the truths held to be self-evident in the Declaration of Independence the very first is that "all men are created equal." This conviction is fundamental because we understand intuitively that it is the equality of persons that justifies universal participation in government. The acknowledged equality of citizens is the ground, the philosophical bedrock of our democracy.

American political practice long failed to respect this ideal in the concrete; in some ways we fail still. But our laws and institutions have grown much more enlightened. We have moved inexorably, even if too slowly, toward the fuller realization of the moral ideal of equality.

Equality became a focus of congressional concern in the years following the Civil War, with the cruel history of black slavery fresh in mind. The Thirteenth Amendment to our Constitution, ratified in 1865, forbade slavery, but it barely dented the racism of the time. A few months later, in the Civil Rights Act of 1866, Congress declared:

> [A]ll . . . citizens of the United States . . . of every race and color . . . shall have the same right . . . to full and equal benefit of all laws and proceedings for the security of person and property . . . and shall be subject to like punishment, pains, and penalties and to none other.

Forceful language—but parity between the conditions of blacks and whites was hardly approached. The principle of human equality needed the enforcement that could only be assured if incorporated into the U.S. Constitution, as it soon was. The first section of the Fourteenth Amendment, adopted in 1868, reads in part: "No State shall . . . deny to any person within its jurisdiction the equal protection of the laws."[1] Voting discrimination on grounds of race was specifically forbidden by the Constitution two years later.[2]

Thus firmly embedded in our highest law, the principle of equality was implemented legislatively in the Civil Rights Act of 1875, whose language was, again, unambiguous:

> [A]ll persons within the jurisdiction of the United Sates shall be entitled to the full and equal enjoyment of the accommodation, advantages, facilities, and privileges of inns, public conveyances on land and water, theaters, and other places of public amusement; subject only to the conditions and limitations established by law, and applicable alike to citizens of every race and color. . . .

Earnestly proclaimed and honestly intended, these declarations of principle did not come close to ending racial oppression in America. Discrimination against blacks and other minorities, flouting the Constitution and federal law and yet enforced by state governments, remained nearly universal until the middle of the twentieth century.

The everyday instrument of this ongoing discrimination was the invidious *segregation* of the races. In the long-governing case of *Plessy v. Ferguson*[3] the U.S. Supreme Court, although affirming the formal ideal of equality, accepted the principle that equality of the races is consistent with their legally enforced separation—thereby inviting another 60 years of racial oppression. The repudiation of that "separate

---

[1]The force of this "equal protection clause" has been contested by the advocates of race preference; those Constitutional arguments are discussed in detail in chapter 6.

[2]In the Fifteenth Amendment (1870): "The right of citizens of the United States to vote shall not be abridged or denied by the United States or by any State on account of race, color, or previous condition of servitude."

[3]163 U.S. 537 (1896). Citations of court decisions, of which there will be many in this book, have four parts: [1] the series of reports in which the decision is published (*United States Reports*, abbreviated as U.S., is one such series), is preceded by [2] the number of the volume in that series and followed by [3] the page number in that volume, with [4] the year of the decision in parentheses concluding the citation. *Plessy v. Ferguson*, as the citation in this footnote shows, was decided in 1896, and published in volume 163 of *United States Reports*, beginning on page 537.

but equal" doctrine did not come until 1954, when state-sponsored segregation was held at last to be inconsistent with the equality guaranteed by the Constitution. In that most momentous decision of the twentieth century, the Supreme Court spoke with one voice:

> We conclude that in the field of public education the doctrine of 'separate but equal' has no place. Separate educational facilities are inherently unequal.[4]

But even before that century had begun, the essence of the evil of policies based on race had been clearly identified by the lone dissenter in *Plessy*, Justice John Harlan, Sr.:

> In respect of civil rights common to all citizens, the Constitution of the United States does not, I think, permit any public authority to *know the race* of those entitled to be protected in the enjoyment of such rights. . . . I deny that any legislative body or judicial tribunal *may have regard to the race of citizens* when the civil rights of those citizens are involved.[5]

As the twenty-first century opens, that spirit begins to recapture the respect of our legislatures and courts. It is rooted in the principle of equality itself. Only ten years after the close of the Civil War, in the congressional debate over what was to become the Civil Rights Act of 1875, a black congressman from North Carolina, Richard Cain, put into words that simple vision of racial justice that a genuine commitment to equality entails. On the floor of the House of Representatives, he said:

> All we ask for is that you, the legislators of this nation, shall pass a law so strong and so powerful that no one shall be able to elude it and destroy our rights under the Constitution and laws of our country. That is all we ask. . . . We do not want any discriminations. I do not ask any legislation for the colored people of this country that is not applied to the white people. All that we ask is equal laws, equal legislation, and equal rights throughout the length and breadth of this land.[6]

---

[4]*Brown v. Board of Education*, 347 U.S. 483 (1954).
[5]163 U.S. 537, at p. 555 (1896). Emphases added.
[6]The Hon. Richard H. Cain, cited by Frances F. Freeman, ed., in *The Black American Experience* (New York: Bantam Books, 1979), p. 116.

The reasonableness and cogency of this plea could not be denied. The civil right movement, imbued with that spirit precisely, later became the nation's conscience. This demand for equality in everyday life was, and is, morally irresistible. Nothing less than genuinely equal treatment for all races, enforced by law, is tolerable in this country.

But the ideal was far easier to express than to achieve. To spur action guided by that ideal, to touch the moral nerve of the American public, heroes of the civil rights movement were obliged to defy discriminatory statutes, often at great personal risk, sometimes even at the cost of life. They knew, as we know now, that the ideal of equal treatment for all must eventually overcome. With gathering momentum after World War II, the United States turned away—reluctantly at first but then with increasing vigor—from long-ensconced patterns of racial oppression.

One full century after the close of the Civil War, the great Civil Rights Act of 1964 was adopted.[7] This federal statute, in its many sections, makes discrimination, exercised by governments or employers in this country "against any individual . . . because of such individual's race, color, religion, sex, or national origin," *unlawful*. The day the United States Senate passed that act (all one hundred members voting), as the House of Representatives had done months before, it might have seemed that the law so long sought had been at last enacted, a law "so strong and so powerful that no one shall be able to elude it."

The words of the Civil Rights Act of 1964 gave specificity and concreteness to the constitutional guarantee of "the equal protection of the laws." In employment, in education, in all spheres of public accommodation, there was to be from that time forward no official favoritism for one race or ethnic group at the expense of others. The intentions of the members of the Congress in adopting this law were clearly and emphatically expressed. The comprehensive and unambiguous purpose of the legislators was again and again made explicit in debates on the floor of the House and the Senate during that summer of 1964. All racial preference was to be eliminated. Choosing their words carefully, representatives and senators,

---

[7]That law now appears as chapter 42 of the *United States Codes*.

one after the other, rose to explain that with the passage of this act the equal treatment (in the public sphere) of all races in America was henceforth to be legally enforced. The clarity and force of the words in the law were repeatedly emphasized; their plain meaning, they said, could not thereafter be mistaken. This Civil Rights Act of 1964 is the law of our nation still; it was politically momentous but also morally fine. In matters pertaining to race it marks the highest point reached in our national consciousness.[8]

[8]The bearing of the Civil Rights Act on contemporary race preferences, and the congressional debate concerning the intent of the law at the time of its passage in 1964, are discussed at greater length in chapter 5.

2

Affirmative Action

In March of 1961, less than two months after assuming office, President John F. Kennedy issued Executive Order 10925, establishing the President's Committee on Equal Employment Opportunity, whose mission was to end discrimination in employment by the federal government and its contractors. This order—still in effect—has required every federal contract from that time forward to include the following pledge:

> "The Contractor will not discriminate against any employee or applicant for employment because of race, creed, color, or national origin. The Contractor will take *affirmative action*, to ensure that applicants are employed, and that employees are treated during employment, *without regard to their race, creed, color, or national origin.*"[9]

Although the words had been used in federal legislation years before,[10] it was this order of President Kennedy that initiated our national commitment to "affirmative action"—our determination to take positive steps to *extirpate* all preference by race.

Three years later the Civil Rights Act of 1964 was adopted. The unambiguous provisions of that great statute (of which much more will be said in chapter 5) could not by themselves bring public racial discrimination to an end. In hotels and restaurants, in industrial employment, in the admission of students to universities, in the letting of government contracts, in housing rentals and sales, in all the nooks

---

[9]Executive Order 10925 (1961). Emphases added.
[10]They were used in the National Labor Relations Act of 1935, in which the aim was to eliminate discrimination against union members.

and crannies of American life, discriminatory practices had become embedded. Everyday procedures had to be reviewed and their discriminatory infections identified; a heightened sensitivity to racial unfairness was essential if that unfairness were to be effectively addressed. Formal organization was essential too, authoritative agencies issuing detailed regulations to cleanse institutions of their discriminatory—often inadvertently discriminatory—elements. Positive steps were still needed to uproot the preferences long given to whites and males.

President Lyndon Johnson had worked assiduously for the passage of the Civil Rights Act. Only months after its adoption he added muscle to the demand for nondiscrimination by issuing Executive Order 11246. The racism that had infected federal employment (and also the work forces of private firms with which the federal government did business) was no longer to be tolerated. President Johnson's order said:

> It is the policy of the Government of the United States to provide equal opportunity in federal employment for all persons, *to prohibit discrimination* in employment because of race, creed, color, or national origin, and to promote the full realization of equal opportunity through a positive, continuing program in each executive department or agency.[11]

This enforceable assurance of *nondiscrimination* extended (and extends still) to every aspect of employment: promotion, demotion, transfer, recruitment, termination, training, and rates of pay. Affirmative action was thus designed as a sustained pattern of efforts—by the federal government in the first instance, and by all those who deal with it as well—to insure that race, creed, color, and national origin were *not* to be the grounds of differential treatment. Those same assurances of nondiscrimination were demanded some two years later with respect to sex.[12]

Where the equal treatment obliged by the Civil Rights Act had been denied, those wrongfully injured by race discrimination were invited by the statute to come to the courts to be "made whole." The

---

[11]Executive Order 11246 (1965), part I, sec. 101. Emphasis added.

[12]Executive Order 11375, issued by President Lyndon Johnson in 1967.

act recognized the likely need for remedial relief, explicitly providing that, when some practice (e.g., in employment or college admissions) is found by a court to have been in violation of the demands of nondiscrimination, that court will have the authority to "order such *affirmative action* as may be appropriate." Affirmative action had the backing of both the president and Congress.

The language of executive orders and federal legislation referring to affirmative action was perfectly clear, its meaning indisputable. Affirmative action was understood to comprise positive steps to insure genuinely *equal* protection. By identifying discriminatory preferences long entrenched, by eliminating them, and where feasible by redressing them, those seeking the *nondiscriminatory* treatment of all persons of all races proudly raised the banner of affirmative action.

So conceived, affirmative action was morally right, as honorable as public policy can be. The ideal of equality had been protected by unambiguous federal statute. The realization of that ideal was now to be advanced by deliberate community efforts. Affirmative action was to be the instrument with which we would expose and uproot unequal treatment of every kind, covert and overt, deliberate or inadvertent. Affirmative action so understood spoke then, and it speaks now, to our condition. It deserved its good name.

3

Race Preference: The Transformation of Affirmative Action

The Civil Rights Act of 1964 forbade ethnic preference in American public life. It was to have given teeth to the guarantee that the laws would be "applicable alike to citizens of every race and color." But less than seven years after its passage, public and private bodies were giving, in the name of "affirmative action," outright preference by race. Affirmative action was rapidly and dramatically transformed.

That transformation has much to teach us. One lesson is this: There are two competing visions of racial justice. The first is that of a society in which race has ceased to be an instrument for invidious classification, a society in which, as Justice Harlan had put it in *Plessy*, no public authority is permitted "to know the race" of those entitled to be protected. The second is that of a society in which the goods of social life are distributed evenly among all ethnic groups, a culture in which racial imbalance has been overcome. This distinction was not at first commonly noted because it was widely supposed that, when the barriers created by racial segregation were at last torn down, balance in the distribution of social goods would quickly follow.

That did not happen. As I write, nearly 40 years after the enactment of the great Civil Rights Act, formal segregation in America is viewed as a long-suffered historical perversion, now forbidden and rightly despised. Many cannot even remember it. But racial balance in a fully integrated society, balanced patterns of residence and employment, an approximately proportionate distribution of wealth and education among our many ethnic clusters—all that is very far from realization. Partly this is due to the persistence of racism. Partly it is due to the nature of human beings, their differing styles of life and their drive to cluster with others like themselves. In many hearts racism is still alive, although it is also true that, as a people, we have become much more enlightened in this sphere. But we have thus far been unable to transform our society into one that is fully integrated, and that failure has not been due entirely to the forces of evil. Powerful social magnets, arising naturally, pull those of similar cultural heritage together and reinforce patterns that, at times, do not advance long-term well-being. In the United States, cultural homogeneity is not at all feasible, and many think it not at all desirable. There are formally desegregated cities in America that are less fully integrated now, in the twenty-first century, than they were in 1964.[13] That reality, having multiple causes of which some are evil and some are not, has greatly complicated the history of affirmative action.

The early results of the 1954 court order in *Brown* to *desegregate* the public schools fell very far short of what had been hoped for. School boards, supported by their state governments, retained dual, segregated school systems in violation of the law. Frustrated federal courts were repeatedly obliged to intervene, to oversee the schools, and then again to *order*—sometimes in anger—the desegregation that the Constitution requires.[14] The continuing obstinate refusal of the states to provide fully equal educational opportunities for those of all races could not be justified. What judges demanded, and the citizenry deserved, was a plan for school desegregation that promised

---

[13]In Boston, for example, 70 percent of all public school students are black, and the balanced integration of the public schools is nearly impossible. In Detroit, where the percentage of public school students who are black is over 90 percent, it is a goal yet more distant.

[14]There was much argument in the courts at that time regarding the speed with which the implementation of *Brown I* was reasonably to be expected. In *Brown II*, the Supreme Court had remanded that case, and other school segregation cases, to the lower courts with the instruction to "take such proceedings and enter such orders and decrees consistent with this opinion as are necessary and proper to admit to public schools on a racially nondiscriminatory basis *with all deliberate speed . . .* " (*Brown II*, 349 U.S. 294, at p. 301 [1954]; emphasis added). But the meaning of the phrase "with all deliberate speed" long remained in dispute.

to work, and (as one court put it in a famous school case more than a decade after *Brown*) "promises realistically to work *now*."[15] We feel the frustration and share the indignation of that federal judge, and we applaud his vigor.

Eventually state-supported segregation of the public schools came to an end. The federal courts used their powers to insure that pupils would be brought, by buses if that were the only way feasible, to schools affording equal opportunity. Federal marshals gave physical protection where that proved essential. The demand for equal treatment was entirely reasonable; the outcome was to be school systems that were *unitary*—separate schools for blacks and for whites no more.[16] Every student in a public school district is *qualified* for equal treatment, and *entitled* to equal treatment. If school boards (or the states) dragged their feet in satisfying this entitlement, they would be forced to obey. They were forced, and eventually they did obey.

That same demand for equality of outcome was extrapolated from the sphere of the public schools to the sphere of colleges, professional schools, and private and public employment, where admission or appointment is competitive and there is no universal entitlement to success. This created a very painful problem because, unlike the case of the public schools, all who sought college admission, or good jobs, were not equally qualified for those goods so limited in supply. Minority applicants were generally less well qualified, and therefore the demand for racial balance could not be satisfied in these contexts, and of course it was not satisfied. Universal equality of outcome by race supposes the universal possession of skills and attainments by race in approximately equal degree. But the proportion of minority applicants able to compete successfully for the limited number of places in academic institutions, and for prestigious professional appointments in private industry and government employment, was

---

[15]*Green v. School Board of New Kent County (VA)*, 391 U.S. 430, at p. 439 (1968).

[16]"Brown II was a call for the dismantling of well entrenched dual systems . . . [School boards] were clearly charged with the affirmative duty to take whatever steps might be necessary to convert to a unitary system *in which racial discrimination would be eliminated root and branch.*" *Green*, pp. 437–38. Emphasis added.

and remains far smaller than the proportion of those minorities in the population at large. The needed qualifications were and remain very far from being distributed proportionally, and no court orders or federal marshals can alter their actual distribution.

The invidious segregation of the races was no longer the chief hindrance to the racial integration of institutions. By the late 1960s, discrimination against minority applicants in higher education had long ceased to be the rule. Universities welcomed minority applicants genuinely, designed programs to encourage and support them, and extended themselves to promote the success of minority students and scholars. Notwithstanding all such efforts, the racial proportionality that had been a reasonable expectation in public school systems remained an unrealistic expectation in law schools and medical schools, in laboratories and newsrooms. For many reasons, but perhaps mainly because of earlier educational deficiencies, the racial balance hoped for was not soon to be achieved, even after discriminatory barriers had been torn down.

This reality was difficult for many to accept. Why, they asked, should the distribution of educational and professional appointments not now be *proportional by race*, at least approximately? Those who had supposed that desegregation, now the law, would soon bring racial balance in its train were bitterly disappointed. Affirmative action had been needed to erase the vestiges of formal segregation, all agreed to that. But the results anticipated had not nearly been achieved. If proportional outcomes were called for by justice but had not ensued, this must be (it was reasoned) because the steps taken to promote them, although "affirmative," had not been sufficiently vigorous.

Affirmative action as originally conceived could not achieve racial proportionality in the short term because it could not alter minority applicants in the ways needed to make them qualified. Well then, came the response in effect, we must take steps that are more penetrating. We must *change the systems* of admission or employment so that minority applicants *will* be qualified. Social justice requires (it was argued) that ethnically proportional outcomes be insured. That has not happened. Therefore we must devise the more powerful machinery that can move us promptly toward racial balance *now*.

Our objectives can be achieved (the argument continued) if the *standards* for qualification are appropriately altered, that is, if race be included as one important element of those standards. Let us re-think the ways in which minority employees are recruited, and minority students admitted. We long labored under the conviction that equality must govern the competition for appointment or for admission. But that was equal treatment, and equal *treatment* leads to stymie, and does not yield the racially proportional *results* that are (they insisted) the hallmark of justice. Equality must govern in a different way, transcending equal treatment. We must not fear the vigorous social engineering required to achieve the racial balance that is our objective. We must take the needed steps. We must design and implement the "race-sensitive" programs that will *produce* a racially balanced society.[17]

This result-oriented social engineering, these race-sensitive programs that "went beyond" equality of treatment, were advanced in the good name of affirmative action. And so it happened that what was thought justified by "affirmative action" was, in a very few years, thoroughly transformed. The outcomes that could not be achieved through equal opportunity were approximated by insisting upon *un*equal opportunity. Race *preferences* were given, and are widely given still, in competitions for admission and for employment. Moral urgency was put to the service of objectives that could not be justly realized. Driven by the mistaken conviction that social arrangements would be fair only when racial balance had been achieved, *racial proportionality* became the unspoken, and for many the unquestioned, measure of success.

At first, very modest preferences for minority applicants in closely competitive situations were thought to be all that was needed. But weighing race as no more than a marginal "plus factor" did not achieve the desired objective. To approximate that objective, the

---

[17]A century before, in Germany, the goal of national unification was held by the Prussian authorities to be overriding, and therefore to justify means that were sly or even brutal. Said Bismarck: "Gangrene will not be cured with lavender water." That was in 1870. In 2002 an academic organization tenaciously committed to the continuation of race preferences in the United States calls itself "BAMN"—an acronym for "By Any Means Necessary."

preferences given had to become, and did become, more and more weighty with passing years. The general public was led to suppose that only minor advantages were being bestowed, while in fact wholesale race preferences of substantial dimensions had been quietly and often secretly introduced. The universities, which had been leaders in the public condemnation of racial favoritism during the 1950s and '60s, grew understandably ashamed of what they were doing in the 1980s and '90s. Race preferences were therefore hidden; when mentioned publicly they were referred to using euphemisms. "Special admissions" programs were designed for minorities only to "give them a break" or "level the playing field." But the verbal cover for the entire enterprise, almost invariably, was "affirmative action."

The phrase "affirmative action" was kidnapped. That honorable expression, originally denoting efforts to *eradicate* all preference by race, had its meaning *inverted*. In the good name of what had been designed to *uproot* preference, preference was now formally *incorporated* and made often obligatory. In pursuit of the desired proportional outcomes, a vast network of ethnic preferences gradually took shape, in both private and public institutions. Cloaked with appeals to racial justice, shielded by words and names that gave lip service to racial equality, affirmative action had been transformed into its own opposite.

The details of this monstrous transformation will be reported and explained in the pages that follow. But all will surely agree that cleansing institutions of the remnants of race discrimination is right. Giving redress to persons who have suffered known injuries because of their race is right. Designing procedures that are truly race neutral is right. Affirmative action, as originally conceived, to advance those honorable objectives is morally right and certainly is not in dispute here. At issue here and now is *unequal* treatment of the races in the name of equality. At issue here and now is *preference* given to persons for no reason other than that they are members of one or another minority group. At issue here and now is *not* affirmative action, but naked *preference* by race. Naked race preference, I will argue, is very wrong and very bad.

PART II

Why Race Preference Is Wrong

4

Race Preference Is Morally Wrong

(1) The Principle of Equality

That *equals should be treated equally* is a fundamental principal of morality. Race preference is morally wrong because it violates this principle.

But who are equals?[18] Identical treatment for everyone in all matters is certainly not just. Citizens have privileges and duties that aliens do not have; employers have opportunities and responsibilities that employees do not have; higher taxes may be rightly imposed upon those with higher incomes; the right to vote is withheld from the very young. Groups of persons may deserve different treatment because they *are* different in critical respects. But what respects are critical? Surely the poor or the elderly or the disabled may have special needs that justify community concern.

The principle of equality does not require that all be treated identically; but this much is clear: if some receive a public benefit that others do not receive, that preference will be unfair unless the advantages given can be justified by some feature of the group preferred. Unequal treatment by the state requires defense.

As a justification for unequal treatment some group characteristics are simply not relevant and not acceptable, all agree. Ancestry we reject. Better treatment for Americans of Irish decent than for those of Polish decent is wrong; we haven't any doubt about that. Sex we reject. Privileges to which men are entitled cannot be denied to

---

[18]Aristotle wrote: "All men admit . . . that equals ought to receive equally. But there still remains a question: equal treatment for equality or inequality of what?" *Politics*, book III, chapter 12.

women. Religion we reject. Opportunities open to Methodists must be open to Baptists. Color we reject. When the state favors white skins over black skins—a common practice for centuries—we are now properly outraged. Such categories cannot determine desert. This matter is morally settled: in dealings with the state, persons *may not* be preferred because of their race, or color, or religion, or sex, or national origin.

Bigots, of course, will draw distinctions by race (or nationality, etc.) in their private lives. But private opinions, however detestable, are not public business. Under rules to be enforced by our body politic, bigotry is forbidden. Persons of all colors, religions, and origins are equals with respect to their rights, equals in the eyes of the law. And equals must be treated equally. Race and nationality simply cannot serve, in our country, as the justification for unequal treatment.

This we do not learn from any book or document. These principles are not true because expressed in the Declaration of Independence, or laid down in the Constitution of the United States. The principles are found in those great documents because they are true. That "all men are created equal" is one way, perhaps the most famous way, of expressing the fundamental moral principle involved. A guarantee that the "equal protection of the laws" is not to be denied to any person by any state (as the Fourteenth Amendment to our Constitution provides) is one way of giving that moral principle political teeth. Our great documents *recognize* and *realize* moral truths grasped by persons everywhere: All the members of humankind are equally ends in themselves, all have equal *dignity*— and therefore all are entitled to equal respect from the community and its laws.

John Dewey, rightly thought of as the philosopher of democracy, put it this way:

> Equality does not mean mathematical equivalence. It means rather the inapplicability of considerations of . . . superior and inferior. It means that no matter how great the quantitative differences of ability, strength, position, wealth, such differences are negligible in comparison with something else—the fact of individuality, the manifestation of something irreplaceable. . . . It implies, so to speak, a metaphysical

mathematics of the incommensurable in which each speaks for itself and demands consideration on its own behalf.[19]

This recognition of the ultimate equality and fellowship of humans with one another is taught by great thinkers in every culture—by Buddha, and St. Francis, and Walt Whitman. At bottom we all recognize, as Walter Lippmann wrote, a "spiritual reality behind and independent of the visible character and behavior of a man. . . . [W]e know, each of us, in a way too certain for doubting, that, after all the weighing and comparing and judging of us is done, there is something left over which is the heart of the matter."[20]

This is the moral standard against which race preference must be judged. The principle of equality certainly entails at least this: It is wrong, always and everywhere, to give special advantages to any group simply on the basis of physical characteristics that have no relevance to the award given or to the burden imposed. To give or to take on the basis of skin color is manifestly unfair.

The most gruesome chapters in human history—the abomination of black slavery, the wholesale slaughter of the Jews—remind us that *racial* categories must never be allowed to serve as the foundation for official differentiation. Nations in which racial distinctions were once embedded in public law are forever shamed. Our own history is by such racism ineradicably stained. The lesson is this: Never again. Never, *ever* again.

What is today loosely called "affirmative action" sticks in our craw because it fails to respect that plain lesson. It uses categories that *must not* be used to distinguish among persons with respect to their entitlements in the community. Blacks and whites are equals, as blondes and brunettes are equals, as Catholics and Jews are equals, as Americans of every ancestry are equal. No matter who the beneficiaries may be or who the victims, preference on the basis of race is morally wrong. It was wrong in the distant past and in the recent past; it is wrong now; and it will always be wrong. Race preference violates the principle of human equality.

---

[19]*Characters and Events*, Vol. ii (New York: Henry Holt & Co, 1929), p. 854.
[20]*Men of Destiny* (New York: Macmillan, 1927), p. 50.

(2) Race Preference Is not Justified as Compensation

What about people who have been hurt because of their race, damaged or deprived because they were black or brown? Do they not deserve some redress? Of course they do. But it is the *injury* for which compensation is given in such cases, not the skin color.

But (some will respond) it is precisely the *injuries* so long done to minorities that justify special consideration for minorities now. Bearing the past in mind, deliberate preference for groups formerly oppressed reverses historical injustice, and thereby makes fair what would otherwise seem to be unfair. They argue that blacks, Native Americans, Hispanics, and other minorities have for many generations been the victims of outrageous discrimination, the sum of it almost too cruel to contemplate. Explicit preference to these minorities now makes up, in part, for past deprivation. Historical wrongs cannot be undone, but we can take some steps toward the restoration of moral balance. At this point in our history, advocates continue, equal treatment only appears to be just. Minorities have been so long shackled by discriminatory laws and economic deprivation that it is not fair to oblige them to compete now against a majority never burdened in that way. The visible shackles may be gone, but not the residual impact of their long imposition. We must *level the playing field* in the competition for employment and other goods. Only explicit race preference can do this, they contend; therefore, explicit race preference is just.

This is the essence of the argument in support of race preference upon which most of its advocates chiefly rely. It is an argument grounded in the demand for *compensation*, for redress. It seeks to turn the tables in the interests of justice. White males, so long the beneficiaries of preference, are now obliged to give preference to others. Past oppression must be paid for. Is turnabout not fair play?

No, it is not—not when the instrument turned about is essentially unjust. The compensatory argument is appealing but mistaken, because preference *by race* cannot serve as just compensation for earlier wrongs. It cannot do so because race, as a standard, is crude and morally blind. Color, national origin, and other accidents of birth have no moral weight. Historical injustices we now seek to redress were themselves a product of moral stupidity; they were inflicted because burdens and benefits were awarded on grounds entirely irrelevant to what was deserved. Blacks and other minorities were not injured by *being* black or brown. They were injured by treatment unfairly *based* on their being black or brown. Redress deserved is redress that goes to *them*, to persons injured, in the light of the injuries they suffered. Many are long dead and can never be compensated. Those ancient injuries are not remedied by bestowing benefits now upon other persons who happen to belong to the ethnic group of those injured.

Using race to award benefits now does injustice in precisely the way injustice was done originally, by giving moral weight to skin color in itself. The discriminatory use of racial classifications is no less unfair when directed at whites now than it was when directed at blacks then. A wrong is not redressed by inflicting that same wrong on others. By devising new varieties of race preference, moreover, we give legitimacy to the consideration of race, reinforcing the very injustice we seek to eradicate. We compound injustice with injustice, further embedding racial categories in public policy and law.

The moral blindness of race preference is exhibited from both sides: *the wrong people benefit, and the wrong people pay the price of that benefit.*

Consider first who benefits. Race preference gives rewards to some persons who deserve no rewards at all, and is thus *over*inclusive. Preferential systems are designed to give special consideration to *all* those having some physical or genetic feature, all those who are black, or female, or of some specified national origin. Hispanics, for example, receive the advantage because they have parents or grandparents (is one enough?) of certain national origins. But have all those of Hispanic origin been wrongly injured? Do all those of that single national origin deserve compensation now for earlier injuries? No one seriously believes that. Discrimination against Hispanics in our country has been (and remains) common, to be sure. But it is also true that many of Hispanic ancestry now enjoy here, and have long enjoyed, circumstances as decent and as well protected as those enjoyed by Americans of all other ethnicities. The same is true of African Americans, some of whom are impoverished and some of whom are rich and powerful. Rewards distributed on the basis of ethnic membership assume that the damage suffered by some were suffered by all—an assumption that we know to be false.

But, knowing the falsehood of that assumption, we remain unable to refine our moral responses in the light of that knowledge where race rules. The University of Texas long gave preference to all blacks seeking admission, claiming that by this preference it was giving remedy for the deprivations suffered by blacks in the Texas public schools. If some of the very finest public school students (and public school teachers) in Texas are black, as they surely are, the university's racial favoritism could not even recognize that fact; the system was unable to attend to morally significant differences. Blackness in itself, naked race, was the ground of preference in Texas, and the finest black students of the Texas schools received preference in admission along with every other applicant whose skin was black. Black applicants to the University of Texas were given preference if they hadn't attended Texas public schools at all. It was their blackness that counted. Graduates of private schools in Dallas or Houston, if they were black, received admission preference as *compensatory relief.* Applicants could have come from any other state, might have attended public or private schools of any description— but if they were black they were given preference at the University of Texas. Even applicants not residing in the United States, graduates of schools in France or in India, were preferred if their skin was the right color. Preference in Texas was by color. Blind to all moral considerations, the university relied solely on skin color to determine who deserved special treatment. The defense of these preferential admissions as compensatory, presented by the University of Texas in lengthy federal litigation, was categorically rejected by the U.S. Court of Appeals.[21]

---

[21]*Hopwood v. Texas*, 78 F. 3rd 932 (5th Cir., 1996). The *Hopwood* decision should have been no surprise in Texas. The former attorney general of Texas, Dan Morales, looking back, said this: "What was going on at the University of Texas was a discriminatory admissions scheme. If you were a minority applicant, you had a lower standard to meet and you went to a separate admission committee. If you were a non-minority applicant, you had a higher standard to meet and went to a different admission committee." See *Dallas Morning News*, 10 January 2002.

Overinclusiveness was unavoidable because racial categories are exceedingly crude, far too blunt to do justice. "Set-asides" for minority contractors also illustrate this crudity. To compensate for past discrimination against minority contractors in the City of Richmond, Virginia, the City Council reserved 30 percent of all city contracts for minority-owned firms. Before that, only a few minority contractors had done business in Richmond, and their portion of city contracts had indeed been small. The allegedly compensatory preference, however, was given not only to Richmond firms that may have suffered unfairly, but to every firm, wherever based, whose owners happened to be in one of certain specified racial categories, including Native Americans, Eskimos, and Aleuts. Discriminatory injustices against Eskimos or Aleuts in Richmond are likely to have been few, but the City Council was not truly seeking to compensate anyone; they were relishing the spoils of municipal power. The 30 percent set-aside was a quantity of business impossible for the existing minority contractors of Richmond to conduct, so the statute indirectly obliged the award of "compensatory" benefits to minority contractors who had never suffered injustice in Richmond or anywhere, and even to minority contractors based far beyond Virginia who, if they had suffered at all, certainly had not been victims of any discrimination by the City of Richmond. Overinclusive to the point of absurdity? Plainly. But racial set-aside programs similar to this one pervade city and state governments in America still, and the federal government as well. Such preferences intensify the moral consequences of race, indirectly confirming the legitimacy of the very instrument of classification that we find repugnant.

Race preference is morally defective also in being *under*inclusive, in that it fails to reward many who deserve compensation. If redress is at times in order, for what injuries might it be deserved? Inadequate education perhaps: teachers poorly qualified, books out of date or in short supply, buildings vermin-infested and deteriorating, schools rotten all around. High school graduates who come to the verge of college admission in spite of handicaps like these may indeed be thought worthy of special consideration—but that would be a consideration given them not because of the color of their skins, but because of what they have accomplished in spite of handicap. *Everyone* whose accomplishments are like those, whose determination has overcome great barriers, is entitled to whatever compensatory relief we think graduation from such inferior schools deserves. Everyone, no matter the color of her skin.

So race preference is morally faulty in what it does not do, as well as in what it does. Seeing only race we cannot see what may truly justify special regard. Blacks and Hispanics are not the only ones to have been burdened by bad schools, or undermined by poverty or neglect, or wounded by absent or malfunctioning families. But those with skins of other colors, however much they too may have been unfairly injured or deprived, get no support from race-based "affirmative action." They are simply left out.

Also left out are most of those blacks and Native Americans who really were seriously damaged by educational deprivation, but who fell so far behind in consequence that they cannot possibly compete for slots in professional schools, or for prestigious training programs, and therefore cannot benefit from the race preferences commonly given. So those most in need of help usually get none, and those equally entitled to help whose skins are the wrong color get absolutely none.

Whatever the community response to adversity ought to be, this much is clear: what is given must be given without regard to the race or sex or national origin of the recipients. It is the injury and not the ethnicity for which relief may be in order, and therefore relief cannot be justly restricted to some minorities only. If some injury or deprivation does justify compensatory redress, whites and blacks who have suffered that injury should be entitled to the same redress. Racial lenses obscure this truth.

A just apportionment of remedies should be designed to compensate most those who were injured most, and to compensate least, or not at all, those who were injured least, or not at all. Therefore a keen regard for the nature of the injury suffered, and the degree of suffering, is critical in giving redress. Remedy for injury is a complicated matter; naked race preference must fail as the instrument in providing remedy because by hypothesis it has no regard for variety or degree. How gravely injured are they who complete undergraduate studies and compete for admission to law school, or medical school? The daughter of a black physician who graduates from a fine college has been done no injury entitling her to preferential consideration in competitive admissions simply because she is black—but she will surely receive it. The principal beneficiaries of "affirmative action" in law schools and medical schools are the children of upper middle-class minority families, for the simple reason that they are the minority applicants most likely to be in a position to apply to such schools. Those whose personal histories of deprivation may in truth entitle them to some special consideration are rarely in a position even to hope for preference in such contexts. It is one of the great ironies of "affirmative action" that those among minority groups receiving its preferences are precisely those least likely to deserve them.

This moral obtuseness is partly a consequence of measuring the success of affirmative action by race *counting*. Acting on the premise that in the absence of oppression the distribution of ethnic groups in educational and employment categories would be proportional to their percentage in the population at large, universities and private firms establish minority admission and employment goals that roughly duplicate the ethnic profile of the larger community. These numerical targets are usually not attainable so long as normal standards are applied. But the political pressure upon administrators to approach these goals is intense; their jobs may depend on the racial numbers they report. In the law schools, for example, the question of whether those receiving favor truly *deserve* those special benefits is not even asked. The compensatory arguments that engendered the preferences are quite forgotten in what becomes a press for minority numbers. Our immediate concern, say the affirmative action bureaucrats in the universities, in private industry, and in government agencies, is our employment or student profile: we must have more black (or brown) faces.

Defending the practice of laying off white teachers with high seniority to protect the jobs of black teachers with much lower seniority, an attorney was asked by a justice of the U.S. Supreme Court *why* the employment preference in question had been given. His answer was blunt but honest: "We want them there."[22] "Them" in such contexts refers to people having the color preferred; it mattered not at all to that school board that those persons had no claim

---

[22]*Wygant v. Jackson Board of Education*, 476 U.S. 267 (1986).

whatever for compensatory relief. At the University of Michigan, where highly qualified majority applicants are rejected in great numbers while minimally qualified minority applicants are accepted in their place, questions by admissions officers about the degree of injury possibly suffered by those minority applicants are rarely asked; whether any discriminatory injury has been suffered is simply not their concern. They have "affirmative action goals" to meet.

One commonly alleged justification for racial goals is "underrepresentation." But the passion to remedy the underrepresentation of minorities is not matched by a concern for the underrepresentation of the white majority. To illustrate: U.S. Department of Housing and Urban Development (HUD) gives preference to Asian males in hiring for its professional work force because the proportion of Asian males (in the year 2002) on that force is only 3.4 percent, while the proportion of Asian males in the larger technical labor force is 3.5 percent. This difference of *one-tenth of one percent* is reported by HUD as a "manifest imbalance" that justifies explicit hiring preference for Asians. But white males constitute just 5 percent of the technical employees at HUD, while the proportion of white males in the larger technical work force is 36 percent. This 31 percent discrepancy does not trigger preferences—plainly because the preferences would then go to the "wrong" group. Surely, if manifest imbalance is to trigger preference (a principle not obviously correct), it must at the very least be considered for all ethnic groups equally. That is certainly not the case at HUD.[23]

---

[23]See Stanley Kurtz, "Fair Fight," *The National Review*, 9 August 2002. Kurtz provides the documented detail of a class action civil suit against HUD (and against the Equal Employment Opportunity Commission, which encourages and supports such preferences in many federal agencies!), *Worth v. Martinez*, filed on 8 August 2002. Kurtz points out that in cases in which a minority (say, Hispanic females) is overrepresented in a category (say, "administrators"), it is the practice of the EEOC to search out a subcategory of administrators, such as "criminal investigator," in which Hispanic females are underrepresented, and institute hiring preferences there. The result is that minorities must be proportionally or more than proportionally represented in every employment subcategory, while white males are bound to be greatly underrepresented overall.

What federal agencies do by formal rule, universities more commonly do informally and surreptitiously; candor is rare in the world of college admissions. But it is easy to see, and painful to note, that race preference often results in the college enrollment of students who are deemed "qualified" only by stretching the concept of qualification until it is meaningless. Standards in the appointment of faculty members are similarly eroded. "Affirmative action hiring goals" result in the hiring of faculty who would not have been hired but for their race. Those favored invariably include many who have been earlier deprived of nothing because of their race.

In sum, race preference gives to those who don't deserve, and doesn't give to those who do. It gives more to those who deserve less, and less to those who deserve more. These failings are inescapable because the preferences in question are grounded not in earlier injury but in physical characteristics that cannot justly serve as grounds for advantage or disadvantage. Whatever is owed persons because of injuries they suffered is owed them without any regard to their ethnicity. Many who may now deserve remedy for past abuse are not minority group members; many who are minority group members deserve no remedy. Preference awarded only to persons in certain racial categories, and to all in those categories whatever their actual desert, invariably overrides the moral considerations that are genuinely relevant, and cannot be rightly defended as compensatory.

(3) Race Preference Imposes Unfair Penalties Upon Those Not Preferred

Not only the benefits, but also the *burdens* imposed by race-based preferences are distributed unfairly. By attending to skin color rather than to what should truly count, racial instruments invariably impose penalties upon those who deserve no penalty at all, persons entirely innocent of the earlier wrong for which the preference is allegedly given, but whose skin is of the wrong color.

Even if those receiving race preference now had been injured earlier because of their race, it is plainly false to suppose that those over whom they are now preferred were in any way responsible for the earlier injuries. A race-based system of penalty and reward is morally cockeyed.

In a competitive setting, advantages given must be paid for by disadvantages borne. If the goods are in short supply—as jobs and promotions and seats in a law school and the like are certainly in short supply—whatever is given to some by race is necessarily taken from others by race. If some are advantaged because of their color or sex, others must be disadvantaged because of their color or sex. This is a truth of logic that cannot be escaped. *There is no ethnic preference that can be "benign."*

Advocates of preference scoff at the alleged burden of race preferences, contending that their impact upon the majority is insignificant. The body of white job applicants, or white contractors, or white university applicants is large, while the number of minority applicants given preference is small. So if those preferences impose a burden, the advocates contend, it is at worst a trivial burden because of the great number over whom that burden is distributed. The complaint about unfairness, the advocates conclude, thus makes a mountain of a molehill. Preferences given to minority applicants are so greatly *diluted* by the size of the majority that their consequences are barely detectable.

This argument is deceptive and its conclusion is false. True it is that only some in the majority are directly affected, and true also that after such preferences are given we often cannot know precisely who among the majority would have been appointed or admitted if that preferential system had not been in place. But it is not true that, because the group from whom the benefits are taken is large, the burden of preference is diluted or rendered insignificant. The price must be paid, and some among that larger group must pay it. Some individual members of the majority must have been displaced, and upon them the burden is as heavy as it is unfair. Injustice is not made trivial because the names of its victims of not known.

Do this thought experiment: Suppose you are the incorruptible admissions officer at the University of Michigan law school (where race preference is very marked), and, with all due diligence, you select those to be admitted by applying, at the direction of the governing faculty, only the criteria for admission appropriate for a fine law school: earlier academic performance, character, promise, related intellectual attainments, recommendations, performance on admissions examinations, and so on. With great care you at last select the list of those applicants who are to be offered admission in a given year. Suppose also that you scrupulously avoid all racial classifications in weighing applicants, giving no preference whatever for ethnic status or any other suspect classification. Some five hundred persons, let us say, are to be sent letters of acceptance, perhaps one out of each ten applicants. You place the name of each one of the applicants accepted on a single long list, starting at the top with those whose acceptance was clear and uncontroversial, continuing with the names of less commanding applicants, completing the list with the names of those applicants who, although succeeding, barely made it above the cut-off line. There must have been a cut-off line because you have confronted many thousands of applicants, and the great majority of them, of course, you must have rejected.

But now suppose that you and your colleagues construct the list of accepted applicants a second time—this time introducing also the preferences for applicants of certain races actually employed at the Michigan law school.[24] Again you write down the names of all those accepted in one long column. This list and the other will not be identical, of course, for if they were, race would not have entered the process in the second listing, as we know it does in fact. Therefore there will be many names on the second list that did not appear on the first—the names of persons who received special consideration because of their race. We will be happy for them. But there will also be—there *must* also be!—some names on the first list that do *not* appear on the second. These are the persons who pay the price of the preferences. They do not pay it just a tiny bit. There is no dilution of the burden for them; they lose 100 percent of what would otherwise have been theirs, because they are not to be admitted. They are rejected—although, by hypothesis, they would have been admitted had there been no racial considerations introduced. It is an inescapable fact that, with

---

[24]The University of Michigan law school uses race in its admissions very heavily, and has become respondent in a federal case—*Grutter v. Bollinger*—now awaiting resolution by the United States Supreme Court.

race weighed, some people must lose out who would not have lost out if race had not been weighed. The burdens of preference are fully borne by them.

In many contexts that penalty, inevitably imposed by preference, is very heavy. Getting a job, or keeping one, is no minor matter. Some folks lose out in their quest for employment *because of their race*. Some employees who might have been promoted in their workplace are passed over. Some who might have been admitted to fine colleges, or law schools, or medical schools, are not admitted because of their race, and must go elsewhere, or perhaps go nowhere. The white applicants squeezed out in this process are, ironically, often the children of first generation Americans, the first members of their families pulling their way into universities and professional life. They, not the established rich, are the ones hit hardest by race preference.

Persons who have been displaced in this way usually do not know, cannot know, that they are the ones who are paying this price. That first list constructed hypothetically in our thought experiment never gets constructed in fact. The names on it are never specified, so we cannot know which among them have been deleted when the second list takes its place. But there *is* such a first list; that is, there is a list of persons who would have been accepted had race not been weighed, and the second list (constructed with race as a factor) *does* take the place of that one. The fact that we cannot name the persons squeezed out of the first list does not make the squeezing any less unfair.

Because the names of those actually displaced cannot be identified, each of those many applicants who thought his chances of admission excellent or at least good is likely to think, when rejected, that *he* is one of those whose race cost him his place. Most rejected white applicants may reasonably suppose that if only their skin color had been darker they would have been accepted. Ugly and awful are the consequences of what is now commonly done with good intentions: some deserving applicants do not get, simply because of their race, what they would have gotten if their color had not been held against them. This outcome is morally unacceptable, but it is an ineluctable consequence of every system of race preference.

The underlying problem is everywhere the same: in deciding upon what is to be given by way of redress for injury the properly critical moral consideration is the injury itself, its nature and its degree—not the race or national origin of the persons compensated. When preference is given to persons because of their race alone, many who are in fact owed redress do not receive it (either because they had been too greatly damaged, or because they happen not to be members of the favored categories), while many who are members of the favored categories receive benefits although owed nothing in the way of redress. And those who bear the burden of the preferential award are totally innocent of wrongdoing, bearing no responsibility whatever for injuries that may have been done to persons of the race preferred. Because both benefits and burdens are a function of race, and are not determined by considerations having genuine moral weight, race preference is perfectly incapable of achieving the compensatory objective offered in its defense; such preference is inevitably unfair and morally wrong.

(4) Race Preference Cannot Be Justified by the Quest for Diversity

Diversity is now widely offered as a justification of race preference. In universities, and where information or argument is reported or discussed, intellectual diversity is indeed a value worthy of pursuit. Among students, teachers, and journalists, a wide range of opinions and perspectives is certainly healthy. But the importance of diversity in these spheres is often greatly exaggerated, and its merits, even when they are substantial, cannot override the principle of equality. The quest for variety cannot justify the suspension of our moral duty not to discriminate by race.

In any case, the term "diversity" (as commonly used in this arena) does not actually mean variety of viewpoint and opinion; in practice it means variety among the *races* in their proper proportions. Colleges and universities that could greatly enrich their *intellectual* diversity do not work very hard at that, except so far as the variety they claim to seek is associated with minority ethnic groups. The almost complete homogeneity of political views on the faculties of major universities—one respect in which diversity would be particularly helpful—is extraordinary, but appears not to be a matter of great concern.[25] And even ethnic diversity, if it does not satisfy the quest for more of those minorities thought to have been earlier oppressed, does not count for much. Diversity of religion, diversity of life-style, diversity along any one of many other dimensions that really could provide more genuine enrichment is commonly ignored. The only "diversity" that is said to justify preference is racial diversity, and the standard by which it is decided whether "diversity goals" have been adequately achieved is the *match* of the proportion of certain minorities entering college (or entering professional schools, owning radio or TV stations, and so on) to the proportion of those minorities in the population at large. "Diversity," as everyone well understands, is today no more than a euphemism for race proportionality. A candid demand for proportionality would require highly objectionable (and probably unlawful) racial quotas, so politically correct institutions insist that it

---

[25]In a survey of 151 Ivy League professors conducted in 2002 *not one* identified himself as conservative. When a reporter for Denver's *Rocky Mountain News* surveyed the humanities and social science departments at the University of Colorado, Boulder, in 1998 he found that of 190 professors with party affiliations, 184 were Democrats; in the psychology, journalism, English, and philosophy departments he discovered not a single Republican. (Meanwhile, there are two hundred thousand more registered Republicans in Colorado than there are Democrats, and both senators are Republicans!) A 1999 survey of major history departments found 22 Democrats and 2 Republicans at Stanford—and no Republicans, not one, among the 29 professors in the history department at Cornell, or among the 10 in the history department at Dartmouth. In the spring of 2001 at Brown University the number of Republicans among the entire liberal arts faculty was 3—but zero in the English department, zero in the history department, zero in sociology and in political science. Also zero was the number of Republicans in the department of Africana studies. At the University of New Mexico, there were 10 Republicans—but none in the departments of history, or journalism, or political science, and only one each in the departments of sociology, English, women's studies, and African American studies. At the University of California, Santa Barbara, 97 percent of all professors were Democrats, and only one Republican professor could be found. Diversity in political views (unlike skin color) probably does have a bearing on how controversial issues are taught—but political diversity is not a great concern in university precincts. See *Jewish World Review*, 28 January 2002, and *The Christian Science Monitor*, 2 May 2002.

is only "diversity" that they pursue—an objective with wide appeal that is superficially race neutral.

But even where the quest for diversity is honest, that quest cannot justify outright unfairness. Preference by race is plainly unfair, as we have seen, and the demand for ethnic diversity simply ignores that unfairness. Are the numbers of black students enrolled, or Hispanic faculty appointed, sufficiently large? Is the racial profile of those employed, or of those winning prizes, or of those going to prison proportionate to the profile of the larger population? *Proportionality* is the unquestioned standard of success in achieving diversity; the racial *numbers* are what count. But ethnicity has no bearing whatever in many spheres, and in such spheres percentages cannot justifiably govern or distort the selection process. The alleged but uncertain benefits of some desired racial distribution do not override moral principles requiring fair treatment.

Suppose we were confronted with very strong evidence that racially *segregated* classrooms improve learning and teaching. Suppose the evidence in support of segregated schools were far more impressive than the very thin materials now offered in support of ethnic diversity. Would we think that such evidence (supposing it reliable) provided a *justification* for the deliberate racial segregation of our classrooms? Of course we would not. On the contrary, we will condemn the imposition of racial discrimination by the state in any case; we will point out that *whatever* the evidence of its consequences may show, racial discrimination is unacceptable, *wrong*, and that any advantages that may flow from it could not begin to justify a policy that is intrinsically unjust. And that is what race preference is.

As it happens, the praises of diversity as an instrument of education are greatly overblown; there is serious doubt that racial diversity has any measurable impact upon the quality of learning or teaching in a university.[26] But even if those claims of benefit had substantial merit, they would carry very little weight in a just society. Racial discrimination imposed by the state is despicable, we

[26]See "Why Justice Powell's Diversity Rationale for Racial Preferences in Higher Education Must Be Rejected," Princeton, N.J. 2001. Available online at www.nas.org.

know. Whichever the race favored by some discriminatory policy, the policy itself is morally intolerable; no studies or scholarship aiming to persuade us of its educative benefits can make it acceptable.

(5) Race Preference Cannot Be Justified by the Need for Outreach

To overcome the racism that has long pervaded American society we have a duty to insure that persons of all races and ethnicities have genuine and equal opportunities in all spheres of social life. Where previously invidious exclusion had been the rule, inclusion must now replace it. Deliberate efforts to accomplish this is a genuine duty deserving emphasis—but that duty cannot possibly justify race preference.

Utilizing truly equal opportunities requires a flow of unrestricted information that must not be reserved for the members of the establishment. In public settings, systems of selection that rely on an inner network of friends or acquaintances are unjust. And because the contributions of those who come from outside the inner circle may be lost, those "old-boy networks" are also often counterproductive. Reaching out to the larger community in announcing opportunities, in offering scholarships, in posting available jobs, and so on is right. Qualified members of all ethnicities, of both sexes, are entitled to have the same educational and employment opportunities that white males have traditionally enjoyed. To extend this inclusiveness, to advertise with the deliberate aim of reaching groups beyond those already well represented and well informed is *affirmative action* in its original and honorable sense. Where the availability of jobs and educational opportunities have traditionally favored some and disfavored others, honest outreach, favoring none, is certainly the duty of the arms of a state.

To illustrate: The State of Florida recently created two new law schools in which race is to play no role whatever in admission. But they are located at universities that have historically attracted a majority of minority students. One of these laws schools, at a fresh location in Orlando, is associated with Florida A&M University, historically black. The other, in Miami, is associated with Florida International University, where most students are Hispanic. This is outreach properly conceived; no preference is involved.[27]

Some varieties of race preference are *disguised* as outreach, and they ought to be condemned. Several examples:

First, when race preference in college admissions was forbidden in Texas by the *Hopwood* decision earlier noted,[28] a plan was devised in Texas to evade the law without giving preference explicitly. The system is ingenious and simple: all those graduating in the top 10 percent of their high school class are admitted to the University of Texas. The high schools in Texas are largely segregated de facto, not by law but because of residential patterns sustained by many socioeconomic factors. By automatically admitting a fixed and generous percentage from each of the de facto segregated secondary schools, the University of Texas is able to admit Hispanics and blacks in roughly the same proportion as when explicit race preference was in force. Maintaining those racial numbers was the principal reason for the adoption of the Texas bill imposing the 10 percent scheme. One of the sponsors of that bill in the legislature was candid: "We hope to increase the number of minority admissions to colleges and universities, which had plummeted with the chill that *Hopwood* had put on admissions."[29] Another sponsor described the bill as "a joint effort to zero out the impact of *Hopwood*."[30] It was, moreover, highly unusual for the Texas legislature to dictate university admissions policy. Now, with the constitutionality of race preference in serious doubt, officials are reluctant to admit that preference to advance racial balance is indeed the objective of the 10 percent plan. But no one is fooled.

[27]The new law school at Florida International University, which opened in the fall of 2002, received 41 percent of its applications from Hispanics, 32 percent of its applications from whites, 19 percent of its applications from blacks, and 2 percent of its applications from Asians. And of those accepted for the first year, 46 percent were white, 43 percent Hispanic, 10 percent black, and 3 percent Asian. Florida *is* reaching out; honest reaching neither requires nor justifies race preference.

[28]78 F. 3rd 932 (5th Cir. 1996).

[29]R. G. Ratcliffe and Lydia Lum, "Senate Approves Bill Designed to Boost Minority Enrollments," *Houston Chronicle*, 9 May 1997.

[30]Renee C. Lee, "State University Admissions Policy Proposed: Bill Seeks to Increase Minority Enrollment after Recent Affirmative Action Ruling," *Fort Worth Star-Telegram*, 15 March 1997.

Texas's success in thus advancing racial goals has led other states to do likewise. In Florida, with de facto segregation as marked as that in Texas, the top 20 percent of each high school class wins automatic admission to the premier state universities; in California it is the top 4 percent. Such systems advance racial proportionality only because the public high schools are segregated de facto. Race neutral on the surface, these are in reality instruments designed mainly to circumvent the prohibition of racial considerations. Fine students are replaced by mediocre students of the right color.[31] Ostensibly introduced as "outreach," these percentage plans are a species of indirect preference of which no one can be proud.[32]

---

[31]The impact of these percentage systems on the intellectual standards of the universities concerned is clearly adverse. In high schools with demanding curricula and many high-performing students, graduates below the top 10 or 20 percent may be very much more suitable for university admission than those with higher rankings from much weaker schools.

[32]Whether programs like the Texas 10 percent plan will stand up under constitutional examination is a question whose answer is not known. On the one hand, the Supreme Court has suggested, in the 1989 case in which a racial set-aside in Richmond was struck down, that it might have been reasonable for the city to rely upon race-neutral considerations to achieve the result sought, which was greater minority participation in certain business spheres. (*City of Richmond v. Croson*, 488 U.S. 469, at p. 507.] On the other hand, the court has also suggested in a 1979 case that a policy has a discriminatory purpose if the state "selected or reaffirmed a particular course of action at least in part 'because of,' not merely 'in spite of,' its adverse effects upon an identifiable group." [*Personnel Administrator v. Feeney*, 442 U.S. 256, at p. 278.]

Percentage plans like that of Texas aim to do indirectly what is plainly unlawful to do directly; in the long run such devices are very likely to be rejected. Antidiscrimination law is about substance, not just form. If it is illegal to require blacks to attend one school and whites to attend another, it must be illegal to require students from one geographic zone to attend one school and students from another geographic zone to attend another, in cases in which those geographic zones are delineated to ensure that most blacks would be in one zone and most whites in the other. That precisely was the decision of the U.S. Supreme Court in *Keyes v. School District No. 1* [413 U.S. 189 (1973)]—and the analogy to the Texas plan is close. Years will pass before this controversy is fully resolved—but it is plain that the Texas 10 percent plan, and others like it, have a racially disparate purpose, and are much more than race-neutral outreach.

Second, scholarships at public universities may no longer be openly reserved for specific racial groups.[33] Nevertheless, at the University of Texas that "technicality" has been overcome in the name of outreach. Special scholarships are offered—not to minorities, but to 130 carefully selected high schools located in the inner cities where enrollment is overwhelmingly black and Hispanic. Race has nothing to do with these special scholarships, we are told. "We're interested in a geographically, culturally, and economically diverse student population," explains the university spokesman, Ahmed El-sweewi. "This is not something designed to recruit minority students." Honest Texans cover their faces.[34]

Third, no race preference may be given in Texas after *Hopwood*. But at Texas A&M, the other huge and wealthy public university in that state, the prohibition is circumvented in yet another way. From a substantial number of specified inner-city high schools (whose students consist largely of minorities) the top 20 percent rather than the top 10 percent of the graduating class are deemed automatically admissible. Because the targeted schools from which the larger percentage of those accepted are racially identifiable, the device is transparently preferential.[35]

Fourth, at the campuses of the University of California, the recent shift to the "comprehensive review" of applicants has opened a back door to preference, giving significant advantage to candidates who claim to have faced hardships. At UCLA, an applicant now receives extra points to supplement his academic credentials if he's been the victim of a shooting; at UC Davis applicants earn up to 250 extra points for "perseverance"—which is inferred if they've faced family disruptions such as divorce or desertion, poverty, or life in "dysfunctional environments." At UC Berkeley good grades count

---

[33]A scholarship program exclusively for blacks was struck down at the University of Maryland at College Park in the case of *Podberesky v. Kirwan*, 38 F. 3rd 147 (1994). I served as an expert witness on behalf of the plaintiff in that case.

[34]See "UT Tailors Scholarship to Minority High Schools," *The Houston Chronicle*, 11 February 2002.

[35]Texas A&M's "top 20" plan was bluntly described by former U.S. secretary of education Lamar Alexander as "a step back toward racial quotas." See "Alexander Criticizes Top 20 Plan," *The Texas A&M Battalion*, 31 January 2002.

more if they have been earned at a poor high school, especially one that is afflicted with gangs, crime, dropouts, and drugs. Applicants from middle-class families that are loving and prosperous are at a distinct disadvantage. The Associated Press reported the pained response of one student with a 4.0 GPA and SAT scores of 1300, a varsity athlete in high school, who was turned down at all three of these campuses: "If my parents had been divorced I would have gotten in." Everyone understands that special boosts to applicants from single-parent homes, to crime victims and graduates of rotten schools, are designed to raise black and Hispanic enrollment. It works; black admissions rose 19 percent, Hispanic admissions 9 percent (with fewer whites and Asians, of course) for the fall term following the introduction of what is sardonically referred to as the "sob story sweepstakes."

Such efforts to evade the prohibition of race preference in the California constitution do more than simply dilute the role of intellect; they teach precisely the wrong lessons. A black professor of linguistics at the University of California, John McWhorter, laments the fact that "this new policy enhances the culture of victimization, teaching students of any color a lesson history will consider curious and misguided. . . . For decades now, students entering college have imbibed a 'victimologist' perspective; now UC's 'hardship' policy serves as a kind of college prep course on the subject."[36]

Nor is there any real doubt about why such preferences are given. McWhorter reports his experience sitting on a university committee that distributes scholarship money: packages once earmarked for "diversity" are now simply labeled as "hardship" bonuses. McWhorter writes: "Of course, the official line is that administrators are deeply concerned about hardship across race lines, but it doesn't wash. How seriously can we take this sudden concern for the coal miner's daughter when we heard not a peep of such class-based indignation during three decades of [outright] racial preferences? . . . [The system of hardship bonuses] is being utilized as a way to revive precisely the racial bean-counting that Proposition 209 outlawed."[37]

[36]John McWhorter, "It Shouldn't Be Good to Have It Bad," *Washington Post*, 4 August 2002.
[37]Ibid.

In their willingness to sacrifice scruples to advance racial balance in these ways, universities humiliate themselves. Outreach that is genuine, that seeks the spread of opportunity to all regardless of race or nationality, outreach that attends in a genuinely race-neutral way to life experiences that enhance individual qualifications, is affirmative action to which we may all subscribe. But acting affirmatively to insure that opportunities are indeed equal does not justify schemes designed to evade the law. Programs introduced in the name of "outreach"—race neutral on their surface but implemented to achieve a preferential outcome—are shameful cheats.

In summary: Race preference conflicts with the principle of equality that every decent society morally ought to respect. Race preference cannot be justified as a compensatory device. It cannot be justified by the quest for diversity. It cannot be justified by the call for outreach. It is morally wrong.

5

Race Preference Is Against the Law

(1) The Civil Rights Act of 1964

Race preference, even when its aims are honorable, is one form of deliberate racial discrimination. That is certain and undeniable. Such racial discrimination is illegal. Race preference clearly violates the Civil Rights Act of 1964.

The Civil Rights Act aimed to prohibit racial discrimination in public settings. The act comprises many prohibitions, grouped into parts called titles, each of which is itself a family of prohibitions. Current reference to the act is usually by title number. Thus Title III forbids race discrimination in places of *public accommodation.* Title VI deals with exclusion or the denial of benefits by race, color, or national origin, by any *institution receiving federal financial assistance*—which includes all public schools and colleges (e.g. the University of Georgia, the University of Michigan, etc.) and most private educational institutions (e.g. Harvard, Stanford, etc.) as well. Title VII forbids discriminatory *employment* practices, in both the public and the private sector. (It is complemented by executive orders: Executive Order 11246 [1965] and Executive Order 11375 [1967] lay down rules that govern public contractors, requiring that federal employment be "without discrimination because of race, color, religion, sex, or national origin.") Title IX forbids discrimination on the basis of *sex.* In the several titles the wording is somewhat repetitive for the sake of unmistakable clarity and precision. This Civil Rights Act of 1964 has been—and remains—the principle law that governs the uses of race in public settings throughout the United States. Its fair and egalitarian spirit is manifest in its plain language. Two key passages of the Civil Rights Act are these:[38]

From Title VI (Federally Assisted Programs, Education):

> No person in the United States shall, on the ground of race, color, or national origin, be excluded from participation in, be denied the benefits of, or be subjected to discrimination under any program or activity receiving Federal financial assistance.[39]

From Title VII (Private and Public Employment):

> It shall be an unlawful employment practice for an employer—
>
> (1) to fail or refuse to hire or to discharge any individual, or otherwise to discriminate against any individual with respect to his compensation, terms, conditions, or privileges of employment, because of such individual's race, color, religion, sex, or national origin, or
>
> (2) to limit, segregate, or classify his employees or applicants for employment in any way which would deprive or tend to deprive any individual of employment opportunities or otherwise adversely affect his status as an employee, because of such individual's race, color, religion, sex, or national origin.[40]

To make it crystal clear that the law was intended to forbid racial preference of every kind, including preferences for minorities, and that such preferences may not be imposed under its authority, the act includes the following passage:

> Nothing contained in this subchapter shall be interpreted to require any employer, employment agency, labor organization, or joint labor-management committee subject to this subchapter to grant preferential treatment to any individual or to any group because of the race, color, religion, sex, or national origin of such individual or group on account of an imbalance which may exist with respect to the total number or percentage of persons of any race, color, religion, sex, or na-

[38]The whole of the Civil Rights Act of 1964 may be found in chapter 42 of *United States Codes*. The passages cited here are identified by section number, within their respective titles.
[39]Civil Rights Act of 1964, Section 601 of Title VI.
[40]Ibid., Section 703(a) of Title VII.

tional origin employed by an employer, referred or classified by any employment agency or labor organization, or admitted to, or employed in, any apprenticeship or other training program, in comparison with the total number of persons of such race, color, religion, sex, or national origin in any community, State, section, or other area, or in the available work force in any community, State, section, or other area.[41]

This comprehensive rejection of discrimination by race pervades all the sections and titles of the Civil Rights Act of 1964. Its several prohibitions are specified with very careful phrasing, in a very emphatic tone and with great lucidity throughout. Years after its passage, one justice of the Supreme Court called attention to the remarkable clarity of the act's language, by calling it "a model of statutory draftsmanship."[42] One need not be a lawyer or judge to grasp its force. No person of adult understanding who can read English can have any doubt whatever that the object of this Civil Rights Act was, and is, to make unlawful (in those spheres to which the law expressly applies) *all* discrimination on the basis of race, color, religion, sex, or national origin.

What is done in the name of "affirmative action" is not exempt from this law. The plain words of the statute can hardly be misunderstood. Employers, university administrators, and all others who discriminate among ethnic groups to give special favor to some *break the law.*

When race preferences given by the University of California were struck down by the Supreme Court in 1978, four justices of that court joined in emphasizing that such preferences could not survive *simply because they violated Title VI of the Civil Rights Act,* which specifically forbids discrimination on the ground of race under any program or activity receiving federal financial assistance.[43] Having noted that the university acknowledges that it receives federal financial assistance, Justice Stevens wrote for that group of four: "The

---

[41]Ibid., Section 703(j) of Title VII.

[42]Justice Antonin Scalia, in *Johnson v. Transportation Agency,* 480 U.S. 616, at p. 647, 1986.

[43]The exact language of Title VI is cited in the third paragraph of this chapter, p. 47. The case described here, *Regents of the University of California v. Bakke* (438 U.S. 265 [1978]), will be discussed in greater detail in the following chapter, which deals with constitutional issues.

plain language of the statute therefore requires" that the judgment of the Supreme Court of California striking down admissions preferences at the University of California be affirmed, and that Mr. Bakke be admitted. He continued:

> Nothing in the legislative history justifies the conclusion that the broad language of Section 601 should not be given its natural meaning. *We are dealing with a distinct statutory prohibition.*[44]

Prohibitions enacted by congressional statutes are distinguishable from those imposed by our Constitution. The law may forbid what the Constitution permits. That is why the fact that the prohibition of race preference flows directly and expressly *from the statute* must be emphasized. Even if it were held that the Constitution is not violated by such preferences, it remains the case that *the law* is clearly violated by them; the prohibition of discrimination in the Civil Rights Act, Justice Stevens takes pains to point out, is not "simply that of a Constitutional appendage."[45] The condemnation continues:

> In unmistakable terms the Act prohibits the exclusion of individuals from federally funded programs because of their race. As succinctly phrased during the Senate debate, under Title VI it is not "permissible to say 'yes' to one person but to say 'no' to another person, only because of the color of his skin." . . . The University's special admissions program violated Title VI of the Civil Rights Act of 1964 by excluding Bakke from the medical school because of his race.[46]

There is no ambiguity in this matter: Race preference (in institutions receiving federal assistance) is impermissible *as a matter of federal law* in the United States of America. No qualifications, no conditions, no uncertainties have place here: *Race preference by institutions receiving federal financial assistance breaks the law.*

(2) Evading the Civil Rights Act

How has it been possible—in the face of a statute so plain and unambiguous—to maintain racially preferential programs that blatantly violate that law? Evasion has been protected in two ways: by

---

[44]*Bakke*, p. 417. Emphasis added.
[45]Ibid.
[46]*Bakke,* pp. 419, 421.

obscuring illegal conduct with *subterfuge* and by defending illegal conduct with *unsound argument*. I take these in turn.

Racially discriminatory conduct has often been hidden, disguised so as to make it appear that the law was being obeyed. Deception has been common; dishonesty has not been rare. "Affirmative action" programs are described as designed to support "disadvantaged" persons when the only disadvantaged persons considered are the members of ethnic minorities for whom preference is intended. Tacitly assuming that all members of certain ethnic minorities are necessarily disadvantaged, advocates misleadingly describe preference for those minorities as no more than support for the disadvantaged.

Compensation for social or economic disadvantage does not violate the Civil Rights Act, of course—so long as race is not a qualification for that support. It is certainly not the case that all disadvantaged persons are members of some ethnic minority, nor is it true that all members of any given minority are disadvantaged. Therefore, to reserve preferences for members of certain races, and then to defend those preferences as no more than efforts to combat disadvantage, is simply cheating. The Civil Rights Act is evaded when the conduct it forbids is obscured by deliberately deceptive description.

Three examples of such cheating: (1) The California court that first struck down the preferential admissions program of the Davis medical school at the University of California noted that the program had been very carefully described by the university, in its letters to applicants, as applying to "applications from economically and/or educationally disadvantaged backgrounds." But, the court found, it was *in fact* a system of preference based only on ethnic status, since no applicants other than those from approved "affirmative action categories" had *ever* been admitted under the special admissions program. The Supreme Court of California, reviewing the matter, agreed.[47] The medical school had deliberately sought to make it appear that its standards were race neutral, but its actual practice made it evident that this was knowing subterfuge. No one having an opportunity to examine the data would be fooled—but the data came to light only in the course of litigation. The California judges were irate, and they scolded the university severely for its deliberate

---

[47]*Regents of the University of California v. Bakke*, 18 Cal. 3rd 34, at p. 55.

obfuscation. Chastened, the university ceased to argue that its program was not racially preferential.

(2) A quarter of a century later, a federal judge found (after a lengthy trial) that the official account of the admissions program at the law school of the University of Michigan was at best deceptive. The law school had insisted that it sought only to enroll a "critical mass" of minority students; the judge found the system to be in fact "practically indistinguishable from a quota system."[48]

(3) Even in federal regulations the word "disadvantaged" is sometimes used when what is really meant is "minority." Cash bonuses are paid to firms contracting with the U.S. government if their subcontractors are minority owned. This is plainly race preference. The preference is hidden by the language of the regulations, which is framed not in terms of "minority" ownership but in terms of "disadvantaged" ownership; the bonus payments are to be made to encourage *"disadvantaged* business enterprises"—DBEs, as they have come to be known. That would appear innocent—except that the *definitions* used provide that *subcontractors who are not members of the white majority are automatically to be treated as "disadvantaged business enterprises."*[49] Administrators in government agencies are skilled in the arts of obfuscation to evade the law.

[48]Judge Bernard Friedman, in his findings of fact in *Grutter v. Bollinger*, 137 F. Supp. 2nd 821 (E.D. Mich. 2001). After having been enjoined from the further use of race in admissions, the University petitioned for a delay in the imposition of this injunction, claiming irreparable harm. The petition was denied; Judge Friedman then added: "The court has found that defendants' use of race is indistinguishable from a quota system, and there is no doubt that racial quotas in this context and for this purpose are unconstitutional. Defendants are not irreparably harmed by an injunction that requires them to comply with the Constitution." 137 F. Supp. 2nd 874, at p. 878.

[49]This statute has given rise to a chain of Supreme Court cases involving a small company, Adarand Constructors, whose bid on a small highway project in Colorado was rejected in favor of a bid by a minority-owned subcontractor. But that successful bid was made feasible only by the federal cash bonus paid to the minority-owned subcontractor. The matter reached the highest court as *Adarand Constructors, Inc. v. Pena* (516 U.S. 200 [1995]). Proceedings in that case were much extended because the devices used by the U.S. Department of Transportation in dealing with contractors were repeatedly altered to protect minority preferences, making the federal agency that gave such preferences a very slippery target.

At colleges and universities euphemistic names given to preferential programs to hide their racial character are common. At the University of Michigan, admissions preference was called "The Michigan Mandate." At Pennsylvania Military College, preferentially admitted students who did not satisfy ordinary admission standards were enrolled in "Project Prepare." (But as one black student so admitted revealed, only persons of certain colors are thus prepared.[50]) At the University of Maryland, the preferential program is called "Upward Bound."

Of all the euphemisms, "diversity" is now the most common. In the *Bakke* decision of 1978, in which preference to compensate for societal "disadvantage" was rejected, Justice Powell expressed the view that diversity may be a justification for the consideration of race in college admissions. His opinion has been heavily relied upon by universities whose admissions officers argue that since diversity is a compelling objective, it must be lawful to give racial preference to achieve it.[51] In university circles the quest for "diversity" now largely *means* a quest for ethnic proportionality. Other code words—"multi-culturalism" and "cultural pluralism"—have similar deceptive functions.

The truth does not fare well in public reports about these matters. The legal prohibition of racial discrimination, on the one hand, and the political need to advance racial balance (to "promote diversity"), on the other hand, put administrators in an awkward bind. To report the "improvement" in diversity numbers, they must (and do) give race preferences that cannot be admitted—so they lie, or deceive. A nonacademic manager at the University of Michigan recounted (as an example) this device: "Recently the University decided to . . . monitor how we do our hiring. . . . They would send us [completed] applications and circle certain minorities. They wouldn't tell you why, but you knew why."[52]

When outright dishonesty is too risky, *doublespeak* may serve in its place. Here are the instructions received by a job applicant from the

[50]"Into the White Ivory Tower," *New York Times Magazine*, 6 February 1994, p. 26.
[51]Whether or not diversity can serve successfully as a "compelling" objective to justify racial classifications under the constitutional standard of strict scrutiny is discussed at length in chapter 6.
[52]"Affirmative Action Not What It Seems," *The Michigan Review*, 1 April 1992.

"Affirmative Employment Division" of the U.S. Air Force Academy: "The Federal Government is an equal opportunity employer and in support of that effort we ask that you voluntarily complete the Standard Form 181, 'Race and National Origin Identification.'"[53] Racial discrimination is against the law, says the Air Force, and we comply with the law. But we prefer minorities. Are you one? Help wanted advertisements in every sphere are commonly concluded with the oxymoron that epitomizes this subterfuge: X-Corp [replace with the name of the company or agency] is an "*Affirmative Action/Equal Opportunity Employer.*" Everyone understands what that means.

Middle-level employees who may object to such cheating are often unable to speak out safely. Within the company the sham is generally recognized, but over time almost everyone is made complicit—so almost all find it most convenient to wink. Violations of law can only be proved using records kept secret; to obtain such records the cost, interpersonal as well as legal, is likely to be high. But in an open society like ours, where freedom of information statutes are common, and where civil litigation obliges full discovery, the truth about such matters cannot be permanently hidden. At the state universities of Virginia, Georgia, and Michigan, and at many other major universities, gross preference by race can no longer be denied.[54]

---

[53]The instruction was included in the letter sent to the applicant by the "Equal Employment Specialist," as reported in *Heterodoxy*, March 1993. "Equal," in this context, generally means something like "Unequal."

[54]A Freedom of Information Act request to the University of Michigan, of which I was the author in 1995, resulted in the disclosure of documents proving the university's earlier denials of race preferences in admission to have been deceptive or dishonest. Data revealed in those documents, subsequently reprinted in the *New York Times* and in other national publications, roused the anger of some Michigan legislators and led to federal litigation that remains in process as I write. In *Gratz v. Bollinger* (respecting undergraduate admission preferences) and *Grutter v. Bollinger* (respecting law school admission preferences) the plaintiffs contend that the race-based practices of the university, hidden no longer, are plain violations of Title VI and of the Constitution. At other universities the race preferences given in admission have been revealed in a series of shocking reports published by the Center for Equal Opportunity, in Washington, D.C. *Gratz* and *Grutter* were argued before the Supreme Court of the United States on 1 April 2003.

(3) Reinterpreting the Civil Rights Act

Some advocates of race preference argue that the Civil Rights Act of 1964 permits what they do, if that law be properly interpreted. In effect they argue as follows:

> The *spirit* of the law is what binds us. The Congress, when it enacted the Civil Rights Act of 1964, aimed to improve the conditions of minorities. Race preference does just that. Therefore, even if they are not strictly "within the letter of the statute," preferential programs are "within its spirit." Protecting and enlarging opportunities for blacks and Hispanics—in employment and education and public accommodation—was what Congress sought to do. Therefore, when an employer or a union now gives employment preference to blacks, or a university gives admission preference to Hispanics, such preferences (because they protect and enlarge opportunities) do not really violate the Civil Rights Act because it cannot be the case that Congress intended to prohibit private or public agencies "from taking effective steps to accomplish the goal that Congress designed [the Civil Rights Act] to achieve."[55]

So long as the benefits of some preference go to persons whom that law was designed to protect (this argument avers), that preference cannot be a violation of the statute properly understood. The argument comes to this:

> The aims of preferential affirmative action are consonant with the aims of Congress. Congress thus could not have intended to forbid such preference. Therefore, if the language of Congress *appears* to say that race preference is forbidden, we must interpret that language to mean what it did not say—for what it does say it surely could not mean.

This argument is wholly without merit. We are obliged to obey the law as it is written. Judges are obliged to enforce the law as it is written, and not as they may think it ought to have been written.

---

[55]This is precisely the argument put forward by Justice Brennan in holding race preference for blacks in industrial employment to be within the spirit of Title VII of the Civil Rights Act. The phrases quoted here are the words of Justice Brennan in deciding that case, *United Steelworkers of America v. Weber*, 443 U.S. 193 (1979).

Congress forbad racial discrimination flatly, explicitly; and its members understood very well the plain words they used in doing so.[56] Those words, applied with their ordinary and straightforward meaning, make race preference unlawful. One of the *goals* of Congress, in adopting the Civil Rights Act, was indeed to improve opportunities for blacks and other minorities. But it does not follow that any and every preferential program having that goal is therefore to be considered lawful under the statute. Two patterns of conduct sharing the same larger objective may differ sharply with respect to their permissibility in advancing it. This is the point of the common observation that "the end does not justify the means." The aphorism is misleading because ends really do serve in justifying means, but the moral point of this homily is the limitation it conveys: even very worthy objectives don't justify *any* means that may be thought effective in achieving them. Broadening opportunities for blacks is an objective very widely supported, but some of the means that some persons now think useful in advancing that objective were forbidden—unambiguously prohibited—by the U.S. Congress in the Civil Rights Act of 1964.

Consider this analogy. Suppose Congress, with the goal of reducing dependence on foreign oil, appropriated funds to explore alternative sources of energy. But suppose in that same bill they had explicitly forbidden the use of the funds for the development of nuclear energy. Would a program that deliberately ignored this

---

[56]Senator Hubert Humphrey, floor manager for the Civil Rights Act of 1964 in the Senate, was asked early in the debate what was meant by the word "discrimination" as it was used in the bill. He answered, on the Senate floor, as follows:

> [T]he word "discrimination" has been used in many a court case. What it really means in the bill is a distinction in treatment . . . given to different individuals because of their different race, religion, or national origin. . . . The answer to this question is that if race is not a factor we do not have to worry about discrimination because of race. . . . The Internal Revenue Code does not provide that colored people do not have to pay taxes, or that they can pay their taxes six months later than everybody else. . . . If we started to treat Americans as Americans, not as fat ones, short ones, tall ones, brown ones, green ones, yellow ones, or white ones, but as Americans . . . we would not need to worry about discrimination. *Congressional Record*, vol. 110, pp. 5864, 5866.

restriction and spent the funds to develop nuclear energy be then lawful? Of course not. Could such expenditures be defended as "within the intentions" of the legislature because (as Justice Brennan argued in defense of employment preferences in *Weber*) "the purpose of the plan mirrors those of the statute"? We know that Congress intended not to permit the advancement of its larger objectives in that way. If the law (in that imagined hypothetical case) had said explicitly that "it shall be unlawful to expend any of the appropriated funds on the development of nuclear energy" we might think that prohibition unwise, but we understand the difference between the larger *purpose* of Congress in appropriating funds for energy research and its explicit *intent* to limit the ways in which those purposes may be advanced. What Congress hopes to achieve is often important to know, but our conduct is nevertheless restricted by what the laws explicitly forbid.

The prohibitions of the Civil Rights Act of 1964 were designed to enlarge opportunities for blacks and to insure racial justice for all. Racial discrimination—because it had so long hindered opportunities—was flatly prohibited for all by that bill. To argue that Congress did not intend to forbid employment discrimination against whites because some discrimination against whites might also advance opportunities for blacks is plainly unsound. When it is argued that under the Civil Rights Act some outright preferences are protected, that act is being used to justify precisely the practices it was explicitly designed to condemn. An interpretation warped in that way, Justice Scalia wrote in another case, *converts* Title VII "from a guarantee that race or sex will not be the basis for employment determinations, to a guarantee that it often will." Such reasoning, he observed, "effectively replace[s] the goal of a discrimination-free society with the quite incompatible goal of proportionate representation by race and by sex in the workplace." [57]

(4) The Intentions of Congress in the Civil Rights Act of 1964

The intent of a legislature may become a matter of importance when the wording of its laws is ambiguous or their meaning unclear.

---

[57]*Johnson v. Transportation Agency*, 480 U.S. 616 (1986).

Interpretation may then be required. Additionally, unforeseen circumstances may give rise to controversies that the language of the statute does not resolve, making it necessary to construe legislative intent at the time of enactment in order to determine how that language should bear upon the newly arisen conditions. Sometimes legislation is formulated in language that is deliberately ambiguous to win its passage—obliging some court later to construe legislative intent in adjudicating the law's application.

No such problems are presented by the Civil Rights Act of 1964. The language of every title within it exhibits, as the chief justice of the Supreme Court later noted, "no lack of clarity, no ambiguity."[58] When an employer, public or private, discriminates against an applicant for employment, or against an employee seeking promotion, simply because he is white—a form of preference now widely given in the name of "affirmative action"—that, in the unambiguous language of the statute, is "an unlawful employment practice."

Has the act been widely interpreted to prohibit discrimination only against blacks but not against whites? No, of course not. When whites and blacks have been treated differently, the Supreme Court concluded, after close examination of the act and its legislative history, that (as Justice Thurgood Marshall wrote) it "prohibits discrimination against the white petitioners in this case upon the same standard as would be applicable were they Negroes."[59] Without doubt the Civil Rights Act applies equally to persons of all races.

A single standard, applicable equally to all persons and all races, has been repeatedly affirmed by the Supreme Court. Unanimously the court held in 1971 that "The objective of Congress in the enactment of Title VII is plain from the language of the statute. It was to achieve equality of employment opportunity. . . . Discriminatory preference for any group, minority or majority, is precisely and only what Congress has proscribed."[60] And again, five years later: "Title VII prohibits *all* racial discrimination in employment, without

[58]Chief Justice Warren Burger, dissenting in *Weber*.
[59]*McDonald v. Santa Fe Trail Transportation Company*, 427 U.S. 273, at p. 280 (1976).
[60]*Griggs v. Duke Power Co.*, 401 U.S. 424, at pp. 429, 431 (1971).

exception for any group of particular employees."[61] Three years after that, the issue of racial *ratios* in employment was before the Supreme Court, whereupon the court concluded: "It is clear beyond cavil that the obligation imposed by Title VII is to provide an equal opportunity for each applicant regardless of race, without regard to whether members of the applicant's race are already proportionately represented in the work force."[62] With respect to the question of whether the Civil Rights Act protects whites equally with nonwhites, there is no trace of ambiguity in the law itself or in Supreme Court opinions that have interpreted it. There is therefore no need to enter the question of legislative intent in enacting this legislation.

Notwithstanding the notable clarity of the statute, the advocates of race preference for minorities claim support for their judgments in the legislative history of the Civil Rights Act. So we must ask: Did Congress intend, when it adopted the Civil Rights Act of 1964, to permit *some* racial preferences for minorities? The categorical answer is no; the proof of this—here following—is overwhelming.

In the U.S. House of Representatives, and in the Senate, the Civil Rights Act of 1964 was debated at length, and the full record of those debates is available to us in the *Congressional Record*. Committee reports to the House are open to us. A scholarly study of the legislative history of Title VII has been published. What was intended by the members of Congress in enacting this legislation is fully, readily, and definitively determinable.[63]

---

[61]*McDonald*, p. 283. Emphasis in the original.

[62]*Furnco Construction Corp. v. Waters*, 438 U.S. 567 (1978).

[63]The congressional debates appear in volume 110 of the *Congressional Record* of 1964, extending intermittently over exactly 13,000 pages of ten massive tomes. The committee reports appear in *House of Representatives Reports*, no. 914, 87th Congress, First Session, 1963. Additional views of particular members, and groups of members, appear there in addition to these reports. The Senate decided to take up the civil rights bill directly, so it was not submitted to committee there, but the full text of lengthy Senate floor debates is open to us. The historical study referred to is that of Francis J. Vaas, "Title VII: Legislative History," in *Boston College Industrial and Commercial Law Review* 7, pp. 431–58. Vaas wrote: "Seldom has similar legislation been debated with greater consciousness of the need for 'legislative history' or with greater care in the making thereof, to guide courts in interpreting and applying the law" (p. 444).

No reasonable person who has examined these materials can doubt what the intent of Congress was, in choosing the words they did choose. Democrats and Republicans both, conservatives and liberals both, insisted repeatedly and at length that the Civil Rights Act of 1964 (Called H.R. 7152 in the congressional debates) would forbid *all* racial preference in public settings for *any* race.

The one great objection raised by opponents of the act (and especially Title VII, pertaining to employment) in both the House and the Senate was this: because of it, racial proportionality might someday be required by a federal agency under color of law. An employer (suggested one critical minority report) *"may be forced to hire according to race*, to 'racially balance' those who work for him . . . or be in violation of Federal law."[64] This fear that racial balance might be imposed under the bill had to be allayed, and the objection overcome, if the bill were to be passed. To this end, proponents of the act repeatedly reassured their colleagues, without reservation, that no such racial balancing was contemplated, that preferential hiring by race could not be required and *would not be permitted* under Title VII. The key section of Title VII was 703(a), which expressly forbad all racial discrimination, and all racial classification that would have any adverse impact upon any single employee. It reads:

> It shall be an unlawful employment practice for an employer—
>
> (1) to fail or refuse to hire or to discharge any individual, or otherwise to discriminate against any individual with respect to his compensation, terms, conditions, or privileges of employment, because of such individual's race, color, religion, sex, or national origin; or
>
> (2) to limit, segregate, or classify his employees or applicants for employment in any way which would deprive or tend to deprive any individual of employment opportunities or otherwise adversely affect his status as an employee, because of such individual's race, color, religion, sex, or national origin.

When the debate in the House of Representatives opened early in 1964, the chairman of the House Committee on the Judiciary, Representative Emanuel Celler (D-NY), clarified the intent of this critical passage. The fear that it would require or permit hiring or

---

[64]*House Committee Reports*, 1963, p. 69.

promotion on the basis of race, he said, resulted from a description of the bill that was "entirely wrong." *Even a court*, he continued,

> could not order that any preference be given to any particular race, religion, or other group, but would be limited to ordering an end to discrimination. The statement that a Federal inspector could order the employment and promotion only of members of a specific racial or religious group is therefore patently erroneous. . . . The Bill would do no more than prevent a union, as it would prevent employers, from discriminating against or in favor of workers because of their race or religion or national origin. It is likewise not true that the Equal Employment Opportunity Commission [EEOC] would have the power to rectify existing "racial or religious imbalance" in employment by requiring the hiring of certain people . . . simply because they are of a given race or religion. Only actual discrimination could be stopped.[65]

This emphatic declaration of intent echoed repeatedly during the debate in the House. Representative Lindsay (R-NY, later to become mayor of New York City) took up the defense of the act:

> This legislation does not . . . as has been suggested heretofore both on and off the floor, force acceptance of people in schools, jobs, housing, or public accommodations because they are Negro. It does not impose quotas or any special privileges of seniority or acceptance. There is nothing whatever in the bill about racial balance. . . . What the bill does do is prohibit discrimination because of race.[66]

With that very clear understanding the bill passed the House, 290-130, on February 10, 1964.

In the Senate the expression of legislative intent was equally unequivocal but much more voluminous. Again, the chief objection of opponents was that a federal inspector might one day require racial balancing under color of law. Again—and again and again and again and again—the defenders of the bill replied with unqualified reassurance, vehemently insisting that such fears were totally unfounded. The key word, appearing repeatedly in the bill, was "discrimination." That word was examined minutely on the Senate floor. Could it be

[65]*Congressional Record*, vol. 110, p. 1,518.
[66]Ibid., p. 1,540.

taken to mean the absence of racial balance? Answer by the proponents: definitely not. Could it be intended as a technical term, whose hidden meaning was "discrimination against blacks but not discrimination against whites"? Answer: certainly not. The majority leader and foremost advocate of the bill in the Senate, Hubert Humphrey (Democratic candidate for president in 1968), put that suggestion permanently to rest:

> [t]he meaning of racial or religious discrimination is perfectly clear. . . . it means a distinction in treatment given to different individuals because of their different race, religion, or national origin.[67]

The only freedom of employers that the bill limits, he emphasized, is the freedom to take action based on race, religion, sex, or national origin.

The Senate did not send the bill to committee; on the Senate floor its advocates were obliged to reply, repeatedly, to the objection that the bill would lead or might lead to race preference. Not so, they said, not *possible*. Senator Humphrey again:

> That bugaboo has been brought up a dozen times; but it is nonexistent. In fact, the very opposite is true. Title VII prohibits discrimination. In effect it says that race, religion, and national origin are not to be used as the basis for hiring and firing. Title VII is designed to encourage hiring on the basis of ability and qualifications, not race or religion.

He goes on to give examples that

> make clear what is implicit throughout the whole of Title VII; namely, that employers may hire and fire, promote and refuse to promote for any reason, good or bad, provided only that individuals may not be discriminated against because of race, religion, sex, or national origin.

He repeats himself in the hope that none will fail to hear:

> The truth is that this title forbids discriminating against anyone on account of race. This is the simple and complete truth about Title VII.[68]

---

[67]Ibid. p. 5,423. Exactly the same account had been given by Senator Humphrey earlier in the debate, as reported in footnote 19.
[68]Ibid., p. 6,549.

Senator Kuchel (R-CA), the Minority Whip and a strong supporter of the Civil Rights Act, explained why the seniority of workers already employed would not be affected by the act:

> Employers and labor organizations could not discriminate in favor or against a person because of his race, his religion, or his national origin. In such matters the Constitution, and the bill now before us drawn to conform to the Constitution, is color-blind.[69]

Senators Clark (D-PA) and Case (R-NJ) were floor captains in the Senate for Title VII. Specifying what that title did and did not prohibit or permit was one of their tasks. It was their duty to refute the charge that Title VII might result in preference for any group. They prepared a memorandum for the Senate, expressing the intent of Title VII unequivocally:

> Any deliberate attempt to maintain a racial balance, whatever such a balance may be, would involve a violation of Title VII because maintaining such a balance would require an employer to hire or to refuse to hire on the basis of race. It must be emphasized that discrimination is prohibited as to any individual.[70]

The Department of Justice prepared a separate memorandum on the same aspect of the act, presenting the same conclusion about the force of its language:

> No employer is required to maintain any ratio of Negroes to whites, Jews to Gentiles, Italians to English, or women to men. The same is true of labor organizations. On the contrary, any deliberate attempt to maintain a given balance would almost certainly run afoul of Title VII because it would involve a failure or refusal to hire some individual because of his race, color, religion, sex, or national origin. What Title VII seeks to accomplish, what the civil rights bill seeks to accomplish, is equal treatment for all.[71]

The opponents of the bill did not trust these assurances. Senators Smathers (D-FL) and Sparkman (D-AL) granted that the bill

[69]Ibid., p. 6,564.
[70]Ibid., p. 7,213.
[71]Ibid., p. 7,207.

did not require the use of racial quotas, but complained of its likely indirect effects. Under this bill, they suggested, employers might be coerced by federal agencies into giving preference by race. Could the proponents guarantee that this would not be permitted? The response, given by Senator Williams (D-NJ) is painful to read today. Opponents of the Civil Rights Act, he said,

> persist in opposing a provision which is not only not contained in the bill, but is *specifically excluded* from it. Those opposed to H.R. 7152 [the Civil Rights Act] should realize that to hire a Negro solely because he is a Negro is racial discrimination, just as much as a "white only" employment policy. *Both forms of discrimination are prohibited by Title VII of this bill.* The language of that Title simply states that race is not a qualification for employment. . . . [A]ll men are to have an equal opportunity to be considered for a particular job. Some people charge that H.R. 7152 favors the Negro at the expense of the white majority. But how can the language of equality favor one race or one religion over another? Equality can have only one meaning, and that meaning is self-evident to reasonable men. Those who say that equality means favoritism do violence to common sense.[72]

But the fear that the proposed legislation might somehow permit or encourage race preference would not die down. Again the floor leader, Senator Humphrey, was obliged to reiterate the intent and the plain meaning of the words of the act:

> [Title VII] does not provide that any preferential treatment in employment shall be given to Negroes or to any other person or groups. It does not provide that any quota systems may be established to maintain racial balance in employment. In fact, the title would prohibit preferential treatment for any particular group, and any person, whether or not a member of any minority group, would be permitted to file a complaint of discriminatory employment practices.[73]

In the face of this parade of unequivocal accounts of the intent of the act, by its authors, one cannot now plausibly maintain that race preference for minorities is "within the intent" of this Civil Rights

---

[72]Ibid., p. 8,921. Emphasis added.
[73]Ibid., p. 11,848.

Act. But the defenders of preference have nevertheless sought to do so, next relying upon the following maneuver: Congress may have intended to forbid preference to *maintain* balance (the argument goes) but did not intend to forbid preference designed to *eliminate existing imbalance*. Preferential affirmative action now is of the latter sort, and that sort of preference really is within the intent of the law.[74]

The distinction is spurious. Senators Clark and Case had written in their joint memorandum:

> Title VII would have *no effect* on established seniority rights. Its effect is prospective and not retrospective. Thus, for example, if a business had been discriminating in the past and as a result has an all-white working force, when the title comes into effect the employer's obligation would be simply to fill future vacancies on a non-discriminatory basis. He would not be obliged—or indeed permitted—to fire whites in order to hire Negroes, or, once Negroes are hired, to give them special seniority rights at the expense of white workers hired earlier.[75]

The Justice Department, in its analysis of the act, also emphasized that Title VII could not be used to alter seniority entitlements because of earlier discrimination in employment:

> [E]ven in the case where, owing to discrimination prior to the effective date of the Title, white workers had more seniority than Negroes . . . assuming that seniority rights were built up over a period of time during which Negroes were not hired, these rights would not be set aside by the taking effect of Title VII. Employers and labor organizations would simply be under a duty not to discriminate against Negroes because of their race.[76]

A distinction between "achieving racial balance" and "maintaining racial balance" was never any part of the understanding of Congress

---

[74]The preferential affirmative action plan adopted by Kaiser Aluminum and the Steelworkers Union in the 1970s was defended by Justice Brennan in just this way. That plan, said he, "is not intended to maintain racial balance, but simply to eliminate a manifest racial imbalance." *Steelworkers v. Weber*, p. 208.

[75]Ibid., p. 7,213. Emphasis added.

[76]Ibid., p. 7,207.

in adopting the Civil Rights Act. The claim that preference is now lawful in the light of that distinction is therefore groundless. For Congress in 1964, as the Civil Rights Act was debated, race preference was simply impermissible, and would be as wrong if undertaken with the one aim as with the other. Moreover, it is evident that current defenders of preference are as ready to use such devices to maintain racial balance as to achieve it; current argument resting upon that spurious distinction is therefore hypocritical. Race preference for any purpose flies in the face of this law.

To meet the repeated objections of implacable opponents, the sponsors of the Civil Rights Act decided to insert an amendment that would lock the matter down, making it impossible for any federal agency later to use the law as justification for race preference. Senators Dirkson (R-IL) and Mansfield (D-MT) devised a subsection, 703(j), that specifically addressed the fear of imposed racial balancing. This section provides that *nothing in the law may be interpreted to require* giving preference to any individual because of his race.[77]

This inserted section was later used, in an ironic turn, by defenders of preference in the following way. The added section (addressed to courts but not to employers) bars the requirement of imposed racial preference, but does not speak to its prohibition. On this ground, it was argued that it must have been the intention of Congress to permit race preference if it were not required! This inference is utterly disingenuous, because the inserted section was

---

[77]It reads in full: "Nothing contained in this subchapter shall be interpreted to require any employer, employment agency, labor organization, or joint labor-management committee subject to this subchapter to grant preferential treatment to any individual or to any group because of the race, color, religion, sex, or national origin of such individual or group on account of an imbalance which may exist with respect to the total number of percentage of persons of any race, color, religion, sex, or national origin employed by any employer, referred or classified by any employment agency, or labor organization, or admitted to, or employed in, any apprenticeship or other training program, on comparison with the total number of persons of such race, color, religion, sex, or national origin in any community, State, section, or other area, or in the available work force in any community, State, section, or other area." 42 U.S. Codes 2000e-2(j).

designed specifically to meet the objection that race preference might someday be required. It did not address "voluntary" race preference by employers for the very good reason that voluntary race preference of every kind had been repeatedly and specifically forbidden by the plain language of the sections just above it. No one in Congress ever supposed that race preference could be lawful under this statute if adopted by an employer "voluntarily," when the law clearly says: "It shall be an unlawful employment practice for an employer to discriminate against any individual, . . . to limit, segregate, or classify . . . in any way that would deprive any individual of opportunities . . . because of race, color, sex, or national origin."[78] "Voluntary" preference—preference given by the employer, or by the employer and the union acting jointly—was precisely what both proponents and opponents understood to be flatly forbidden by the unambiguous wording of Section 703(a), which banned any employment practice that would discriminate against any individual because of that person's race. The prohibition was not repeated in the inserted Section 703(j) because that would have diluted the force of that specially added section aimed narrowly at the objection that race preference might someday be imposed by government, and because it would have been plainly redundant to do so.

The difference in the phrasings of Sections 703(a) and 703(j) makes clear the difference in their targets and functions. The general prohibition of preference, Section 703(a), is addressed to employers and begins: "It shall be an unlawful employment practice for an employer . . . " But section 703(j) is addressed to possible enforcement agencies and courts and therefore begins with words plainly meant for them: "Nothing in this subchapter shall be interpreted to require . . . " To infer that Congress did not intend to prohibit preference from the fact that this added section does not repeat the prohibition already explicit in the preceding sections is transparently unsound.

After Section 703(j) had been inserted, the debate on the Senate floor continued. Defending Title VII (with 703[j] included), Senator Saltonstall (R-MA) summed up its full meaning:

---

[78]The full text of the key section, 703(a), which formulates the prohibition in detail, appears at the outset of this chapter on page 47.

the legislation before us today provides no preferential treatment for any group of citizens. In fact, it specifically prohibits such treatment.[79]

Still, the skeptics remained unsatisfied. Senator Ervin (D-NC) suspected that the act "would make the members of a particular race special favorites of the laws." Senator Cooper (R-KY) replied, again seeking to put Ervin's suspicions to rest:

> As I understand Title VII, an employer could apply the usual stan-
> dards which any employer uses in employing, in dismissing, in pro-
> moting, or in assigning those who work for him. There would be only
> one limitation: he could not discriminate, he could not deny a person
> a job, or dismiss a person from a job, or promote on the sole ground
> of his color, or his religion, other factors being equal.[80]

Senator Clark, answering Senator Ervin more emphatically, said, "The bill does not make anyone higher than anyone else. It estab-lishes no quotas." The normal judgment of employers, he continued, would continue to rule in their own business activity—but

> [a]ll this is subject to one qualification, and that qualification is to
> state: "In your activity as an employer, as a labor union, as an employ-
> ment agency, you must not discriminate because of the color of a
> man's skin." That is all this provision does. . . . It merely says, "When
> you deal in interstate commerce you must not discriminate on the ba-
> sis of race."

Then, to avoid any possible misinterpretation, Senator Clark re-peated himself:

> All it [Title VII] does is to say that no American, individual, labor
> union, or corporation, has the right to deny any other American the
> very basic civil right of equal job opportunity.[81]

Today, nearly half a century after the adoption of the Civil Rights Act, anyone who argues that some race preference is "within the in-tent" of that act must be either ignorant of its legislative history or

---

[79]*Congressional Record*, 1963, vol. 110, p. 12,269.
[80]Ibid., p. 13,078.
[81]Ibid., p. 13,079–80.

willfully deceptive. There is no evidence that would support a construction of that act under which preference might be lawful. Scour
those thousands of pages of *The Congressional Record* as one will,
one finds not a single speech, not one account of the proceedings
of that historic summer, that can support the claim that race preference under that act might afterward be lawful. If there were any
such passage that might contribute even in some strained way to the
defense of preference, we can be sure it would have been fastened
upon by its contemporary advocates—but they never mention such
a passage because it does not exist.

Congress did make (in Sec 703[i]) one explicit exception to its
prohibitions, providing for narrowly marked-off preferences given to
Indians living on Indian reservations:

> Nothing contained in [Title VII] shall apply to any business or enter-
> prise on or near an Indian reservation with respect to any publicly an-
> nounced employment practice of such business or enterprise under
> which preferential treatment is given to any individual because he is
> an Indian living on or near a reservation.[82]

The great care with which this exception is set forth confirms the
judgment that if there had been any other exceptions they would
have been made no less precisely, and that, absent such explicit qualifications, the prohibition of race preference in the Civil Rights Act
was intended to apply to all. No other exceptions appear in the act.

To restate the matter summarily: If Congress had intended to permit private or "voluntary" race preference by universities or labor
unions or corporations, it would surely have expressed that intention explicitly in the law. No such expression, either in the act itself
or in the debates preceding its adoption, is to be found. Therefore,
Congress cannot plausibly be supposed to have had that intent.

Justice Thurgood Marshall, writing for the Supreme Court in a
later analysis of the intent of Congress in adopting the Civil Rights
Act, quoted Representative Celler, who said in the 1964 debates that
the act was intended to "cover white men and white women and all
Americans."[83] Citing Senators Humphrey, Clark, Case, and Williams

---

[82]42 U.S. Codes, 2000(e)–2(i).
[83]*Congressional Record*, 1963, vol. 110, p. 2,578.

in passages such as those quoted here, Marshall concluded: "[Title VII's] terms are not limited to discrimination against members of any particular race." This conclusion he further substantiates by extended reference to the interpretation of Title VII given by the Equal Employment Opportunity Commission. The EEOC, wrote Marshall,

> whose interpretations are entitled to great deference, . . . has consistently interpreted Title VII to *proscribe racial discrimination against whites on the same terms as racial discrimination against non-whites*, holding that to proceed otherwise would constitute a derogation of the commission's Congressional mandate to eliminate all practices which operate to disadvantage the employment opportunities of any group protected by Title VII, including Caucasians.[84]

This history of legislative intent in adopting the Civil Rights Act, said Thurgood Marshall then, is "uncontradicted."

Is the horse dead, or may we flog it yet again? Racial discrimination thrives today in every college and university that gives preference in admission, in every private corporation that gives preference in hiring and promotion, in every government agency that gives favor in licensing or in contracting, and so on and on. Overtly or covertly, the law of the land is being widely ignored, shamefully defied. So it is not unreasonable to report here once again what the understanding of the United States Congress was in the final hours of its long debate in that spring and summer of 1964. The House having acted earlier, and President Johnson having expressed his vigorous support of the bill, the Senate would decide the matter. The decision was at hand. Advocates took their final opportunity to present their understanding of the bill they knew was about to pass: Here are two of those final statements, characteristic of most of the rest:

> Senator Muskie (D-ME): It has been said that the bill discriminates in favor of the Negro at the expense of the rest of us. It seeks to do nothing more that to lift the Negro from the status of inequality to one of equality of treatment.[85]

---

[84]*McDonald v. Santa Fe Trail Transportation Co.*, pp. 278–80, 283. Emphasis added.

[85]*Congressional Record*, 1964, vol. 110, p. 14,328.

Senator Moss (D-UT): The bill does not accord to any citizen advantage or preference; it does not fix quotas of employment or school population; it does not force personal association. What it does is to prohibit public officials and those who invite the public generally to patronize their businesses or to apply for employment, to utilize the offensive, humiliating, and cruel practice of discrimination on the basis of race. In short, the bill does not accord special consideration; it establishes equality.[86]

Very self-consciously, fully aware that it was making history, the Senate passed the amended civil rights bill on June 19, 1964, by 73 to 27, every member voting. The bill was then returned to the House, approved as amended, and signed into law by President Johnson. It was the product of one of the most protracted and intense legislative struggles in the history of the United States. The meaning and force of every line and every phrase in the act had been scrutinized, argued, and explained with scrupulous care. The legislators knew precisely what they were prohibiting, and we know exactly what they understood themselves to be prohibiting because they, very deliberately, put their explanatory accounts on record.

The subsequent history of what has been loosely called "affirmative action" must give some pain to every honest American citizen. Racially preferential schemes in our universities and in private industry have been widely adopted, sometimes in response to threats by the Office of Federal Contract Compliance. Even when nondiscrimination has been honestly respected, the allegation of "underutilization" has forced employers to pursue racial balance, to hire by ethnic numbers. One of the most tenacious opponents of the Civil Rights Act, Senator Sparkman of Alabama, repeatedly warned that no matter what was promised by its defenders, federal agencies would misuse the act to give preference to minorities. He was hooted down on the floor of the Senate. He countered that "the 'suggestion' will surely be made to some small business with a government contract that if it does not carry out the preferences proposed to the company by some inspector, its government contract will not be renewed."[87] To our shame we have proved that man prescient.

[86]Ibid., p. 14,424.
[87]Ibid., p. 8,618.

No honest and impartial person—administrator, employer, or judge—may now in good conscience defend the claim that the Civil Rights Act of 1964 was intended by Congress to permit preference by race. Preference by race is wrong; plainly and indubitably it is a violation of federal law.

6

Race Preference Violates the Constitution

(1) The Equal Protection of the Laws

Equality is the philosophical base upon which democracy is built. Equality of right—the opportunity to participate equally in the life of the community and to benefit equally from its laws—is grounded in the fundamental equality of persons. For if some class of persons are thought inferior by birth (as was long the case in human history), the several classes—nobles and commoners, patricians and plebeians, freemen and slaves—will naturally differ in their entitlements. Where there is no commitment to the fundamental equality of persons, democracy cannot be justified and is unlikely to succeed.

Therefore, until slavery was forbidden with the ratification of the Thirteenth Amendment to the U.S. Constitution in 1865, full democracy could not be realized in the United States. After that great change, the principle of universal equality could be explicitly incorporated into the Constitution, and that was done three years later. From that time forward all persons, whatever their race or color, were to be recognized, in our country, as equals. However much we may differ in wealth or strength or wisdom, *before the law* no racial distinctions will be recognized. The first section of the Fourteenth Amendment formulates this guarantee of equality of right in one magnificent clause:

> nor shall any State . . . deny to any person within its jurisdiction the equal protection of the laws.[88]

[88]The Fourteenth Amendment to the U.S. Constitution, ratified in 1868, has five sections: the second deals with the apportionment of representatives; the third, with qualifications for federal office; the fourth, with the validity of

The sweeping force of these words is beyond doubt. The guarantees of equal protection, said the Supreme Court in 1886, "are universal in their application . . . without regard to any difference of race, of color, or of nationality. . . . "[89] If today any State, or any agency of any State, gives preference to any group of persons simply because of their race, or color, or national origin, that preference violates our Constitution. Distinguishable from this constitutional prohibition are the prohibitions of the Civil Rights Act of 1964, forbidding race preference independently, as I have recounted in the previous chapter at some length. But were that law (or any law) to be somehow construed to encourage preference, it could not stand under our Constitution, which plainly forbids all discrimination by race.

(2) Suspect Classifications and Race Consciousness

Slavery had been justified by the alleged inferiority of blacks, who were thought to be different in essence from the European whites who bought and sold them. That ancient view of mankind as falling naturally into classes, some by nature fit to be slaves and others by nature fit to be masters, gave pseudo-respectability to systematic oppression. How decent and thoughtful people could have defended that invidious and intolerable classification of humans we find difficult today to understand. In our own country, human beings were sorted and their fates determined by their skin color; we are shamed by those arbitrary and odious practices and their consequences, which remain horrible to contemplate.

---

public debt; the fifth gives Congress the power to enforce the whole. The first section of the Fourteenth Amendment, in which is formulated the principle that renders race preference unconstitutional, reads in full:

All persons born or naturalized in the United States, and subject to the jurisdiction thereof, are citizens of the United States and the State wherein they reside. No State shall make or enforce any law which shall abridge the privileges or immunities of citizens of the United States; nor shall any State deprive any person of life, liberty, or property, without due process of law, nor deny to any person within its jurisdiction the equal protection of the laws.

[89]*Yick Wo v. Hopkins*, 118 U.S. 356 (1886).

Never forgetting the nasty purposes so long served by racial classifications, we are rightly suspicious of any racial sorting now, *whatever* the reason given for it. In any public place or under any public law—in commerce or in schools or in some government offices—every classification by race is, we say, inescapably *suspect*. That is the adjective—"suspect"—with which classifications by race are regularly described by the United States Supreme Court.[90]

The equal protection of the laws does not forbid *every* racial classification. Blacks and others who have been clearly injured by unlawful discriminatory practices may come to the courts for remedy, and a just remedy may require that the race of those who were earlier injured be taken into account. To give victims what they are due, the courts may be obliged to use the racial categories by which victims were earlier deprived of what they were due. In one of the justly famous school desegregation cases of the 1970s, the Supreme Court agreed that

> Just as the race of students must be considered in determining
> whether a constitutional violation has occurred, so also must race be
> considered in formulating a remedy.[91]

But the objective of that remedy must be entirely nondiscriminatory "to eliminate from the public schools all vestiges of state imposed segregation."[92] Consciousness of race may be at times unavoidable, but its application to public business remains always problematic. Even when the aim is desegregation, as in those famous school cases of the 1970s, race consciousness may enter only as the unavoidable instrument of closely measured redress; no *preference* by race is to be given.

The distinction—between race *consciousness* (essential in some circumstances to give remedy) and race *preference* (introduced to achieve racial balance)—is profound. The slippery passage from justifiable consciousness of race to unjustifiable preference helps to

---

[90]Other arbitrary and invidious classifications—by national origin, sex, religion, color, etc.—are similarly held suspect. Here and in what follows I use "classification by race" as shorthand for all suspect classifications.

[91]*Swann v. Charlotte-Mecklenburg Board of Education*, 402 U.S. 1, at p. 45 (1971).

[92]Ibid., p. 6.

explain the ambivalence widely felt about what is today called "affirmative action." Steps designed to eradicate discrimination we are likely to support, even when they may be race conscious. Steps designed to achieve racial proportionality by giving race preference we reject. But which of those aims underlies what is loosely called "affirmative action" is often unclear. The real moral controversy in this arena is thus not about "affirmative action," whose range is uncertain, but about race preference, which is readily identifiable.

(3) The Standard of Strict Scrutiny

Because every racial classification is suspect, every use of such a classification must be closely scrutinized to determine whether the constitutional guarantee of equal protection has been preserved. In making that determination, the standard applied is the most rigorous contemplated by law—the standard of *strict scrutiny*. The U.S. Supreme Court has repeatedly reaffirmed that where race is the basis of a legislative or administrative classification, the standard of constitutional permissibility must be the very strictest possible. Shortly after the enactment of the Civil Rights Act of 1964, Justice Byron White wrote:

> We deal here with a classification based upon the race of the participants, which must be viewed in light of the historical fact that the central purpose of the Fourteenth Amendment was to eliminate racial discrimination emanating from official sources in the States. This strong policy renders racial classification "Constitutionally suspect" and subject to *the most rigid scrutiny*. . . . [I]nvidious official discrimination based on race . . . bears a heavy burden of justification, as we have said, and will be upheld only if it is necessary, and not merely rationally related, to the accomplishment of a permissible state policy.[93]

Three years later, Chief Justice Earl Warren made the point again:

> At the very least, the Equal Protection Clause demands that racial classifications . . . be subjected to the most rigid scrutiny, and, if they are ever to be upheld, they must be shown to be necessary to the accomplishment of some permissible state objective, independent of the

[93]*McLaughlin v. Florida*, 379 U.S. 184, at pp. 192, 196 (1964). Emphasis added.

racial discrimination which it was the object of the Fourteenth Amendment to eliminate.[94]

Warren there cited Justice Hugo Black, who had opened his opinion in a famous 1944 case with these words:

> It should be noted, to begin with, that all legal restrictions which curtail the civil rights of a single racial group are immediately suspect. That . . . is to say that courts must subject them to the most rigid scrutiny.[95]

Justice Black, in turn, had cited a famous passage, authored by Chief Justice Stone and joined by every member of the court in 1943, that has reappeared in many decisions since:

> Distinctions between citizens solely because of their ancestry are by their nature *odious to a free people* whose institutions are founded upon the doctrine of equality.[96]

That unanimous court, in its turn, had cited a decision handed down only 21 years after the adoption of the Fourteenth Amendment:

> The Fourteenth Amendment to the Constitution is not confined to the protection of citizens. . . . [Its] provisions are universal in their application, to all persons within the territorial jurisdiction, without regard to any differences of race, of color, or of nationality; and *the equal protection of the laws is a pledge of the protection of equal laws.* It is accordingly enacted by section 1977 of the Revised Statutes that 'all persons within the jurisdiction of the United States shall have the same right, in every state and territory . . . to the full and equal

---

[94]*Loving v. Virginia*, 388 U.S. 1, at p. 11 (1967).

[95]*Korematsu v. United States,* 323 U.S. 214, at p. 216 (1944).

[96]*Hirabayashi v. United States*, 320 U.S. 81, at p. 100 (1943). Emphasis added. Years later Justice Tom Clark held what was called "the minority transfer rule" unconstitutional, observing that "racial classifications are obviously irrelevant and invidious." *Goss v. Board of Education of Knoxville*, 373 U.S. 683 (1963). Justice Potter Stewart, in that same year, noted that (in the light of *Brown v. Board*) classification on racial lines is in itself, "per se," impermissible. "Our Constitution presupposes that men are created equal, and that therefore *racial differences cannot provide a valid basis for governmental action.*" *School District v. Schempp*, 374 U.S. 203, (1963) at p. 317. Emphasis added.

benefit of all laws and proceedings . . . and shall be subject to like punishment, pains, penalties, taxes, licenses, and exactions of every kind, and to no other.'[97]

In 1978, when the race preferences of the University of California were at issue in *Regents v. Bakke,* Justice Powell, announcing the decision of the court, left no doubt that there would be no departure from that settled principle of constitutional law:

> Racial and ethnic distinctions of any sort are inherently suspect and thus call for the most exacting judicial examination.[98]

In 1995 that highest court not only reaffirmed the principle that strict scrutiny must be applied to every racial classification, but expanded the reach of the standard to apply not just to legislation of the several states, but to legislation of the United States government as well:

> Federal racial classifications, like those of a State, must serve a compelling governmental interest, and must be narrowly tailored to further that interest. . . . When [political judgments regarding the necessity of any classification] touch upon an individual's race or ethnic background, he is entitled to a judicial determination that the burden he is asked to bear on that basis is precisely tailored to serve a compelling governmental interest. The Constitution guarantees that right to every person regardless of his background. . . . [A]ny person, of whatever race, has the right to demand that any governmental actor subject to the Constitution justify any racial classification subjecting that person to unequal treatment under the strictest judicial scrutiny.[99]

This demand—the application of this settled constitutional principle—was yet again reiterated in 2001.[100]

What this test of strict scrutiny means in practice was explained in plain words by Justice Powell in 1986:

> There are two prongs to this examination. First, any racial classification must be justified by a compelling governmental interest. Second,

---

[97]*Yick Wo v. Hopkins,* p. 369. Emphasis in the original.
[98]*Bakke,* p. 291.
[99]*Adarand Constructors v. Pena,* p. 235.
[100]*Adarand Constructors v. Mineta,* 534 U.S. 103 (2001).

the means chosen by the state to effectuate its purpose must be narrowly tailored to the achievement of that goal.[101]

To meet this standard, any legislation using a racial classification
must serve an interest that is not merely reasonable, or substantial,
or even important; its objective must be overriding, *compelling.* And
the racial classification used must be shown to address that compelling need with precision, imposing no burdens that do not bear
directly and narrowly on that overriding objective.

This demand for a "narrowly tailored" relationship between the law
and its purpose is the jurisprudential way of expressing a moral principle intuitively clear to us all: a just remedy must *fit* the wrong; the
instrument must *fit* its object. If we aim to give redress, what we do
must compensate in appropriate form and degree for the injury actually suffered; it must compensate those persons who suffered that
injury and not some other set of persons who may happen to share
their skin color or nationality. Any instrument using suspect classifications can be defended successfully only if it is "narrowly tailored"
to accomplish the compelling need to which it is said to respond.

This standard of strict scrutiny is meant to be very demanding, meant
to be a test that suspect classifications will not easily pass. That no state
may deny to any person within its jurisdiction the equal protection of
the laws is a constitutional pledge not to be broken; therefore, no instrument of any state, no local government, no state university or any
other public institution, may be allowed to apply laws differently to
persons because they are of different racial or ethnic groups *unless an
overriding demand of justice itself requires that differentiation.*

There is one such demand—but only one—generally agreed to
be so compelling that it may justify racial classification. Persons to
whom a known injury has been done must be made whole so far as
that is possible. When the injury was done by using a racial classification, there may be no way to devise appropriate relief for those
who were so injured without attending once again to race. In such
circumstances, a racial classification may prove defensible, but it will
be a *remedy,* not a preference, devised in the light of the injury to
be redressed. A racial classification, if permitted for the purpose,

[101]*Wygant v. Jackson Board of Education.*

will be particularized, not universal; it will be addressed to an identified set of deserving persons, not an entire racial group.[102]

Preference awarded to members of one or another ethnic group simply because they are members of that group—naked preference—can never pass this test of strict scrutiny. Preference cannot satisfy the first prong of the strict scrutiny standard because no state interest is so compelling that it can justify burdening innocent members of the disadvantaged group only because of their skin color or nationality. Naked preference cannot satisfy the second prong of the strict scrutiny standard because no generalized classification by skin color or nationality could ever be tailored narrowly enough to serve a specific remedial need that might be genuinely compelling.

(4) Allegedly Compelling Needs

The justifications most commonly put forward to show the constitutional acceptability of race preference—that is, the state interests that are alleged to be "compelling"—are these:

- to compensate for societal discrimination and oppression
- to achieve racial balance in some population
- to achieve diversity in schools, colleges, and other contexts
- to provide role models for minority students
- to provide better professional services for minorities
- to desegregate a public body
- to integrate a public body

[102]An illuminating illustration of this distinction arises in *Franks v. Bowman Transportation Company*, 424 U.S. 727 (1976). In this case, the known black victims of racial discrimination by a trucking company sought, as a remedy, to be placed in the seniority lists of that company where they would have been placed if they had not been earlier victimized. Giving that remedy would require that the existing seniority ranking of white employees be adversely affected—but it was a remedy to which these plaintiffs were plainly entitled. The court rightly held that to do justice in such circumstances there was no way to avoid classification by race. Without it, the victims of earlier wrongdoing would remain subordinate to persons who, had it not been for identified racial discrimination in that company, would now be their juniors. Those who were adversely affected by the remedy (even though possibly innocent themselves) had plainly benefited, in seniority, from the specific discriminatory practice for which remedy was being given. In such cases, racial classification may be defensible—although it remains always subject to strict scrutiny, of course.

Not one of these alleged justifications can pass the test of strict scrutiny set forth in the preceding section. I take them in order:

(4a) **Race Preference to Compensate for Societal Discrimination**

Earlier we saw why race preference cannot be *morally* justified by the demand for compensation. Where *race* is the condition of the preference, it cannot justly meet a compensatory need because it will always prove to be both *over*inclusive and *under*inclusive, awarding benefits to many who are not entitled to them because injury has not been suffered by them and failing to award benefits to many others who (even if plausibly entitled to relief) are of such a color (or nationality, etc.) that they get nothing. The underlying difficulty is that color of skin is not itself the injury and therefore cannot be in itself the instrument of preferential remedy.[103]

As a matter of constitutional principle the same objections apply. The appeal to compensation to justify race preference fails in constitutional terms because the interest served by race preference is *not compelling*, and because even if it were thought to be compelling, race preference *cannot be narrowly tailored* to any need shown. The words of the Constitution itself reinforce the rejection of this defense of preference: the first section of the Fourteenth Amendment guarantees the equal protection of the laws to every single person *individually:* "it is the individual who is entitled to judicial protection against classifications based upon his racial or ethnic background because such distinctions impinge upon personal rights . . . "[104] Generalized race preference cannot stand with that guarantee in force.

Race preference is *group* preference, advantage given to persons of a given ethnicity simply on the ground of their ethnicity. But the equal protection clause identifies what it protects as the rights of single *persons*; they are individual rights, not rights held by any group. They are rights understood distributively, not collectively. Therefore any single individual who is denied, because of his (or her) race, some benefit to which he (or she) is otherwise entitled will have had *his* (or *her*) rights under that clause infringed.

---

[103]See chapter 4, sections (2) and (3).
[104]Justice Lewis Powell, in *Bakke*, p. 299.

The historical oppression of minorities in America has left an ineradicable stain. But that historical oppression cannot serve as the constitutionally compelling need that might justify the use of racial classification because the preference cannot be shown to remedy identifiable injuries done by identifiable institutions. Only if the nature and source of the earlier injury could be specified, and those injured individuals identified, might compensation to them be justifiable. This is the force of the *individualized* locus of the right to equal protection.

Again and again, the U.S. Supreme Court has cited the following famous passage, from a 1948 decision in the case of *Shelley v. Kraemer*:

> The rights created by the first section of the Fourteenth Amendment are, by its terms, guaranteed *to the individual*. The rights established are personal rights.[105]

But all race preferences are, essentially and by their nature, awarded to racial groups. To seek compensation for ethnic groups is to suppose that those groups have entitlements, that there are group rights. But rights are not possessed by groups. The same right may belong to each member of a group, of course, but *the group*—"the Jews" or "the blacks" or "the Hispanics"—*cannot* be the holder of rights. Rights—the right to equal protection above all—are held by individual persons, not by groups.

Therefore, to justify a racial classification in some compensatory way, it must be shown that every member of the preferred racial group did in fact suffer the injury for which redress is proposed. Justice Stewart put it eloquently:

> A judicial decree that imposes burdens on the basis of race can be upheld only where its sole purpose is to eradicate the actual effects of illegal race discrimination. . . .

> The hostility of the Constitution to racial classification by government has been manifested in many cases decided by this Court. And our cases have made it clear that the Constitution is wholly neutral in forbidding such racial discrimination, whatever the race may be of those who are its victims. . . . *Under our Constitution, the government may*

[105]334 U.S. 1, at p. 22 (1948). Emphasis added.

never act to the detriment of a person solely because of that person's race. The color of a person's skin and the country of his origin are immutable facts that bear no relation to ability, disadvantage, moral culpability, or any other characteristics of constitutionally permissible interest to government. "Distinctions between citizens solely because of their ancestry are by their very nature odious to a free people whose institutions are founded upon the doctrine of equality." The command of the equal protection guarantee is simple but unequivocal: "No state shall . . . deny to *any* person . . . the equal protection of the laws."[106]

Preference given to some persons over others on the basis of race or national origin, without inquiry into the injury suffered by those preferred, plainly violates the constitutional rights of those who are disadvantaged by the preference given.

The advocates of preference contend that the advantages given to minorities today are designed to make up for the inequalities of yesterday. So grave and long continued has discrimination against minorities in our country been, they reason, that only by discriminating *for* them can justice be done. But the moral blunder reappears when it is supposed that the grievances lie *in* some skin-color group, and that *to* some skin-color group redress may be awarded. When the Constitution is seen to protect rights held by *individuals* and to recognize no rights of racial groups, such reasoning must fail.[107]

---

[106]*Fullilove v. Klutznick*, 448 U.S. 448 at p. 524 (1980). Emphasis added.

[107]The attorney general of the State of Virginia, in April 2002, formally and explicitly warned the presidents and governing boards of all Virginia colleges and universities that certain common arguments offered in support of race preference were unacceptable as a matter of law. The Virginia state solicitor wrote: "The question that must be addressed is whether . . . public institutions of higher education may lawfully use remediation as a basis for race-conscious programs. The answer to this question turns upon the facts as they may be found to exist at any given institution; however, we are aware of no facts that would justify *any* Virginia college or university in using remediation as a basis for race-conscious admissions or scholarship programs. Upon a review of the law and the facts, it appears that any institution that operates race-conscious admissions or scholarship programs—based on a remedial justification—is almost surely acting unlawfully and is exposed to substantial legal liability." Memorandum, Office of the Attorney General, Commonwealth of Virginia, Richmond, 22 April 2002.

Race preferences given as compensation by universities, and other subordinate public bodies, face another insurmountable constitutional barrier: the institutions awarding such preference do not have the *authority* to use race in this way. The University of California argued explicitly (in *Bakke*) that its admission preferences were justified "to counter the effects of societal discrimination." This justification was rejected by the Supreme Court for the moral reasons given in this section, but also because no arm of government may use suspect classifications to help once-victimized groups at the expense of others (for example, to give preference to blacks at the expense of whites), *unless* there have been "judicial, legislative, or administrative *findings* of constitutional violations"[108] for which redress may be in order. After such findings have been made, the rights of the once-victimized persons may deserve vindication, and an appropriate remedy devised by a court or a legislature. But without such findings of constitutional or statutory violations, no court or government agency can be justified in taking from some and giving to others. Preferences burden those not preferred; absent some finding of earlier violation no government agency is authorized to impose such a burden. The University of California, as Justice Powell points out,

> does not purport to have made, *and is in no position to make*, such findings. Its broad mission is education, not the formulation of any legislative policy or the adjudication of particular claims of illegality. . . . [I]solated segments of our vast governmental structures are not competent to make those decisions. . . . Before relying upon these sorts of findings in establishing a racial classification, a governmental body must have the authority and capability to establish, in the record, that the classification is responsive to identified discrimination.[109]

Universities do not have the authority to establish such a record and *are not competent* to respond appropriately to an earlier violation of law.

This argument devastates even the most well-meaning efforts by universities and like bodies to give redress for what they perceive to have been "societal discrimination"—a notion described by Justice Powell as "an amorphous concept of injury that may be ageless in

[108]*Bakke*, p. 307.
[109]Ibid., p. 309. Emphasis added.

its reach into the past."[110] The telling constitutional conclusion is framed by the context of the *Bakke* case, but is widely applicable:

> Hence, the purpose of helping certain groups whom the faculty of the Davis Medical School perceived as victims of "societal discrimination" does not justify a classification that imposes disadvantages upon persons like respondent [Alan Bakke], who bear no responsibility for whatever harm the beneficiaries of the special admissions program are thought to have suffered. To hold otherwise would be to convert a remedy heretofore reserved for violations of legal rights into a privilege that all institutions throughout the nation could grant at their pleasure to whatever groups are perceived as victims of societal discrimination. That is a step we have never approved.[111]

Indeed it is a step that no court would be wise to approve under our Constitution, for to do so would be to abandon not only strict scrutiny, but nearly all scrutiny. Were the authority to make such determinations (to justify race preference) given to middle-level bureaucrats working behind closed doors, it would be uncontrollable, inviting its use to advance the social vision of those bureaucrats. A university, a government agency, a private employer simply does not have the authority to give preferences to racial groups on the ground that in *its* wisdom such preferences are thought an appropriate remedy for oppression that *it* believes has been long suffered. This is a procedural objection to the compensatory justification of preference, but a very powerful one. Under our Constitution, race preferences designed (by universities and other such institutions) as compensation for societal injuries are thus forbidden, for reasons both procedural and substantive.

(4b) Race Preference to Achieve Racial Balance

Many assume that in the absence of racial discrimination, the ethnic profiles of student bodies in colleges, and of work places in industry, would be racially *balanced*—that the percentage of minorities in any given school, or firm, would roughly equal the percentage of that minority in the population at large. This assumption is false. Racial discrimination often reinforces such clustering, but patterns of interest

---

[110]Ibid., p. 307.
[111]Ibid., p. 310.

and performance are not merely the product of discrimination. Some clustering of racial and ethnic groups is perennial and natural, and therefore eliminating every racial imbalance is certainly no demand of justice. Indeed, the effort to preclude such clustering—are there proportionally too many Jews at Harvard? too many black players in the National Basketball Association?—may be plainly unjust.

That quest for racial balance has often been put forward as a justification of race preference. The University of California sought (as many universities still seek) to "reduce the historic deficit of traditionally disfavored minorities"[112] in its student body. Even if this be thought an appropriate objective, it cannot serve, under the standard of strict scrutiny, as the *compelling* objective that might justify race preference. The racial imbalance complained of may have resulted from decisions freely made by members of the minorities themselves. To assume that minority members would decide and act just as those in the racial majority decide and act, in proportions just like theirs, is as patronizing as it is unwarranted. To rely upon that assumption as the implicit ground for an allegedly compelling need is plainly unsound. Justice Powell, addressing this argument in *Bakke*, disposed of it crisply:

> If [the University of California's] purpose is to assure within its student body some specified percentage of a particular group merely because of its race or origin, such a preferential purpose must be rejected not as insubstantial but as *facially invalid*. Preferring members of any one group for no reason other than race or ethnic origin is discrimination for its own sake. This the Constitution forbids.[113]

---

[112]Brief of the University of California in *Bakke*, cited by Justice Powell at p. 306.
[113]*Bakke*, p. 307. Emphasis added. It is also worth noting that racial balance, if it were an acceptable objective, would require—at the University of California— a far greater enrollment of Caucasians, the racial group most seriously underrepresented. In the late 1990s, about 51 percent of the California students who met state requirements for admission were Caucasians, but Caucasians constituted only about 31 percent of the newly admitted students. Asian Americans, on the other hand, were 23 percent of those qualified for admission, but 45 percent of those admitted. See: Serge Herzog, "Making Admissions Decisions in the Name of Diversity," *Chronicle of Higher Education*, 5 July 2002. The practical impact of the quest for racial balance is a sharp *reduction* in the number of Asian Americans enrolled. Advocates of preference commonly say that they seek no quotas—but it is precisely ethnic quotas to which their views must lead.

Yet the claim that racial balance does justify preference continues to reappear. The school board in Jackson, Michigan, joined by the teachers' union, defended employment preference for minority public school teachers on the ground that minority teachers were "substantially and chronically underrepresented." Their argument relied upon the supposed compelling need for balanced ratios, their goal being a ratio of black teachers to white teachers that would mirror the ratio of black students to white students. But the factors governing the availability of teachers are very different from those affecting the racial profile of student populations, and the racial proportionality sought was utterly unattainable. Nevertheless, in pursuit of that goal, the school board protected minority teachers ("employees who are black, American Indian, Oriental, or of Spanish descendancy") against layoffs even when white teachers with much higher seniority had to be laid off in their stead. This rationale for preference, as well as the preference itself, was rejected by the U.S. Supreme Court.[114]

At the time that the seventh layoff of the same high-seniority white teacher led to Supreme Court review, blacks constituted a much greater percentage of the teachers and administrators in that school district than they did of the Michigan population. But because the proportion of black students in that district was higher still, even the most junior minority teachers were never threatened by a budget-imposed layoff. Only white teachers could lose their jobs, and they did.

When this preferential scheme was defended in oral argument before the U.S. Supreme Court, Justice Sandra Day O'Connor noted that the court must seek to determine "whether the government can demonstrate a compelling state interest to justify such a [racial] classification." She then asked: "Now what is the compelling state interest that the School Board asserts here? Is it to maintain faculty-student ratio, or is it some other purpose? What do you rely on today?" The Board's attorney replied that the need for "integration" and the need for a "diversified faculty" were both motivating factors. The oral exchange then continued:

> *Justice O'Connor:* So the Board does rely essentially on a faculty-student ratio and the role-model rationale?

---

[114]See *Wygant v. Jackson Board of Education.*

Attorney for the Board: Justice O'Connor, I didn't say that and I didn't mean that. I think what I was looking at specifically was, was it their duty to integrate, how to go about that integration.

Justice O'Connor: Integrate in hiring. You are talking about hiring employees?

Attorney for the Board: . . . If you're not going to do something about layoffs is it going to be considered by the public as a good faith effort to integrate?

Justice O'Connor: Maybe I can't get an answer, but I really would like to know what the compelling state interest is that you are relying on for this particular layoff provision, in a nutshell.

Attorney for the Board: [Swimming!] . . . to protect the gains made that was going to allow us to do that as we looked at what we certainly thought were some of the factors we ought to be looking at like faculty and wanting a diverse ethnic faculty, to protect that we had to have [the layoff provision].

Justice O'Connor: To protect a faculty-student ratio that the Board thought was appropriate?

Attorney for the Board: . . . We wanted them there. We had to have a method of protecting them.[115]

The Jackson schools were by that time very well integrated, and minority teachers were employed there in substantial numbers. The school board and the union had nevertheless insisted upon striving for a numerical ratio of blacks to whites that they believed was ideal. That—we now see—cannot serve as the compelling need that might justify race preference.

Numerical reports of minority representation can be insidious when they are framed to imply that, in a particular sphere of work or study, only random or racially proportional distribution would be

---

[115]Official Transcript of Proceedings before the Supreme Court of the United States, 6 November 1985, case # 84-1340, pp. 30–33.

reasonable or just, and that anything short of that is a failure. Typical is this recent report in the *Washington Post*:

> More than 14 percent of this year's entering class [at the University of Texas–Austin] is Hispanic; about 3.5 percent is black.
>
> Still, those numbers fall well short of the overall minority population in Texas, which is about 30 percent Hispanic and 12 percent black. . . . Of this year's freshman class at UT-Austin, nearly 15 percent are Asian Americans, although they constitute scarcely 2.7 percent of the state's population.[116]

But deviations from arithmetic proportionality are certainly not proof of racial discrimination. Even if comparisons are made with the "relevant pool" of students or workers, ethnic proportionality is not to be expected, because patterns of work and skills, patterns of interest in study, patterns of residence and styles of life, differ sharply among ethnic groups for reasons having nothing to do with discrimination. Ethnic balance is a crude standard, wholly unsuitable as a societal ideal, and the quest for it is certainly not a constitutional justification of race preference.[117]

(4c) Race Preference to Achieve Diversity

Diversity—of opinion, of perspective, of background and interest—is valuable in many spheres. It enriches our lives and enhances the democratic process. Diversity of race, if it brings different perspectives on controversial issues to a public forum, may also be a worthy objective.

But ethnic diversity does not insure intellectual diversity. Persons of different races often hold similar views; persons with different views are often of the same race. In some contexts—in the study of mathematics or chemistry, for example—ethnic diversity is hardly relevant. In other contexts—a religious seminary, for example—diversity may have negative consequences. In colleges and universi-

---

[116]11 November 2002.

[117]To make such invidious uses of race counting impossible, an initiative in California—*Classification by Race, Ethnicity, Color, or National Origin* [*CRECNO*]—will be on the state ballot in March of 2004. Widely known as the Racial Privacy Initiative, it was initiated by the American Civil Rights Coalition; if adopted it will amend the California constitution so as to *prohibit* (with certain narrow exceptions) state and local government from classifying individuals on the basis of race.

ties, where moral and political debate is very much in order, a diverse student body is a healthy and reasonable objective.

Diversity was not the objective of ethnic preferences when they were first introduced by colleges and employers. Before the *Bakke* decision in 1978, that objective was rarely mentioned. Preferences were originally devised to give compensation, to "level the playing field," or to advance racial balance. When it became clear that racial balance to account for societal discrimination cannot justify racially preferential programs under our Constitution, the defenders of race preference turned to diversity as their best remaining hope. What had earlier been no more than a tertiary consideration was then put forward as a (suddenly discovered) compelling need. The diversity rationale for preference is now ubiquitous at colleges and universities. The Center for Equal Opportunity found that racial and ethnic "diversity" is promoted in some fashion on the website of every state flagship institution.

Ordinary people are not likely to think that diversity, even if admittedly a good thing, is an interest rightly described as "compelling." Many communities are ethnically homogenous, or nearly so, and not at all distressed by that reality. Intellectual inquiry should be unrestricted, but its genuine openness does not entail researchers of different nationalities or sexes. University administrators are now heard to contend that diversity is absolutely critical for higher education, that only through ethnic diversity can education succeed, and that to meet this utterly compelling need, racially discriminatory programs are absolutely essential. These extravagant claims, claims that strain credulity when taken literally, may be explained as the only recourse left open by our constitutional history.

The compensatory justification for race preference was firmly rejected by the Supreme Court in *Regents v. Bakke.* Justice Powell, having agreed wholeheartedly in that case that the university admissions preferences in question were a violation of the equal protection clause, nevertheless sought to soften the absolute preclusion of racial considerations that had been demanded by the earlier opinion of the California Supreme Court. To this end, he pointed out that some constitutional interests (in open and robust debate) are furthered by the intellectual diversity of college classes, which (he emphasized) is much more than racial diversity. He held, therefore, that it would not be unreasonable for an admissions officer, in considering the several merits of *individual* applicants, to consider race also as a "plus factor" in the effort to achieve diversity. Race (on that view) might enter into admissions decisions sometimes—but only in evaluating the files of *particular* applicants, not as a factor that could justify systematic preference. A sharp line, he thought, divides the kind of racial consideration for individuals that might be weighed for the sake of diversity, and the wholesale race preference given by the University of California then (and many others today), which exhibit on their face the intention to discriminate generally by race.

This introduction of "diversity" into the discussion of university admissions appears in Justice Powell's opinion only; it was not joined, or even mentioned, in the opinions of the other eight justices in that case. Nor has his willingness to accept the constitutional relevance of ethnic diversity been affirmed by any Supreme Court justice since that time. The argumentative reed is a frail one, but universities have relied upon it, upon Powell's discussion of diversity, as their last and best defense. Four justices of the court were then disposed to support race preferences in a compensatory spirit. Now the advocates of preference claim that these four justices really *would have joined* Powell if they had thought that useful. We are to overlook the fact that they specifically declined to do so. On this supposition it is now argued that diversity is the "compelling need" that the justification of race preference requires.[118]

This matter is before the Supreme Court as I write. It will be enough, for the present, to observe:

a) Four of the justices now on the Supreme Court (Justices O'Connor, Kennedy, and Scalia, and Chief Justice Rehnquist) have expressed their rejection of the diversity justification (in the realm of broadcast journalism) in no uncertain terms, insisting that racial classifications may be used by government only to respond to an identifiable demand of justice. They wrote:

> Modern equal protection has recognized only one [compelling state] interest: remedying the effects of [identified] racial discrimination. The interest in increasing the diversity of broadcast viewpoints is clearly not a compelling interest. It is simply too amorphous, too

[118]This was the argument presented to defend the use of race preferences by the University of Michigan in *Grutter v. Bollinger*.

insubstantial, and too unrelated to any legitimate basis for employing racial classifications.[119]

Diversity is a consideration less weighty in university admissions than it is in journalism; the constitutional reasoning that leads to its rejection in the latter context will almost certainly do so in the former.

b) As a moral argument, the claim that an improvement in the education of university students (assuming it could be shown) justifies outright racial discrimination is totally without merit. I have discussed this argument at length in chapter 4.[120]

c) The factual premise upon which the diversity defense relies— the claim that there are enormous and indispensable benefits produced by ethnic diversity in classrooms—is very doubtful. Evidence submitted[121] by the University of Michigan in its defense of admission preferences, purportedly showing their great educational benefits, has been subjected to meticulous review by reputable social scientists and statisticians. One set of critics concluded, after careful review of all that is known in this sphere, that the empirical claim that there is a correlation between campus racial diversity and positive educational outcomes is not supported by any data, including that offered by the University of Michigan.[122] The crucial test of that claim is multivariate regression analysis, a statistical technique applied to complex settings with many variables to determine where causality may (and may not) be reliably inferred. This powerful tool,

---

[119]*Metro Broadcasting, Inc. v. FCC*, 497 U.S. 547, at p. 612 (1990). Justice Clarence Thomas, who has repeatedly expressed his strong objections to race preference on any ground whatever, joined the court after this case had been decided.

[120]See chapter 4, section (4).

[121]In *Gratz v. Bollinger*.

[122]The database used by the university is that developed by the Cooperative Institutional Research Program (CIRP) of the American Council on Education. Alexander Astin, the director of research at the time of data collection, aimed to determine the impact of ethnic peer groups upon the college experience. After thorough statistical analysis of the data, Astin concluded that, with respect to African American, Asian American, and Latino peer groups, "*outcomes are generally not affected by these peer measures, and in all but one case the effects are very weak and indirect.*" A. W. Astin, *What Matters in College? Four Critical Years Revisited* (San Francisco: Jossey Bass, 1993); emphasis added. In the light of such findings, the claim that the educational need for such peer groups is "compelling" cannot be successfully defended.

concluded the National Association of Scholars, "actually *discon-firmed* the claim that campus racial diversity is correlated with educational excellence.[123] The study on which the university chiefly relied as evidence was given a second, detailed examination and was found not to meet even minimal standards on every major dimension: research design and methods, measurement, sampling, statistics, and statistical interpretation.[124]

More recently the empirical question has been examined more deeply by three impartial statisticians and social scientists of highest repute.[125] They rejected the methods of the University's carefully enlisted supporters, who asked questions like "How much has a diverse student body in law school helped you to work more effectively and/or get along better with members of other races?" and "Do you feel that diversity enhances or detracts from how you and others think about problems and solutions in classes?"—questions that "push responses" in the direction desired. Such manipulative questions, these researchers observe, "are disturbing to find in research on which such far-reaching decisions are based."[125a]

---

[123]See: Thomas E. Wood and Malcolm J. Sherman, *Race and Higher Education: Why Justice Powell's Diversity Rationale for Racial Preferences in Higher Education Must Be Rejected*, National Association of Scholars, Princeton, NJ, 2001.

[124]See: Robert Lerner and Althea K. Nagai, *A Critique of the Expert Report of Patricia Gurin in Gratz v. Bollinger*, Center for Equal Opportunity, Washington, D.C., 2001.

    In May of 2003 Lerner and Nagai published "Diversity Distorted: How the University of Michigan Withheld Data to Hide Evidence of Racial Conflict and Polarization," in which they report the content of university documents uncovered by an industrious researcher, Chetly Zarco, while the matter was being deliberated by the Supreme Court. These documents, a partial analysis of the data upon which Prof. Gurin's study was built, show that the diversity policies of the University of Michigan led, during the 1990s, to sharply increasing perceptions of interracial tension, by both black and white students, and plummeting numbers of interracial friendships. The longer students were enrolled at Michigan the more likely they were to perceive racial conflict on the campus. The university's own charts and figures, withheld from the discovery process, show that "diversity," as practiced at Michigan, produced among the races not greater harmony but greater antagonism.

[125]Stanley Rothman, Seymour Martin Lipset, and Neil Nevitte, "Does Enrollment Diversity Improve University Education?," *International Journal of Public Opinion Research*, Vol. 15, No. 1, (2003), pp. 8–26.

[125a]Ibid., p. 12.

Rather than asking members of the university community how they felt about the effects of diversity on campus—questions whose "correct" answers are well understood—they asked thousands of students, faculty, and administrators, randomly chosen from 140 institutions of different sorts, simply to evaluate aspects of their educational experience and campus environment. These responses were then correlated with an independent empirical measure of enrollment diversity on those campuses.

If, as the University of Michigan argues, diversity is beneficial to the entire campus community, it will produce a better educational environment in general, greater satisfaction with the quality of education, and better relations between students of different races. On this "diversity model" increasing proportions of black student enrollment should be positively associated with more favorable responses to the queries on educational quality.

But no such positive association was found. Indeed, what was found in this large and careful sample, was that

> In every case, the significant correlations were in the direction opposite those predicted by the diversity model. As the proportion of black students enrolled at the institution rose, student satisfaction with their university experience dropped, as did assessment of the quality of their education, and the work efforts of their peers. In addition, the higher the enrollment diversity, the more likely students were to say that they personally experience discrimination. . . . [I]t is unusual for hypothesis testing of such a clearly specified model to produce a reversal of signs on all operational measures that produce statistically significant correlations.[125b]

For faculty members and administrators sampled, "the same pattern held" for the evaluation of the educational environment, although assessments of race relations were, for those samples, in line with the model's predictions.

This careful study, which investigated the *actual* effects of diversity rather than what some people *say* about diversity, shows that earlier survey instruments and designs

> were flawed in ways that undermined their claims. . . . Indeed the case of enrollment diversity may be a cautionary lesson of the pitfalls

[125b]Ibid., p. 15.

of basing legal and policy decisions too readily on social science research.[125c]

This much we may conclude (from the size of the sample in this
study and the robustness of its results) with virtual certainty: The argument that enrollment diversity improves the educational and racial
milieu at American colleges and universities has not been given reliable support. The claim that diversity is a *compelling need* is wholly
unwarranted. Whatever the meaning of "compelling" may be, the
need for enrollment diversity, if there is one, certainly falls short.

d) Empirical doubts about the benefits of diversity are justified, but secondary. The primary point is this: however great such
benefits may possibly be, they could not justify outright discrimination.[126] Classifications based on race can be very damaging, Justice
O'Connor observed in her opinion for the Supreme Court majority
that struck down a racial set-aside, "[u]nless they are *strictly reserved
for remedial settings*."[127] Even if, in some context, intellectual di-

---

[125c]Ibid., p. 24.

[126]In 1954, the states defending segregated schools in *Brown v. Board of Education* submitted a great deal of evidence claiming to show that segregation was
really very good for minorities and for majority alike. The state of Virginia (in
a companion case) "presented 4 educators, a psychiatrist, and 2 psychologists,"
all "eminent men"—including the chairman of the psychology department at
Columbia University—whose work was supported by "other outstanding scholars" and who testified that "segregated education at the high school level is best
for the individual students of both races." Several years before that, in the case
that resulted in the first integration of public universities (*Sweatt v. Painter*, 339
U.S. 629 [1950]), the state of Texas had presented evidence aiming to show that
segregated education was truly advantageous for those segregated. A sociolog-
ical expert testified: "a very large group of Northern Negroes came South to attend separate colleges, suggesting that the Negro does not secure as
well-rounded a college life at a mixed college, and that the separate college offers him positive advantages; that there is a more normal social life for the Negro in a separate college; that there is greater opportunity for full participation
and for the development of leadership; that the Negro is inwardly more 'secure'
at a college of his own people." In response, a unanimous Supreme Court, finding racial classification in education unacceptable and unjustifiable, gave all such
evidence the attention it deserved. They ignored it.

[127]*Richmond v. Croson*, p. 493. Emphasis added. Her words have been echoed
in the Fourth Circuit Court of Appeals: "classifications based on race must
be reserved, understandably, for remedial settings." *Podberesky v. Kirwan*,
956 F. 2d 52 (1992), at p. 55.

versity were thought to be a critical need, preference by *ethnic* group cannot be narrowly tailored to meet that need. Under the standard of strict scrutiny, diversity cannot serve as the compelling need that might justify race preference.

(4d) Race Preference to Provide Role Models for Minorities

The role model justification of preference was categorically rejected by the Supreme Court in 1986, when it was advanced by the Jackson (Michigan) School Board to defend preferences in the employment of minority teachers. The court held that such a defense is really no more than one variant of the defense based on "societal discrimination" discussed earlier.

The role model argument goes like this: the historical oppression of minorities has relegated them to employments in the lower economic strata. To support and encourage their employment in more prestigious positions, it is essential for minority school children to have, as role models, teachers and administrators who are themselves minority members. Without such role models, it is argued, there is too little self-esteem among minorities, too little hope, too much self-deprecation.

This, the court pointed out in response, is simply another way of contending that past societal discrimination is what justifies race preference now. Justice Powell wrote the forceful majority opinion rejecting the argument:

> This Court has never held that societal discrimination alone is sufficient to justify a racial classification. Rather, the Court has insisted upon *some showing of prior discrimination by the governmental unit involved* before allowing limited use of racial classifications in order to remedy such discrimination.[128]

The "role model theory" ignores the need for that direct relationship. Powell continues:

> [T]he role model theory employed by the District Court has no logical stopping point. The role model theory allows the Board to engage in discriminatory hiring and layoff practices long past the point required by any legitimate remedial purpose.

---

[128]*Wygant v. Jackson Board of Education.* Emphasis added.

As a claimed justification of preference, the theory therefore fails to satisfy the requirement of a compelling need. But it also fails to satisfy the requirement that any racial classification be closely fitted to address some purported need. Powell continues:

> Moreover, because the role model theory does not necessarily bear a relationship to the harm caused by prior discriminatory hiring practices, it actually could be used to escape the obligation to remedy such practices by justifying the small percentage of black teachers by reference to the small percentage of black students. Carried to its logical extreme, the idea that black students are better off with black teachers could lead to the very system the Court rejected in *Brown v. Board of Education*.[129]

Powell sums up:

> Societal discrimination, without more, is too amorphous a basis for imposing a racially classified remedy. The role model theory announced by the District Court and the resultant holding [reversed in this decision] typify this indefiniteness. . . . No one doubts that there has been serious racial discrimination in this country. But as the basis for imposing discriminatory *legal* remedies that work against innocent people, societal discrimination is insufficient and over expansive. In the absence of particularized findings, a court could uphold remedies that are ageless in their reach into the past, and timeless in their ability to affect the future.[130]

Role models are important. The role models truly needed by minority students and indeed by all students are teachers with open minds, who are diligent and competent and devoted to their work; teachers delighted by books and ideas, and enthusiastic in their teaching. The color of their skin is of little consequence. Providing minority role models cannot serve, under the standard of strict scrutiny, to justify race preference.

(4e) Race Preference to Insure Better Professional Services for Minorities

Several years before the *Bakke* case reached the Supreme Court, race preference in university admissions had been confronted in an-

---

[129]Ibid.
[130]Ibid. Emphasis in the original.

other case. At the University of Washington law school, a preferential admissions policy had been devised, it was argued, to provide better legal services for minorities in Washington.[131] If black clients are to be adequately served, the law school contended, black lawyers must be produced to serve them. An analogous argument was later presented, in *Bakke,* in defense of the minority admission program at the UC Davis medical school. Preference was essential, it was held, to produce the black doctors who are most likely to provide the health care needed in black communities.

The argument was rejected by the U.S. Supreme Court. One's doctor, or one's lawyer, does not need to share one's skin color to give good professional service. Black professionals may be more likely than whites to build their practices in black communities, but it does not follow that preferring blacks in admission to law and medical schools is the right way to address the need for professional service to minorities.

Justice Powell addressed this argument explicitly. Even were the State's interest in facilitating health care so compelling as to support the use of a suspect classification, he wrote in his *Bakke* opinion, there is no evidence that the preferential admissions program at the University of California was needed to promote that goal, or that it was in any way designed to achieve it. Powell quotes the Supreme Court of California, which, in holding that Mr. Bakke had indeed suffered a constitutional injustice, wrote:

> There are more precise and reliable ways to identify applicants who
> are genuinely interested in the medical problems of minorities than by
> race. An applicant of whatever race who has demonstrated his concern
> for disadvantaged minorities in the past and who declares that practice
> in such a community is his primary professional goal would be more

---

[131]*DeFunis v. Odegaard*, 416 U.S. 312 (1974). Marco DeFunis, the white plaintiff in this case, had been admitted to the law school by the order of a lower court in which he had prevailed. By the time his case reached the U.S. Supreme Court, he was about to graduate from the law school. The university agreed in oral argument that his performance there had been good and gave assurance that he would not be ejected even if their preferential admissions system were upheld. The Supreme Court thereupon found that nothing in that case remained at issue and held the case moot.

likely to contribute to alleviation of the medical shortage than one who is chosen entirely on the basis of race and disadvantage. In short, there is no empirical data to demonstrate that any one race is more selflessly socially oriented or by contrast that another is more selfishly acquisitive.[132]

It cannot be shown that preference by race is essential to improve health care or legal services. That racial classifications are likely to have *any* significant effect on the problem has not been shown, Powell observes. It is false that only black lawyers can serve black clients adequately, or that Hispanics, when sick, require Hispanic physicians, or that white defendants cannot be fairly tried before black judges. The supposition that conscientious fulfillment of professional function is dependent upon sameness of race or heritage between client and practitioner is unfair and destructive. The record of professional services completely transcending difference of race or religion or nationality is long and honorable.

Minority communities are indeed often underserved, but the needed improvement in professional service is far more dependent upon economic considerations than upon the color of practitioners. To defend preference on the ground that minority needs will be better served thereby is to build upon a tacit *expectation* that minority lawyers (and doctors) will, as a matter of course, practice mainly in minority communities. That expectation is worse than parochial—it exerts heavy and unfair pressure on minority professionals to limit the sphere of their practice.

But do not blacks and other minorities need lawyers and doctors who share their race and cultural heritage? Are they not likely to *feel* more comfortable with professionals who are sensitive to their attitudes and circumstances, who can truly understand them? This defense of preference is troubling and dangerous. If "comfort" really were a satisfactory ground for race preference, firms whose clientele is largely of one color might plausibly defend outright discrimination against job applicants of some other color. "Our white clients cannot be *comfortable* with black attorneys [we will hear], and good profes-

---

[132]18 California 3d, p. 56.

sional service to our clients requires that we retain their psychological confidence. That is possible only with community of heritage."

The argument mistakenly supposes a unity and distinctness of interest shared by almost all members of some racial category and by very few outsiders. The genuine and extensive variety of circumstances and opinions among blacks, and among whites, is thus overridden by racial identification. Discrimination *against* minority professionals was long justified by the very same appeal to racial "comfort." That appeal revived will be quietly welcomed by bigots of every color. We are urged, with the best of intentions, to think with our blood.

Of all the most liberal justices in the history of our Supreme Court, perhaps the most passionate in his liberalism was William O. Douglas. Justice Douglas gave a direct and eloquent response to the argument that ethnic communities need the support of racial discrimination. Himself a graduate of the University of Washington law school, he was angered by that school's parochial defense of its discriminatory admissions program, which came before him and the court in *DeFunis v. Odegaard,* in 1973. Learning that Marco DeFunis was in any case sure to graduate from the Washington law school, a majority held the case moot; Douglas dissented vigorously, writing:

> The state, however, may not proceed by racial classification to force strict population equivalences for every group in every occupation, overriding individual preferences. The equal protection clause commands the elimination of racial barriers, not their creation in order to satisfy our theory as to how society ought to be organized. The purpose of the University of Washington cannot be to produce Black lawyers for Blacks, Polish lawyers for Poles, Jewish lawyers for Jews, Irish lawyers for the Irish. It should be to produce good lawyers for Americans.[133]

(4f) Race Preference to Desegregate a Public Body

Ours is a free country; private association is not, among us, the business of government, and we know that people often group them-

---

[133]*DeFunis v. Odegaard,* p. 342.

selves, voluntarily, by race or religion or national origin. But for the community as a whole the case is very different; segregation imposed by the state, in schools or other public institutions, violates the U.S. Constitution.[134] For a unanimous Supreme Court, Chief Justice Warren wrote, in *Brown v. Board of Education*:

> Education . . . is a right which must be made available to all on equal terms. . . . Does segregation of children in public schools solely on the basis of race, even though the physical facilities and other "tangible" factors may be equal, deprive the children of the minority group of equal educational opportunities? . . . It does.
>
> [I]n the field of public education the doctrine of "separate but equal" has no place. Separate educational facilities are inherently unequal. Therefore . . . the plaintiffs and others similarly situated . . . are, by reason of the segregation complained of, deprived of the equal protection of the laws guaranteed by the Fourteenth Amendment.[135]

Desegregation, the *elimination* of any system of governmentally authorized separation by race, was held in this great case to be a command of justice. Separate facilities are inherently unequal facilities, and therefore to *segregate* by race is to deprive some of their rights under the equal protection clause. *Desegregation* is, plainly, a *compelling* state interest.

But race *preference* was never envisaged as an instrument to combat segregation. On the contrary, preference (for whites!) was precisely what had to be rooted out. Only months after *Brown* was decided came a set of related cases, called *Brown II*,[136] in which the need to *implement* desegregation was addressed. How was the right to nondiscriminatory admission to the public schools to be secured? Courts were directed to use their powers in equity to review the plans proposed by previously segregated school systems, and thus to effect the "elimination of a variety of obstacles in making the transition to school systems operated in accordance with the Constitutional principles set forth in *Brown I*." The lower federal courts were ordered "to take such proceedings, and to enter such orders and de-

[134]*Brown I.*
[135]Ibid.
[136]349 U.S. 294 (1954).

crees . . . as are necessary and proper to admit to public schools *on a racially nondiscriminatory basis.*"[137] No preference by race was dreamed of in these implementing cases, none was suggested, and none was permitted.

But the unambiguous command to desegregate the public schools was defied, and subverted, and deviously evaded by school systems all over the American South. The struggle to make desegregation a reality was long and bitter. In Charlotte, North Carolina, for example, 15 years after *Brown I* had outlawed state-imposed racial segregation, two-thirds of the black students attended 21 schools whose students were 100 percent (or 99 percent) black. Racially identifiable schools were duplicitously maintained. School systems that were ostensibly unitary were dual in fact; the wrongful segregation of pupils on the basis of race was tenaciously protected. That had to be stopped.

"[T]o break up the dual school system" that had been surreptitiously maintained, and "to eliminate from the public schools all vestiges of state-imposed segregation," the district courts found it essential to introduce *race-conscious remedies,* drastic remedies that were subsequently approved by the Supreme Court in *Swann v. Charlotte-Mecklenburg Board of Education.* Noncontiguous school zones were paired and grouped. Busing—the much-hated transport of elementary school pupils, blacks to formerly white schools and whites to formerly black schools—was ordered and approved "as one tool of school desegregation."[138] There was affirmative action! But it was affirmative action in the original sense of that term—positive steps to achieve desegregation without a hint of preference by race. The implementing measures were indeed race *conscious* because only in that way could remedy be provided for earlier wrongs done by the state. The Supreme Court wrote:

> *Absent a constitutional violation there would be no basis for judicially ordering assignment of students on a racial basis.* All things being equal, with no history of discrimination, it might well be desirable to assign

[137]Ibid. Emphasis added.
[138]Ibid. The courageous district court judge in the *Swann* case was James B. McMillan (now deceased), a man of the finest character and intellect, whom I am proud to have known.

pupils to schools nearest their homes. But all things are not equal in a
system that has been deliberately constructed and maintained to enforce racial segregation. The remedy for such segregation may be administratively awkward, inconvenient, and even bizarre in some
situations, and may impose burdens on some; but all awkwardness and
inconvenience cannot be avoided in the interim period when remedial
adjustments are being made to eliminate the dual school systems.[139]

The constitutional legitimacy of such race-conscious remedies
gives no warrant for the claim that the desegregation of the public
schools required then, or justifies now, any *preference* by race. *Equal*
treatment for all was precisely and only what was ordered.

All of the famous "school cases" of the 1960s and 1970s were decided in that same spirit of remedy for earlier identified wrongs by
the states. When the University of California later argued that those
school cases could serve as precedents for its system of admissions
preference in 1978, Justice Powell, looking back, rejected that claim.
He wrote:

> Each [of the earlier school desegregation cases] involved remedies for
> clearly determined constitutional violations. E.g. *Swann v. Charlotte-
> Mecklenburg Board of Education,* 402 U.S. 1 (1971); *McDaniel v. Bar-
> resi,* 402 U.S. 39 (1971); *Green v. County School Board,* 391 U.S. 430
> (1968). Racial classifications thus were designed as remedies for the
> vindication of constitutional entitlement.[140]

But when that remedy has been given, and the discriminatory segregation of the school board has at last been overcome and eradicated, the use of race in the assignment of students could no longer
be justified. The procedures of the Charlotte-Mecklenburg School
District were overseen by the courts for more than 30 years. In 2001,
the Court of Appeals for the Fourth Circuit upheld a lower court
ruling that that school district was now "unitary," no longer unjustly
segregated, and that, therefore, the refusal (on racial grounds) by
administrators of that district to assign a student to a school to which

---

[139]*Swann,* p. 28 Emphasis added.
[140]*Bakke,* p. 300.

she was otherwise qualified, in their effort to maintain "racial balance," could not be justified under the Constitution.[141]

White students burdened by state uses of race are in circumstances "wholly dissimilar" (as Justice Powell observed) to that of pupils bused from neighborhood schools in compliance with a desegregation decree. What the University of California did to Alan Bakke was not done in order to desegregate the Davis medical school. The university's preference was not designed to remedy an injustice. On the contrary, the university *did* an injustice, by "den[ying] him admission, and may have deprived him altogether of a medical education."[142]

There are some who say that were ethnic preferences to be ended, the universities would become resegregated. But that is a patronizing claim (because it supposes that minorities are incapable of winning places on their own merits), and it is utterly false. Racial preferences have already been ended in California, and Texas, Florida, and Washington, and the university systems in these states have by no means become resegregated. In short, a demand for desegregation cannot be the "compelling need" that might justify deliberate race preference.

(4g) Race Preference to Integrate a Public Body

Integration and desegregation are very different. The nondiscriminatory admission of all students to public schools is a right constitutionally guaranteed. Desegregating public schools was and is, therefore, a constitutional command. Integrated schools, schools in which pupils of different races enroll in fact, are an ideal, widely and rightly sought. An integrated school system must be desegregated *a fortiori*—but the converse does not hold. Truly desegregated school districts are often not integrated, or fully integrated, for reasons having nothing to do with state action or state policy.

The ideal of racial or ethnic integration has been rejected, in recent years, by some minority groups who do not wish to become a

---

[141]*Belk v. Charlotte-Mecklenburg Board of Education,* 269 F. 3d 305 (2001) at p. 311.
[142]*Bakke,* p. 300, footnote 39.

part of a mixed or blended community that is mainly white. The grand and honorable dream of Martin Luther King, Jr., that blacks and whites might live and work and study together, attending not to skin color but to the content of character, was one that most of us share. But not all blacks, or all whites, do share it.[143]

Religious minorities are often deliberately parochial, fearing that the integration of their students with those of the majority may sap the vitality of their convictions, or may (as they believe) corrupt the religious upbringing of their children. The goods and evils of parochial schools need not be judged here. Although segregation in the public schools is strictly forbidden, parents may (and often do) seek out residential communities in which the preponderant ethnic heritage is that of their own religion, their own nationality, or their own race, in order that their children may be deeply imbued with those traditions. This is not always wrong. Even those who think such self-separation unfortunate must agree that it does not violate the Constitution, and it is certainly not a practice that must be uprooted in order that constitutional values be safeguarded.

In the decades that have elapsed since school busing and other vigorous remedies were introduced to break down segregated school systems, some communities, after approaching integration, have self-separated themselves once again. The loss of school integration resulting from unforced residential patterns, however much we may not like it, is not proof of deliberate segregation by any public body. Where that outcome is not the result of state action or policy it is not an injury that can justify a racially preferential remedy.

One illustration: Forty years ago, a federal district court found that the schools in Oklahoma City were intentionally segregated; a school busing plan was eventually devised, ordered (in 1963), and

---

[143]In *Kwanzaa and Me: A Teacher's Story* (Cambridge: Harvard University Press, 1995), an experienced elementary school teacher, Vivian G. Paley, raises seriously the question of whether white schools (or "integrated" schools) are bad for black children. One black professor of sociology (she reports) told her that he would "rather have his child go to an all black school, no matter how bad, than to an integrated school." Another black professor (she reports) refuses to send his daughter to a white school because he won't have her feeling "dumb and ugly." Such views are extreme and may be mistaken—but their growing currency shows that racial integration is certainly not a universal ideal.

implemented to demolish the dual system. The desegregation of the schools there was enforced by the authority of the courts. Many years later, when that busing plan was finally dropped, attendance in many elementary schools began to return to the racially clustered pattern of their residential neighborhoods. Some parents then sought to have the old remedial decree reinstituted. But the federal district court concluded, after a careful review of the local situation, that the later racial patterns in residence were the products of private choices, not of deliberate segregation, and that, therefore, the school busing order could no longer be justifiably forced upon that school system. This conclusion was ultimately upheld by the U.S. Supreme Court in 1991:

> From the very first, Federal supervision of local school systems was intended as a temporary measure to remedy past discrimination. . . . [School desegregation] decrees are not intended to operate in perpetuity. . . . Dissolving a desegregation decree after the local authorities have operated in compliance with it for a reasonable period of time properly recognizes that "necessary concern for the important values of local control of public school systems dictates that a Federal Court's regulatory control of such systems not extend beyond the time required to remedy the effects of past intentional discrimination."[144]

By 1985, racial clustering in Oklahoma City was so attenuated that it could no longer be rightly called a "vestige" of earlier school segregation. The unitary status of the school system had long been maintained by the school board in good faith. The assignment plan (by residential neighborhood) that they sought to implement "was not designed with discriminatory intent." In such circumstances, now fairly common in our country, the Supreme Court concluded that "the previous injunctive decree should be vacated and the School District returned to local control."[145] When "the vestiges of *de jure* segregation had been eliminated as far as practicable" (as in Oklahoma City decades after the original desegregation decree), a race-

---

[144]*Board of Education v. Dowell*, 498 U.S. 237, at p. 248 (1991).
[145]Ibid., p. 243.

conscious order, even one that does not give preference, is no longer justifiable.

Desegregation is indeed a constitutional obligation; integration is not, and cannot be forced upon a community whose members freely choose not to have it. When that is the choice they have made, "the displacement of local authority by an injunctive decree in a school desegregation case is a violation of the constitution."[146]

The race-conscious remedies of the 1960s and 1970s were justified by the constitutional demand for the desegregation of the public schools, not their integration. Now we rightly work for the racial integration of our communities and our schools. But if, as we have seen, integration cannot justify even race-conscious devices that are not preferential (such as school busing), it certainly cannot serve as the compelling need that might justify race *preference* under the standard of strict scrutiny.

In sum: Bearing the standard of strict scrutiny always in mind, and reviewing the application of this standard by the U. S. Supreme Court to the allegedly "compelling needs" that have been put forward over the past several decades

- to compensate for societal discrimination and oppression;
- to achieve racial balance in a particular population;
- to achieve diversity in schools, colleges, and other contexts;
- to provide role models for minority students;
- to provide better professional services for minorities;
- to desegregate a public body; and
- to integrate a public body,

we may confidently conclude that none of them can justify naked preference by race, and that such preference does indubitably violate the Constitution of the United States.

---

[146]Ibid., p. 248.

PART III

Why Race Preference Is Bad

7

Race Preference Is Bad for the Minorities Preferred

Race preference is plainly unfair, unjust—but many who admit this will say that its unfairness must be tolerated because its consequences are needed and good. All things considered, however, the consequences of preference are by no means good. Consider:

1. preference *divides* the society in which it is awarded;
2. it establishes a dreadful precedent in *excusing admitted racial discrimination* to achieve political objectives;
3. it *corrupts* the universities in which it is practiced, sacrificing intellectual values and creating pressures to discriminate by race in grading and graduation;
4. it *breeds hypocrisy* within schools and encourages a scofflaw attitude among college officials;
5. it *obscures the real social problem* of why so many minority students are not competitive academically;
6. it *obliges a choice of some few ethnic groups,* which are to be favored over all others;
7. it compels a *determination of how much blood is needed* to establish race membership;
8. it *removes incentives* for academic excellence and *encourages separatism* among racial and ethnic minorities;
9. it *mismatches students and institutions*, greatly increasing the likelihood of failure for many minority students;
10. it *injures race relations* over the long haul.

These consequences of preference I will explain—but its worst consequences, with which I begin, are the injuries it inflicts upon the racial minorities preferred, *creating widespread resentment, reinforcing stereotypes,* and *humiliating its purported beneficiaries* in the eyes of their classmates, colleagues, workmates, teachers—and even in their own eyes. Race preference has been an utter catastrophe for the ethnic minorities it was intended to benefit.

Some individual members of the favored minorities are advantaged by preference, of course. But the minority as a whole is undermined. Preference puts distinguished minority achievement under a cloud. It imposes upon every member of the preferred minority the demeaning burden of presumed inferiority. Preference *creates* that burden; it *makes* a stigma of the race of those who are preferred by race. An ethnic group given special favor by the community is *marked* as needing special favor—and the mark is borne prominently by every one of its members. Nasty racial stereotypes are reinforced, and the malicious imputation of inferiority is inescapable because it is tied to the color of skin.

Competitive appointments, promotions, and admissions, in institutions of all kinds, are now substantially influenced by consideration of the race of competing applicants. This is no longer in doubt, and has now been generally acknowledged. At the University of Michigan, for example, where competition for admission is stiff, minority applicants automatically receive 20 points for their race in a system requiring about 100 points for acceptance.[147]

Such preferences embedded in otherwise competitive systems have unfortunate consequences for *minority* candidates. If unsuccessful in spite of their special advantage, they are disgraced. And if successful, minority candidates are undermined because many of them—not all, of course, but we cannot be sure which—are known to occupy their places *because* of their race. This is universally understood but cannot be openly acknowledged because it is so very humiliating. The

---

[147]The impact of preference on American universities is discussed more fully in the following chapter. Two prominent federal cases involving the University of Michigan (*Gratz v. Bollinger*, addressed preference in undergraduate admissions, and *Grutter v. Bollinger*, addressed preference given by the Michigan law school) have exposed the preferential machinery there.

sting of it is there, nevertheless, in frequent references to "affirmative action hiring" and to programs for "special admits."

Minority admissions or appointments are not based exclusively upon race, of course; experience and credentials count heavily. But the weight given to skin color or ethnicity is often the critical factor that accounts for success. The regard for skills and attainments in such appointments (admissions, promotions, etc.) is therefore *relatively* reduced; this fact is inescapable, and it follows that many who receive such appointments would not occupy their present places had they been white. This is painful to say, but it is true, and everyone recognizes, although not everyone will admit openly, that it is true. The evidence for its truth has been compiled and lamented by blacks as well as whites.[148]

In law schools and medical schools, race preference is nearly universal; admission is commonly awarded to minority applicants *much* less qualified than their majority counterparts. Some are admitted who, had they been white, would have been *summarily* rejected, not even seriously considered for admission. The statistical gap between the past performances of those admitted on normal competitive criteria and those admitted preferentially is wide. The Association of American Medical Colleges reported that in 1992 the mean scores of blacks admitted to medical school that year were in some institutions as much as 18 percent lower than the mean scores of accepted whites, and as much as 4 percent lower than the scores of white applicants who were *rejected* for admission.[149] The editor of *The Journal of Blacks in Higher Education*, acknowledging extensive preference for black medical school applicants, puts it this way: "Over half the 15,000 white students *rejected* for admission to U.S. medical schools scored above the mean for black students who were *admitted*. . . . Affirmative action plays a huge, if not almost determinative, role in the admission of African Americans to professional schools."[150] Admission under such circumstances is no favor to the black minority.

---

[148]The *Journal of Blacks in Higher Education* has reported this evidence in much detail, in many issues from 1994 to the present.

[149]Theodore Cross, "Minority Students in Medical Education: Facts and Figures," *Journal of Blacks in Higher Education*, #9, autumn 1995, p. 47.

[150]"What if There Was No Affirmative Action?" *Journal of Blacks in Higher Education*, spring 1994, p. 44. Emphasis added.

Selective undergraduate colleges also give substantial admission preference by race. At the eight Ivy League schools (Brown, Cornell, Columbia, Dartmouth, Harvard, Princeton, University of Pennsylvania, and Yale), admissions officers were interviewed in 1994 by the editors of *The Journal for Blacks in Higher Education*; statistical data about applicants and matriculants in these schools were then correlated with Scholastic Aptitude Tests, which remain the best predictors of academic success. Those tests are in two parts, verbal and quantitative, with a maximum possible combined score of 1600, 800 on each part. Using Harvard as illustrative of the preferences given at the most selective institutions, the editor of *JBHE* wrote: "We know for certain that in the freshman class that came to Harvard College in the fall of 1991 the mean SAT score of black entering freshmen was 160 points below the average of admitted whites. Blacks [entering Harvard] averaged combined scores of 1290 and whites averaged combined scores of 1450. . . . Very few black students in the nation score at this level. Only 102 blacks [nationwide] had scores above 750 on either the math or verbal SAT in 1992, yet over 15,000 whites scored at that level."[151] To enroll the number of minority students sought, very substantial preferences are given—at Harvard and at selective colleges across the country.

Students admitted as a result of such preference are much less prepared to undertake the studies required of them than their non-minority peers. It is not surprising that they often perform at a lower level than their peers admitted without preference; sometimes they are cruelly humiliated; failure is not rare. Extracurricular tutoring is commonly offered to preferred students; remedial courses are designed for them; special counselors are hired to guide and support them. The intellectual gap arising over 17 years of life is to be closed, it is hoped, in a summer or a semester of catch-up—but success is spotty and the attrition rate is high. Dispensations—often in the form of opportunities to retake examinations failed—are commonly given to those preferentially admitted so that they do not flunk out early.

In spite of all this, preferred students will fare poorly if standards remain high and the same standards are applied to all. But since

---

[151]Ibid., p. 47.

preferred students must not be allowed to fare poorly, standards do not remain high or the same standards are not applied to all. The gap between the performance of those admitted on established academic merit and those admitted with heavy reliance on race is wide, so the inadequacies of specially admitted students must be excused or overlooked, leniency shown in their evaluation. By hook or by crook, a sufficient number of minority lawyers, doctors, or bachelors of arts must be got through. In professional schools, minority students very rarely flunk out. And everyone—instructors, roommates, competitors, the students themselves—knows what is going on. The colleges and professional schools are corrupted, of course—but the worst result is this: all minority students are stamped (as Justice Clarence Thomas has put it) "with a badge of inferiority."

Minority students who cannot compete successfully *after* having been admitted must again be preferred in the interest of racial balance. In most law schools, for example, "making law review" has long been the achievement of only the most accomplished law students, a prize hard won. Race preference has changed even this. The great law reviews—like the *Michigan Law Review* (*MLR*) in Ann Arbor—have knuckled to the pressure for more "diversity." Recent events there illustrate the damage race preference to achieve proportionality does to minority students.

Until 1992, only the very most talented students made the *Michigan Law Review*. In that year, a new policy was adopted, designed to insure "the same percentage of minorities on its staff as there are minorities in the Law School."[152] Under this new policy, students seeking positions on the *Review* submit writing samples that are graded blindly; the applicants' grade point average in completed law classes is then factored in. This competition, if unmodified by race, would yield law review appointments racially "unbalanced," so the ethnicity of the applicants is then also weighed to *fix* the outcome. The policy reads:

> If the above procedures fail to identify a sufficient number of minority candidates for positions on the Law Review, we will supplement these

[152]Memorandum from the Michigan Law Review Association, Ann Arbor, Michigan, 3 April 1992.

procedures by considering an applicant's *affirmative action eligibility*
. . . that is, on the basis of whether an applicant is a Black American,
Mexican American, Native American, or Puerto Rican raised on the
American mainland.

Minority students are identified (by the law school office) as having
"affirmative action eligibility" (i.e., being African American, or Native American, etc.), and this is noted on their writing entries. In the
end, "a sufficient number of positions will be offered to those applicants from minority groups with the highest writing scores or aug-
mented grades."[153] What number is "sufficient" is not specified. But
the essence of the policy is clear enough: when minority applicants
aren't good enough to make it on their own, the best minority applicants available will be appointed to insure the racial numbers
sought. To avoid the risk of dreadful embarrassment by the appointment of persons utterly incompetent, the *Michigan Law Review* policy concludes with the following proviso: "Positions will not
be offered to applicants who score a zero in the writing competition
and whose grades fall below a threshold to be determined by the
Editor-in-Chief and Managing Editor."

What would one expect to be the impact of this policy upon the
spirit of black law students? I report the responses of one outstanding
law student, identified here only by his initials, MKF, who was appointed to the editorial board of the *Michigan Law Review* on merit
before the adoption of that policy. Learning of the newly proposed
preferential system for editorial appointments, and greatly distressed, he explained (in a long letter to his fellow editors) the consequences of such preference *for black students* like himself:

First, the reputation of all black students who make law review,
whether by preference or by merit, is undermined within and without
the school. In the competition for jobs, he observed, law review "on a
minority student's resume [now] signifies merely that one did not both
write a competition piece worthy of a zero and fall below a minimum
grade point average of an unknown level—hardly a distinction."[154]

---

[153]Ibid.

[154]From an unpublished letter, in my files, written by MKF to the Editorial
Board of the *Michigan Law Review*, 23 March 1992. As an undergraduate,
MKF had been my student—an excellent student—in logic.

Within the law school, "[m]inority law students [appointed as editors] face subtle and explicit doubt in the eyes of non-*Review* students" and also face resentment from white students who applied but were not accepted. In the eyes of other minority students, "the credibility of minority *Review* members is impeached." And *even in their own eyes,* those minority students who rely upon ethnic preference must "live with their own doubt. Meeting the *Law Review* challenge is a frightening experience. How much more difficult is it for minority students who have reason to believe that they wouldn't have qualified but for their race? How scary it is for one who can think, as many *Review* members have thought, 'I'm not good enough for this.' "[155] And those who fail to make the *Review*, although their "affirmative action eligibility" was duly noted, are simply devastated.

Second, the preferential policy teaches minority students a very destructive lesson. MKF:

> Minority students in general are assumed to be less qualified than the white applicants. And to the extent that we are, we are told by the *Law Review* that we need not work hard to develop ourselves as other *Law Review* hopefuls do; the *Law Review* will take us for less. Instead of expecting excellence from minority students, and in turn minority students expecting excellence from ourselves, we need only expect to be average. (That's a guess, of course; how low the *Review* will go is a secret.) In this way the *Law Review* offers little incentive to work hard to make it.

> Personally, I'm tired of having my achievements doubted. When my wife told her workmates that I had been accepted by the U of M Law School, one person muttered, "it's no wonder, he's black and he's blind." [MKF's vision is seriously impaired.] On the *Law Review* I thought I could attain recognition for my merit rather than my color. . . . Unfortunately, my membership is tainted. . . . Isn't it ironic to have blind grading tickets for everyone and colored grading tickets for minorities? Sometimes I wonder whether I deserve to be on the Editorial Board or whether I stand as a token for our progressive *Law Review*."[156]

[155]Ibid.
[156]Ibid.

At another law school one black student wrote:

> I'll never forget my first week of law school. The message was clear:
> we were the 'slow' kids. A meeting between the dean and a group
> from my section confirmed this. That experience left no one with the
> illusion that we were anything but charity cases. We wanted to com-
> pete but apparently the law school had some doubt that we could. We
> were only there for diversity's sake.[157]

In engineering as well as in law, the product of preference is bitterness. A minority mechanical engineering student at the University of Michigan in his fifth year writes poignantly: "Nobody expects
you to know what you're doing. . . . You're always the last lab part-
ner picked."[158]

Preference humiliates even at the highest levels. When a black
administrator, Dr. Yolanda Moses, was appointed president of the
City College of New York in 1993, she was correctly described by
the *New York Times* as a "little known vice-president from California."[159] A professor at Penn State University responded with dismay
that this description made "Dr. Moses appear an affirmative action
appointment."[160] And everyone knows what that means.

Some of those appointed on racial grounds are just not up to the
job, and that may prove highly embarrassing, as the following anecdote illustrates. Two black women were routinely assigned the task
of editing a manuscript submitted to the *Harvard Law Review* in
1993; the president of the *Review* at that time, Emily Schulman,
called the assignment a disaster. Her problem was this: The manuscript in question had been submitted by a black assistant professor
at the Harvard law school (who is now, in 2003, a full professor there)
and was to be his "tenure article," the piece upon which his career
at Harvard might depend. Ms. Schulman understood how race had
infected the appointment of editors at the *Harvard Law Review*.
Was she to allow this fine author's work to be prepared for publication by persons whose competence as editors she knew to be

[157]*New York Times*, 25 May 1993.
[158]*Michigan Daily*, 21 October 1993.
[159]*New York Times*, 25 May 1993.
[160]*New York Times*, 7 June 1993.

doubtful? She took it upon herself to investigate the actual capacity of the women assigned to do the requisite editorial work. That investigation provoked general outrage at the law school, but preference demoralizes everyone involved. Those most enraged were black law students, of course, who were universally humiliated.

When preference is given to an ethnic group, *every* member of that group is readily identifiable as one who is likely to have received preference—*whether or not* special favor has in fact been given to him or to her, and whatever that person's true level of talent or achievement. A black gastroenterologist from New York, Carlyle Miller, whose attainment and promise won him scholarships to Columbia University and to Cornell medical school, resentfully called affirmative action (i.e., race preference) "a one-way ticket." As a medical specialist, you may prove your abilities beyond doubt and win appointments without favor. No matter, says he, "All along the way everyone is questioning you."[161] In Cleveland, an outstanding high school student, valedictorian of her graduating class, was recruited by the best colleges in the country—but their message to her was degrading. "I should have been the kind of person that anybody would have wanted in their college," she observed, "but the letters almost always read 'Dear Black Student. . . . ' "[162] An 18-year veteran of the Chicago police force, repeatedly denied promotion to sergeant while Hispanics and females with lower scores than his were given the higher-ranking positions set aside for those groups, observed that, since he himself is black, when at last he gets his promotion, that achievement is likely to be so *tainted* by "affirmative action" that he will be perceived as (in his own words) a "quota sergeant."[163] An assistant corporation counsel in Chicago reported that, having worked in an eastern law firm for 18 months, he was never sure whether he was, in his words, "an affirmative action hire," but he always felt like one.

You always want to believe that you were hired because you were the best. You work seven days a week, you wear Brooks Brothers suits,

[161]*New York Times*, 15 September 1991.
[162]Ibid.
[163]*Time*, 27 May 1991.

you play golf. *But everything around you is telling you you were brought in for one reason: because you were a quota.* . . . No matter how hard I worked or how brilliant I was, it wasn't getting me anywhere. It's a hell of a stigma to overcome.[164]

Advocates of preference who believe they are doing minorities a great favor must suppose that those they patronize are not bright enough to appreciate the insult. Stephen Carter, a professor at the Yale University law school, puts it like this: "[A]s long as racial preferences exist, the one thing that cannot be proved is which people of color in my generation would have achieved what they have in their absence."[165] The psychological impact of preference upon those preferred is epitomized in the remark of a black student at the University of California: "I feel like I have AFFIRMATIVE ACTION stamped on my forehead."[166]

When affirmative action seeks to award with preference what only intellect can achieve, it *forges a link* between minority status and weak performance. The suggestion that minorities are intellectually inferior is a canard, false and outrageously unfair. But preference encourages just that belief. Benevolently intended preference by race has done more, in two decades, to damage the intellectual reputation of blacks and other minorities than all the bigots had done in the half century before.

Do this thought experiment. Suppose that height were made a critical consideration in university admissions. Suppose preference were widely given, in law schools or medical schools or undergraduate colleges, to overcome the disadvantage that short stature imposes. Absurd, but suppose it. Some short applicants, minimally qualified, would be admitted because of that extra credit given to all "shorts." Then shorts overall would, *as a group*, prove to be weaker students, because many of them, marginally qualified, were not so well suited for academic work as their peers who were selected wholly on grounds related to attainment or promise. With

---

[164]*New York Times*, 15 September 1991. Emphasis added.

[165]*Insight*, 20 June 1994.

[166]Reported by Troy Duster, a sociologist at the University of California, in *Time*, 27 May 1991.

remedial instruction, patient tutoring, some wincing and some winking, the specially admitted shorts are pushed through to graduation somehow. Charts showing the growing numbers of shorts in the student body and among the faculty are displayed by administrators who express pride and satisfaction in the increased numbers of short professionals admitted and graduating, while yet insisting that much work remains to be done to further improve the "stature numbers."

Some of the very most talented applicants and graduates will of course always be short; there is obviously no conflict between shortness and intellectual excellence. But where shortness has been systematically introduced into the selection process it must, indubitably, dilute the importance of intellectual excellence in selection. The shorts *will* be poorer students as a group, not because they are short, but because many of them (unlike the class of nonshorts) will have been selected on a lower intellectual standard by hypothesis: that is what preference by height entails. The outcome? Everyone soon learns that the credentials of noticeably short students, or short doctors, or short lawyers, are suspect. Suspicion will burden all shorts because no one can be sure—not even the shorts themselves—whether their selection for certain positions were made wholly in virtue of their merits, or (in some good part) because of their shortness.

Expressing this distrust of shorts publicly will be unacceptable, of course, a stature slur. To call attention to the inferior performance of the short group (it will be said) shows prejudice, some deep and irrational antipathy toward shorts. But that would not be true. When the selection is known to have been deliberately diluted by the consideration of some physical characteristic, members of groups in whose favor that dilution was designed are inescapably suspect.

The individual talls displaced by such preferences (and all those who for good reason *believed* that they were so displaced) would harbor justifiable resentment, no doubt. But talls as a group would not suffer. Shorts as a group, on the other hand, would suffer mightily. Poorly prepared shorts, marginally qualified shorts who would not have been admitted if they were not short, would rarely fail to recognize their own relative unsuitability for the roles into which they had been thrust. The internal burden they bear would be heavy.

And their tall colleagues (or classmates or competitors or patients), knowing or reasonably presuming the part that shortness had played in their selection, would view them with silent disdain.

But all shorts, whatever the level of their true talent, would find themselves under an intellectual cloud, a cloud created by—could it be?—their height! Even outstanding performance by shorts would be likely to win less than full credit because it would be seen, by talls and shorts alike, through a veil of skeptical doubts and lowered expectations. The known preference gives rational ground to conjecture, regarding each short, that she had been given favor because she was short; behind her back she is likely to be referred to, with a knowing look, as the short candidate. Any individual short appointed or admitted could never be sure what had accounted for her selection.

Short people in the real world may be thankful that all this is fantasy, that we have not done this terrible thing to them. Black students and black professionals have not been so fortunate. For them not height but skin color, equally unrelated to intellectual excellence, has been transformed into onus. The insidious injury that would be done to shorts in this absurd thought experiment is truly being done, constantly, to blacks and other minorities, and in some cases to women, in institutions of every description.

The common journalistic focus upon the color of one who achieves distinction, rather than upon the reasons for the honor given, often gives unintended but nevertheless humiliating insult. The appointment of a new president at Wayne State University, in Detroit in 1997, illustrates this subordination of personal distinction to race. Here is the opening of the report of his appointment in a major Michigan newspaper:

> In a time when affirmative action is being criticized throughout the United States, Wayne State University has appointed its first African-American President. In December 1996, Wayne State's former President, David Adamany, announced his retirement. Seven and a half months later, at an August public Board meeting, Irvin Reid was named the University's ninth president, making history by being the first black face among his eight predecessors. . . . Wayne State Board of Governors Chair Denise Lewis said . . . "he's one of the leading

African-Americans in higher education because he's been in higher education for some 30 years."[167]

Is this not painful? Offensive? Condescending? Is race preference good for President Reid and all other distinguished black administrators? Individual members of minority groups will sometimes benefit from favors, no doubt—but the minority as a whole is in such ways *subverted* by preference. Invidious racial comparisons are invited by selection processes tied to race. Nasty stereotypes of racial inferiority are *reinforced*, given apparent substance by the preferential devices that were supposed to be offering support to previously disadvantaged groups.

Had racists set out deliberately to besmirch minorities, to impose a subtle but substantial handicap on groups they despised, no more cruelly effective device could have been chosen to "prove" that inferiority. Persons preferred on grounds of race or ethnicity do sometimes perform at a level that is embarrassingly inferior. This is certainly not because they are minorities, of course, but because, having been selected for reasons irrelevant to the tasks to be performed, they are less competent at those tasks. If some demon had sought to concoct a scheme aimed at undermining the credentials of minority scholars, professionals, and students, to stigmatize them permanently and humiliate them publicly, no more ingenious plan could have been devised than the system of preferences now defended as a social need and great favor to minorities. With friends like these, as the saying goes, who needs enemies?

And yet, among minorities themselves, support for preference remains substantial in spite of the humiliation to which it leads. Why? Because each member of a group preferred may reasonably say to herself, or himself, that the system is one in which I am myself a possible, perhaps a probable beneficiary. Everyone will weigh his own advantages most heavily, of course, and no one is to be faulted for defending programs under which he, or she, is more likely to receive favorable consideration. It is not unreasonable for one to hope for such advantage, or to support a program that, although not good

---

[167]*Ann Arbor News*, 26 August 1997, p. A1.

for the group as a whole over the long run, may promise substantial personal benefit. If the rules provide such benefits, one who accepts them—even if the preferential system is unjust in the large—does nothing wrong.

Minority support for preference is reinforced by the advocacy of celebrated persons called "civil rights leaders," whose positions may depend upon preferential programs, and whose influence is enhanced by their enlargement. Designing preferences—and advocating, implementing, enforcing, and assessing them—has become a profession, well paid in money and prestige. Reiterated claims of victimhood that are held to justify preference become the principal themes of those who make their livelihood exploiting racial divisions.

But what about the white advocates of preference—is the damage that preference does to minorities not seen by them? Some black scholars, troubled by the impact of preference on blacks, contend that it is the feeling of guilt for the historical oppression of minorities that causes many whites to make what they think to be a form of restitution. One black scholar asserts that American institutions, when it comes to race, "are driven entirely by white guilt." Critical capacities are suspended, says he, and the strategy of white officials is always one of appeasement.[168]

Perhaps. But guilt feelings probably play no larger role than the mistaken conviction that preferences are benign, that in giving them no real damage is done. The stigmatization of minorities by preference is not a genuine threat, they suppose, because the greater frequency of poor performance among the minorities will be obscured (they think) by the great spread of performance quality among the mass (of students, or professionals or appointees of every stripe). Objective differences in talent are not reliably measurable anyway, it is said, so disparities in performance by group will go unnoticed—and hence that feared damage to the minority will not arise.

This belief is seriously mistaken. If preferences were given only to those with blue eyes, the weaker performance of the blue-eyed as compared to the non-blue-eyed might not be much noticed. But when the preference is given by *race*, by physical factors that are

---

[168]See Shelby Steele, *A Dream Deferred: The Second Betrayal of Black Freedom in America* (New York: HarperCollins, 1998).

prominent and almost unavoidably noted, the relative weakness in the performance of those preferred (the racial minorities), as compared to those not preferred (the racial majority), is quickly and universally observed. As an objective, statistical matter, those preferred will perform less well. That inferior performance comes to be tied in the public mind to the color of those preferred.

In the world of athletics, where performance is public and graded by all, race preference will not be tolerated. Our sports teams play to win, not to display a racially balanced array of participants. In the National Basketball Association and the National Football League, most of the players are black—a percentage vastly greater than that of blacks in the population at large. Blacks are in those team lineups for no reason other than that they are good, *very* good.

Here is another thought experiment: Suppose it were decided that basketball teams must exhibit racial proportionality. Suppose a system had been devised to insure that, in every college and professional basketball game, the percentage of whites on the court must reflect the approximate racial proportionality in the population at large. Substantial preference would have to be given to inferior white players, of course. Picture the scene as the teams take the floor: three or four whites are in the starting lineup of each team of five; black players known by all to be markedly superior to them remain on the bench. The relative mediocrity of the white players preferred is there for every eye to see. Put aside the unfairness to blacks, whose earned places are taken by preferred whites. What must the fans, the coaches, the players of all colors be thinking *about the whites* who play in that corrupted system? What will be assumed about the abilities of *every new white player* who enters the game? If that white player is highly skilled and yet errs, as every player will on occasion, *to what will his error be attributed*? If that white player is relatively unskilled, what will everyone in the audience suppose to be the real reason that duffer is out there playing?

This is fantasy, of course, because ethnic disparities on sports teams are universally accepted, not as an evil but as the product of many cultural factors; it is an outcome we see no need to eliminate. Forcing race proportionality on basketball or football teams is a notion that strikes us as silly. What counts on a sports field is not the color of the players but their skill and endurance. We want our teams to *win*. The importance of winning may be minimized in elementary school, where all boys and girls benefit from the experience of team play, whatever the outcome. But at the high school and college level, and certainly in the world of professional sports, *winning* is the object of the game.

The case is no different in any field of serious work or study. In a courtroom, where criminal punishment or money damages may be at stake, winning—securing a favorable verdict—is the overriding objective. In the operating room, where life itself may be at stake, the success of the medical procedure, winning, is all that counts. We no more care whether the surgeon be black or the lawyer Hispanic than we care whether the quarterback is black or the center Samoan. We are certainly right not to care.

The percentage of minorities enrolled in the nation's law schools and medical schools has been artificially inflated by race preferences; when preferences are eliminated, that percentage will drop, at least for a while. That is a regrettable consequence of the level of preparation of minority youngsters, just as the domination of some athletic teams by minorities is a consequence of their superior training as youngsters. We will not change the standards of performance on the basketball court to achieve racial balance among the players. No more ought we change the standards for performance in the hospital to achieve racial balance among the doctors. In the important spheres of life, skin color is simply not relevant.

Preference to achieve racial balance in the professions is even more counterproductive than it would be in professional sports. The mistakes of less-competent doctors, journalists, scientists, and lawyers are not so widely displayed as fumbled footballs or missed baskets. But human lives and fortunes rest in those professional hands; weak skills in those arenas are very costly, and they will certainly be recognized, if not by the public at least by clients and colleagues. Those in need of professional help seek the very best service they can find and afford; skin color simply doesn't count.

Nor do we think for a moment that the performance of the lawyers we hire, or the doctors who treat us, cannot be fairly judged. Intellectual strength and attainment is an objective matter. Evaluating professional performance, like judging the skill of a quarterback, may not be quantitatively precise, but in both spheres evaluations by experts are generally quite accurate. My colleagues in surgery at the Michigan medical school make judgments of the proficiency of their juniors in the operating room every bit as reliable as the judgments of our football coach on the gridiron. I teach logic; I can tell you with some precision who among my students have a solid grasp of the principles of correct reasoning, and who among them understand the material less well, or poorly. For the intellectual rigors of veterinary medicine, or accountancy, or for graduate study in mathematics or philosophy, students who are well prepared can be quite readily distinguished from those who are not. Intellectual talents—the ability to master complex theoretical materials, to apply theory to complicated fact situations, to undertake careful analyses and make subtle distinctions—are no harder to identify than talents on the athletic field. Where performance standards are high, the inability to perform effectively or compete successfully is quite readily ascertainable by those skilled in that activity. Race cannot make up for it.

Wherever inferior performance is found regularly to accompany some physical characteristic disproportionately—as it must when ethnic characteristics are given weight in a selection process for intellectual functions—the bearers of that physical characteristic become unavoidably suspect. The fact that some who possess that characteristic are also among the very best cannot ward off the natural inference associating that physical characteristic with inferiority. Therefore ethnic preferences, wherever in the world they have been introduced, *brand* racial groups as inferior, inflicting upon the members of those groups the very injury they least deserve to suffer. By thrusting minorities into positions in which their relative performance must prove statistically weaker, "affirmative action" has given maddening plausibility to the judgments that persons of some colors are not capable of meeting the standards of performance imposed on those of other colors.[169]

---

[169]The process works also in reverse. Not long ago, the quota for Jewish students in some Ivy League universities (where they were distinctly unwelcome) was tiny; those who made the cut had to be exceedingly able. The myth of the Jews as supersmart was given support by the rational inference, then, that any Jew enrolled at Harvard, or Columbia, must indeed have been very brainy!

In that mythical world in which shorts are given preference over nonshorts in college admission, who is done greater injury: the class of talls among whom some are displaced by favored shorts? Or those many shorts who would have won their places fairly through intellect and energy but who are nevertheless forever suspect because of their shortness? Many among the "affirmative action" minorities also needed no preference, wanted none and got none, yet cannot gain the respect of colleagues and clients who have good reason to suspect that those places had been gained through race preference. Minority professionals who have *not* been preferred, whose intellect and character would have won them universal esteem without any regard for color, are thus undermined by preference. No matter their industry, their talent, their hard-won attainments, they are *seen* to be black or brown and *believed* (by majority and minority members both, and perhaps even by themselves) to be where they are by virtue of a preference having nothing to do with their talents. Among the favored groups, even those who excel and receive no favor cannot escape distrust.

Nor is there any way for them to cleanse themselves of the taint. When minority law students are interviewed by judges for clerkships (MKF observed in his critique of preference on the *Michigan Law Review*) or interviewed by law firms for employment, they are not asked whether they took advantage of their "affirmative action eligibility." That question cannot be asked without offense, and it should not be asked. But if in fact they have accepted no such racial advantages, how can that be made known? To report on a resume that a preference was offered but declined would be indiscreetly vain, and would indirectly undermine others who had not declined. Such a report, even if true, simply cannot be given. "We are as qualified as well-qualified whites," MKF wrote, "but nobody knows it, and, in fact, outsiders have a legitimate reason to doubt it."[170] The net of preference is inescapable.

White students who gain prestigious editorships on law review, MKF notes with irritation, "remain unimpeachable, while they congratulate themselves for helping a lot of minority students." Preference on the

[170]MKF, letter of 23 March 1992, p. 2.

Review, he observes, is there to "soothe the consciences" of those not subject to it. He continues:

> Who is the policy intended to benefit anyway? Is the *Law Review* concerned with the development of minority students or with appearing politically correct? This type of policy—we simply lower our standards—is the easy way out.[171]

A policy truly respectful of the capacities of minority students, writes MKF, would expect of them

> the same excellence that the *Law Review* expects of others. Isn't that how white students are encouraged to develop themselves, by being recognized for excellence when they achieve it? Minority students can achieve excellence, and we should be expected to do so if we want to be recognized for it. . . . Can real development and actualization come any other way than by effort and study? All law students, and especially those of us on the Editorial Board of the *Michigan Law Review* know the answer to this question. No pain, no gain.[172]

This resentment, on the part of black scholars, of policies that systematically minimize minority achievements, is perfectly understandable. John McWhorter, the distinguished professor of linguistics at the University of California, puts it this way:

> Affirmative Action in education denies black students the incentives to do their very best. . . . [They will not do their best when] they are told they only have to do pretty well. That will never raise a group to parity with whites and Asians. That is my reason for not liking affirmative action—because it keeps black students down.[173]

High-achievers among the minorities often find it difficult, in spite of the unfairness and the hurtfulness of preference, to be as

---

[171]Ibid. It will be recalled that MKF, a member of the editorial Board who had himself received no preference, was writing to his fellow members who planned to give preference.

[172]Ibid., p. 5.

[173]John McWhorter, in an interview with Lee Hubbard on 10 January 2002, as reported online at www.African.com. Professor McWhorter's critique is presented and defended at length in his book *Losing the Race: Self-Sabotage in Black America* (New York: Simon and Schuster, 2000).

outspoken in criticism as Professor McWhorter and MKF have been. But equally outspoken is Stephen Carter, now professor at Yale. As a youth, Carter won the National Achievement Scholarship awarded to "outstanding Negro students." But the award he really yearned for was the National Merit Scholarship, so he inquired: If he accepted the former, might he be considered for the latter? No. And must he decide on this right away? Yes—but no matter, he was told: you "wouldn't win a National Merit Scholarship anyway. . . . the people who get National Achievement Scholarships are never good enough to get National Merit Scholarships." Carter continues:

> I was stunned—the more so when, later, a number of white students with lower test scores than mine and similar grades were awarded National Merit Scholarships. The lesson was that the smartest students of color were not considered as capable as the smartest white students, and therefore would not be allowed to compete with them, but only with each other.
>
> It is called the "best black" syndrome, and all black people who have done well in school are familiar with it. We are measured by a different yardstick: first black, only black, best black. The best black syndrome is cut from the same cloth as the implicit and demeaning tokenism that often accompanies racial preferences. "Oh, we'll tolerate so-and-so on our faculty, because she's the best black." Not because she's the best qualified candidate, but because she's the best qualified black candidate. She can fill the black slot. And then the rest of the slots can be filled in the usual way: with the best qualified candidates.

And who is responsible for the spread of this "best black" syndrome? Carter explains:

> This dichotomy between the "best" and the "best black" is not something manufactured by racists to denigrate the abilities of professionals who are not white. On the contrary, it is reinforced from time to time by those students who demand that universities commit to hiring some pre-set number of minority faculty members. What they are really saying is: "Go out and hire the best blacks." And it is further reinforced by faculty members who see these demands as nothing more than claims for simple justice.

The best black syndrome creates in those of us who have benefited from racial preferences a peculiar contradiction. We know, because we are told over and over, that we are the best black people in our fields, whatever those fields may be. . . . At the same time we long for more. We yearn to be called what our achievements often deserve: simply the best—no qualifiers needed!

No, what I describe isn't racism, but it is in its way every bit as tragic. It is nearly as insulting. The best black? There are the best people—that's one category—and there are the best black people— that's another. And those twain don't meet.

Racial preferences must certainly reinforce the best black syndrome. . . . The best black syndrome is demeaning and oppressive and ought to be eradicated. . . . [But] in an era when so many doubt the talents of those of us who have benefited from preferences, "best black" can be a substitute for "best affirmative action baby."[174]

Race preference purports to help minorities, but, as my friend and former student MKF puts it bluntly, such preference "insults and harms" them. Of all the hurts race preference inflicts, this is the deepest, the longest lasting, and the worst.

[174]Stephen L. Carter, "The Best Black, and Other Tales," *Reconstruction* 1, no. 1 (winter 1990), p. 7. This account reappears in Carter's book: *Reflections of an Affirmative Action Baby* (New York: Basic Books, 1991).

8

Race Preference Is Bad for the Universities that Give Preference

Race preference pervades American institutions of many kinds, but it is chiefly encountered now in four spheres: *employment, voter redistricting, contracting,* and (most commonly) *school admissions.* Employment preferences are cruel, and their consequences painful.[175] Voting districts gerrymandered to give race preference, although rejected by the Supreme Court, have not yet been stamped out. Contract preferences given by state and local governments are a scandal, continuing in spite of the fact that there has been an almost unbroken succession of court cases in which such blatant racial discrimination has been struck down.[176]

But the widest and deepest penetration of race preference has been in college and university admissions, where it is firmly ensconced and routine. The very bad consequences of these preferences *for the educational institutions themselves* are my concern in the pages that follow. Similar evils attend race preference in the other spheres noted, but universities—in which I have had long and direct experience—are the institutions I know best.

Universities are *corrupted* by race preference. To give such preference, they must engage in extensive, self-conscious hypocrisy. The

---

[175]See Carl Cohen, *Naked Racial Preference* (New York and London: Madison Books, 1995), parts C and D.

[176]As recently as March 2002, a preferential contracting program in Charlotte, North Carolina, euphemistically called the "Minority and Women's Business Development" program, has been ordered replaced by one that is race and gender neutral.

equal treatment of all is earnestly professed at the very time policies of unequal treatment are being secretly implemented. Institutions that ought to serve as models of honorable and principled conduct *cheat*. The contrast between what is professed and what is practiced is appalling.[177] Our universities are humiliated and shamed by systematic dishonesty in matters of race.

Once a college or university is committed to a policy of race preference, duplicity becomes inescapable because giving preference entails lowering academic standards, but *acknowledging* lowered standards is simply out of the question. University representatives always *say* that the striving for excellence is their governing principle, and insist that students and faculty are selected on the highest feasible intellectual standards. But this is no longer true in America's premier universities, and it has not been true for decades. Standards have been deliberately and knowingly lowered—because only by lowering standards can the number of minority students enrolled, and the number of minority faculty appointed, come close to satisfying "affirmative action goals." This is readily ascertainable fact, as I will show, but any college president who acknowledges in public the inescapable connection between ethnic targets and lowered standards may as well submit his resignation the same day.

There is no inconsistency between membership in any ethnic minority and the highest intellectual attainment. This important truth should be spelled out in letters so large that he who runs may read it. Blacks, Hispanics, and Native Americans exhibit every excellence of human kind, as do members of all ethnic and racial groups. The

---

[177]While outright preferences for minority applicants to the law school and the undergraduate college were being acknowledged in legal proceedings, each of the published catalogues of my university carried this formal disclaimer: "The University of Michigan is committed to a policy of non-discrimination and equal opportunity for all persons regardless of race, sex, color, religion, creed, national origin or ancestry . . . in employment, educational programs and activities, and admissions." Many references to the University of Michigan will appear in the following pages, partly because its procedures were at the time of this writing the subject of notorious civil litigation, and partly because (since I am a member of the Michigan faculty) the facts at this institution, to which I am devoted, have been driven home to me.

lowering of standards obliged by preferential admissions and appointments is *not* the consequence of the intellectual inferiority of the groups favored. It is the consequence of the sharp imbalance between the number of minority members insisted upon as "goal" or as a "target", on the one hand, and the number of minorities available to satisfy that demand using established intellectual standards, on the other hand. The latter falls far short of the former; that is a troubling reality, a fact that no special admissions program or "opportunity hiring" program can change.

Advocates of race preference suppose that this imbalance can be overcome by *forcing* a change in the ethnic ratios of those appointed or enrolled. But altering criteria for selection cannot improve the applicants. Manipulating admissions and appointments so that the proportion of the races among students and faculty will mirror (or approach) those proportions in the population at large cannot affect the capacities of the persons admitted and hired. When the demand for the number of minority students (and faculty) far exceeds the number available on established intellectual standards, only lowering those standards can satisfy that demand.

But what accounts for that demand? The imperative arises because *ethnic proportionality* has been taken to be the measure of justice. This proportionality has been the explicit objective of our universities for years.[178] That objective unquestioned, the lowering

---

[178]Illustrations abound; four will suffice. (1) In the year 2000, Ohio State University, one of the largest and best of our state institutions of higher learning, made no bones about its target, formulated by its president and its provost: "[T]he short term goal . . . [of Ohio State University] is to create a faculty, student and staff profile that reflects the demographic profile of the state." (2) From the California Master Plan for Higher Education, adopted in 1988 by that state's legislature: "Each segment of California public education shall strive to approximate by the year 2000 the general ethnic, gender, economic, and regional composition of high school graduates, both in first year classes, and subsequent college and university graduating classes." (3) In the enforcement of Title IX (which prohibits sex discrimination in college athletics), proportionality has for some years been the explicit test applied by the federal Office of Civil Rights in determining institutional compliance: if a student body is 60 percent women and 40

of standards follows inexorably. College administrators aver repeatedly that their standards are never lowered, but no one with open eyes will believe them. The evidence, presented at some length in what follows, is irrefutable.[179]

Official accounts of admissions practices are pervaded by equivocation, and sometimes by dishonesty. Such chicanery was long difficult to document because the mechanics of preferential programs had been so carefully concealed.[180] But inquiries under the Freedom of Information Act, followed by the process of discovery in civil litigation, have brought many blatantly discriminatory practices to light. The fear that disclosure would trigger embarrassing litigation was well founded. So long as preferential policies were hidden, university officials could describe them in misleading language, assuring the public that double standards were not being applied *while applying them*. With the veil of secrecy largely down, we learn how

---

percent men, that school's sports teams must consist of 60 percent women and 40 percent men. It doesn't matter if the percentage of men who want to play sports is far greater than the percentage of women; it doesn't matter if every woman who wants to play sports is actually playing on a school team. All that matters is whether the *proportions* of men and women on sports teams mirror their proportions in the student body as a whole. Only gender proportionality is safe harbor. See "The Inequity of Gender Equity," *Chronicle of Higher Education*, 3 May 2002. (4) An explicit commitment to "effect in each entering class the black representation in the general populace" (i.e. 12–13 percent) was made in 1968 by Brown University, which recommitted itself to similar measures in 1975, and did so again in 1985. See K. Ishihara, "Regressing to Our Racist Roots" *Brown Daily Herald*, 6 December 2001.

[179]A typical device is entry requirements that differ for the races. At the University of Michigan, a very desirable six-year program (called "Inteflex") that combined undergraduate and medical studies had very high entry standards for white applicants, but different and markedly lower standards for black or Hispanic applicants; it was the only way that the targeted number of minorities could be enrolled.

[180]Guidelines identifying the preferences to be given, distributed to admissions counselors at the University of Michigan, are marked—still, in 2002—in bold print: **"Confidential: For Internal Use Only."**

great institutions have abased themselves in the name of "affirmative action."[181]

Before turning to the defenses given for such conduct, I note that discriminatory admissions practices are very widespread. In *The Shape of the River*, a 1998 book frequently cited by those defending "race-sensitive" admission policies, the authors, William Bowen and Derek Bok, acknowledge studies estimating "a marked degree of racial preference" in 20 percent of all four-year institutions, and a lesser degree of preference in another 20 percent of them. But Bowen and Bok also assert that "only about 20 to 30 percent" of colleges and universities are at all selective—so we may reasonably conclude that the only schools that don't discriminate on the basis of race are the ones that admit all applicants.

The pervasiveness and severity of racial and ethnic discrimination was probably understated in *The Shape of the River*. Careful studies of the admissions policies of 57 different schools in eight states (California, Colorado, Maryland, Michigan, Minnesota, North Carolina, Virginia, and Washington); six medical schools (in Georgia, Maryland, Michigan, Oklahoma, New York, and Washington); and three law schools (all in Virginia) have been conducted by the Center for Equal Opportunity, a nonprofit research and public-advocacy institution. The data were supplied by the schools themselves, pursuant to freedom-of-information laws, and were subjected to regression analyses by professional statisticians; they demonstrate

---

[181]For a full account of the details at the University of Texas, the University of Michigan, and some other institutions, see Carl Cohen, "Race, Lies, and *Hopwood*," *Commentary* 102, no. 2 (August 1996). The details of preferences given by private institutions such as Stanford University and Williams College, not governed by the Freedom of Information Act, remain for the most part undisclosed. One great public institution, the University of Wisconsin, battled to avoid disclosure of its admissions patterns from the time it was confronted with a Freedom of Information Act request submitted by the Center for Equal Opportunity (CEO) in 1998—but UW lost that battle in July 2002 in the Supreme Court of Wisconsin, which agreed with the CEO that student privacy could be protected by removing all names, while allowing an examination of admission procedures and results by ethnic group. The University of Michigan, recognizing the legitimacy of such Freedom of Information Act requests in 1995 and responding to them, was legally obliged to disclose records that, by exhibiting very substantial race preferences, trig-

conclusively that every state system studied manifests significant race discrimination.[182]

How do the colleges respond to such revelations? The first line of defense by administrators is purely semantic. In their institutions, we are told, *un*qualified students are never admitted. True by definition. Since admissions officers themselves determine who is "qualified," all whom they admit are qualified in the sense that to be admitted by them is to be qualified. But if "qualified" means exhibiting intellectual attainments and capacities that have traditionally served as the prerequisites for admission to scholarly institutions, the claim is false. The intellectual level of some who are admitted preferentially in order to reach racial goals is scandalous. At leading law schools and medical schools, it is common for the average of the test scores and the grade point averages of *admitted* minority applicants to be below the average of Asian and white applicants who were *rejected*.[183]

The second line of defense is a statistical deceit. The grade point average (GPAs) of all admitted students together, including those given preference, has gone up; these figures are exhibited to show

---

gered the litigation—*Grutter v. Bollinger* and *Gratz v. Bollinger*—before the Supreme Court of the United States in 2003.

[182]These studies are readily available on the website of the Center for Equal Opportunity: www.ceousa.org.

Several publications of the center, authored by its statisticians, Robert Lerner and Althea K. Nagai, address portions of that data: All the undergraduate schools (except for those in Maryland) are discussed in *Pervasive Preferences* (2001). All the medical schools (excepting that of Maryland) are discussed in *Preferences in Medical Education* (2001). Maryland undergraduate admissions are discussed in *Preferences in Maryland Higher Education* (2000); Maryland's state medical school is discussed in *Racial and Ethnic Preferences and Consequences at the University of Maryland School of Medicine* (2001). The law schools are discussed in *Racial and Ethnic Preferences at the Three Virginia Public Law Schools* (2002). Highlights of many of these studies appear in an article by Lerner and Nagai: "Reverse Discrimination by the Numbers," *Academic Questions*, vol. 13, no. 3 (summer, 2000).

[183]The decision of the federal appellate court in a case involving the University of Texas law school reports that contrast at UT: "These [racially] disparate standards greatly affected a candidate's chance of admission. For example: by March of 1992, because the presumptive *denial* score for whites was a TI

that preferences do not lower standards. No such thing is shown. First, schools have engaged in a steady inflation of all grades, so overall averages rise with this inflation. Second, *averages* reveal nothing about the range or clustering of the numbers averaged; by reporting only the averages of *all* those admitted, schools obscure the intellectual profiles of the *groups* admitted; different admission standards applied to ethnic subsets are hidden. In fact, the grade point averages and test scores required of those preferentially admitted are markedly lower than those required of standard applicants.[184] But in calculating the averages, the splendid records of those not preferred (for whom intellectual selectivity has been increased) outweigh the dismal records of those who are preferred. Race preferences are buried within the larger averages. Double standards by race are common in American universities.

The third line of defense is a verbal deceit: the process of admission depends upon many more factors than test scores and grades, and therefore differing numerical records do not report all that is known about admitted students; what may appear to be ethnic preference (we are told) is the result of weighing, for minority students with poor records, nonquantitative factors pertaining to character and experience.

[Texas Index—a combination of other scores] of 192 or lower, and the presumptive *admit* TI for minorities was 189 or higher, a minority candidate with TI of 189 or above almost certainly would be *admitted*, even though his score was considerably below the level at which a white candidate almost certainly would be *rejected*. Out of the pool of resident applicants who fell within this range (189–192 inclusive), 100 percent of blacks and 90 percent of Mexican Americans, but only 6 percent of whites, were offered admission." [*Hopwood v. University of Texas:* emphases in the original.] That contrast is even more marked in professional schools that are more selective.

[184]At the law school of the University of Virginia, for example, where the relative odds of admission of a black over a white applicant were overwhelming, the gap between the median GPA of black and white students was, in 1998 and 1999, one-third of a point on a four-point scale; the black-white gaps in Law School Admission Test (LSAT) scores at that law school were 10 points and 8 points those two years—equivalent to approximately 100 points on the undergraduate SATs. At the University of Michigan, applicants for undergraduate admission with identical academic credentials—applicants with the very same scores and same GPAs—have long been admitted or rejected depending only upon their race, with blacks being admitted and whites rejected.

Personal factors do enter every admission process, of course. But in institutions receiving many thousands of applications each year, the categorization of applicants by quantitative measurement of past performance remains central and indispensable. Such quantitatively measured performance, however, is *weighed differently for applicants of different skin colors.* Different cut-off scores are applied to different ethnic groups. Marks of good character—leadership, determination, past community service—are alleged to provide the rationale for the admission of minority applicants whose academic records are seriously deficient, but such virtues of character, perhaps appropriately considered by admissions officers, are in fact no more common or more notable among the racial groups preferred than they are among Asians and whites. Yet fine character will be of little help to a white male applicant whose scores are low. The real objective lying behind much current talk about character and nonquantifiable merit is increasing minority enrollment; to that end, applicants of certain ethnicities are given deliberate favor by resorting to "individualizing" factors that are weighed for them as they are not weighed for others.[185]

---

[185]At Bucknell University, the dean of admissions, Mark Davies, reports that average SAT scores there are 1280, but that "appealing minority candidates are not held to that standard or even close to it." See "Fine-Tuning Applicants," *New York Times*, 6 May 2002. "Tests just don't do it for them," says Mr. Davies. "Tests don't measure motivation." High motivation on the part of white students with low SATs is not likely to render them similarly "appealing."

At Colgate University, a black professor of English writes, "[S]eparate tracks of expectation, performance, and success for black students have been the most disheartening aspect of my experience here. . . . [E]very professor I know has observed it. . . . The double standard leaves its mark on black students long after graduation." A white professor of political science at Colgate pointed out that "minority students were often seduced into unchallenging courses where liberal professors, who were 'sensitive' to their needs, gave them inflated grades." See Phillip Richards, "Prestigious Colleges Ignore the Inadequate Intellectual Achievement of Black Students," *The Chronicle of Higher Education*, 13 September 2002.

At Temple University, a professor of mathematics (who asks to remain anonymous) remarks: "I am teaching kids who should not be in college, but I can't fail them." *Chronicle of Higher Education*, 30 January 2002.

The fourth line of defense for the lowering of intellectual standards is the claim that judgments of intellectual merit and potential cannot be made objectively in any case. After all, test scores and grades do not guarantee student success or failure in college. This is surely true. Anecdotes of ill-prepared ghetto students who prove brilliantly successful are offered in evidence, and there are such cases, of course. But to infer from anecdotes of failure or of success that there can be no objectivity in intellectual judgment is a silly mistake.

Reliable judgments of achievement and promise have long been made, and are now commonly made. No predictive system is perfectly reliable, of course; some applicants overcome dreadful beginnings, others fail to realize great promise. But *on the whole* we can quite accurately determine, among those who apply for admission to universities and professional schools, who are most likely to succeed, and who most likely to fail. The claim that we cannot do this is simply false.

Good colleges and professional schools *must* appraise the intellectual potential of their applicants. The tone and atmosphere of an institution depend largely upon the quality of the students admitted; the plainest mark of the intellectual quality of a college is the intellectual profile of its students. Fine schools therefore depend upon their predictive judgments about the intellectual potential of applicants; their success helps to account for the high ratings of premier institutions. First-rate institutions enroll students who, at the time of their application, are known to exhibit enormous potential; colleges and community colleges of the second and third tier are obliged to enroll applicants who may be fairly described as less distinguished. Some in that latter category will prove themselves outstanding in the end, true enough—but that does not begin to show that objective judgments of merit cannot be made.

Admission systems vary greatly, but there are three measures almost universally relied upon by universities in some degree: 1) the applicant's grade point average in previous schooling, with performance in more difficult substantive materials given greater weight; 2) the applicant's rank in class in the secondary school (or in the undergraduate college, for professional school applications), where the standards of that previous school are also known and taken into account; and 3) the applicant's performance on a standardized test, such as the SAT, ACT, LSAT, or MCAT (Medical College Admission Test). Differing weights will be given to these intellectual factors, but one or more of them will play a central role in the admissions systems of all respectable colleges.[186]

Although imperfect, these instruments have been much refined over the years; their reliability and validity have been repeatedly tested and are well established. Using them (but not them alone), admissions committees can identify the strongest applicants for admission. Such measuring instruments serve the scholarly purposes of a university well. To the extent that they are subordinated to wholly non-intellectual considerations—race, personal connections, money—the integrity of the admission process is undermined. Every dilution of intellectual measure drives the enrolled student population, statistically, toward mediocrity. This applies not only to dilution by race: the "dumb jock" is not a myth but a reality; so much preference has been given for athletic talent that a varsity athlete with a B average is now an intellectual star. But the irrelevant consideration that has most corrupted admissions in recent years is ethnicity.

The percentage of minority students who perform with excellence on those objective intellectual measures is substantially lower than the percentage of minority students in the population at large.[187] This, I repeat, is certainly *not* because race is a mark of inferiority. It is a statistical reality that must be confronted. To mask that reality, the advocates of preference use two devices; the first is to attack the reliability of standard examinations, and the second is to report intellectual performance in a deliberately misleading way.

---

[186]The replacement of the SAT I (an examination testing general aptitudes) with the SAT II (an examination testing achievements in specific subject matters) has recently been much discussed. But there are few who would abandon standardized examinations entirely. If they were abandoned, of course, much less manipulation would be needed to reach racial target numbers. In reality, SAT and other test scores have generally been a factor in admission much less significant than grade point averages in previous schooling.

[187]Studies of scores of universities, by the Center for Equal Opportunity (see footnote 182), reveal that black-white gaps in SAT verbal and math scores of 100 points or more are common, with corresponding disparities in graduation rates among different racial groups.

1) Consistently poorer performance by Hispanic and black students on standardized aptitude exams like the SAT I, it is claimed, is merely a consequence of the prejudice built into the tests themselves. Racially disparate outcomes are said to be the product of the "cultural bias" with which those exams are constructed.

But the central premise of this complaint is false; it has been repeatedly shown to be false by exhaustive scientific inquiry. Distortion resulting from cultural bias became a concern of psychologists and testing services years ago, and it has been scrupulously eliminated from the standardized exams now used for college admissions. Every single question on the standardized exams now widely given is subjected to a rigorous "fairness review."[188] The tired claim that the differing levels of performance by ethnic groups are explained by hidden racism is simply without warrant.

The predictive power of aptitude tests is widely misunderstood. At the extremes, the predictive power of the SATs is *very* great, as no one can deny: at Oberlin or Michigan, a student scoring 800 on the combined SATs is *far* likelier to flunk out than is a competitor scoring 1500. Good schools therefore rely on these tests to filter out students quite unlikely to succeed. But among those accepted whose scores are, say, in the range of 1100 to 1300, the predictive power of the score differences is moderate, because for such students other variables—maturity, self-discipline, home environment, etc.—may override small score differentials. Advocates of preference, hoping to eliminate the tests, call attention to the variability of success within the narrower range of scores of those accepted—betraying their failure to grasp their principal, filtering function. Abandoning such tests completely would result in a very different set of acceptances.

Independent scholars of fair testing now agree that carefully constructed and well-validated scholastic aptitude tests are among the very best instruments for making reliable judgments of intellectual promise. At the RAND Corporation in Santa Monica, a senior research scientist has given admission criteria for law schools the most scrupulous review; he has shown that admissions criteria that include using standardized tests actually *favor* minority candidates. He concludes:

[188]See: "For SAT Writers, Questions Can Matter as Much as Answers," *New York Times*, 10 June 2002.

Thus although blacks earn lower UGPAs [undergraduate grade point averages] and LSAT scores than their classmates, these scores still yield an inflated estimate of their chances of earning good grades in law school. The combination of UGPA and LSAT provides a more accurate (less biased) prediction, but it still favors black candidates. There is a similar pattern for Hispanic and Asian students, but with considerably less over-prediction. In short, if there is any bias in the LSAT, it is in the direction of favoring the minority applicants by over-predicting their law school grades.[189]

Similarly, it has been found in literally *hundreds* of validity studies that, for the prediction of success in undergraduate study, the combination of SAT and high school grades is significantly more accurate than are high school grades alone.[190] But even the SAT has been repeatedly shown to *favor* blacks by over predicting their performance in college.[191] It is now beyond doubt that in the measurement of intellectual promise of college applicants and professional school applicants, disparities in performance by race[192] cannot be evaded by blaming those disparate results on the measures themselves.

2) The GPAs of students in their previous schooling also exhibit marked racial disparities. These averages report the outcome of years

[189]Stephen P. Klein, "Law School Admissions, LSATs, and the Bar," *Academic Questions* 15, no. 1 (winter 2001–02).

[190]Wayne J. Camara and Gary Echternacht, "The SAT I and High School Grades: Utility in Predicting Success in College," *Research Notes*, Office of Research and Development, College Board, Report No. 2000-10.

[191]Brent Bridgman, Laura McCamley-Jenkins, and Nancy Ervin, "Predictions of Freshman Grade-Point Average from the Revised and Recentered SAT I: Reasoning Test," College Board Research Report No. 2000-1. See also Frederick E. Vars and William G. Bowen, "Scholastic Aptitude Test Scores, Race, and Academic Performance in Selective Colleges and Universities," in *The Black-White Test Score Gap*, C. Jencks and M. Phillips, eds. (Washington, D.C.: The Brookings Institution, 1998).

[192]Disparities are great. Minority students generally earn significantly lower scores than their white classmates on the SAT, and much lower scores on the LSAT. See S. Klein and R. Bolus, "The Size and Source of Differences in Bar Exam Passing Rates among Racial and Ethnic Groups," *The Bar Examiner* no. 4 (1997). See also: L. Wightman, *LSAC National Longitudinal Bar Passage Study* (Newton, PA.: Law School Admission Council, 1998).

of study, and at most colleges they are much more heavily weighed than are standardized tests.[193] To evade these disparities, a technique called "race norming" has been commonly employed. Its principle is simple. If applicants are grouped by race, the standing of any member of a given group can be reported in relation to other members of that group only. We may learn, for example, that the performance of a given minority applicant is at the eighty-first percentile (top fifth) of her group, and from this infer that she is a desirable candidate for admission. But if the scores had been race-normed, that percentile number, although accurate, may indicate that she is within the top fifth of only *minority* applicants, while among *all* applicants she may rank in the bottom fifth. By reporting the records of minority applicants only as they rank among the records of other minority applicants, performance can be made to appear far better than it really is.

The resort to race-norming illuminates the fundamental problem of ethnic proportionality as the criterion of success. There simply is no way to achieve racially proportional admissions if all candidates are evaluated on the same objective standards. Manipulating the reports of performance is a desperate alternative when efforts to discredit the objective evaluations themselves have failed. One way or another, educational institutions determined to give race preference (in the name of "affirmative action") must lower their standards. The demand for proportionality permits no escape.

Another pattern of evasion attacks the standards not by imputing racial bias to the tests or by race-norming, but by insisting that *all* numerical measures whatever are unsatisfactory because a wise admission process must give thoroughly *individualized* attention to the entire record of each applicant. But individualization, a very worthy objective difficult to realize in large institutions, can be fair, as noted earlier, only if undertaken in a race-neutral way. If applicants with poor academic records are to be given special consideration because

---

[193]This is probably due to the belief that high school grades are better predictors of success, or perhaps the conviction that the applicants themselves think that they are. It turns out, in fact, that as predictors of success, high school grades have roughly the same value as the SAT. See Camara and Echternacht 2000.

their previous schools have been bad, or because they have overcome great adversity, or because they manifest unusual enthusiasm,
or for any other reasons of that subjective kind, considerations of
the very same kind must be weighed for all applicants without regard to their color. The current enthusiasm for the "individualization" of admissions in select universities may be accounted for in
part by the fact that such "individualization" often serves, in reality,
as a way of hiding race preferences given under the table.[194]

The admission of some preferred students on a lower standard
(apart from its adverse impact on the minority as a whole, and upon
the majority students displaced) directly damages the university itself. The intellectual fabric of a college is mainly supported by fine
students. The quality of learning in classrooms and laboratories, of
debates in common rooms and seminars, of discussions in residence
halls, of extracurricular activities as well as curricular performance—
all depend directly or indirectly upon the intellectual capacities and
enthusiasms of talented students. Faculty scholars are drawn to institutions that enroll the best students. Keen and demanding students bring out the best in their instructors and in their classmates;
they set the critical tone of intellectual seriousness; they *make* the
university.

When the intellectual quality of entering students is deliberately
lowered, therefore, the adverse impact on the institution is serious;
when that lowering is sharp and obvious, the impact can prove

---

[194]The University of California changed its admissions system in 2001 to one
in which a "comprehensive" examination of all features of a student's background would be applied to all applicants, rather than (as formerly) to only
some of them. Softening the grip of objective standards permits a larger number of Latino and black admissions in a state whose constitution now prohibits race preference. The university system's vice chancellor for legal affairs,
Joseph Mandel, explained candidly that the new UC policy is "the University's way around proposition 209." Yes. And when in the fall of 2002 "comprehensive review" was for the first time universally applied, minority
admissions did of course go up: 19.1 percent of those offered admission to
the University of California in the fall of 2002 were minorities, compared
with 18.8 percent in 1997, the last year race preferences were given. (See
"Admission Up for Minorities in California," *New York Times*, 7 April 2002.)
Everyone in the University of California system well understands what is going on.

catastrophic. Proof of this came vividly in the recent history of the City University of New York, long known as CCNY, City College. One of the premier centers of learning in the United States for generations, CCNY generally attracted students who were the children of recent immigrants, often poor and disadvantaged. But the academic standards at CCNY were *very* high, and its graduates became leaders in every intellectual arena. It was called "the poor man's Harvard"—but in intellect it surpassed Harvard, because at CCNY intellectual distinction was never diluted by money or by family or by anything else. If you couldn't cut it, you didn't stay.

Political pressures that could not (or would not) be resisted resulted in the introduction of a system of "open admissions" at the (renamed) City University of New York during the 1970s. Standards for admission were drastically reduced, and with sickening speed that great institution sank from high distinction to low mediocrity. Some graduates of the new CUNY were nearly illiterate. Touching success stories there were also, but they only highlighted the generally depressed level of intellectual activity. Remedial teaching became a central function there, because the ability to read and write (at least at the high school level!) is indispensable for college work. But the performance of many admitted students was abysmal; although they had fine character and great enthusiasm, their very poor preparation commonly obviated their chances for college success. The steep downward path of the student body was paralleled by that of the morale of the faculty, causing the early departure of many of the best among them. City College, the traditional home of brilliant students and distinguished scholars, had transformed itself by lowering its admissions standards. Its senior colleges came to be called "schools of last resort." High school guidance counselors now described it as "the absolute dregs."[195]

That transformation of CCNY was an extreme and singular case, but the process that led to its degeneration is well understood; that very same process, different in tempo but not in essence, is currently underway in many great centers of learning. When intellectual standards are systematically lowered—the inevitable

---

[195]See "To Raise Its Image, CUNY Pays for Top Students," *New York Times*, 11 May 2002.

consequence of admission based on nonintellectual factors—a university goes down. Energetic teaching, generous funding, and thoughtful planning, all marshaled with earnest good will, together cannot reverse the slide.

Remedial instruction like that forced at CUNY is already common in many universities; students lured to come by preference and who cannot swim must not be left to sink. Serious scholars find remedial teaching distasteful, but the alternative—the large-scale failure of the preferentially admitted—is politically intolerable. Courses designed to teach ill-educated underclassmen how to write a simple essay have become central in the program of English departments. Students who ought never to have been admitted in the first place must be taught how to study, how to draw inferences, how to take notes, how to write a coherent paragraph. Now common are "mentoring programs," in which students deficient in the most basic skills are assigned to individual faculty members for guidance and remediation. Special academic support and counseling programs, especially to improve writing, are ubiquitous, their names euphemisms: "Upward Bound," or "the Bridging Program," or "the Office of Academic Enrichment." In larger institutions, there are separate minority counseling offices with "peer counselors" to tutor, badger, pull, or push marginal students through. In medical schools, where race preference is common, designated remedial staffs give elementary instruction in biology and chemistry to "affirmative action admits." Much of what was once required for admission to medical school is required no longer, for if it were, the targeted number of ethnic minorities could not be approached.

None of this comes cheap. During the decade from 1975 to 1985, the administrative staffs of American universities increased by 60 percent—but the number of students enrolled actually declined by about 10 percent. Most of those new administrators added little or nothing to the normal teaching and research functions of the university; many were hired mainly to support students who ought never to have been admitted, and then to recruit more of them. Academic and guidance counseling offices, financial aid and scholarship offices, tutoring centers, performance monitoring agencies—all with their complement of managers and assistant managers—have grown steadily, consuming ever larger chunks of college resources.

The numbers of students of different colors and ethnicities must be counted and reported; there must be separate counselors for each, and often separate physical facilities for each as well. Between ethnic clusters—blacks and Hispanics, minority and majority—tensions arise that are addressed with workshops in "diversity management" conducted by "experts" who helped to create the problems they are hired to solve. The compilation of data can only be justified by its subsequent analysis and appraisal, so detailed reports must be written. The writers of those reports thrive on the recruitment of minorities, so the reports themselves generally call for an intensification of minority recruitment efforts and an enlargement of support for minority students—and, of course, more funding to achieve that. Politically correct conclusions, rarely contested, rise from one level of the bureaucracy to the next for discussion and implementation. Racial goals are steadily revised upward, always remaining out of reach. To pursue them, new "affirmative action plans" must be concocted, which in turn must be reviewed and approved, and then implemented (with uncertain success) through affirmative action subsections of the admissions and employment offices. This implementation in various units and subunits will call for repeated reevaluation, and every new assessment will yield a fresh report likely to call for additional "diversity initiatives." 'Task forces' are established to overcome the "gap"—the disparity in the performance of racial groups. "Achievements" are reported in self-congratulatory booklets and newsletters, slickly prepared and distributed at considerable expense to alumni and the press. These almost invariably conclude by lamenting the enormous distance that must yet be traversed to achieve racial balance, and with a reminder that progress demands much greater funding. The "affirmative action" industry thus feeds upon itself, creating new race-oriented programs, from which arise new demands, politically difficult to resist, to be managed and monitored by yet more staff, who justify their employment by devising more new programs, and so on without respite. The morass of bureaucracy devised to advance and protect preferential admissions has imposed very great costs upon our universities, costs that cannot be calculated in money alone.

Perhaps the most distinguished contemporary critic of American education, Chester Finn, has implored the president of Harvard to respond vigorously to the family of afflictions now widespread among the best of American universities: "the sundering of the campus into self-absorbed enclaves, identifiable by race, ethnicity, gender or sexual preference, each devoted to studying (only) its own 'culture' and adamant that the university resources—from budgets to student places to faculty berths to dining hall provender—be divvied up according to intricate calculations of proportional shares, unburdened by any uniform standards, concern for the common good, or shared definition of truth."[196]

All this (we were told) was to be temporary. Preferences would be needed only to overcome historical inequities; diversity once achieved would be self-sustaining. Preferentially admitted students would quickly "come up to speed"—or, old-fashioned standards having been put to rest, their "speed" will no longer be measured. This supposed transience of preference has been a delusion. The objective of ethnic proportionality on a single standard is in fact not attainable for the foreseeable future, and race preference will be employed, covertly if not overtly, so long as proportionality is the measure of success. Once having taken root, preference flourishes and does not wither.[197]

Efforts within the university to reduce preference and thin the affirmative action bureaucracy are likely to be condemned as evidence of "institutional racism."[198] Bloated university offices are overseen by state and federal regulatory agencies largely staffed by members of the very groups preferred. "Affirmative action personnel" move from

---

[196]"An Open Letter to Lawrence H. Summers," *Policy Review* 113 (June 2002).

[197]Nevertheless, the claim that it is all no more than temporary is repeated endlessly. An editorial in *Detroit News* on 10 December 2001 concludes by saying that after affirmative action "help[s] minorities reach the point where they are allowed to compete on their own merit and rise as high as their individual abilities will take them, . . . affirmative action can fade away." Fat chance!

[198]So much is the charge of racism feared that at the highest levels of university administration, even some who privately find race preference repugnant will support it publicly. One member of the publicly elected regents of the University of Michigan (as the *Ann Arbor News* reported on 15 March 2002) admitted in a letter to a colleague that although he is personally against preferential policies, he had, as regent, voted for them.

one level of the bureaucracy to another, from one institution to another, creating what can only be called "diversity fiefdoms." At Harvard medical school, there is the "Office for Diversity and Community Partnership"; at the University of California, Berkeley, there is a "Diversity Committee" and a "diversity officer"; at George Mason University, there is an "Office for Diversity Programs and Services" and a "Diversity Advisory Board"; at Brown (where a "Diversity Institute" and an "Affirmative Action Office" now exist), a new senior post is soon to be filled: "director of diversity." The list is endless.

Zealous students, some indirectly justifying their own preferential admission, learn the art of cowing college administrators, who knuckle to the demands of demonstrators as the price of a peaceful campus. The next set of student "demands" is likely to include the creation of a new ethnic studies unit, probably requiring more minority faculty, or perhaps the appointment of a new "affirmative action vice-provost," with additional staff, and so on.[199] Resisting such demands will produce tension and may even trigger disorder but giving in to them is easy because doing so meets no organized opposition and the costs can usually be hidden.

The longevity of the preferential enterprise is assured by the steady escalation of racial demands, since the higher the numerical targets become the more difficult it is to reach them, and the more essential it becomes to lower standards for admission and appointment—which, in turn, brings continuing need for monitoring to insure compliance and greater need for remedial support. Admissions officers, department heads, deans, even presidents make public apology

---

[199]Harvard is now being called upon by the Foundation for Intercultural and Race Relations to establish a new Center for the Study of Race and Ethnicity, and to fund four new professorial chairs in Latino studies, Native American studies, comparative ethnic studies, and the like. *Boston Globe*, 11 October 2002.

Demands of this sort can have an aesthetic dimension as well: Said an administrator at Harvard, "We want to make Harvard buildings literally more multicultural by having artwork portraying minorities by minorities." *Daily Crimson*, 29 April 2002. In Ann Arbor, where music is queen, the University of Michigan Business and Finance Diversity Choir sings the praises of diversity in a choral program entitled "Celebrating Diversity."

for past failures to meet "affirmative action goals," following those apologies with earnest promises of renewed efforts to "do better." Whatever is necessary to advance toward racial proportionality, first in enrollment and eventually in graduation, must be done.[200]

Blatant preference by race, at times the product of this machinery and at times its cause, largely escapes public notice. Devices giving preference are normally disguised; policies are either unwritten or well hidden. In private institutions, where accountability to the public is much reduced (although federal financial assistance is almost invariably received), the process remains largely secret still.

Now and then, a cat gets out of the bag. Here follow three cases— but in *hundreds* of American colleges and universities, race preference is as pervasive, if better hidden.

1) At the law school of Georgetown University, in Washington, D.C., marked race preferences were discovered by an editor of the school's *Law Weekly*, Timothy Maguire, who had been working in the admissions office. When the details were published in the *Weekly*, Maguire was vilified by the dean and efforts were made to expel him. Administrators ordered the confiscation of all copies of the issue in which the preferences were disclosed. The dean announced that the consideration of race was no part of the law school admission policy. But the facts were these: Of all those nationally who took the LSAT that year (1990/91), Georgetown students were, on average, in the nintieth percentile—but the average LSAT score of all Georgetown's black students was at the seventy-fifth percentile, and in 1989 at the sixty-ninth percentile. To be *considered* for admission at Georgetown, white applicants needed to be in the top 15 percent of all those taking the LSAT that year, but black applicants were told they had "a strong chance of acceptance" if they were in the top 40 percent. The grade point average of white students enrolled was 3.7 (just below A); the grade point average of black students enrolled was 3.2 (just above B).[201]

---

[200]This is not an exaggerated account. No devices are foresworn; the acronym for the student corps that relentlessly agitates in support of race preference is BAMN: By Any Means Necessary.

[201]A full account of the scandal at Georgetown law school is to be found in an essay by Timothy Maguire, "My Bout with Affirmative Action," *Commentary* 93, no. 4 (April 1992).

The dean refused to discuss these uses of race because (on her own account) doing so might cause people to judge individual members of the benefited groups inappropriately. And then came the standard academic responses: a) all students at Georgetown "are qualified to meet the standards to graduate," and b) grade point averages at the school had risen since affirmative action had been introduced. Our law school, said the dean, has been sorely embarrassed by this "very painful event." The pain, it appears, lay not in the reality of the preferences but in their disclosure.

2) Race preferences at the University of Michigan law school, in Ann Arbor, were found a few years later to be much more pronounced. Details were revealed in a federal court trial at which the university was obliged to defend itself against the suit of a 43-year-old white woman with a superb record who claimed that the racial skewing of the admission system under which she had been rejected violated the law and the Constitution.[202]

The following facts (hundreds more like them were presented at trial) will give the reader a sense of what was going on: At the Michigan law school many thousands of applicants compete for about 380 places. In 1995, applicants with good (B+) undergraduate records and very good LSAT scores (156–163) had less than a 3 percent chance of admission (7 of 238)—if they were "Caucasian Americans." But for "African American" applicants to the Michigan law school with those identical grades and scores, the admission rate was 17 out of 17—100 percent.[203]

To measure the extent of racial preference, the "odds ratios" for admission are commonly calculated. An odds ratio of 1 is equivalent to a correlation coefficient of 0—no relationship between the two variables is found. Odds ratios (of one group to another) greater than 1 indicate the greater likelihood of the one group's being

---

[202]This case, *Grutter v. Bollinger*, is before the Supreme Court of the United States at the present writing; its outcome there may bring resolution to many of the issues confronted in this book.

[203]Figures come from admissions grids prepared by the University of Michigan Law School Admissions Office, for "Caucasian Americans" and for "African Americans" for the year 1995, delivered in response to a Freedom of Information Act request submitted in the autumn of 1995. I was the author of that request.

admitted.[204] To put the matter in perspective, in medical investigations the goal is to find a drug that may double or triple the odds of cure—an odds ratio of 2 or 3 to 1 is thus highly prized. Any odds ratio for a medical treatment greater than 100 to 1 would be hailed as nothing short of a scientific miracle. In this light, consider the odds for admission to the law school of the University of Michigan: Over the six years between 1995 and 2000, the odds ratio for the admission of African American applicants compared to that of "Caucasian American" applicants was—reader, hold your hat—*over 234 to 1!* For the year 2000 by itself, the odds ratio was *over 443 to 1!* This means that whatever the chances for admission a white applicant with a given set of credentials had, a black applicant with the identical credentials had chances of admission *443 times as great.*[205] But even the Michigan law school is outdone by the law school of the University of Virginia, where, in 1998, the odds in favor of black applicants were an astounding *650 to 1*, and in 1999, *730 to 1.*

Why do selective law schools—Georgetown, Michigan, Virginia, and their peers—give such admission preference by race? Because (as noted earlier) they cannot meet their minority enrollment targets in any other way. The reality of percentage targets for minorities is never admitted, but the ethnic makeup of first-year classes at several leading law schools leaves little doubt about them. At Harvard and at the University of Pennsylvania, 11 percent of the first-year students (in 2002) are African American; at Duke it is 9 percent; and at Georgetown 12 percent. That same range is approximated at law schools across the country; at Michigan, the range in recent years has generally been 10 to 12 percent.

Suppose, estimating conservatively, that the first-year classes of 50 fine law schools each contain 50 or more black students. From where might they have been recruited? The year of the Georgetown exposure, all applicants admitted there were, on average, in the

---

[204]For a more detailed account of this kind of measurement, see David W. Hosmer and Stanley Lemeshow, *Applied Logistic Regression* (New York: John Wiley and Sons, 1989).

[205]These figures are carefully documented in the findings of fact by Judge Bernard Friedman, of the federal district court of the Eastern District of Michigan, 137 F. Supp. 2nd 821, (2001), at pp. 836–843.

ninetieth percentile of all those taking the LSAT; at the Harvard, Duke, and Pennsylvania law schools, the average percentile would have been higher. But the number of black graduating seniors around the country who scored at that percentile or above on the LSAT, and may therefore have been (using that established standard) eligible for those law schools, was miniscule. At Howard University and Morehouse College, historically black undergraduate institutions, of all those taking the LSAT that year, more than half were in the *bottom* 10 percent of all takers nationwide. At Hampton University, 61 percent; at Jackson State College, 74 percent; and at Grambling University, 84 percent of those taking the LSAT had scores at the tenth percentile or lower. In the late 1980s, the director of admissions of the University of California law school at Berkeley observed with distress that "only five blacks who took the LSAT had scores and GPAs that equaled [Berkeley's] average." The pool of black applicants surely does contain some very fine young scholars—but it plainly does not contain a sufficient number of excellent applicants to provide the select law schools with the number of black students they are determined to enroll.

Those racial objectives are nevertheless usually met—by admitting minority students whose records are very much poorer than those of applicants admitted without regard to race. The arithmetic leaves no doubt; the number of black applicants who could qualify for admission to the top-tier law schools on the standards regularly applied to white applicants does not *approach* the number needed to reach the minority enrollment percentages those schools report. Law schools, determined to achieve proportionality by race, sacrifice their standards to enroll minority students. What is true of law schools is true of most other professional schools as well.

3) Among applicants to undergraduate colleges, the number of outstanding black candidates coming from the secondary schools is far greater, but the competition among select colleges seeking to enroll them is greater still. Demand again far exceeds supply.[206] Any

---

[206]The National Assessment of Academic Progress, last administered in 2001, found that only a minority of all twelfth graders (i.e., high school seniors who might apply for college admission) was "proficient" in history—that is, exhibited "solid academic performance" based on knowledge of important

black high school student with a good academic record and good SAT scores is likely to be bombarded with offers of four-year scholarships from several (or many) fine colleges, all tuition and expenses paid. Well-endowed universities can afford to *pay* for "diversity" with cash. But no money price can increase the supply. Where "affirmative action targets" cannot be achieved with standards intact, corrupted standards take the place of dollars.

At those same well-endowed universities, white applicants (who may be superbly qualified) compete desperately, and often unsuccessfully, for admission. Full scholarships for white students are a rarity. Many will drain their family's resources if they do gain admission. This contrast in the circumstances of white and black applicants is the fruit of the aggressive search for the few minority students who are well qualified on the normal standard.[207]

Long experience with race preference in the state of California is instructive. Today in California all preference by race is forbidden by Article 1, Section 31, of the state constitution.[208] Prior to the

---

events and trends in history. But of the black students examined, only 3 percent—3 *percent!*—were thus proficient. See "Students, Especially 12th Graders, Do Poorly on History Tests," *New York Times*, 10 May 2002.

[207]*New York Times* reported in detail the experience of typical students competing for college admission during the winter of 2002. One white student profiled, having outstanding credentials, including notable accomplishments in theater and superb SAT scores (1500 out of a possible 1600), was ultimately rejected in April 2002 by the Ivy League college he had hoped to attend. Another student, black, with good but not distinguished credentials, had by February 2002 received acceptances from Manhattan College (which offered extra scholarship money); Clarkson University (which offered him a $6,000 "incentive" scholarship); SUNY at Buffalo; Lafayette University; and Bucknell University, where he was offered a financial "package" ($28,500 from the school + $2,750 from a federal Pell grant + $2,625 from a federal Stafford loan + an on-campus job that would pay at least $1,500) totaling $35,375 for his freshman year.

[208]The California Civil Rights Initiative, widely known as Proposition 209, was adopted (becoming a part of the state constitution) by a substantial majority in a statewide referendum in 1996. It reads: "The state [California] shall not discriminate against, or grant preferential treatment to, any individual or group on the basis of race, sex, color, ethnicity, or national origin in the operation of public employment, public education, or public contracting."

adoption of that section in 1996, however, Californians had extensive familiarity with ethnic preferences; they knew well what they came at last to forbid. Since what California did during the 1980s and 1990s is now being nearly duplicated in other states, that history is worthy of brief reflection.[209]

The academic performance of minority high school graduates in California during that period had been distressingly poor; multiyear efforts to narrow the gap between minority and nonminority graduates had had little success. In 1994, a report of the California Department of Education put the matter bluntly: "[T]he mean academic scores of blacks are so low that fewer than 5% of black students have the grades necessary to enter the University of California system."[210] Nevertheless, they *did* enter the UC system in great numbers because the demand for "affirmative action" required it. But ethnic proportionality was overshot! By the mid-90s, blacks were overrepresented at UC Berkeley by 40 percent, Hispanics overrepresented by 10 percent, and whites *under*represented by 47 percent!

How was this possible, one asks, if there were so very few qualified minority applicants? Answer: by manipulating the criteria for "qualification." For Asians and whites admitted to Berkeley during 1987 and 1988, the average SAT score was 1270; the average SAT score for Hispanics was 1037, and for blacks it was 979. That very large numerical gap between the stronger and the weaker performers is roughly indicative of a four-year difference in academic preparation. As the number of whites admitted went down, the intellectual selectivity for those whites who were admitted went up—and the gap between the two racial groups grew wider. Academic standards for white and Asian applicants at Berkeley steadily rose (partly because of competition among them for a declining number of places),

[209]The admissions data appearing in the paragraphs that follow have been gathered from several authoritative sources: a) *Working Together for the Education of All Students* (Sacramento: California Department of Education, 1994); b) "Freshman Admissions at Berkeley: A Policy for the 90's and Beyond," The Academic Senate, University of California at Berkeley Division, 1991; c) Vincent Sarich, "The Institutionalization of Racism at the University of California," *Academic Questions* (winter 1991).

[210]*Working Together for the Education of All Students*, 1994.

and thus the *overall* SAT averages at UC were maintained. But the reality is that by the middle 1990s the entering classes at UC Berkeley comprised two quite distinct components, one component consisting of whites and Asians whose records were outstanding, the other consisting of Hispanics, African Americans, and Native Americans whose records were markedly inferior. Race preference at Berkeley "produced two student populations whose academic levels barely overlap."[211]

An internal document at the University of California from that period distinguished three groups of students: those admitted through "affirmative action"; those admitted by "special action" (discretionary devices for enrolling athletes and additional minority students); and those admitted normally, on the basis of their "academic index scores," which combine the intellectual factors constituting the standard entrance requirements. Of the thousands of students newly enrolled in 1987, for example, the number of black students admitted on the basis of academic index was *one*, and the number of Hispanics 27. But of the entire entering class of many thousands that year, 12 percent were black, 17 percent Hispanic. Did the University of California lower its standards for undergraduate admission in order to increase minority enrollment? There can be no doubt of it.

Of our 50 states only two, California and Washington, now forbid race preference by law.[212] But there are more than three thousand colleges and universities in our country, and very many of them have committed themselves to increasing the number of blacks and other minorities in quantities that necessitate giving preference by race. Competition for those minority applicants with records good enough to qualify for admission to a fine university without preference is ferocious, but, of course, most schools are doomed to lose out. High-performing minority students are quickly soaked up— *bought up* with scholarships and grants—by a tiny number of elite

---

[211]Sarich 1991.

[212]In California it is a constitutional prohibition, resulting from the adoption of Proposition 209, as noted above. In Washington the nearly identical prohibition is a statute appearing in the Revised Code of Washington (RCW 49.60.400) as a result of the passage of a statewide initiative (known as I-200) in 2000.

schools that are also very rich. What are the rest to do? In undergraduate recruitment as in law school recruitment, the arithmetic is inescapable:

Black high school seniors who registered for the College Admissions Testing Program numbered approximately 71,000 in 1983. Of these, 66 received verbal SAT scores over 699 out of a possible 800. Black seniors with math SAT scores over 699 numbered 205. The number of black students, nationwide, with verbal SAT scores of 600 or above—a level not high enough for white applicants to have a serious chance for admission to a fine university—was less than 1,000 (and 2,000 for the math SATs). These results (distributed evenly) would yield one or two moderately qualified black applicants for every three colleges in the country. And the racial gap since 1983 has become yet wider.[213] The shortage of qualified minority applicants is so severe that even the most distinguished universities cannot reach their goals unless standards are lowered substantially.[214]

Having gone to extraordinary lengths to find minority students and to support them financially, the universities simply cannot in good conscience allow them, once admitted, to flunk out. If they are good enough to enroll, the reasoning goes, they must be good enough

---

[213]In 1996, of all graduating seniors in California, 3.8 percent of the Latino graduates, and 2.8 percent of the African American graduates—but 30 percent of Asian American graduates—were qualified for admission to the University of California. See "Diversity Urged to Boost Minority Enrollment," *Whittier Daily News*, 7 May 2002. The *Chicago Tribune,* on 15 November 2002, reported "startling disparities at some of the most highly touted suburban [Chicago] schools. . . . At Naperville Central High School, for example, 88 percent of white juniors passed state math tests, compared with 36 percent of African-Americans. At Barrington High School, 85 percent of white students met standards in reading, versus 27 percent of Hispanics."

[214]At the University of Michigan, the odds ratio, blacks to whites, for undergraduate admission, was carefully calculated (in 1998) and shown to be 173.7 to 1. This means that whatever the chances of admission for a white student with a given set of credentials that year, the admission chances of a black student with identical credentials were *173 times as great.* See Robert Lerner and Althea K. Nagai, *Racial Preferences in Michigan Higher Education*, Center for Equal Opportunity (Washington, D.C.: 1998). In a *Washington Post* editorial, the Michigan program was described as "giving an edge" to minorities!

to graduate. And so the special academic support services earlier noted are established, special counselors appointed, special tutors provided. But graduation rates do not reach parity. "Institutional racism" must be the culprit—although what that means and how it is to be overcome no one can clearly say.

The demand for graduation rates in proportion to racial numbers leads to yet another kind of corruption within the universities—corruption in the academic curriculum itself. Normal academic requirements are eased; intellectually challenging requirements—a sequence in chemistry, courses in a foreign language—are waived; if favor by race becomes too obvious, the embarrassment is avoided by eliminating those requirements for all. Very few fine colleges now retain the mastery of a second language as a requirement for graduation. Even doctoral studies now commonly dispense with the requirement of second or third language facility. The intellectual achievements required for graduating from our universities today amount to something less than admission to them entailed a century ago.

Some requirements remain, however, and within them some courses may prove difficult. To avoid having to fail students who were preferentially admitted, indulgences are given. Courses and exams failed may be repeatedly retaken until some success is achieved. It is not rare for such dispensation to be given a third and even a fourth time—until a passing grade is obtained. Giving such privileges to blacks and Hispanics but not to others would be plainly outrageous, so all students are given the opportunity to retake those exams, lest academic burdens become too onerous. In the professional schools today, and in the medical schools above all, students must prove themselves repeatedly and obstinately irresponsible to flunk out.

Undergraduate grade point averages are lifted by the availability of assorted ethnic studies courses—black studies, Chicano studies, and so on—in which classroom activity may consist largely of the informal discussion of victimhood; grades in these courses, as might be expected, are uniformly splendid. Timothy Maguire, whose revelations scandalized the Georgetown law school, encountered in his research one (unnamed) black applicant to that law school whose undergraduate average was suspiciously high in the light of her very poor LSAT score. After checking her transcript, Maguire wrote, "There, alongside a C+ in

Shakespeare, a C in Economics, and an F in calculus, were 8 A's in African American courses."[215] A single anecdote proves nothing, but the contrast that record revealed is not rare.

Faculty members often *internalize* the spirit of race preference. In evaluating borderline student performance, professors commonly favor minority students whose failure might prove awkward. This favoritism is deeply concealed, and very rarely admitted by those who know themselves complicit. A former member of the University of Michigan faculty wrote me this illustrative report: He had given a failing grade to a minority student whose work in his course had been very poor. The student complained, insisting that the examinations given did not adequately reflect his understanding of the material, and that he (the student) had been burdened with especially high expectations because of his race. The professor, aware that there would be an ugly scene if such groundless charges were made public, discussed the matter with the chairman of his department. The chairman was sympathetic but not helpful, saying essentially this: "You can stick to your guns, which would be just but will probably result in a terrible mess for our department—or you can make a minor change in the student's grade, easily done, easily justifiable, and of little consequence in the long run. You choose." To me this professor wrote: "I am ashamed to admit (and would never admit publicly) what I did. I avoided the mess and changed the grade."

But most of those who do likewise tell no one, and may not admit it even to themselves. Excuses are made for inferior work by students who presumably come from disadvantaged backgrounds; standards go down, grades go up. A little extra generosity, after all, won't cause the heavens to fall. Applying normal intellectual standards to the work of students who ought not to have been admitted in the first place becomes too costly.

This problem is partly circumvented, and sometimes completely buried, by changing the scales on which college work is evaluated. The fewer the categories distinguished, the less frequent will be the need for invidious intellectual comparisons. Levels of performance are often collapsed into three: honors, pass, and fail. Virtually no one fails. The distinction between pass and honors becomes invidious in

---

[215]Maguire 1992.

turn, and almost everyone becomes an honors student. Of the graduating seniors at Harvard in 2001, it was revealed that 91 percent had graduated with honors.

An even surer way to avoid having to give bad grades to students admitted preferentially is to refrain from grading altogether. Grades are said to be a distraction, causing embarrassment and creating a competitive atmosphere in which minority students don't thrive. So the categories of evaluation are (in many contexts) reduced to two: credit and no credit. Everyone who shows up gets credit.

But the sense of shame has not dissipated completely; if better grades are given to inferior students than their work deserves, that favoritism is commonly obscured by raising the grades of all other students as well. At the most competitive universities, where race preference is common, grades are retained in most courses, but the fraction of all students receiving an A or at least an A − (often well more than half) is extraordinary. Grading in many college courses has become a bad joke.

In the appointment of faculty, as well as in the admission of students, race preference brings the lowering of standards. The pressure is always downward because, here again, the number of minorities sought cannot be obtained if high standards remain in force. The president of Xavier University (an institution historically black) was criticized in 1995 by some of his students because too many of the newly appointed faculty there were white. But the problem that confronted him confronts all universities, including those predominantly white: Xavier's president was hard pressed to *find* qualified black professors. Said he: "We're doing everything possible to increase the number of minority and African-American faculty. The clamor is going to be for more. But where are they going to come from?"[216]

Where indeed? More pressure does not solve this problem; it merely intensifies the competition for the few who are qualified. Approximately 16,000 doctoral degrees are awarded each year to U.S. citizens in the liberal arts—English, mathematics, philosophy, etc.,—in which a doctorate is the normal prerequisite for a faculty appointment. Of these, the number awarded to American blacks has

[216]*Chronicle of Higher Education*, 3 March 1995.

been under four hundred, or less than 3 percent.[217] In some academic fields—astronomy, botany, classics, comparative literature, European history, geography, Russian, Italian, Chinese, and Arabic language and literature—there was (in the year 1988, for example) not one single black Ph.D. in the entire country. In mathematics and computer science that year, there were 2, out of a total of more than 600; and in earth, atmospheric, and marine sciences there were another 2. Even in American history, which includes African American history, the number of recent black Ph.Ds is countable on one's fingers. One member of the U.S. Commission on Civil Rights, Abigail Thernstrom, remarks: "Students and concerned faculty often argue that schools that really care will at the minimum employ a black scholar to teach Afro-American history. Where will they find them?"[218]

Research universities make extraordinary efforts to attract black graduate students, and to increase the flow of black Ph.Ds. Minority graduate students receive the most generous welcome and support, which usually includes both tuition and living stipend. But most black and Hispanic graduates with fine records choose to pursue careers in more prestigious professions, far more lucrative than careers in the academic world. The supply of qualified minority faculty remains exceedingly small.

This fact does not lessen the zeal of those who insist, at hundreds of universities, that the number of black faculty simply must be increased. The University of Wisconsin adopted a five-year plan (in 1988) to increase minority faculty by 75 percent. Duke University pledged to add one minority faculty member to every department by 1993 (but revoked that pledge after finding that it simply could not be done with respectable standards intact). In California (before race preference was prohibited there), a legislatively imposed minority quota of 30 percent was imposed on all new faculty appointed to the community colleges of the state; "affirmative action job fairs"

---

[217]See A. M. Thernstrom, "On the Scarcity of Black Professors," *Commentary* 90, no. 1 (July 1990), pp. 22-26, in which the data are gleaned from reports of the National Academy of Sciences, the National Research Council, and the American Council on Education.

[218]Ibid., p. 23.

were held to meet the quota. Yale, Wellesley, Michigan, and other colleges and universities publicly announce their determination to increase markedly the number of minority faculty. Success for all is out of the question.[219] The resulting desperate competition produces bidding wars of almost ludicrous proportions when it appears that a distinguished minority scholar may be pried loose from his or her institution. And all such auctions must have more losers than winners.[220] To placate demands issuing from the board of governors or the legislature, standards for the appointment of minority faculty who remain in the market grow yet lower.

To beat the market, colleges often employ a device called "opportunity hiring," which works like this: When a reasonably qualified minority faculty person has for some reason become available, the normal process of searching and vetting is bypassed, and, however little need there may be for a person in his field of study at that time, the appointment may be authorized by administrative fiat. Intellectually unjustifiable perhaps, but—heaven be thanked!—it increases minority numbers. This is common practice.

In 1997, the Nebraska state legislature imposed the mandate that its state university be among the top 50 percent of peer institutions in the number of women and minorities on its faculty by August 2002. The university was explicitly threatened with the reduction of its general fund appropriation if that goal were not reached. But using normal standards it could not be reached. So in 1998, the university formally adopted a plan to "increase diversity" by appointing

---

[219]In November 1998, the University of New Hampshire signed an agreement with its Black Student Union that established the following goals: adding 50 black students each year until a target of 300 is reached in 2004, having a total of 10 black tenure-track faculty by 2003, and hiring no fewer than 2 black visiting scholars per year through 2003. "Goals" like these inevitably become quotas; imposing them will certainly result in other candidates' being discriminated against.

[220]Iowa State University, at Ames, has been one of the recent losers. But while losing out, ISU vainly offered minority journalism faculty higher salaries and perks than their nonminority peers—leading to a near revolt by a group of bitterly resentful white colleagues much less well cared for, and the forced resignation of some administrators. See "Pursuit of Diversity Sparks ISU Tension," *Des Moines Register*, 8 May 2002.

faculty "without benefit of a formal search process, to take advantage of an exceptional and usually serendipitous opportunity . . . [when] doing a search would serve no useful purpose." Departments were advised to apply to the Office of Academic Affairs to request "bridge funds" made available from a special fund that, according to the University of Nebraska associate vice-chancellor, "supports the hiring of underrepresented groups."[221] The university counsel candidly admitted that at Nebraska race and gender have now become plus factors in hiring. One professor of philosophy remarked, "Like it or not, what affirmative action has turned into at Nebraska is a quota system. They [the University] won't call it that, but that is what they are doing."[222] Nebraska is only one of many institutions engaged in the same chase.

Distinguished minority scholars are undermined by such devices, stigmatized, as noted earlier. Professor Stephen Carter, of the Yale law school, points out that when law schools give preference by race in hiring, the consequences are likely to be disastrous. A school sets out to hire "the best blacks," and as a result attracts scholars who "produce work of lower median quality than the work produced by those hired simply because they are the best potential scholars."[223] Universities put their heads in the sand, he writes, "pretend[ing] that the costs [of racial preferences] do not exist." But they do; such preferences "carry an implicit denigration of the abilities of scholars of color, the unspoken suggestion that we cannot really compete." Law schools, and indeed all schools, he urges, ought to count their costs carefully—"including the costs to . . . their beneficiaries—the 'best blacks.'"[224]

When scholarly standards differ by race, Carter observes, we create a two-track system overtly or covertly, whose premise—"an insult"—is that scholars of color would not survive under the hiring standards normally employed. Two-track systems are designed to bring into the university those who could not be appointed using the normal criteria, so there is every likelihood that, as Carter gently

---

[221]Reported by Gwen Tietgen in the *Daily Nebraskan*, 14 December 2001.
[222]Ibid.
[223]Carter, "The Best Black and Other Tales," p. 46.
[224]Ibid.

puts it, "the scholarship of those who are hired because of racial preferences will not be as good as the scholarship of those who are not." Everyone in our universities sees this plainly, yet it is rarely acknowledged. That silence, Stephen Carter concludes, "can only be ascribed to a fear of attacking the shibboleth of preferences."[225]

In sum: Race preference is counterproductive in all institutions, but as long experience proves, it is particularly injurious to universities because it entails the lowering of standards for admission and for appointment, because it corrupts the institutions that vainly seek to hide their racial double standards, and because it reinforces the stereotype of minority intellectual inferiority. Widely practiced for three decades, race preference has seriously damaged our universities.

[225]Ibid.

9

Race Preference Is Bad for Society as a Whole

Racial oppression and racial discrimination have plagued our nation from its earliest days. Americans created these hostilities; it is our moral obligation to do, in our lifetimes, the very best we can to heal racial wounds, and to eliminate racism root and branch. Fulfilling this duty is greatly hindered by race preference.

Injustice is only part of the problem. Race preference does indeed violate our laws and our deepest moral principles, of which none is more important than equality before the law. But preference does damage to our society that goes beyond injustice. Mutual respect among the races is undermined. Racial divisions are intensified. Distrust is engendered. Disharmony, even anger, is provoked.

Ethnic preferences presuppose some generally understood sorting of the community into ethnic categories, necessary for the award of advantages to this group or to that one. Each person must be *identifiable*—by others and by himself—as a member of one ethnic group or another. To receive the benefits reserved for any minority, the beneficiaries must be seen, *and see themselves*, as members of that minority. Without identifiable memberships, preferences make no sense. But the pervasive application of racial classifications is malignant in a civil society. What obliges individuals to identify themselves by group divides the groups, builds barriers between them.

"Black" and "white," "Hispanic" and "Asian," and all the now-common names for ethnic groups are attended by confusion and many absurdities. Preferences didn't create those ethnic labels, but by preferences they are made more sensitive, and their importance is magnified. Of course, we want a society in which cultural attachments are protected and heritage preserved, but also one in which no citizen is by birth inferior to any another. We honor our origins, but no one's origins are second class. We strive for a community in which ethnic membership is a source of satisfaction, yet cannot impinge on any individual's rights or opportunities. The American ideal is that of a society in which neither race nor national origin are given *official* function.

This ideal is subverted by formally awarded ethnic preferences. When corporations, universities, and government agencies first classify and then reward and penalize their employees or applicants by race, the categories of race are hardened, entrenched. This hardening has very bad consequences for society at large.

First comes the *separation* of racial groups. The term "segregated" describes oppressive communities in which the races are *kept* apart by rule or law—segregated waiting rooms, segregated buses, segregated lunch counters, and so on. Segregation in the public schools, condemned by our Supreme Court half a century ago, yields inequality unavoidably, and is of course intolerable in a democracy.[226] The divisions obliged by contemporary preferences have a gentler face. Not segregation, but in its place the *separation* of the races is what preference promotes.

Separation is now rarely enforced by rules, but it is certainly encouraged by policies under which ethnic groups are treated differently. Separation is often *sought* by ethnic groups as one response to that different treatment. Persons obliged to think of themselves as being of this or that color (or nationality) in work or study are understandably drawn toward others similarly categorized. Preferences do not forbid an embrace across racial boundaries, but they do make genuinely integrated social life exceedingly awkward.

Barriers that had divided the races for generations began to melt under the heat of the civil rights movement in the middle years of the twentieth century. That movement reached its apogee in the 1960s, rousing the conscience of the nation. In 1964, most racial discrimination in public settings was forbidden by Congress, and the

[226]*Brown I.*

prospect for increasing racial harmony was very promising. That promise withered when the race preferences of the 1970s and 1980s, producing new racial tensions, led once again to the rise of informal but insidious barriers between the races.[227]

Evidence of this regrowth surrounds us today. Students—in high school and college almost always, and often even in the lower grades—now regularly sort themselves by color. In lunchrooms and libraries and lounges and classrooms, blacks cluster with blacks, and whites with whites, all keenly aware of their color. That color-consciousness is not moderated but is on the contrary intensified by their institutions. The orientation for entering students at a university or college will not have concluded before each new student has been repeatedly reminded of his racial group, the minority student among them invited to a racially exclusive gathering and urged to join racially oriented clubs. All new students will probably be warned of the racism of the white majority.[228] Some facilities in public institutions (lounges and study halls in college dormatories, for example) are now reserved exclusively for one race or another. In public schools, on beaches, and in playgrounds, racial identity has once again become, has been *made*, a central and separating fact about one's life.

Students, like all citizens, have a perfect right to gather and socialize with whomever they choose, of course. We tolerate no formal rules imposing either segregation or integration. But established institutional preferences put all students (or workers) of a given race in the same psychological boat, and those of other races in different boats. The choice to separate is made freely, but it is a choice strongly encouraged where race preference is pervasive. The increasing separation of

[227]The transformation and inversion of affirmative action is recounted at length in chapter 3.

[228]Special slots are often set aside for "minority peer advisors" in college residence halls who are *trained* to teach racial separation. One of the assigned readings for novice advisers at the University of Michigan ("Uprooting Racism") explains how "white people" ought to use their oppressive history to benefit those they "subjugate." Another assigned reading ("Identity") teaches that most whites passively accept inequities and advantages, but that their racism is "correctable" when their "whiteness" is redefined in "non-racist" terms.

At Wellesley College, there is a separate "pre-orientation program" each year for incoming minorities—in addition to an annual retreat for black students only. See *Boston Globe*, 10 November 2002.

the races that ensues ought not surprise us. In places of entertainment, of residence, of study—even in legislatures and on juries—we are, as a people, more deeply separated by race than by anything else. Preference by race leads almost inevitably to separation by race.[229]

Separation is not all the damage done. Discomfited and ashamed, we might resign ourselves to a society in which the races choose to live apart, and to entertain themselves separately. But the disintegrating process penetrates more deeply. Separated by race, citizens become *distrustful* by race. Trust requires candor, but candor is difficult to preserve across the racial divide. Embarrassing aspects of race preference, and resulting ethnic tension, cannot be openly discussed for fear of misunderstanding. Lips are buttoned and resentment boils. Opposition to race preference is very widespread but cannot be comfortably expressed. Ninety-two percent of randomly selected American adults, in 2001, supported the statement that admissions and hiring judgments "should be based strictly on merit and qualifications"—92 *percent!* Only 5 percent thought that race or ethnicity should be a factor in admissions or hiring. But that poll, by the *Washington Post,* was anonymous; public statements on

---

[229]At the University of California at Los Angeles in 2001 (as in many other universities), commencement exercises were—by the vote of the students graduating—held separately for the several ethnic groups; that year, there was a "Raza Graduation" for Latinos; a separate graduation for African Americans; and a "Lavender Graduation" for lesbian, gay, bisexual, and transgender students. At California State Polytechnic University, there was a graduation ceremony exclusively for blacks. And at the University of Texas at Austin, a graduation celebration separately conducted for ethnic minorities—Hispanics, Native Americans, and African Americans—*excluded* Asian Americans. See *Los Angeles Times,* 26 July 2001. At the University of Michigan, incoming black students are formally gathered by black administrators at a Black Student Convocation, called Umoja, the word for "unity" in Swahili. One arriving student there observed enthusiastically that as a result of that convocation she "became aware of her status as a minority student." See the *Michigan Daily,* 5 September 2002. At Brown University each fall term, a racially *segregated* orientation is conducted—the Third World Transition Program for "students of color" only.

Graduating ceremonies for black students exclusively were held, in the spring of 2003, at Vanderbilt University, the University of Pennsylvania, Michigan State University, the University of California-Berkeley, and Washington University in St. Louis, among others. See: "Diversity or Division on Campus?" *Washington Post,* 19 May 2003.

the subject might cause one to suppose that general attitudes were very different. Even the reality of the race preferences now common is obscured; the ubiquity of the phrase "affirmative action" is partly accounted for by its usefulness in blurring the truth, acknowledging only obliquely the preferences whose forthright recognition would be indelicate or even offensive. Better to keep our mutual distance and keep silent.[230]

Sometimes resentment boils over. On the campus of the University of Michigan, I witnessed the following scene: The president of our university, my friend and colleague, was invited during the winter of 1995 to talk informally with students of the small college within the university in which I teach. The floor of the college lounge was packed with undergraduates. Questions on any topic of mutual concern were invited; a young female student rose to speak. She was angry. The burden of her complaint to the president was this: "You promised us more black lounges, but in this residence hall we have only one black lounge, and we see that you do not keep your promises. When will you fulfill the commitment to create more black lounges?" Nearby, several white male students were clustered, one of whom did not wait to be called on to respond loudly: "*More* black lounges are what you want? Why should you have *any* black lounges at all? Are there *white* lounges?" He also rose, as did his friends with him. Racial hostility in that lounge on that occasion was almost palpable. Had the president not been calm and adroit, a physical clash between races might have erupted that winter afternoon. Such an incident probably will come, on our campus or some other, if preference by race is not eliminated.[231]

---

[230]See Paul M. Sniderman and Thomas Piazza, *The Scar of Race* (Cambridge: The Belknap Press, 1993).

[231]Monica Kern, professor of psychology at the University of Kentucky, confirms the point: "Most University of Kentucky faculty and students agree that there is a high degree of racial tension on campus. Affirmative action [i.e., race preference] instead of easing that tension only exacerbates it by creating the mistaken impression that blacks are not capable of competing on a level playing field. . . . Most institutions with selective admissions, including the University of Kentucky . . . admit black students who would not have been accepted if their skins were white." See "Affirmative Action Unfair in Practice," *Lexington Herald-Leader*, 6 January 2002.

When "they" are known to be seeking a greater share from the common pot, "we" must strategize to protect our share of it. What *they* win by special treatment will in the end be paid for by *us*. When the goods are limited and distributed by race, *their* interests, the interests of that race, are necessarily in conflict with *our* interests, the interests of our race. If they unify we must unify in response. If what *they* seek will reduce the share that *we* have come to expect, their interests and ours cannot be mutually supportive. *Race preference inevitably breeds racial resentment.* Self-chosen separation exacerbates resentment. Resentment leads to mutual suspicion, and then to outright hostility.[232]

This downward spiral has been growing wider and deeper for some years. Between blacks and whites, tensions have multiplied and intensified. Racial slurs, and then accusations of racism from all sides, have become more frequent. Preference is condemned as modern racism. Critics of preference are condemned as racists. Look at the racists who are calling us racists, say the whites. Only whites can be racists, say the blacks in return. One recognized leader of blacks says point blank, "I don't trust white Republicans or white Democrats; I want a black party!"[233]

Hostility grows into hate. Hate talk—mostly in private, but also on much talk radio—becomes acceptable. "Honkey" and "whitey" are words commonly heard, now even in formal settings. The uses of "nigger" become the subject of scholarly inquiry, and there is public argument about who is entitled to use the word. The organizers

[232]In Benton Harbor, Michigan, ethnic "goals" have driven hostility to an acute level. The school board, the administrators of the Benton Harbor schools, and the great majority of the public school principals there are black; the formally adopted school hiring policy that aims for 60 to 70 percent minority teachers—a proportion impossible even to approach without discriminating against white teachers—has produced not only angry litigation but community-wide racial bitterness. See *Benton Harbor Herald Palladium*, 29 September 2002. In Prescott, Arizona, racial hostility was intensified when, at Northern Arizona State University, *all* minority faculty members, but not one white faculty member, received substantial salary raises, even though an internal university analysis showed that there had been no statistically meaningful difference between salary levels of nonminority male professors and minority professors. See *Arizona Daily Sun*, 19 December 2000.

[233]The Reverend Jesse Jackson, quoted in *Time*, 13 December 1993.

of white hate, and the advocates of black hate like them, are grudgingly admired. Sister Souljah tells her audience, to laughter and applause: "If black people kill black people every day, why not take a week off and kill white people?" What cannot be said safely about blacks is said readily about whites; on the best-seller lists of 2002 is a cheaply written book entitled *Stupid White Men.*[234] Boycotts are organized by race: Buy white! Buy black![235] Interest groups by race multiply; exaggerated and even absurd claims for minority cultures go uncontested for fear of retaliation. Athletic competition in Catholic schools is infected with racial hostility, black teams leaving leagues dominated by whites.[236] A Broadway production of *West Side Story* is denounced because the white producer is allegedly unable to speak for the Puerto Rican experience in New York.[237] Double standards by race are everywhere. But of all the thorns, *preference* is the sharpest; the unfairness of preference results, as Senator Joseph Lieberman rightly puts it, in "breaking the ties of civil society."[238]

Friction arises also *among* the minorities, each competing to protect and enlarge its portion of the spoils. Foundations offer grants by race.[239] Public universities offer scholarships by race.[240] Blacks and Puerto Ricans battle for turf in New York; Latinos and Asians battle for turf in California. Among competing minorities animosity becomes more evident. In south Florida, Cuban Americans and Haitian Americans are at each other's throats. In major cities, the bitter tension between Koreans and African Americans has come to blows. The Hispanic minority, rapidly growing in size, registers its claim for preference in medical schools, cutting into what blacks had thought were their entitlements. Preference for Hispanics, some blacks complain angrily, are "shutting blacks out."[241]

---

[234]The author is Michael Moore (New York: Harper-Collins, 2001).

[235]*New York Times*, 23 May 1993.

[236]*New York Times*, 10 March 2001.

[237]*New York Times*, 18 August 1991.

[238]Ibid.

[239]*New York Times*, 29 November 1994.

[240]By the University of Maryland, for blacks only. See *Podberesky v. Kirwan*, 38 F. 3rd 147.

[241]See *Chronicle of Higher Education*, 17 August 1994, and *Ann Arbor News*, 22 December 1993.

If the pie is going to be divided by race, we—whoever "we" may be—had better get organized quickly to insure that we get our share. What racial groups will next coalesce to register demands? Chinese Americans? Japanese Americans? If suffering past injustice be the principal criterion, many groups not now receiving preference deserve it. Shall we introduce additional preferential schemes for Polish Americans or Italian Americans, or other nationality groups? Will it be thought unreasonable when religious groups long persecuted—Mormons, Christian Scientists, Jews—unify to stake their claims? The evils promoted by race-based policies were noted astutely by Justice Sandra Day O'Connor, who wrote for the Supreme Court majority when it struck down a racial set-aside in Richmond, Virginia:

> Classifications based on race carry a danger of stigmatic harm. Unless they are strictly reserved for remedial settings, they may in fact promote notions of racial inferiority and *lead to politics of racial hostility.*"[242]

The distribution of public goods by ethnicity is simply wrongheaded; it is sure to produce anger. There *cannot* be any pattern of distribution by ethnic group that is fair. Racial proportionality is an internally incoherent ideal because the many ethnic classifications are not even drawn on the same dimension, and *there is no scheme—however much proportionality may be sought—that ever could satisfy all the ethnic competitors.* Even if ethnically proportional distribution were achievable in principle (which it is not), its outcomes could not be stable in a world in which competition by race is fomented by racial politics, and in which changing populations constantly alter political outcomes.

Beyond the hostility it breeds, preference demands a social apparatus that is nearly as ugly as hate. We must be able to specify the authorized beneficiaries of the preferences given. That specification requires criteria for determining who are, and who are not, members of the preferred group. But any criteria formulated or applied lead quickly to social discord.

Who is black? Who is white? Are persons called "multiethnic" to be counted as one, or the other, or both? Conflicting views about

[242]*Richmond v. Croson*, p. 493. Emphasis added.

race membership are trivial disputes so long as nothing hangs on their resolution, but when a great deal is at stake, the need for consistent and rational answers becomes pressing. Who are to receive the preferences to which those of some races, but not all races, are entitled?

Are the races merely categories constructed by society? Are they natural divisions of human kind? Whether race is a construct or a natural kind there must be—found or invented—some criteria that can be applied objectively and with some degree of consistency to determine who gets the advantages that the preferred race gets, and who does not. Preferences oblige us to employ our racial categories with at least apparent rationality.

How much "blood" of a given race is enough to justify one's claim that she is of that race? Is "one drop" enough? If the absurd "one drop" rule were applied to "Caucasians," we might agree that since the drops of white blood are very widely spread, we are all whites. But if one parent identifies as black and the other white, most of us expect the offspring to classify themselves as black. One black grandparent is commonly thought sufficient to establish blackness. But what if only one great-grandparent were black?

Congressional legislation in 1888 directed the federal census to "take such steps as may be necessary to ascertain . . . the birth rate and death rate among pure whites, and among negroes, Chinamen, Indians and half-breeds or hybrids of any description . . . as well as of mulattoes, quadroons, and octoroons." An "octoroon" (according to *The American College Dictionary*) is "a person having one-eighth Negro ancestry; offspring of a quadroon and a white." Those categories were indeed counted in the census that followed.

Early in the twentieth century, a *Dictionary of Races and Peoples* was issued by a congressional commission seeking to cope with the identities of immigrants then flooding into the United States. *Forty-five* "nonwhite" racial subgroups were distinguished, including Slavs, Poles, Italians, and Russians. For Jews there was a separate racial category, "Hebrews."[243] This system of classification, happily, did not become embedded in the law. The racial categories in common use

---

[243]S. Moore and R. Fields, "The Great White Influx," *Los Angeles Times*, 31 July 2002.

have changed, but the essential questions remain unanswered. In the year 2000, six racial options were offered to respondents in the U.S. Census: 1) white; 2) black or African American; 3) American Indian or Native Alaskan; 4) Asian; 5) Native Hawaiian or other Pacific Islander; 6) other. Racial categorization remains arbitrary, inconsistent, and often deliberately invidious.

The ubiquity of race preferences nevertheless obliges us to specify how such categories are to be applied in the world of work and study, because the race in which persons are classified by employers, schools, and governments now materially affects their opportunities. Racial and ethnic categories used in various federal programs were devised by the Federal Interagency Committee on Education. Confronting that committee were questions such as this one: Shall persons from India be categorized under the "Asian and Pacific Islander" category, or under the "White/Caucasian" category? Bitter dispute ensued. Why? Because the award of major benefits results from some answers but not from others. In the trial directive of the committee, one scholar reports, persons from India were classified as "Caucasian." But then all preferential benefits would be lost! In the final version, they were reclassified as "Asian"—"most likely in response to Asian Indian lobbying to ensure racial minority status."[244]

Consider this repulsive question: if a person is an octoroon, is he (or she) now to receive preference when preference is given to blacks? Questions of that general form are unavoidable where preference is given, and the answers must be either yes or no; one is entitled to the preference or one is not. In the hope of evading awkward uncertainties, institutions often leave racial identification to the individual concerned, allowing him to decide whether he is (or is not) to be considered a member of this group or that one. That can be tolerated on census forms, where respondents are permitted now even to check more than one category—but self-identification is not acceptable when the racial classification is consequential and contested. If each person were authorized to adjudicate his own case, outcomes would be painfully inconsistent and unfair. Classification by race must be at least superficially rational. But how is that rationality to be achieved?

---

[244]Melissa Nobles, *Shades of Citizenship* (Stanford: Stanford University Press, 2000).

If one-eighth ancestry is not enough to justify minority classification, an "octoroon" who makes the claim for preference—say, a
student claiming the preference given to Hispanics because one
great-grandparent was born in Mexico—must be advised that he is
not entitled to it. But if one-eighth *is* sufficient "racial blood" (of this
or that category) to permit the minority racial identification to be
made, the question inevitably reappears at the next level: Is one-
sixteenth enough (a great-great-grandparent)? And one thirty-
second (a great-great-great-grandparent)? Controversy must continue until we can say with some precision what determines membership in the race preferred. Who *is* black? Who *is* Hispanic? When
a minority is to be given a preference that many covet, who is to be
counted as a member of that minority?

The rational implementation of ethnic preferences in the twenty-
first century cries out for a new "dictionary of races." Consider:

Many American families have arisen from the union of a white
slave master and his female slave; the union of Thomas Jefferson
and Sally Hemmings is only the most well known of these. Are all
the descendants of such unions black? If response is evaded by again
resorting to self-identification, we rejoin: Very well then, are all the
descendants of Sally Hemmings (and other black slaves treated as
she was treated) entitled to *choose* to be considered black? Does the
option never end, or does it expire after the passage of many generations? How many? Six generations? Seven? There must be some
line on one side of which there is an entitlement to preference, and
on the other side of which there is no such entitlement; the implementation of any preferential program that claims to be just demands
that such lines be clearly drawn.

Consider the even greater difficulties presented by unions between whites and American Indians, very frequent in our history.
We have no word precisely analogous to "octoroon" in this context—
but there are very many Americans whose great-grandparents
include one American Indian. Are they Indians? (or Native Americans?) The State of Michigan guarantees a college education to qualified Michigan Indians, because, in a nineteenth-century treaty, it
was agreed that in exchange for certain lands of which the state
university took possession, the descendants of the Indians from
whom the land was taken would be entitled to free tuition in that

state university. This is a preference of substantial significance. How do we decide who is entitled to benefit from it?

Yet greater difficulties are encountered in classifying persons as "Hispanic," a minority commonly targeted for preference. In Jackson, Michigan, the school board gave marked employment preference to teachers "of Spanish descendancy"—but who are they?[245] One Hispanic parent is almost certainly sufficient; perhaps one Hispanic grandparent is also sufficient. So Juan Santiago, whose paternal grandfather was Carlos Santiago, gets the preference. But what of John Taylor, whose suburban upbringing incorporated no tincture of Hispanic heritage, but whose *maternal* grandfather was Carlos Santiago? Is he not equally entitled to the preference? And if Carlos Santiago is the *great*-grandparent on one side or the other, what then? Hispanic "octoroons" are uncountable in America. Does their entitlement to preference depend only on their choice of ethnic self-identification? Does it depend on their last name?

Confusion is compounded by the fact that some preferences in contemporary America are given to Hispanics of one subcategory but not to Hispanics of another. In the American West, institutional preference is commonly guaranteed to "Chicanos," they being Mexican Americans, but not to Hispanics whose families are from Spain, Argentina, or Puerto Rico. In our northeastern states, preference is often given to Puerto Ricans, but not to Hispanics from Mexico or elsewhere. Yet more complication arises because in awarding this preference, a distinction is commonly drawn between *mainland* Puerto Ricans, i.e., those whose families have migrated to New York or other cities in the United States, who do get the preference, and those whose families continue to reside in Puerto Rico, who do not.

Worldwide family migration and a great mix of ancestors make all such distinctions, for all ethnic groups, thoroughly absurd. Preferences do not create the tangles, but giving preferences elevates and intensifies them by making it essential that they be somehow untangled. Important goods are to be distributed, and the details of ancestry cannot plausibly govern that distribution until the rules have been spelled out.

---

[245]See *Wygant v. Jackson Board of Education*.

Quarrels unending and seething hostility is what the advocates of preference must confront.[246] The impact of arbitrarily assigned ethnic identities—a federal contract secured, employment obtained, admission to a fine university gained—is not a trivial matter. Preferences create powerful incentives to make the claim of this or that ethnicity for the purpose of winning the advantageous allocation. The benefit to be distributed is often a good that only a few, and by no means all, can be given. We may then expect that some who are not entitled to that benefit will make fraudulent claims of minority status. Knowing this, those who lose out in the quest for preference are very likely to believe that they, and the community, have been defrauded. A new need arises: formally agreed-upon *rules* for the determination of ethnic category.

In Germany, in the 1930s, precisely that problem was confronted by the Nazi Party in awarding significant preferences to Aryans over non-Aryans such as Gypsies and Jews. For many generations, Jews had lived and thrived in Germany, playing a major role in the cultural life of that country. Many Jews had been thoroughly assimilated; some had converted to Christianity. The marriage of Jews and non-Jews had become common, and the offspring of such unions, and their offspring, were very numerous. Since, by law, the Nazis gave preference to Aryans over Jews, they found it essential to issue regulations that would specify the ancestry that would result in the deserving status of Aryan, and the undeserving status of non-Aryan. It became exceedingly important to know who really was an Aryan.

---

[246]Since Congress allotted $42 million to the Seminole Nation of Oklahoma, that nation has torn itself apart quarreling over who is and who is not a Seminole. Blacks were part of the Seminole tribe from the beginning, owning land, serving as interpreters and negotiators with whites, teaching other Seminoles how to grow rice. Black Seminoles were made full members of the tribe in 1866, but a recent election for tribal positions—with only "blood Seminoles" allowed to vote—resulted in a new chief who insists that blacks never had equal rights in the tribe and are not entitled to them. Some 1,500 black Seminoles, who cannot trace one-fourth of their ancestry to blood Seminoles, are now kept from sitting on the tribal council. One of the black Seminoles put his finger on the problem: "We were just like brothers and sisters until this little money come up." See "Money Splits Tribal Members," MSNBC News, 23 September 2002.

These regulations, the so-called Nuremberg laws, were arbitrary and outrageous, of course—but race preferences enforced by government made them indispensable. Methodical German bureaucrats needed to be able to decide consistently who was what. In America today, we have the same need. Every society in which ethnic preference is formally ensconced must have its own set of Nuremberg laws.

Even the most carefully formulated rules conscientiously applied will not resolve all controversy. The twists of intermarriage and mixed ancestry will present puzzles that require some interpretation of the rules, and hence another need arises—for persons authorized to apply the rules. There must be a board, or a committee, or an appointed officer to make the needed racial determinations in disputed cases. The Nazis had that need, and we have it too. Those who contest the racial category in which they have been placed must have an opportunity to argue their case before the board, to submit evidence to demonstrate that they are indeed (or are not) of some specified ethnicity. Such an "ethnicity board" or "racial identity committee" must in turn formulate standards of practice in deciding the marginal cases that inevitably arise.

This is not fantasy. Disputes of this kind already multiply in the United States. Students who have enjoyed preference in gaining admission to some universities have later been brought up on charges questioning the legitimacy of their ethnic claims. Appointments or promotions in police or fire departments, now often partially a function of race, present serious controversies over the legitimacy of the racial claims asserted. Requests for change of racial status are common: some are honest and some fraudulent.

Indian tribes with very few remaining members come, by the renewed application of long-forgotten treaties, to acquire lands on which rich deposits of oil or minerals have recently been found; members of some tribes may fish waters forbidden to nonmembers; some tiny tribes have received preference in the award of licenses to operate gambling casinos in states where that is forbidden to non-Indian citizens.[247] A sudden flow of great wealth is to be divided among iden-

---

[247]The Buena Vista Me-Wuks, in Ione, California, are a federally recognized Indian tribe, and therefore a sovereign nation. Membership in that tribe became a matter of heated controversy when, in 2000, plans were announced

tified members of the tribe. And lo! The number of those claiming a share on ethnic grounds doubles and triples. Who will decide what genealogical standards apply to determine who really are members and who are not, when being a member yields great benefit? Objective criteria, applied by a public body with legislatively delegated authority—blood types perhaps, or these days, DNA samples[248]—are needed.

Ethnic identification begins to saturate everyday life. We must be able to prove *what* we are. You are an American, yes—but an American of *which kind*? We need well-defined racial *categories*; we need *rules* to apply them; we need a *court* formally authorized to interpret the rules and to enforce them. These are the ugly and inevitable products of special entitlements by race. Readers will find the very thought of ethnic rules and identity boards detestable—but where preferences become formally ensconced, we have no choice but to employ them. Race preference does this terrible thing to our community and ourselves; it compels us to do what the Nazis urged—to "think with our blood."

Advocates of preferential "affirmative action" earnestly say—not intending irony—that they aim to achieve greater understanding among the races and to promote interracial harmony. But the outcome of what they do is quite the opposite of what they hope for, as growing racial antagonism on university campuses, in police and fire departments, and in government agencies makes evident.[249]

---

to build a $150 million casino on the tribe's rancheria 35 miles from Sacramento. Only three members of the tribe had recently been recognized, but now—no surprise!—the question of who is and who is not really a member of the Me-Wuk tribe has become a matter hotly contested in the Bureau of Indian Affairs and in the federal courts. Many more such quarrels are sure to come. See "Whose Tribe Is It, Anyway?" *New York Times*, 10 April 2002.

[248]DNA samples are already being collected for this purpose. DNAPrint Genomics, a company in Sarasota, Florida, offers a genetic testing service that will confirm one's continent of origin; this test, explains the company, will "validate your eligibility for race-based college admissions or government entitlements."

[249]Where race preference is most evident, racial hostility is most common. The director of community relations service of the U.S. Department of Justice, Rose Ochi, reported in April 2002 that "there is no place where hate crimes are occurring with more visibility and hostility and increasing frequency than in institutions of higher education."

Race preference, flowing from the demand for ethnic proportionality, obliges everyone to think early and often about his ethnic identity. Race becomes the irritant underlying almost every public issue, the intensifying ingredient of community controversy, and the salt in social wounds. Consciousness of racial identity comes to share center stage with consciousness of citizenship. Racial identification is first authorized, then promoted, then supposed and even ordered by government decree. Employers are judged suitable for government contracts, and colleges are judged worthy of accreditation, in the light of the approximation to racial proportionality among their employees or staff. The ratios of ethnic distribution become the measures of social justice. Employers count their employees by race, hire by race, promote by race; universities admit by race and give scholarships by race, even distribute prizes by race. Symphony orchestras categorize their players by race and audition competing candidates by race.[250] Artists exhibit their paintings by race.[251] Librarians are assigned by race.[252] Even motel owners are sorted by ethnicity.[253] Among applicants for appointment to a college faculty, race is carefully considered. We count crimes by race, and criminals by race, and the victims of crimes by race. We give honors by race and note achievements by race.[254] Even juries must be

[250]The Detroit Symphony Orchestra, abandoning its long-established audition method in which candidates play behind a screen so that they can be heard by the judges but not seen, removed the screen in order that the number of minorities appointed be increased. See *New York Times*, 29 November 1994.

[251]"Race-based exhibitions," wrote the *New York Times* reviewer of The National Black Fine Art Show, held in New York City in February 2002, "tend to ghettoize, giving the impression that minority artists are to be judged by standards different from those of the mainstream art world. . . . [but in this show] there is still too much mediocrity and kitsch . . . too much pseudo-Africanism, pseudo-folk art and pseudo-primitivism." See "From Mouse Ears to Poetic Pop," *New York Times*, 2 February 2002.

[252]In Atlanta, Georgia, the Fulton County Library demoted eight librarians from its central branch to smaller branches to reduce the number of white employees working downtown. "There are too many white managers," said a member of the library board. See "Atlanta Libraries Face Stiff Fines for Transferring White Employees," Fox News, 17 January 2002.

[253]See "When Origin Becomes a Competitive Issue," *New York Times*, 11 May 2002.

[254]When Charles Barron, newly elected New York City Council member and formerly a Black Panther, was sworn in, he announced that many portraits hang-

balanced by race.[255] In every sphere, those who would advance in their work must be seen (and come to see themselves) as a member of this race or that one, as black or white, as Hispanic or Native American. The events and trials of daily life in America come to be seen by everyone through the lens of race. Preference by race yields *dis*harmony, *dis*trust, and *dis*integration.

Success in maintaining a democracy does not require that citizens like one another, or that they be like one another. Homogeneity of religion, of culture, of background is certainly not essential, and is not possible in a democracy like ours. But democratic government does require that the members of the community see one another as *fellow* citizens, as members of the body politic with *equal standing* in the commonwealth—equal in their opportunity to participate, equal in the protection received from the laws. That vision of equal citizenship is inconsistent with race preference. If ever we are to approach our common goal of racial comity and wide civic decency, all such preference by race must end.

Advantage and disadvantage formally tied to race lead inexorably to racial conflict. In an American society of many races, ethnic preference is deeply corrupting. It is wrong, morally and legally and constitutionally, as the earlier chapters of this book have shown—but it is also very *bad* for us. Race preference is bad for our society as a whole, particularly bad for the universities in which it has become commonplace—and for the minorities who were to be helped by it, its consequences are bad beyond measure.

---

ing in City Hall (including that of Thomas Jefferson) must be removed. Said he: "Sixty-five percent of New Yorkers are people of color. We should have a majority of pictures on the wall." See www.newsmax.com, 21 January 2002.

[255]A federal judge in New York, David Trager, fearing an acquittal in the trial of a black defendant who stabbed an innocent Jewish passerby in Brooklyn, manipulated the selection of jurors to insure that it included enough Jews, one of those Jewish jurors being seated in spite of his confessed reservation about his own impartiality. The wanted verdict was obtained—at the cost of a jury quota. The conviction was vacated in January 2002 by the Second Circuit Court of Appeals, rightly insisting that "race discrimination be eliminated from all official acts and proceedings of the State." See "Bad Result, Good Precedent," *Washington Times*, 15 January 2002.

EPILOGUE

The Future of Race Preference

The Supreme Court of the United States has agreed to decide whether the uses of race in admissions by the University of Michigan violate the Constitution or the law; its rulings will shape the future of race preference in this country. Two cases—*Gratz v. Bollinger*[256] and *Grutter v. Bollinger*[257]—are now before the court because preferences given in the undergraduate college of the university differ from those given in its law school. The central issues, however, are the same in both cases.[258]

Preferences given by the University of Michigan had for many years been kept hidden; a request under the Michigan Freedom of Information Act obliged the university to disclose, in 1996, documents giving indisputable evidence of substantial discrimination by race. Testimony on the content of these documents was given before committees of the Michigan legislature, whereupon some legislators, angered by what they thought to have been duplicity on the

---

[256]*Jennifer Gratz and Patrick Hamacher, for themselves and all others similarly situated, Plaintiffs v. Lee Bollinger, James J. Duderstadt, and the Board of Regents of the University of Michigan, Defendants:* 135 F. Supp. 2nd 790 (2000) (District Court); absent decision of the Sixth Circuit *certiorari* granted 2 December 2002, U.S. Supreme Court, No. 02-516.

[257]*Barbara Grutter, Plaintiff v. Lee Bollinger, Jeffrey Lehman, Dennis Shields, Regents of the University of Michigan, and The University of Michigan Law School, Defendants:* 137 F. Supp. 2nd 821 (2001) (District Court); 288 F. 3d 732 (2002) (6th Cir.); *certiorari* granted 2 December 2002, U.S. Supreme Court, No. 02-241.

[258]Brief references to these cases appear in chapter 5, note 54, and in chapter 8, note 7.

part of the university, resolved to take action. Aware that a similar system of preferential admissions at the University of Texas had been struck down by a federal court only a short while before,[259] the Michigan legislators enlisted the support of the Washington non-profit public interest law firm that had taken on that Texas case, the Center for Individual Rights. Once evidence of racial discrimination at Michigan had been gathered, appropriate plaintiffs were sought, in whose behalf legal proceedings in Michigan might be undertaken. Scores of persons who had been rejected by the University of Michigan and who suspected that its admissions system was biased against them came forward; from among these Jennifer Gratz, Patrick Hamacher, and Barbara Grutter became, in 1997, the lead plaintiffs in the two cases.[260] These plaintiffs did not contend that they have a right to admission; they contended that they were entitled to an admission review that was not racially skewed against them. I conclude with a brief account of these cases, and some observations about the probable future of race preference in their light.

Gratz v. Bollinger

Applicants for undergraduate admission at the University of Michigan (from 1995 to 1998) were sorted into "cells," using grids marked on the vertical axis with GPAs, and on the horizontal axis with test scores (SAT or ACT). Applicants in the same cell did not always receive the same response from the university admissions office, however. In cell after cell, applicants with a given set of credentials were rejected if they were white but accepted if they were from a targeted minority—African American, Hispanic American, or Native American. Admission rates for minorities were, in the critical cells, much higher than rates for white and Asian applicants. These em-

---

[259]*Hopwood v. Texas.*

[260]To carry the burdens of protracted federal litigation, the Center for Individual Rights enlisted the *pro bono* support of the Minneapolis law firm of Maslon, Edelman, Borman, and Brand, LLP; Kirk O. Kolbo became lead counsel for the plaintiffs. The two cases were soon certified by the courts as class action suits, the plaintiffs representing not only themselves but also all others similarly situated.

barrassing grids the university eliminated when it changed the mechanics of its undergraduate admissions system in 1999. The newer system, which remains in force in 2002, is based on point totals: out of a possible 150 points, 100 normally suffice for admission, with minority applicants receiving 20 points automatically. By contrast, 12 points are given for a perfect SAT score and 6 points for a very poor SAT score.

In the Federal District Court in Detroit, both sides in *Gratz* sought summary judgment; in December 2000, Judge Patrick Duggan granted that in two very different parts. The older, pre-1999 system he found to be a violation of the Constitution[261]; but with respect to the preferences currently given, Judge Duggan granted summary judgment to the university, holding that the newer point system crosses the "thin line" into permissibility.[262]

Grutter v. Bollinger

In the law school case, a trial was ordered by Judge Bernard Friedman because, although the university acknowledged that race was considered in admission there, the weight given to race in the law school was much in dispute. Law school administrators argued in that lengthy trial that race was merely one minor factor among many considered, but they contended also that if they were not permitted to continue to use race in admitting students, the Michigan law school would be devastated. Professing an abhorrence of all target numbers and race quotas, the law school insisted that it sought no more than a "critical mass" of minority students. A critical mass was regularly found when the number of minority admissions reached 10 to 12 percent. Charts prepared by the law school, separately for "Caucasian Americans" and for "African Americans" and other minorities, revealed that the admission rate for whites in many cells was 2 or 3 percent while, in those same cells, the admission rate for blacks was 100 percent.

---

[261] Because Jennifer Gratz and the class of plaintiffs she represents had applied for admission during the years that older system was in force, they won their suit without need for a trial.

[262] *Gratz v. Bollinger*, 135 Fed. Supp. 2nd 790 (December 2000).

The plaintiffs' victory in this trial was overwhelming. The admission system employed by the law school was described by Judge Friedman in his findings of fact as "practically indistinguishable from a quota." In findings of law, he held that diversity could not serve as a compelling need under the standard of strict scrutiny, that in any case the law school system was not narrowly tailored to any need, and that the uses of race by the law school certainly do violate the equal protection clause of the Fourteenth Amendment. He ordered the university to cease "using applicants' race as a factor in its admissions decisions."[263]

The Intervenors

Because the University of Michigan defends its race preferences (in both cases) only on the ground that the need for diversity on the campus is compelling, a group of Detroit high school students sought to intervene to present the compensatory arguments that the university had forgone. Early in the proceedings, the Sixth Circuit Court of Appeals, overruling the district courts, granted those students formal status as intervenors. Their argument, that race preference in admission is appropriate redress for injuries done to minorities by the University of Michigan over the years, was heard in both courtrooms; in both (as later in the appellate court as well), that defense of preference as compensation was once again rejected.

Appellate Outcomes

Both cases were appealed. The U.S. Court of Appeals for the Sixth Circuit, which includes Michigan, decided not to employ the normal three-judge panel in this matter but instead to hear the two cases *en banc*—that is, all nine justices deliberating. The appeals were heard in Cincinnati on December 6, 2001.

Plaintiffs argued, in *Gratz*, that if the older system of race preference using grids were unconstitutional, as the district court had

---

[263]*Grutter v. Bollinger.* The university later petitioned Judge Friedman to stay his order pending appeal, on the ground that its immediate imposition would do the law school irreparable harm; Judge Friedman denied that petition, remarking that "Defendants are not irreparably harmed by an injunction that requires [them] to comply with the Constitution."

found, the newer system replacing it must be equally so, because the university itself had repeatedly asserted that the new system "changed only the mechanics, not the substance" of admissions practices—which makes perfect sense, since the university's explicit objective was to achieve the same result. In devising the newer system, the university had decided upon the number of points to be awarded for minority status by determining statistically how many points would be needed to insure the *same number of minority admissions* as the old system. But the constitutionality of the point system was not definitively addressed by the appellate court; for reasons unknown, a decision by the Sixth Circuit Court in the *Gratz* case was never issued.

In *Grutter*, the appellate court did act, reversing the trial court by a vote of 5 to 4. The majority found that diversity was a compelling state need that justified the racial classification, and that the law school quest for a "critical mass" of minority students was reasonably designed to address that need. The minority, in a strongly worded dissent, argued that under the standard of strict scrutiny, the majority was mistaken on both counts. Conflict between majority and minority was manifestly bitter.[264]

Supreme Court Action

The plaintiffs immediately petitioned the U.S. Supreme Court to hear the *Grutter* case for final resolution; the university urged the court not to accept it. The plaintiffs also petitioned the Supreme Court to exercise a very rarely used provision of its rules to consider the *Gratz* case, even though the normal appellate process in that case had not been consummated. For reasons unspecified, the Supreme Court had, in recent years, declined to hear cases involving the use of race in admissions. They had denied *certiorari* where the plaintiffs had prevailed, involving the University of Texas in the Fifth Circuit,[265] and also where the university had prevailed, involving the University of Washington in the Ninth Circuit.[266] These

---

[264]*Grutter v. Bollinger*, 288 F. 3rd 732 (6th Cir.), May 2002.

[265]*Hopwood v. Texas*, 518 U.S. 1033 (1996).

[266]*Smith v. University of Washington Law School*, 532 U.S. 1051 (2001).

two Michigan cases, however, the Supreme Court did agree to decide—not only *Grutter*, but *Gratz* as well, even though that latter case had not been resolved at the circuit level.[267] A final resolution of these two cases came from our highest court in 2003.

Issues to Be Decided

The record in these cases is complete and detailed. While the particulars of race usage in the two colleges differ, there are in both cases two primary questions that must be confronted.

(1) Do the ethnic preferences given by the university violate the equal protection clause of the Fourteenth Amendment? Any uses of racial classifications by the state will be subject to the standard of strict scrutiny; therefore, response to this most fundamental question will oblige the court to answer one (or possibly two) subsidiary questions.

> First: Does *diversity* rightly serve as a compelling state interest that can justify race preference under strict scrutiny? If the answer is no, the defense of race preference in this arena fails.
>
> Second: If the answer is yes (that is, if diversity is found to be a compelling state interest), are the admission preferences given by the university *narrowly tailored* to address that need? If the answer is no, the preferences cannot stand.

Only if both of these questions are answered affirmatively can the preferences be upheld.

The second of the two primary questions goes beyond the Constitution to federal statutes.

(2) Do the ethnic preferences given by the University of Michigan violate Title VI of the Civil Rights Act of 1964, which forbids institutions receiving federal financial assistance from discriminating by race, color, or national origin?

Since the University of Michigan is indeed a recipient of much federal financial assistance, and since its admissions systems do ad-

---

[267]See U.S. Supreme Court, *Order List*, 2 December 2002.

mittedly discriminate on the basis of race and national origin, it would appear that an affirmative answer to this question is inescapable. However, the Supreme Court may find that there is no violation of the Civil Rights Act if *and only if* the court finds both a) that the preferences are not a violation of the equal protection clause of the Constitution, and b) that the Civil Rights Act does no more than implement the prohibitions of that constitutional clause, and thus has no statutory reach that extends beyond it.

The university's race-based admissions systems will stand only if *all* of these conditions are realized. If the court finds that diversity is *not* a compelling state interest that can justify racial classifications under the standard of strict scrutiny; or if the court finds that, although diversity may be thought compelling, the admissions preferences given are *not* narrowly tailored to serve that interest; or if the court finds that, even though diversity may be a compelling interest and the admissions preference may be narrowly tailored to serve it, the Civil Rights Act is *not* limited to implementing the equal protection clause but has independent statutory force, the plaintiffs will prevail and the university's efforts to defend race preference will prove unsuccessful.

Probable Outcome

That one or more of these three negative answers will be given is strongly suggested by the vigorous language used by the court in rejecting racial classifications in other contexts, recounted in detail in chapter 6. The same outcome is suggested also by one highly unusual feature of recent developments. When the Supreme Court granted *certiorari* in *Gratz v. Bollinger*—pulling up that case for resolution even though the normal appellate process had not yet been completed—it relied on a procedural rule that was last used in 1974. The evident desire to address *both* cases is very probably an indication that the court intends to produce a ruling that will have extensive *reach*, addressing undergraduate as well as graduate admissions, and perhaps other spheres as well. Some impatience on the part of the Supreme Court may also be inferred. All this is fully consistent with the intense disapproval of racial discrimination by state agencies that has been expressed by five of the nine justices over recent decades.

Wider Implications

When racial discrimination by the universities has been condemned, we may expect that such discrimination—however generously motivated—will fall into disrepute well beyond the universities. Preference will become more difficult to defend in employment and in government contracting. Public rejection has been further increasing the pressure against it. Two states (California, by referendum in 1996, and Washington, by initiative in 2000) have explicitly forbidden all preference by race. Propositions barring race preferences have been approved by substantial majorities, even in the face of highly organized and well-financed opposition. In states more conservative than Washington and California, the rejection of race preference by ballot is likely to prove yet more emphatic. Preference is widely repugnant in our nation. Legislators across the country, sensitive to the current of public opinion, are quite unlikely to introduce or extend race-based instruments. In the courts, such instruments will find—after *Gratz* and *Grutter*—no refuge.

All things considered, I conclude that the days of race preference in the United States are now numbered and short.

SECTION TWO

Defending Affirmative Action, Defending Preferences

James P. Sterba

Affirmative action is one of the most controversial debated issues in the United States today. Unfortunately, this debate has not always been productive. Many defenders and critics of affirmative action have only a hazy grasp of the legal history of affirmative action; many cannot even agree on how affirmative action should be defined. I think we can do better. In this essay, I start out with a brief legal history of affirmative action in the United States and go on to propose a definition that should be agreeable to all sides in this debate. I then set out a defense of the various forms of affirmative action—outreach, remedial, and diversity affirmative action—captured by this definition, and consider a number of objections to affirmative action so defined. I conclude with a brief discussion of how affirmative action is pursued outside the United States.

1

A Legal History of Affirmative Action in the United States

The first use of the phrase "affirmative action" is usually attributed to Executive Order 10925, issued by President John Kennedy in 1961.[1] Two years later, when Kennedy proposed the legislation that finally became the Civil Rights Act of 1964, he and leading liberals of the 1960s assumed that by simply banning discrimination government could create a level playing field where equal opportunity prevailed. It was an assumption that they borrowed from baseball, where Jackie Robinson and other black players had eventually thrived once racial barriers were removed, and from school desegregation cases in the South that were successful in dismantling dual educational systems.

The Civil Rights Act of 1964 prohibits any employer from discriminating because of an "individual's race, color, religion, sex, or national origin." The act also requires that "no person in the United States shall, on the grounds of race, color, or national origin, be excluded from participation in, be denied the benefits of, or be subjected to discrimination under any program or activity receiving

[1] The term was actually first used in the 1935 National Labor Relations Act. There it meant that an employer who was found to be discriminating against union members or union organizers would have to stop and take affirmative action to place those victims where they would be without the discrimination. For a fuller account of the relevant history, see John Skrentny, *The Ironies of Affirmative Action* (Chicago: University of Chicago, 1996); Barbara Bergmann, *In Defense of Affirmative Action* (New York: Basic Books, 1996); Robert J. Weiss, *We Want Jobs* (New York: Garland Publishers, 1997); Eric Schnapper, "Affirmative Action and the Legislative History of the Fourteenth Amendment," *Virginia Law Review* 71, 1985, pp. 753–98.

Federal financial assistance." This feature of the act proved to be especially important to its implementation.

To secure passage of the Civil Rights Act of 1964 over a southern filibuster that consumed a record 83 working days, it was necessary to deprive the Equal Employment Opportunity Commission of cease-and-desist authority as well as the power to sue. Accordingly, the EEOC was initially left with the task of being a conciliator.

Sixteen days after the act was passed, a riot erupted in Harlem in response to an alleged incident of police brutality. The following week, riots erupted in Brooklyn and Rochester. That summer also saw riots in Philadelphia; Jersey City, Paterson and Elizabeth, New Jersey; and Dixmoor, Illinois. But these were nothing compared to what was to come the following summer in the Watts section of southern Los Angeles. The riot in Watts lasted six days. Thirty-four people were killed, 1,072 injured (the vast majority black), 977 buildings destroyed or damaged, and over 4,000 arrested. These riots and more to come (290 just between 1966 and 1968, according to one study) formed the background during which the Civil Rights Act of 1964 was initially implemented.

To implement the act, President Lyndon Johnson issued to all executive departments and agencies of the federal government Executive Order 11246, which required that "each executive department and agency shall establish and maintain a positive program of equal employment opportunity." In response, the Department of Labor created an Office of Federal Compliance Program (OFCP) to implement Section VI of the act. This left the EEOC with the core responsibility of enforcing a private right of nondiscrimination under Section VII by responding administratively to individual complaints. By 1967, the EEOC had received almost 15,000 complaints. Of these, 6,040 had been earmarked for investigation, and the tiny agency's overwhelmed investigators had completed inquiries on only 3,319. It achieved conciliation with respect to only 110 cases (involving 330 complaints). By 1968, its complaint backlog exceeded 30,000. A decade later, that number had grown to 150,000. In recent years, the EEOC has received about 63,000 complaints annually and has been able to bring suit in no more than 500 a year. Moreover, where suit is brought, cases, as a rule, take the better part of a decade or more to reach a legal resolution.

About the same time that the EEOC was taking on its conciliatory role under the Civil Rights Act of 1964, the Department of Labor's OFCP began collecting employment records by race and using them to evaluate hiring practices. It also started a program by which contractors who had received government contracts would be required to demonstrate that they were prepared to meet affirmative action obligations. As this program was to be applied in Philadelphia (where there was only 1 percent minority membership in the craft unions), those who had received government contracts had to "provide in detail for specific steps to guaranteed equal employment opportunity keyed to the problems and needs of minority groups . . . for the prompt achievement of full and equal opportunity." During Johnson's administration, however, the Philadelphia Program ran into difficulty with the General Accounting Office for introducing further requirements after contracts were awarded. There was also the worry that the affirmative action requirements of this program would run afoul of the Civil Rights Act's prohibition of quotas. However, during the Nixon administration, a revised Philadelphia Program was put forward that specified its affirmative action requirements in terms of a target "range" of minorities (for 1970, it was 4 to 9 percent) that the contractor would try to meet. The program thus was able to eventually withstand a federal district court challenge that it was employing quotas. Moreover, because there were no negotiations after bids were opened in the revised Philadelphia Program, Congress determined that the plan was able to meet the objection of the comptroller general. The success of the Philadelphia Program led the Nixon administration to issue a new set of affirmative action guidelines that now applied to all government contractors with 50 or more employees and at least $50,000 in government business. The guidelines required contractors to take into consideration "the percentage of the minority work force as compared with the total work force in the immediate labor areas," and on the basis of that ratio, to design "specific goals and timetables" to correct any hiring problems.

These actions of the OFCP were clearly more effective at improving the situation of minorities than those the EEOC was able to achieve through its conciliatory approach. Moreover, Congress had a chance, in the Civil Rights Act of 1972, to turn back the racial preference policies adopted by the OFCP (specific amendments were offered to that effect), but it refused to do so.[2] In fact, Congress extended the requirements of the act to state and local governments. Nevertheless, visitors to government contractors in 1994-95 who inquired about their compliance with affirmative action requirements found that 75 percent were in substantial noncompliance. In fact, since 1972 only 41 contractors have been debarred from the list of approved federal contractors out of the thousands whose performance was judged unsatisfactory. In addition, only four of those who have been debarred were large corporations, and in these four cases, the debarment lasted less than three months. One study found that most agencies responsible for nonconstruction contractors reviewed less than 20 percent of all federal contracts. One local office had two people monitoring 29,000 contracts.

Relevant U.S. Supreme Court Cases

The first U.S. Supreme Court decision relevant to affirmative action was *Griggs v. Duke Power Company* (1971). In *Griggs*, the African American petitioners argued that their rights under Title VII of the Civil Rights Act had been violated because Duke Power used criteria for hiring and promotion that adversely affected them but were unrelated to job performance. In an eight-to-zero decision, the court agreed. That was the one and only unanimous decision by the Supreme Court on affirmative action. However, a later Supreme Court with different members overturned this very decision with a five-to-four vote.

The issue of affirmative action in education was first addressed in *DeFunis v. Odegaard* (1974), but there the court decided that the case was moot because DeFunis had already been admitted to the University of Washington law school and was just about to complete his degree. It was only in *Regents of the UC V. Bakke* (1978) that

---

[2]One proposed amendment prohibited "discrimination in reverse by employing persons of a particular race, . . . in either fixed or variable numbers, proportions, percentages, quotas, goals or ranges." Another would have made Title VII's prohibition of preferential treatment applicable to executive orders. Both were voted down (22–44 and 30–60, respectively).

the Supreme Court addressed the issue of affirmative action in education on its merits, and there the court significantly restricted its practice. In that decision, a majority of the court found both the use of quotas in the affirmative action program of the Davis medical school and the school's goal of remedying the effects of societal discrimination to be in violation of the Civil Rights Act and the equal protection clause of the Fourteenth Amendment. However, a different majority (with only Justice Powell as the common member) seemed to allow that taking race and ethnicity into account as a factor to achieve diversity does not violate the equal protection clause of the Fourteenth Amendment.

Thus, the legal effect of the *Bakke* decision was to still allow affirmative action programs in education, but to significantly limit the way that they could be practiced and justified. The *Bakke* court also required strict scrutiny of any race-based affirmative action program in education. This meant that an affirmative action program in education was only permitted if it was narrowly tailored to meet a compelling government interest. This constraint was taken to be required by the equal protection clause. However, the same Congress that passed the Fourteenth Amendment in 1867 also passed race-conscious statutes providing schools and farmland to both free blacks and former slaves that do not appear to satisfy the constraints that the *Bakke* majority found implicit in the Fourteenth Amendment. So it is difficult to see how the constraints on the use of racial classifications imposed by the *Bakke* court could be grounded in the Fourteenth Amendment as that amendment was understood by those who enacted it.

After the *Bakke* decision, there followed a number of U.S. Supreme Court cases concerning affirmative action in employment. In *United Steel Workers v. Weber* (1979), a majority of the court found that a voluntary affirmative action program requiring a temporary quota to eliminate traditional patterns of conspicuous racial segregation was permissible under Title VII of the Civil Rights Act of 1964. In one particular plant where the program was to be applied, the craft work force was less than 2 percent African American, even though the local work force was 39 percent African American. In *Fullilove v. Klutznick* (1980), the Supreme Court found that a congressional affirmative action program that required that

10 percent of a federal grant for public works projects be used to procure the services of minority business enterprises did not violate equal protection under the Fifth or Fourteenth Amendments or the Civil Rights Act of 1964. The court judged the program to be within Congress's power to attempt to eradicate what it determines to be the effects of past discrimination. At the time, it was noted that only 1 percent of all federal procurement was concluded by minority business enterprises, although minorities comprised 15 to 18 percent of the population. Nine years later, however, the court, with three new conservative appointees—Sandra Day O'Connor, Antonin Scalia, and Anthony Kennedy—reversed itself, ruling in *City of Richmond v. Croson* (1989) against a similar affirmative action program of the city of Richmond. In *Wygant v. Jackson Board of Education* (1986), the Supreme Court further required that any institution that sought to compensate for past discrimination must itself be guilty of that same discrimination in the past.

When Ronald Reagan came into office in 1981, he made sure that his key civil rights appointees shared his opposition to affirmative action. To run the EEOC, Reagan selected future supreme court justice Clarence Thomas, who did not hesitate to describe himself as "unalterably opposed to programs that force or even cajole people to hire a certain percentage of minorities." Between 1981 and 1983, the budgets of the EEOC and the OFCCP (the Office of Federal Contract Compliance Program) were respectively cut by 10 and 24 percent, their staffs by 12 and 34 percent, and travel funds for EEOC investigations were eliminated. During the Reagan era, affirmative action under the federal government's contract compliance program virtually ceased to exist.

In *Wards Cove Packing Company v. Antonio* (1989), the Supreme Court again reversed itself, this time rejecting its earlier *Griggs v. Duke Power Company* decision (1971), which had held that employers were ultimately responsible for showing the "business necessity" of any employment practice that was shown to have discriminatory impact on minorities. In this new decision, the court held that it was the employees who had to prove discriminatory intent in such cases, something that is very difficult to do. This decision, however, ultimately sparked a legislative response in the form of the Civil Rights Act of 1991. Initially, President

George H. W. Bush opposed the act, calling it a "quota bill," and in fact vetoed an earlier version. But in the wake of the public debate over Anita Hill's charge that Clarence Thomas, Bush's Supreme Court nominee, had sexually harassed her, Bush's options became limited, and he signed the bill into law. This new civil rights act shifted the burden of proof in disparate-impact cases back to the employer. It required a company with an employment practice that resulted in disparate impact on minorities to demonstrate that its practice was both "job related" and "consistent with business necessity."

With Clarence Thomas taking Thurgood Marshall's seat on the Supreme Court, the court sought to impose further restrictions on affirmative action. In *Adarand Constructors v. Pena* (1995), the court, in a five-to-four decision, struck down two of its earlier decisions, ruling that a standard of strict scrutiny applied to race-based action by the federal as well as state and local government.[3] The presumption of this standard of strict scrutiny is that raced-based actions are seldom relevant to any constitutionally acceptable purpose. The court also held that its standard of review "is not dependent on the race of those burdened or benefited by a particular (race-based) classification." Justice O'Connor denied that this now meant that affirmative action was to be equated with invidious discrimination (or more colorfully, as Justice Stevens put it in his dissent, that a welcome mat was to be equated with a "No Trespassing" sign). But Justices Thomas and Scalia, for their part, endorsed this identification. In Thomas's words, "government-sponsored racial discrimination based on benign prejudice is just as noxious as discrimination inspired by malicious prejudice."

Recent Developments

More recently, in *Hopwood v. Texas* (1996), the United States Court of Appeals for the Fifth Circuit argued that an educational institution can only justifiably implement an affirmative action program if it is designed simply to correct for the past discrimination of that

---

[3]The decisions struck down were *Fullilove v. Klutznick* (1980) and *Metro Broadcasting v. Federal Communications Commission* (1990), with respect to the need for strict scrutiny when dealing with racial classifications.

very institution. The goal of educational diversity was also no longer judged sufficient to justify an affirmative action program.[4] In response to *Hopwood,* the Texas State Legislature passed a law requiring the University of Texas at Austin and Texas A &M University to admit all applicants who graduated in the top 10 percent of their high school class. By 1999, under this 10 percent plan, undergraduate enrollment at the University of Texas at Austin was as diverse as the last class enrolling prior to the *Hopwood* decision (1996).

In the same year that the *Hopwood* decision took effect in Texas, voters in California approved Proposition 209, called the California Civil Rights Initiative.[5] It amended the state's constitution so as to rule out "preferential treatment to any individual or group on the basis of race, sex, color or national origins." Earlier in 1995, following intense lobbying by then Governor Pete Wilson, the University of California Board of Regents voted to end racial preferences in its university system. In 2001, however, the California Regents reversed themselves, rescinding their earlier ban on racial preferences. In this same year, California began admitting the top 4 percent of each high school in the state's graduates, regardless of the students' SAT scores, provided that they had taken certain required courses. As a consequence of these and other measures, the UC system admitted 18.6 percent black, Hispanic, and American Indians first year undergraduates for the fall of 2001, just shy of 1997's 18.8 percent, the last time racial preferences were used in admissions. However, a significant disparity can still be found at the system's flagship campuses of UCLA and Berkeley, as well as at San Diego and Santa Barbara.

---

[4]Actually, the legal jurisdiction of the *Hopwood* decision by the Court of Appeals for the Fifth Circuit included Texas, Louisiana, and Mississippi, but its legal effect is only being felt in Texas because Louisiana and Mississippi are still under court orders to desegregate their public universities.

[5]In 1998, a similar amendment was passed in the state of Washington (Initiative 200).

2

A Definition of Affirmative Action

Surprisingly, it turns out that the degree to which people in general are in favor of affirmative action depends in large measure on how that policy is described. For example, a *Los Angeles Times* poll showed that 58 percent of African Americans "opposed special preferences based on race and not merit," while a *Washington Post*/ABC poll showed that roughly two out of three women "oppose preferential treatment for women." On the other hand, according to pollster Lou Harris, every poll that has asked simply whether people "favor or oppose affirmative action—without strict quotas" has obtained a similar result: people favor affirmative action. Support runs 55 percent in favor to 40 percent against in more recent polls, down from the average majority of 60 percent in favor to 38 percent against in polls taken over the past 25 years. Moreover, when people in California were asked whether they would still favor Proposition 209 if it outlawed all affirmative action programs for women and minorities, support for 209 dropped to 30 percent while opposition rose to 56 percent. In addition, if you ask people about affirmative action programs at their workplaces, 80 percent of Euro-American workers strongly support the programs they know about and that directly affect them. According to another study, affirmative action programs were less palatable when they were applied to African Americans and most acceptable for the elderly and people with disabilities. Programs for women and the poor fell somewhere in between.[6]

---

[6]The Supreme Court just recently ruled, however, that Congress does not have the authority to require that states ensure that the handicapped have certain (access) rights. See *Board of Trustees of the University of Alabama v. Patricia Garrett* (2001).

As one might expect, this lack of clarity as to how to characterize affirmative action has affected the debate over whether affirmative action can be justified. Frequently, the affirmative action that critics attack is not the affirmative action that most people defend.[7] Accordingly, it would seem that if we are going to bring this debate any closer to a resolution, we need some agreement on what we should call affirmative action. In this regard, I think it is more appropriate for critics of affirmative action to take their characterization of affirmative action from those who defend it rather than devise characterizations of their own. In this way, critics of affirmative action, assuming there are any left once we get straight about its proper characterization, can then avoid missing their target.[8] It would also be helpful if defenders of affirmative action were to formulate their definitions of affirmative action so as to avoid as much as possible the criticisms that have been directed against it. At least this is what I will try to do in this essay.[9]

Here I propose to define affirmative action as a policy of favoring qualified women and minority candidates over qualified men or nonminority candidates, with the immediate goals of outreach, remedying discrimination, or achieving diversity, and the ultimate goals of attaining a colorblind (racially just) and gender-free (sexually just) society (see diagram).

---

[7]For example, what I defend as affirmative action is not captured by what Louis Pojman calls "strong affirmative action." Yet, it should also be noted that Pojman combines his opposition to affirmative action with support of a range of more radical welfare and environmental programs, which I too support, but which, unlike affirmative action, are politically unfeasible at the present time. See, in particular, his "Straw Man or Straw Theory: A Reply to Mosley," *International Journal of Applied Philosophy* vol. 17 (1998), pp. 169–80, and his "Pedaling Power: Sustainable Transportation," in his *Environmental Ethics,* 3rd ed. (Belmont, CA: Wadsworth Publishing, 2001), pp. 549–51.

[8]Critics of affirmative action need to target the most morally defensible form of affirmative action if they really want to show that affirmative action, however it is characterized, is morally objectionable. In other words, critics of affirmative action need to address their strongest opponents.

[9]I have also proposed a definition that allows that particular affirmative action programs can be justified or not depending on how well or ill they instantiate the goals of affirmative action.

Affirmative Action
   Its Immediate Goals
      -Outreach
      -Remedying Discrimination
         Putting an End to Discrimination
         Compensating for Past Discrimination
      -Diversity
   Its Ultimate Goals
      -A Colorblind (Racially Just) and Gender-free
        (Sexually Just) Society

A colorblind society is a society in which race has no more significance than eye color has in most societies. A gender-free society is a society in which sex has no more significance than eye color has in most societies. It is a society in which the traits that are truly desirable and distributable in society are equally open to both women and men.[10] The ultimate goals can be understood to be racial justice and sexual justice. Since our society is far from being either colorblind (racially just) or gender-free (sexually just), it is generally recognized that to make the transition to a racially just or a sexually just society, we will have to take race and sex into account. For example, after the U.S. Civil War, Congress funded programs explicitly for the benefit of free blacks and former slaves, and after World War II, the West German government approved large compensations to individual Jews and to the newly created state of Israel. In addition, the U.S. government from time to time compensates American Indians for past injustices against them. For example, in 2000, the U.S. Congress approved giving a New Mexico Indian tribe $23 million and about 4,600 acres to settle lawsuits over land claimed under a grant from the king of Spain more than three hundred years ago. In general, if we want to get beyond any kind of significant

[10]For further discussion of the ideal of gender-free society, which I also call an androgynous society, see my books *Justice for Here and Now* (New York: Cambridge University Press, 1998), and *Three Challenges to Ethics* (New York: Oxford University Press, 2001).

wrongdoing, we need to take into account who wronged whom, and what were the consequences, and then try to set things right. There is no other morally acceptable way to get beyond significant wrongdoing.

Even the strongest critics of affirmative action acknowledge that to advance toward a colorblind (racially just) and gender-free (sexually just) society, we will sometimes have to depart from the status quo, for example, by favoring qualified women or minority candidates over qualified men or nonminority candidates when the qualified women or minority candidates have themselves directly suffered from proven past discrimination. They will consider such cases to be justified uses of racial or sexual classifications, and *not* consider them to involve racial preferences. However, these critics will typically object to any use of any kind of sexual or racial proportionality as a means for achieving a colorblind (racially just) or gender-free (sexually just) society. They will regard such uses of sexual or racial proportionality to involve racial or sexual preferences, and thereby to be unjust. So these critics will favor some instances of affirmative action captured by my definition and be against others. But the same will hold for defenders of affirmative action. They too will favor some instances and be against others. Defenders and critics of affirmative action just disagree about which instances of affirmative action we should support and which we should oppose.

As I define it, affirmative action can have a number of immediate goals. It can have the goal of outreach, with the purpose of searching out qualified women and minority candidates who would otherwise not know about or apply for the available positions, and then hiring or accepting only those who are actually the most qualified. Affirmative action can also attempt to remedy discrimination. Here, there are two possibilities (see diagram on p. 201). First, an affirmative action program can be designed simply to put an end to an existing discriminatory practice, and to create, possibly for the first time in a particular setting, a truly equal opportunity environment. Second, an affirmative action program can attempt to compensate for past discrimination and the effects of that discrimination. The idea here is that stopping discrimination is one thing and making up for past discrimination and the effects of that discrimination is another, and that both need to be done. Still another form of affirmative action has the goal of diversity, where the pursuit of diversity is, in turn, justified either in terms of its educational benefits or in terms of its ability to create a more effective workforce in such areas as policing or community relations.[11] Here it might even be said that the affirmative action candidates are, in fact, the most qualified candidates overall, since candidates who do not bring diversity would not be as qualified.[12] As it turns out, all other forms of affirmative action can be understood in terms of their immediate goals to be either outreach, remedial, or diversity affirmative action, where remedial affirmative action further divides into two subtypes; one subtype simply seeks to end present discrimination and create an equal playing field, the other subtype attempts to compensate for past discrimination and its effects (see diagram on p. 201).

Assuming that these are the basic types and subtypes of affirmative action, we need to examine them to determine when specifically they can be justified. Let us begin with outreach affirmative action.

[11]I am defining affirmative action for a context in which the benefits of diversity can serve the ultimate goal of colorblindness (racial justice) rather than just being compatible with it, as would obtain in a colorblind or racially just society.

[12]One might wonder how diversity affirmative action candidates could be the most qualified, given that, as I will argue later, they may still need remedial help for a certain period of time. The reason for this is that the qualifications that affirmative action candidates lack can be remedied, whereas the qualification that nonaffirmative action candidates clearly lack—diversity—usually cannot be remedied. It is in this sense that nonaffirmative action candidates are not the most qualified.

3

A Defense of Outreach Affirmative Action

Outreach affirmative action is easily the most defensible form of affirmative action. Even strong critics of affirmative action, like Louis Pojman and Thomas Sowell, defend this particular form of affirmative action. Thus, Pojman supports what he calls "weak affirmative action," which includes the "widespread advertisement to groups not previously represented in certain privileged positions." Similarly, Sowell holds that "Racial discrimination is [an] obvious area where merely to 'cease and desist' is not enough. If a firm has engaged in racial discrimination for years and has an all-white force as a result, then simply to stop explicit discrimination will mean little as long as the firm continues to hire its current employees' friends and relatives through word of mouth referrals. . . . Clearly, the area of racial discrimination is one in which positive or affirmative steps of some kind seem reasonable."[13] There is also considerable evidence that outreach affirmative action is needed. Social scientists have discovered that many employers tend to recruit selectively and informally, directing their efforts at neighborhoods, institutions, and media outlets that have relatively small minority populations or constituencies, as compared to the general population.[14] For instance, in one study of Chicago-area employers, it was found that in an effort to screen

[13]Thomas Sowell, *Affirmative Action Reconsidered* (Washington, D.C.: The American Enterprise Institute for Public Policy Research, 1975), p. 3. Likewise, Supreme Court Justice Clarence Thomas at his confirmation hearings spoke passionately of his support for outreach affirmative action.
[14]Kathryn M. Neckerman and Joleen Kirschenman, "Hiring Strategies, Racial Bias and Inner-City Workers," *Social Problems* 38 (1991), pp. 433, 437–41.

potential applicants, employers engaged in a variety of race-neutral recruitment mechanisms that had the effect of "disproportionately screen[ing] out inner-city blacks." For example, 40 percent of employers failed to advertise job openings in newspapers and relied instead on informal employee networking to generate job applicants. Of those employers who did advertise job openings, two-thirds advertised in neighborhood or "white ethnic" newspapers rather than in "black newspapers." While some employers recruited in both metropolitan and suburban schools, many of these employers gave applications from suburban schools more attention. According to another study, about 86 percent of available jobs do not appear in classified advertisements, and 80 percent of executives find their jobs through networking. Thus, there is much that businesses and educational institutions can do by way of outreach affirmative action to ensure that minorities and women know about the availability of jobs and positions that in the past were foreclosed to them.

Summing up the main requirement for outreach affirmative action is the following:

> All reasonable steps must be taken to ensure that qualified minority and women candidates have available to them the same educational and job opportunities that are available to nonminority or male candidates.

4

A Defense of Remedial Affirmative Action

(1) The Remedy of Compensating for Past Discrimination

Virtually everyone also accepts the justification of at least some form of remedial affirmative action. Although the U.S. Supreme Court has adopted different positions at different times, it has always held that it is permissible to adopt remedial affirmative action in an institution as compensation for identifiable acts of purposeful discrimination committed by that very institution. Of course, it is rare for an institution that is engaging in affirmative action to actually admit that it has committed identifiable acts of purposeful discrimination, or at least to admit that it did so in the recent past. This is because such an admission would render the institution vulnerable to still further claims of compensation from other victims. Consequently, institutions frequently engage in remedial affirmative action of this sort only when they have been found guilty of discrimination, or, more likely, when they have been "forced" into accepting a legal settlement.

In 1973, AT&T reached a settlement with the Justice Department in which it agreed to restructure its hiring and promotion policies. Up to that time, half the company's 700,000 employees were women, but all of the women were either telephone operators or secretaries. The company had been categorizing virtually all of its jobs as either men's work or women's work. Women, along with minority men, were virtually excluded from the higher paying positions in the company. The agreement required AT&T to pay $15 million in back wages to 13,000 women and 2,000 minority men, and to give $23 million in raises to 36,000 employees who had been harmed by previous policies.[15] More

---

[15]*EEOC v. AT&T*, 365 F. Supp. 1105 (1973); Cynthia Epstein, "Affirmative Action," *Dissent* (fall 1995), pp. 463–65.

recently, in 1993, Shoney's Restaurant chain settled a racial discrimination case against it.[16] Shoney's had been tracking blacks into kitchen jobs so that most employees in the dining area would be white. The case arose when two white managers complained that they had been pressured by their supervisors to restrict blacks to kitchen jobs, and that they had been fired when they had resisted that pressure. As more evidence was gathered, the case grew into a class-action suit against Shoney's nationwide. This case was settled out of court for $105 million. Even more recently, in 1997, Texaco reached a settlement in a class-action suit against it charging that the company systematically passed over black employees for promotions in favor of less experienced whites, and that the company fostered a racially hostile environment. Some participants in the suit reported that they were called "uppity" for asking questions; others said that black employees were called "orangutans" and "porch monkeys." The agreement was reached after disclosure of a secret tape recording of senior Texaco executives, revealing them planning the destruction of documents demanded in the lawsuit and belittling black employees, referring to them as "black jelly beans" and "niggers." The settlement for $176 million is the largest race-discrimination settlement in U.S. history. It called for lump-sum payments averaging around $63,000 to about 1,300 black employees. In addition, salaried blacks still with Texaco got an 11 percent pay raise worth an estimated $26 million over five years, and Texaco also paid $35 million for a five-year task force that revised its personnel programs. Peter Bijur, who was Chair and CEO of Texaco at the time, said that the racial discrimination problems at his company represented just the "tip of the iceberg" in corporate America.[17]

---

[16]Steve Watkins, *The Black O: Racism and Redemption in an American Corporate Empire* (Athens: University of Georgia Press, 1997). The title of this book derives from the company's practice, not found in any corporate manual, of color-coding minority job applications by blackening the "O" in Shoney's to make sure they were passed over for certain jobs.

[17]Alison Frankel, "Tale of the Tapes," *The American Lawyer* (March 1997); *New York Times*, 4 November 1996; "Texaco Chairman Says Company's Bias is 'Tip of the Iceberg' in Corporate American," *Jet*, 16 December 1996, p. 5. There was also a dispute about exactly which belittling remarks were spoken on the tape. See *New York Times*, 11 November 1996.

Most recently, in 2000, the Coca-Cola Company agreed to settle a racial discrimination case in which it was accused of erecting a corporate hierarchy in which black employees were clustered at the bottom of the pay scale, earning an average of $26,000 a year less than white workers. One plaintiff, who worked for Coca-Cola for 13 years, said she made less than white workers she supervised. The settlement of $156 million provided as many as 2,000 current and former black salaried employees with an average of $40,000, while the four main plaintiffs received up to $300,000 apiece.[18]

(2) The Remedy of Ending Present Discrimination

Since, in all four of these cases, compensation was paid to those who claimed they were harmed by the discriminatory practices of their companies, few opponents of affirmative action have objected to remedial actions of this sort. But there are other forms of remedial affirmative action in which the individuals who benefit are not the ones who were actually discriminated against by the institution that is providing the remedial affirmative action.[19] For instance, in *Local 28 of the Sheetmetal Workers Union v. EEOC* (1986), the U.S. Supreme Court upheld a compensatory affirmative action program that required Local 28 of the Sheetmetal Workers Union in New York City to increase its minority membership by admitting into its training program one minority apprentice for each nonminority apprentice until the union reached a 29 percent minority membership. The goal of 29 percent minority membership was based on the number of minorities in the relevant labor pool in New York City at the time. From 1964 to 1986, Local 28 had been found in contempt of every legal attempt to get it to admit minorities into its virtually all-white union. In fact, in 1966 minority applicants, benefiting from a tutoring program, were awarded 9 of the top 10 scores and 75 percent of the top 65 scores on the union's own apprenticeship test, but that year the union refused to abide by the results of its own test.

Clearly, the main beneficiaries of the court's decision were to be minorities who were subsequently admitted into the union by way

---

[18]*New York Times*, 17 November 2000.
[19]Actually, this sort of remedial affirmative action was also mandated by other parts of the AT&T and Shoney's, Texaco, and Coca-Cola settlements.

of its apprenticeship program; these beneficiaries would not be, for the most part, persons who had been previously discriminated against by the union. Yet this is just what we would expect given that the main goal of the court was to get the union to stop discriminating against minorities. Thus, there is no reason to think that those who would benefit, once the union stopped discriminating, would be limited to persons whom the union had actually discriminated against in the past. Rather, they would be minorities who now, under conditions of equal opportunity, would be admitted into the union roughly in proportion to their availability in the relevant labor pool.[20] So it is possible to view the Supreme Court's decision here as simply an attempt to create an equal opportunity playing field from which minorities would rightly benefit, even if they hadn't been harmed by Local 28's past discriminatory practices.[21] Yet sometimes remedial affirmative action will attempt to do more than simply create an equal opportunity playing field. It will also attempt to correct for the harm done by present and past discrimination, as the AT&T, Shoney's, Texaco, and Coca-Cola cases demonstrate.

[20]Moreover, given that at the time only a fraction of minorities who had satisfactorily completed apprenticeship programs were actually admitted into New York craft unions, it was reasonable to admit minorities into Local 28's apprenticeship program at the higher rate, one to one, if one hoped to have minorities actually admitted into the union in proportion to their availability in the local labor pool. In fact, of 600 minorities who successfully completed other union training programs in New York City some years before this Supreme Court case was decided, only 40 actually received union books. See Weiss 1997, p. 215.

[21]I also think that it is possible to interpret or justify some earlier court decisions in the same way that I have done with this court case. In *Contractors Association of Eastern Pennsylvania v. Secretary of Labor* (1973), which dealt with the Philadelphia Program, the federal court was concerned with a five-county Philadelphia area where minorities were 30 percent of all construction workers but only 1 percent of the workers in six craft unions. The federal government's Philadelphia Program (see p. 193) conditioned the granting of federal construction money upon acceptance of a set of goals and timetables for improving minority apprenticeship or membership with respect to these unions. In this case, the court found the Philadelphia Program to be an acceptable way of increasing equal opportunity for minorities in the Philadelphia area. Likewise, in *United Steel Workers of America v. Weber* (1979), the factual situation was quite similar. Blacks represented 39 percent of the local

(3) Statistical Disparities

In making the case for remedial affirmative action, it is generally useful to be able to appeal to statistical disparities (disparate impact) as prima facie evidence of a discriminatory practice. The fact that 50 percent of AT&T's work force during the late 1960s and early 1970s was women, at the same time that they were almost totally absent from management or craftworker positions, was assumed to be prima facie evidence that AT&T had discriminated against them. Similarly, the fact that there were virtually no minority members in Local 28 in New York City, when minorities made up 29 percent of the relevant labor pool at the time, was assumed to be prima facie evidence that Local 28 was discriminating against minorities. Of course, it is always possible that such prima facie evidence of discrimination can be rebutted, but it is important, once such evidence has been provided, that the burden of proof should shift to the employer or union to show why this disparity was unavoidable.

There is also good reason to think that the use of statistical disparities (disparate impacts) to establish a prima facie case for discrimination should be more broadly applied throughout society. Thus, Barbara Bergmann has shown that if you look at American industry by occupational sectors, there is considerable variation among businesses within each section with respect to their hiring of women

---

population in Gramercy, Louisiana, but only 2 percent of the craftworkers and 15 percent of the unskilled workers at the plant, up from 10 percent in 1969, when the company began to hire unskilled workers at the gate on a "one white, one black" basis. However, the company continued the practice of hiring skilled craft workers, from virtually all-white craft unions outside the Gramercy area, and this policy accounted for the small percentage of minorities in craft positions at the plant. Under pressure from the federal government, Kaiser Aluminum and the unions agreed to jointly manage a craft apprenticeship program that would accept one minority worker and one white worker from two different seniority lists until the percentage of minority workers approximated the percentage of minorities in the Gramercy area. Since neither Kaiser Aluminum nor the unions nor Weber, who brought suit against the apprenticeship program, was interested in justifying the program as a means for putting an end to discrimination at the Gramercy plant, the case was argued and decided on other grounds. Nevertheless, the case could have been argued and decided on grounds similar to those that were used in the cases from New York City and Philadelphia.

and minorities.[22] For example, within the auto industry, General Motors has three times as many women managers as Ford, and among retail businesses, McDonald's has four times as many minority managers as Safeway Stores and twice as many as Kroger. Disparities such as these need to be further investigated to determine whether or not they might provide grounds for remedial affirmative action.

It is sometimes objected that statistical disparities (disparate impacts) do not provide suitable grounds for claims of discrimination. Thomas Sowell has argued that discrimination alone cannot explain the presence or absence of statistical disparities among different ethnic groups.[23] Thus, Sowell points out that groups such as the Japanese and Chinese in the United States have fared very well despite racial discrimination against them.[24] But while Sowell is right that an *absence* of statistical disparities may be due to the fact that racial discrimination has been overcome with respect to some groups (e.g., Japanese and Chinese in the United States), this does not show that the *presence* of disparities with respect to other groups in the United States (i.e., African Americans, American Indians, and Hispanic Americans) is not due to more virulent forms of racial discrimination that have yet to be overcome. Nor does it show that a government committed to both equal opportunity and rectifying for past discrimination would not want to correct for these more virulent forms of discrimination with remedial affirmative action. In fact, such utilization of statistical disparities has been endorsed by the U.S Supreme Court itself:

> There is no doubt that where gross statistical disparities can be shown, they alone in a proper case may constitute prima facie proof of a pattern or practice of discrimination.[25]

---

[22]Bergmann, chapter 2.

[23]See Thomas Sowell, *Civil Rights: Rhetoric or Reality?* (New York: William Morrow, 1984); *Preferential Politics: An International Perspective* (New York: William Morrow, 1990); and *Race and Culture* (New York: Basic Books, 1994).

[24]There is also evidence that Asian Americans tend to be concentrated at the extremes, at both the high and the low ends of social status indicators, and that even when Asian Americans are successful, they still tend to experience a "glass ceiling" that limits their success. See Deborah Woo, *Glass Ceilings and Asian Americans* (Lanham, MD: Rowman and Littlefield, 2000).

[25]*City of Richmond v. J. A. Croson Co.* (1987), p. 501. The court held this even as it rejected a particular affirmative action program as being unconstitutional.

There is good reason, therefore, to recognize that statistical disparities can serve as prima facie evidence of discrimination, which then must be shown to be operationally necessary for the business, union, or institution involved in order to preclude the need for remedial affirmative action.[26]

---

[26]Of course, sometimes statistical disparities, even between whites and blacks, provide no evidence at all of discrimination, as in the high proportion of African Americans in the National Basketball Association and in other professional sports. Fortunately, professional sports is one area where talent, or the lack of it, is easily manifest. Moreover, given the general favoritism enjoyed by whites in U.S. society, surely no professional team in the United States is going to prefer a clearly less-talented African American player over a more talented white player.

5

Remedial Affirmative Action and the U.S. Supreme Court

What we need to determine is exactly when remedial affirmative action is justified. The current legal answer in the United States, which has been defended by a number of five-to-four votes of the Supreme Court, is that remedial affirmative action is justified when the following two requirements are met:

1. The past discrimination that is to be remedied must be proven discrimination by the institution that is engaging in the affirmative action in question. Thus, using race-based affirmative action to remedy unproven discrimination, usually referred to as "societal discrimination," or even to remedy proven discrimination that cannot be attributed to the institution engaged in the affirmative action in question cannot be justified. (This approach was first endorsed in *Bakke* [1978] and later in Wygant [1986].)[27]

2. Racial classifications must be regarded as presumptively suspect; it does not matter whether the classifications are intended to remedy the results of prior racial discrimination or whether they are intended to foster or maintain racial discrimination. Accordingly, any use of racial classifications must satisfy a strict scrutiny analysis, that is, it must be narrowly tailored to meet a compelling government interest, where the presumption is

[27]It is important to note here that societal discrimination is simply unproven discrimination. If discrimination can be proven, then it is not societal discrimination in this sense, even if it can be proven to be caused by society as a whole.

that only seldom will such use of racial classifications be justified. (This concept, first endorsed in *Bakke* [1978], was later reaffirmed in *Croson* [1987].)

Although the U.S. Supreme Court defends these two requirements as being either necessitated by or compatible with the Civil Rights Act of 1964 and/or the U.S. Constitution, particularly the Fourteenth Amendment, most of the arguments for these two requirements are found within the Supreme Court decisions themselves, beginning with the *Bakke* decision in 1978. It is important, therefore, to examine the arguments the court provides for these requirements to determine whether they are successful.

(1) The First Requirement

Consider the first requirement—the limitation of remedial affirmative action to proven discrimination by the institution engaged in the affirmative action in question. Surely, it would be unreasonable for anyone today to deny that African Americans and other minorities suffer not only from current discrimination but also from the continuing effects of past discrimination.[28]

Evidence of Racial Discrimination

In the United States today, almost half of all black children live in poverty. Black unemployment is twice that of white, and the median

[28]See *New York Times*, 12 July 1994; Gerald Jaynes and Robin Williams, eds, *A Common Destiny* (Washington, D.C.: National Academy Press, 1989); Andrew Hacker, *Two Nations* (New York: Ballantine Books, 1992); Gertrude Ezorsky, *Racism and Justice* (Ithaca: Cornell University Press, 1991); *Hunger 1995: Fifth Annual Report on the State of World Hunger* (Silver Spring: Bread for the World Institute, 1995); Todd Michael Furman, "A Dialogue Concerning Claim Jumping and Compensatory Justice," *Teaching Philosophy*, 21 (1998), pp. 131–51; Deborah Jones, "The Future of Bakke: Will Social Science Matter?" *Ohio State Law Journal* 59 1 (1998), pp. 1054–67; George Curry, ed., *The Affirmative Action Debate* (Reading, MA: Perseus Books, 1996); Tom L. Beauchamp and Norman Bowie, *Ethical Theory and Business*, 5th ed. (Upper Saddle River: Prentice-Hall 1996); Bryan Grapes, ed., *Affirmative Action*. (San Diego: Greenhaven Press, 2000), Introduction; Weiss, 1997; M. V. Lee Badgett, *Economic Perspectives on Affirmative Action* (Washington, D.C.: Joint Center for Political and Economic Studies, 1995).

net worth of white families is ten times that of black families. The infant mortality rate in many black communities is twice that of whites. Blacks are twice as likely as whites to be robbed, seven times more likely to be murdered or to die of tuberculosis. A male living in New York's Harlem is less likely to reach 65 than a resident of Bangladesh. Blacks comprise 50 percent of the maids and garbage collectors but only 4 percent of the managers and 3 percent of the physicians and lawyers. According to a United Nations study, white Americans, when considered as a separate nation, rank first in the world in well-being (a measure that combines life expectancy, educational achievements, and income). African Americans rank twenty-seventh, and Hispanic Americans thirty-second. According to the U.S. Federal Reserve Board, the loan rejection rate for blacks in the highest income bracket is identical to the rejection rate of whites in the lowest income bracket. According to another study, minority applicants are 50 percent more likely to be denied a loan than white applicants of equivalent economic status. In a study by the Urban Institute, equally qualified, identically dressed, white and African American applicants for jobs were used to test for bias in the job market for newspaper-advertised positions. Whites and African Americans were matched identically for age, work experience, speech patterns, personal characteristics, and physical build. The study found repeated discrimination against African American male applicants. The white men received three times as many job offers as equally qualified African Americans who interviewed for the same positions. According to a 1998 study conducted by the Fair Housing Council in Washington, D.C., minorities in the United States are discriminated against 40 percent of the time when they attempt to rent apartments or buy homes. Another study revealed that African American and Hispanic American job applicants suffer blatant and easily identifiable discrimination once in every five times they apply for a job. African American men with bachelor's degrees earn as much as $15,180 less than their white counterparts. While native-born white males make up only 41 percent of the U.S. population, they comprise 80 percent of all tenured professors, 97 percent of all school superintendents, and 97 percent of senior managerial positions in Fortune 1000 industrial and Fortune 500 service companies. African Americans hold only 0.6 percent, Asian

Americans 0.3 percent, and Hispanic Americans 0.4 percent of the senior managerial positions. For 1993, it was estimated that the failure to employ blacks in jobs using simply their *current* skills for that year represented a $137 billion loss to the U.S economy. This means that rather than being in jobs for which they are underqualified, many blacks are actually *overqualified* for the jobs they hold. One study done in the Los Angeles area found that race and skin color affected the probability of obtaining employment by as much as 52 percent. While whites and light-skinned African Americans were relatively likely to find employment when searching for a job, dark-skinned men were not. In fact, dark-skinned men were twice as likely as others to remain unemployed. According to another study, only 10.3 percent of light-skinned African American men with 13 or more years of schooling were unemployed, compared with 19.4 percent of their dark-skinned counterparts with similar education. Among men who had participated in job-training programs, light-skinned blacks actually had a lower jobless rate than their white counterparts—11.1 percent, compared with 14.5 percent. Yet the rate for dark-skinned African American men with job training was 26.8 percent. Thus, there is plenty of evidence that, at least in the United States, African Americans and other minorities not only are discriminated against but also suffer from the continuing effects of past discrimination.[29]

Given the widespread evidence of current discrimination and the continuing effects of past discrimination in the United States, no defender of affirmative action would have reason to object to restricting remedial affirmative action to discrimination that can be proven in some appropriate way. The U.S. Supreme Court itself has allowed that such discrimination can be proven by judicial, legislative, or administrative findings. The real worry here, however, is that the court has chosen to impose too demanding a standard of proof, making it far too difficult for institutions to correct for past discrimination.

---

[29]In a recent undergraduate class, most of my white students regarded discrimination against minorities as so severe that they would not agree to change their skin color, even if it were possible, for a half million dollars! I didn't try to see if they would accept a higher sum.

City of Richmond v. Croson

Consider the decision the U.S. Supreme Court reached in *Croson* (1989). Here the court held that a generalized assertion of past discrimination in the entire construction industry (the basis of the federal set-aside accepted in *Fullilove* [1980]) was insufficient to justify a minority set-aside by the city of Richmond. The court also ruled that further evidence, showing that while the population of Richmond was 50 percent black, less than 1 percent of the city's construction business had been awarded to minority-owned enterprises, and all the building trade associations in Virginia had at most one or two black members, was insufficient to justify the city's affirmative action program. The court further held that the relevant comparison in this case was not between the percentage of blacks in Richmond and the percentage of the city's construction business that had been awarded to minority-owned enterprises, but rather between the number of minority-owned enterprises in Richmond and the percentage of the city's construction business that had been awarded to those enterprises. The court's general view here was that when special qualifications are required to fill particular jobs, the relevant comparison is not to the general population, but rather to the smaller group of individuals who possess the necessary qualifications. But if discrimination had been as rampant in the construction industry nationwide, and in the city of Richmond, as the evidence indicated, then clearly not many minority-owned enterprises would have been able to survive in that environment. Thus a small number of minority-owned enterprises in the Richmond area is exactly what one would expect if there had been significant discrimination. Accordingly, we cannot use the existence of a small number of minority-owned enterprises to indicate the absence of discrimination. In fact, without an explanation to the contrary, it would be reasonable to infer that a small number of minority-owned enterprises in the Richmond area is evidence of discrimination. Why else would minorities in the Richmond area not have taken advantage of the construction opportunities present there? In the South, under slavery, more than 80 percent of those working as masons, blacksmiths, carpenters, and painters were slaves, according to a census taken in 1865. Even in the case at issue, Croson, the owner of the white-owned, Ohio-based enterprise, actually lost his contract with the city of Richmond because Brown, the owner of the minority-owned, Richmond-based firm that Croson tried to subcontract, astutely took advantage of the opportunity provided to bypass Croson and deal directly with the city.

In any case, the evidence of past discrimination in the *Croson* case is overwhelming. There were the numerous national studies documenting discrimination in the construction industry, some of them commissioned by Congress, none of which gave the least indication that the construction industry in Richmond was an exception to this national pattern. And then there was the particular evidence presented before the Richmond City Council, all of which supported the view that discrimination in the local construction industry was widespread. In fact, no one presented any contrary evidence to the City Council, although some members of the council did oppose its decision, and so would presumably have introduced such evidence had it been available. Thus, when the U.S. Supreme Court concludes that there was insufficient evidence of discrimination to justify a five-year set-aside remedial affirmative action program by the city of Richmond, it is obviously making it far too difficult to correct for past discrimination.

In addition to setting an overdemanding standard for proof of discrimination, the court further requires that any institution that seeks to compensate for past discrimination must itself be guilty of that very discrimination. While such a restriction might have seemed appropriate when it was first imposed by the Supreme Court on a race-based layoff policy in Jackson, Michigan, it is surely inappropriate when it is used to invalidate the finding of discrimination in the construction industry in the Richmond area. In *Croson*, the court found against the city of Richmond because the city did not sufficiently implicate itself in the past discrimination that it sought to correct. But most institutions that are considering whether to engage in remedial affirmative action would understandably be quite reluctant to implicate themselves in the very discrimination they are seeking to correct because that would, in turn, open them up to further liability and censure. Moreover, once sufficient evidence of discrimination has been provided, there seems to be no reason to impose the additional requirement that the agent engaged in the affirmative action program must also be implicated in the discrimination it is

seeking to correct.[30] Given these considerations, the first requirement as to when remedial affirmative action is justified should be:

> The past discrimination that is to be remedied must be proven dis-
> crimination, but the institution that is engaging in the affirmative ac-
> tion need not be implicated in that proven discrimination in order for
> the affirmative action in question to be justified.

(2) The Second Requirement

Turning to the U.S. Supreme Court's second requirement for remedial affirmative action, we find that it begins with a reasonable
assumption that racial classifications should be presumptively suspect. Surely, in the United States, there are good historical reasons
to assume that racial classifications are presumptively suspect.

New Deal Policies

Even the New Deal policies of Franklin Delano Roosevelt significantly discriminated against blacks and other minorities.[31] For example, the Social Security Act of 1935 was purposefully designed to
exclude blacks and Hispanics by denying benefits to servants and
agricultural workers in places where they were overwhelmingly

---

[30]The *Hopwood* court has further restricted the scope of the discrimination for
which an institution can claim to be responsible. Thus, the court held that law
school at the University of Texas could only seek to correct discrimination engaged in by its own law school and so could not justify its affirmative action
program as a partial attempt to remedy discrimination in the State of Texas's
educational system as a whole, even though that system was still under desegregation orders when the *Hopwood* case was being tried. By contrast, the
Sixth Circuit (*Hopwood* was tried in the Fifth Circuit) upheld a district court
ruling that refused to limit its review of Tennessee's professional schools to
past discrimination at each individual school and also took into account discrimination in the State of Tennessee's educational system as a whole. The
Sixth Circuit reasoned that "applicants do not arrive at the admissions office
of a professional school in a vacuum. To be admitted they ordinarily must
have been students for sixteen years." *Geier v. Alexander*, Sixth Circuit (1986).
[31]See Douglas Massey and Nancy Denton, *American Apartheid* (Cambridge:
Harvard University Press, 1993); Robert Post and Michael Rogin, eds., *Race
and Representation: Affirmative Action* (New York: Zone Books, 1998), pp.
117–19.

employed. The Wagner Act of 1935, called by some the Magna Carta of labor, was also explicitly amended to permit racial exclusion in labor contracts. In addition, the Federal Housing Authority's guidelines for granting housing loans, issued in 1939, explicitly used race as the single most important criterion: "If a neighborhood is to retain stability, it is necessary that properties shall be continued to be occupied by the same social and racial classes." The Federal Housing Authority (FHA) further created segregation in suburban areas by recommending that "developers place [racially restrictive] covenants on all housing that they built to ensure its future worth." A bias in favor of the suburbs was also evident in FHA practices and regulations, which favored the construction of single-family homes. In addition, the FHA made its easier and cheaper for a family to purchase a new home than to renovate an older one.[32] As a result, the vast majority of FHA and Veteran's Administration (VA) mortgages went to white middle-class suburbs; very few were awarded to black neighborhoods in central cities. For example, FHA lending in the New York City suburb of Nassau County per capita was 11 times that of Kings County (Brooklyn) and 60 times that of Bronx County (the Bronx). By the late 1950s, many inner cities were locked into a spiral of decline that was both encouraged and supported by federal housing policies.

During the 1950s and 1960s, local authorities were also encouraged and supported by the federal government to carry out widespread slum clearance in growing black neighborhoods that threatened white business districts and elite institutions. Public housing was then used to house black families displaced by the razing of neighborhoods undergoing renewal. Multi-unit projects of extremely high density were built to house within the ghetto as many blacks as possible. As a result of these federal policies and programs,

---

[32]Before the creation of the FHA, mortgages generally were granted for no more than two-thirds of the appraised value of a home, and frequently banks required half the assessed value of a home before making a loan. The FHA, by contrast, required only a 10 percent downpayment, and, moreover, it extended the repayment period to 25 to 30 years, thus resulting in low monthly payments. In this way, many more families were able to purchase homes than would otherwise have been possible.

blacks and minorities in the United States actually became more separated and isolated than they ever had been before.[33] Congress even specifically excluded federal mortgage insurance from coverage under the Civil Rights Act of 1964, so as to allow the widespread discrimination in the FHA and VA loan programs to continue.

However, in 1968, following the assassination of Martin Luther King and the accompanying urban riots, Congress passed the Fair Housing Act, which banned discrimination in the sale or rental of housing. Unfortunately, the price of its enactment was that its enforcement provisions were systematically gutted. Under the act, the Department of Housing and Urban Development (HUD) was authorized only to investigate complaints of housing discrimination made to it by "aggrieved persons," and if it chose to pursue a complaint, it was then only empowered to engage in "conciliation" to resolve the problem. Thus, according to one study, only 20 to 30 percent of complaints that were filed reached formal mediation, and nearly half of these complaints remained in noncompliance after conciliation efforts had terminated. Since HUD had no power of enforcement, the act's main enforcement mechanism was private suits, but even when successful, these suits were limited to only the actual damages and a $1,000 punitive award. In addition, the act held plaintiffs specifically liable for all court costs and attorneys' fees unless they were unable to pay for them. In practice, therefore, the Fair Housing Act of 1968 allowed a few victims to gain redress, while permitting an extensive system of institutionalized discrimination, for the most part, to remain in place. That is why only about four hundred fair housing cases have been decided since 1968, compared with more than two million incidents of housing discrimination that are estimated to occur each year.

---

[33]In fact, before 1900, blacks and whites usually lived side by side in American cities. In the North, the small native black population was scattered widely throughout white neighborhoods. Even Chicago, Detroit, and Philadelphia, cities that are now known for their large black ghettos, were not segregated then. In southern cities, such as Charleston, New Orleans, and Savannah, black servants and laborers lived on alleys and side streets near the mansions of their white employers.

Twenty years later, over stiff opposition from President Reagan, Congress passed the Fair Housing Amendments Act of 1988, which extended the time to file a housing discrimination complaint; allowed attorneys' fees and court costs to be recovered by prevailing plaintiffs; and increased the punitive awards to $10,000 for first and second offenses, $50,000 for a third offense. Unfortunately, this new act still relied heavily on individuals who are willing to sue, so-called private attorney generals, rather than on federal authorities.[34] As a consequence, the high level of segregation found in U.S. cities has changed hardly at all since the passage of the Fair Housing Act of 1968.[35]

Accordingly, given 250 years of slavery in the United States, a hundred years of Jim Crow, and discriminatory practices that continue right up to the present day, there is very good reason to regard racial classifications as presumptively suspect.

A Colorblind (Racially Just) Society

Of course, if we lived in a colorblind society, racial classifications would no longer be presumptively suspect because in such a society a person's race would be no more significant than eye color is in most societies.[36] In most societies, people frequently don't even notice a person's eye color. Except for the mildest aesthetic preferences, eye color tends to be an unimportant trait. Very little turns on what eye color you have. Accordingly, if we lived in a society where a person's race was no more significant than eye color is in most societies, there would be little reason to treat race with any kind of legal scrutiny. In a colorblind society, many cultural

---

[34]In this respect, the ineffectiveness of the Fair Housing Act of 1968 parallels the ineffectiveness of the Civil Rights Act of 1964, after which it was modeled.

[35]According to one survey, while 88 percent of white respondents agreed that black people should have a right to live wherever they can afford to, only 43 percent would feel comfortable in a neighborhood that was one-third black. According to another survey, while 57 percent of white respondents felt that white people did not have a right to discriminate against black people, only 35 percent of white respondents would vote for a law stating that a homeowner could not refuse to sell to someone because of his or her race.

[36]For further development of this idea, see Richard Wasserstrom, "Racism, Sexism and Preferential Treatment, *UCLA Law Review* vol. 24 (1977) 581–622.

differences would remain, but they woundn't be based on race. As a result, the cultures that were constituted by these differences would be open to members of all races in much the same way that most religions today are open to members of all races.

But obviously we don't live in such a colorblind, or, if you prefer, racially just society. In U.S. society, it is not at all difficult to find present discrimination as well as the continuing effects of past discrimination. Hence, in the United States, it is reasonable to assume that racial classifications should be presumptively suspect.

Benign and Invidious Racial Classifications

Nevertheless, the U.S. Supreme Court understands the assumption that racial classifications are presumptively suspect in a fairly specific way. It takes the assumption to imply that it does not matter whether the classifications are intended to remedy the results of past discrimination or intended to foster or maintain that discrimination; the court regards both uses of racial classification as equally suspect. As the court put it in *Adarand v. Pena* (1995), actually quoting *Croson* (1986):

> Absent searching judicial inquiry into the justification for such race-based measures, there is simply no way of determining what classifications are "benign" or "remedial," and what classifications are in fact motivated by illegitimate notions of racial inferiority or simple racial politics. Indeed, the purpose of strict scrutiny is to "smoke out" illegitimate uses of race by assuring that the legislative body is pursuing a goal important enough to warrant use of a highly suspect tool. The test also ensures that the means chosen "fit" this compelling goal so closely that there is little or no possibility that the motive for the classification was illegitimate racial prejudice or stereotype.

In his dissent in *Adarand*, Justice Stevens interprets the majority here as claiming that it is difficult to distinguish between benign or remedial uses of racial classifications, on the one hand, and that invidious discrimination, which was so characteristic of the United State's racist past, on the other. However, as Stevens graphically puts it, the distinction that needs to be made here is between a welcome mat and a "No Trespassing" sign. But this distinction, Stevens argues, is one we not only can, but do make fairly easily, with respect to both the motives and the consequences of these two uses of racial classifications.

Consider some of the motives underlying traditional racial discrimination in the United States. Blacks were not hired or admitted into schools because it was thought that contact with them was degrading and contaminating to whites. These policies were based on contempt and loathing for blacks, on a belief that blacks were less than fully developed human beings suitable only for subordinate positions in society. By contrast, under remedial affirmative action, whites are not being passed over for any of these reasons. No defender of affirmative action thinks that contact with whites is degrading or contaminating, that whites are contemptible and loathsome, or that whites, by their nature, should be subordinate to blacks. Similarly, the consequences of these two uses of racial classifications are radically different. Affirmative action does not stigmatize whites, and it does not perpetuate negative stereotypes about them; it is not part of a pattern of discrimination that makes being white extremely burdensome. Nor does it increase an already dominant group's supply of power, authority, opportunity, and wealth, as did traditional racial discrimination. On the contrary, it results in a more egalitarian distribution of these social and economic goods.[37]

On closer examination, however, it appears that the majority of the court in *Adarand* is not denying that we can easily distinguish between paradigm cases of benign and invidious racial classifications. Instead, the court is worried that those who are advancing so-called benign and remedial uses of racial classifications may have less than ideal motives. For example, instead of being motivated to rectify for past injustices and to give minorities what they deserve, those favoring remedial affirmative action may believe that minorities are naturally inferior and so need special help (the racial paternalism that Justice Thomas seems to fear), or, more likely, they may simply be trying to secure a special advantage for minorities without really justifying it as a remedy for past wrongs. No doubt we should not want to approve of affirmative action programs that are driven

---

[37]For a fuller discussion of this comparison, see Edwin Hettinger, "What Is Wrong with Reverse Discrimination?" *Business & Professional Ethics Journal* 6 (1987), pp. 39–55.

by these less worthy motives. But no evidence of such motives has been provided in the affirmative action cases that have come before the Supreme Court. All the evidence in the *Croson* case, for example, pointed to significant past discrimination in the construction industry in the city of Richmond. So, even assuming that racial classifications are presumptively suspect, we should still be able to use such classifications to remedy proven past discrimination. Unfortunately, the Supreme Court in its recent decisions has elevated the standard for proof of past discrimination so high as to make it extremely difficult to effect such remedies.

From the assumption that racial classifications are presumptively suspect, the court infers the need for a strict scrutiny analysis, which means that it must be possible to show that the use of a racial classification is narrowly tailored to meet a compelling government interest. Given that ending racial discrimination and eliminating the burdensome effects of past discrimination are clearly compelling (government) interests, everything turns on how narrowly tailored the affirmative action program has to be in serving those interests. And here too the U.S. Supreme Court and some lower courts have been unreasonably demanding.

Consider again the *Croson* decision. Richmond's affirmative action plan specified the eligible beneficiaries as being "citizens of the United States who are Blacks, Spanish-speaking, Oriental, Indians, Eskimos or Aleuts," actually using the same specification of minorities that Congress had employed in fashioning its own affirmative action set-aside program on which the Richmond program was patterned. Now it is arguable whether this part of the plan is narrowly tailored since no evidence was given for including Spanish-speaking, Oriental, Indian, Eskimo, or Aleut contractors in the Richmond affirmative action program. Nevertheless, it could have been argued that opening up the construction industry in Richmond to members of these other groups would also serve to break down discrimination against African Americans. Yet, even accepting the majority's view that Richmond's ordinance was overbroad, it does not follow that this should invalidate Richmond's ordinance as a whole. After all, as this affirmative action program functioned in the city of Richmond, only African American contractors actually benefited from it.

6

Racial Discrimination v.
Sexual Discrimination

It is also important to recognize here that the U.S. Supreme Court does not demand the same standard of proof in dealing with sexual discrimination that it does for racial discrimination. Of course, no one doubts that women are currently subject to a great deal of discrimination, as they have been in the past.[38]

(1) Evidence of Sexual Discrimination

In the United States today, 20 percent of women are raped at some time during their lives; between one-quarter and one-third of women are battered in their homes by husbands and lovers; 50 percent of women in the workplace say they have been sexually harassed; and 38 percent of little girls are sexually molested inside or outside the

[38]See Mary Koss, *I Never Called It Rape* (New York: Harper and Row, 1988); Committee on the Judiciary, United States Senate, *Violence Against Women, A Majority Staff Report* (Washington, D.C.: U.S. Government Printing Office, 1992); Ron Thorne-Finch, *Ending the Silence: The Origins and Treatment of Male Violence against Women* (Toronto: University of Toronto Press, 1992); Albert Roberts, *Helping Battered Women* (New York: Oxford University Press, 1996); Cherly Gomez-Preston, *When No Means No* (New York: Carol Publishing Co., 1993); Ellen Bravo and Ellen Cassedy, *The 9–5 Guide to Combating Sexual Harassment* (New York; John Wiley & Sons 1992); Diana Russell, *The Secret Trauma* (New York: Basic Books, 1986); Diana Russell, "The Incidence and Prevalence of Intrafamilial and Extrafamilial Sexual Abuse of Female Children," *Child Abuse and Neglect: The International Journal* 7, no. 2 (1983), pp. 133–46; Tom L. Beauchamp, "In Defense of Affirmative Action," *The Journal of Ethics* 2 (1998), pp. 143–58.

family. Women employed full-time still earn only $.72 for every dollar men earn. Women now hold 70 percent of white-collar positions but only 10 percent of management positions. There are only two women CEOs in Fortune 1000 companies. College-educated Hispanic women annually earn $1,600 less than white male high school graduates and nearly $16,000 less than college-educated white men. College-educated black women annually earn only $1,500 more than white male high school graduates and almost $13,000 less than college-educated white men. College-educated white women earn only $3,000 more than white male high school graduates and $11,500 less than college-educated white men. Women with identical credentials are promoted at approximately one-half the rate of their male counterparts. A National Bureau of Economic Research project sent equally qualified pairs of male and female applicants to seek jobs at a range of Philadelphia restaurants. This "audit" found that high-priced restaurants offering good pay and tips were twice as likely to offer jobs to the male applicants than to their equally qualified female counterparts. Thus, there is plenty of evidence that women in the United States are not only discriminated against but also suffer from the continuing effects of past discrimination.

(2) The U.S. Supreme Court's Arguments for Different Treatment

Despite the widespread evidence of sexual discrimination, the U.S. Supreme Court has advanced a number of arguments for treating sexual discrimination differently than racial discrimination. In *Bakke* (1978), Justice Powell argued that in the case of sexual discrimination, there is just one oppressed group—women—and just one oppressor group—men—so it is easier to determine what sort of remedies are appropriate. By contrast, in the case of racial oppression, there are rival groups that can claim that they too are oppressed, and moreover, the groups that can reasonably make this claim vary over time, so the argument for remedying racial discrimination must be made on a case-by-case basis. But the same holds true for sexual discrimination; the argument for rectifying sexual discrimination must also be made case by case. The courts have not accepted, nor should they accept, the argument that women have generally been discriminated against by men and so are generally entitled to remedial affirmative action. For example, it is unlikely that women employed in the nursing profession today deserve remedial affirmative action. But there are other areas, like the construction industry, in which remedial affirmative action would be appropriate for women. The argument for remedial affirmative action for women therefore has to be made on a case-by-case basis, just as the argument for remedial affirmative action for minorities has to be made on a case-by-case basis. There is no difference in this regard.

The U.S. Supreme Court has also argued that racial discrimination is a more invidious harm than sexual discrimination, and that, for this reason, we should require a higher standard of proof for using racial than sexual classifications. Now, it is not clear that it is any more useful to try to rank the evils of racism and sexism in our society than it is to try to rank the evils of black slavery and the Holocaust.[39] Even if we assume, for the sake of argument, that racial discrimination is more invidious than sexual discrimination, by imposing a higher standard of proof with respect to the use of racial classifications, the Supreme Court makes it more difficult to correct for racial discrimination than to correct for sexual discrimination. But this is just the opposite of what the court should be doing under its assumption that racial discrimination is more invidious than sexual discrimination.

Interestingly, the court's stance here does make sense, but only in nonremedial contexts in which we are simply concerned with preventing discrimination rather than stopping or correcting for it. Thus, assuming that racial discrimination is more invidious than sexual discrimination, it does make sense in nonremedial contexts to impose a higher standard of proof on the use of racial classifications than on the use of sexual classifications. But in remedial contexts, if we assume that racial discrimination is more invidious than sexual discrimination, it does not make sense to make it more difficult to correct for racial than for sexual discrimination, as the court is presently doing. Given that I have argued that the standard of proof that the court is using for race-based remedial affirmative action is too high, it would make sense to lower that standard to the one re-

---

[39]On this point, see Lawrence Thomas, *Vessels of Evil: American Slavery and the Holocaust* (Philadelphia: Temple University Press, 1992).

quired for correcting for sexual discrimination. This would allow race- and sex-based remedial affirmative action to be similarly justified when reasonably related to the justifiable state purpose of ending and compensating for discrimination against women and minorities in U.S. society.

7

A Better Standard of Proof for Remedial Affirmative Action

Assuming that the standard of proof for remedial affirmative action for minorities were appropriately lowered, it would then be far easier to use race-based affirmative action to correct and compensate for widespread discriminatory practices in U.S. society. For example, it is generally recognized that in many parts of the country, there are de facto segregated primary and secondary educational systems whose existence is clearly rooted in past discrimination. In fact, American primary and secondary schools are now becoming even more segregated than they were in the past.[40] In the South, the most integrated region of the country, the percentage of black students in majority-white schools fell from a peak of 43.5 percent in the late 1980s to 34.7 percent in 1996, which is lower than it was in 1972. National trends parallel those in the South. Nationwide, the percentage of black students in majority-white schools peaked in the early 1980s and has now declined to the levels of the 1960s. Nationwide, the percentage of Hispanics in majority-white schools has

[40]See Paul Wellstone and Jonathan Kozol, "What Tests Can't Fix," *New York Times*, 13 March 2001; Gary Orfield and John Yun, "Resegregation in American Schools," *The Civil Rights Project* (Cambridge: Harvard University, 1999); Gary Orfield, "The Resegregation of Our Nation's Schools," *Civil Rights Journal* (fall 1999); William Celis, "Study Finds Rising Concentration of Blacks and Hispanic Students," *New York Times*, 14 December 1993; Micaela di Leonardo, "White Lies, Black Myths," *The Village Voice* 22 September 1992.

declined from 45 percent in 1968 to 25 percent today. In terms of both resources and race, American schools have become at least as segregated as they were in the 1960s. In large cities, 15 of every 16 black and Hispanic students are enrolled in schools where most of the students are nonwhite. In medium-size cities, 63 percent of blacks and 70 percent of Hispanics attend such schools. White suburban schools have approximately twice the funds per student as do urban schools, where black and Hispanic students are concentrated, although people living in urban school districts are taxed more heavily to support their poorer schools. Moreover, much of this racial segregation in primary and secondary schools in the United States can be traced to the widespread discrimination in housing noted earlier. The financial resources of schools are primarily dependent on the wealth of the school districts in which they are located.

Ideally, it would surely be preferable to correct for these educational disparities with an equal education opportunity program that, within a short period of time, would provide every child in the United States with equally good educational opportunities. This program would cover preschool through twelfth grade and might cost an additional $25 billion a year. Moreover, if we had to choose between existing affirmative action programs and such an equal education opportunity program—if we could not have them both—then there would be no question among defenders of affirmative action as to which one to choose.[41] If these were our options, then surely every defender of affirmative action would favor the proposed equal education opportunity program over affirmative action. Of course, in the real world in which we live, we do not have the option of having the proposed equal education opportunity program. This alternative to maintaining and developing existing affirmative action programs is simply not a feasible option in our current social and political context, at least in the United States.

What then should we do? Recognizing that the poorer educational and residential experiences that minorities have in the United

---

[41]Of course, if these were our options, it might turn out that critics of affirmative action would favor retaining affirmative action over such a radical equal educational opportunity alternative. But my point here is simply that defenders of affirmative action would not favor retaining affirmative action in this case.

States are the result of present or past discriminatory practices, both institutions of higher education and employers could use affirmative action programs to make up for that discrimination. These affirmative action programs would favor qualified minority candidates who have been discriminated against in the past over equally or more qualified nonminority candidates who have not been similarly disadvantaged. In fact, it should be the case that those who are passed over by such programs have themselves benefited from the discrimination suffered by these affirmative action candidates, for example, the discrimination found in their unequal educational and residential opportunities.[42] Yet, to be justified, such affirmative action programs must favor only candidates whose qualifications are such that when their selection is combined with a suitably designed educational enhancement program, they will normally turn out, within a reasonably short time, to be as qualified as, or even more qualified than, their peers. Such candidates must have the potential, to be as qualified as, or more qualified than, their peers, although that potential will not yet have been actualized because of past discrimination. Affirmative action of this sort, with its suitably designed educational enhancement program, purports to actualize just that potential.[43] In this way, persons who receive this form of affirmative action are like runners in a race who, for a time, are forced to compete at a disadvantage with the other runners, for example, by having weights tied to their legs, but later are allowed to compete against those other runners by first having the weights removed and

---

[42]Of course, if someone passed over by an affirmative action program could make the case that he or she had not benefited from the discrimination suffered by the relevant affirmative action candidates (something it would be very difficult to do in the United States given its level of racial and sexual discrimination), that would have to be taken into account.

[43]The question arises as to how we might implement such an affirmative action program. But clearly there are ways to do so. At Georgia Tech, the performance gap between white and minority first-year engineering students was eliminated through the institution of an intensive five-week summer course for the minority students. See Susan Strom and Lani Guiner, "The Future of Affirmative Action: The Innovative Ideal," *California Law Review*, vol. 84 (1996), p. 10

then receiving some special assistance for an appropriate period of time, so that the results of the race will turn out to be fair. Affirmative action of this sort, therefore, is a policy that is directed at only those minority candidates who are highly qualified, yet, because of past discrimination and prejudice, are less qualified than they would otherwise be; it seeks to provide such candidates with a benefit that will nullify the effects of past injustices by enabling them to become as qualified as, or more qualified than, their peers. Thus, once the standards of proof for race-based remedial affirmative action are suitably lowered to those that are used for sex-based remedial affirmative action, it should be possible to correct for a broad range of present and past discriminatory practices.

Summing up, then, the requirements as to when remedial affirmative action is justified should be the following:

1. The past discrimination that is to be remedied must be proven discrimination, but the institution that is engaging in the affirmative action need not be implicated in that proven discrimination in order for the affirmative action in question to be justified.

2. Although, in a colorblind (racially just) society, racial classifications would no longer be presumptively suspect, in the United States, racial classifications must be regarded as presumptively suspect because of the 250 years of slavery, 100 years of Jim Crow, and discriminatory practices that continue right up to the present day. However, the standard of proof required to justify the use of racial classifications in remedial affirmative action should not be unreasonably high, as it is in the *Croson* case. It should not be easier to correct for sexual discrimination in society than it is to correct for racial discrimination. Accordingly, remedial affirmative action still has a significant role in combating proven past and present discrimination in housing, education, and jobs, unless more broadly conceived and much better funded corrective policies are undertaken.

3. Programs may admit only those candidates whose qualifications are such that when their selection is combined with a suitably designed educational enhancement program, they will normally turn out, within a reasonably short time, to be as qualified as, or even more qualified than, their peers.

4. Those who are passed over by such affirmative action programs would have themselves been found to have benefited from the discrimination suffered by the affirmative action candidates, for example, the discrimination found in their unequal educational and residential opportunities.[44]

(1) Affirmative Action Scholarships

One thing that clearly could be done, as a form of remedial affirmative action, is to set up scholarship programs. Affirmative action scholarships specifically for minorities, used to be a widely accepted form of affirmative action in the United States. In the past, federal government Pell grants provided minorities who needed financial support with scholarship money to attend college. During the time these Pell grants were offered, the rate at which African Americans who graduated from high school attended college began to approach the same rate that whites who graduated from high school attended college. During the Reagan administration, that all changed. Pell grants became loans rather than scholarships, and since the median net worth of white families is ten times that of black families, white students were in a better financial position to secure these loans than were black students. As a consequence, the numbers of African Americans attending college began to drop off.

Another setback occurred in 1994, when the U.S. Court of Appeals for the Fourth Circuit in *Podberesky v. Kirwan* ruled against a minority scholarship program that had been recently established by the University of Maryland at College Park (UMCP). In 1968, the U.S. Department of Health, Education, and Welfare's Office of Civil Rights (OCR) began pressuring the state of Maryland to integrate its institutions of higher learning, as required by Title VI of the Civil Rights Act of 1964. In response, the UMCP in 1970 proposed an initial compliance plan that offered enhanced academic programs in order to attract African American students from the

---

[44]Of course, if someone passed over by an affirmative action program could make the case that he or she had not benefited from the discrimination suffered by the relevant affirmative action candidates (something it would be very difficult to do in the U.S. given its level of racial and sexual discrimination) that would have to be taken into account.

state's predominantly black colleges. In 1973, the OCR rejected this plan as ineffectual. The state then proposed a new plan in 1974, but a year later the OCR found that the state failed to promptly and vigorously execute its own plan. In 1978, a new master plan for the University of Maryland system was developed, but this plan did even less for minority recruiting. So, not surprisingly, it was also rejected by the OCR. In 1980, the UMCP submitted a fourth compliance plan, which the OCR still found inadequate. However, continued negotiations with the OCR resulted in a fifth plan, submitted in 1985, that included the Banneker Scholarship Program as one of the UMCP's most important recruiting efforts. Each year, the program provided four-year scholarships to approximately 20 academically talented black students. These students were expected to play an active role in the recruitment and retention of other black students at the UMCP. The annual cost of the program was about $600,000 or approximately 1 percent of the UMCP's total financial aid budget. In 1985, the OCR accepted the 1985-90 plan as "compliance with Title VI [of the Civil Rights Act of 1964] for the life of the plan." In 1990, the UMCP decided to continue to implement the plan with its Banneker Scholarship Program until it was notified by the OCR that it was finally in full compliance with Title VI.

Around the same time, in the fall of 1989, Daniel Podberesky, a Hispanic male who had been admitted to UMCP, sued the university for rejecting his request to be considered for a Banneker scholarship, claiming that the university was denying his equal protection rights under the Fourteenth Amendment. Since Podberesky could not himself receive a Banneker scholarship, the legal relief that he was seeking was the closing of that opportunity to others. The money that would thus be saved if the Banneker program were eliminated would be redirected to other means of recruiting and retaining black students. It would not go into a general scholarship fund from which nonblack students could benefit.

In light of U.S. Supreme Court decisions on affirmative action, especially *Croson* (1989), it was taken for granted that any race-conscious affirmative action program, such as the Banneker Scholarship Program, must satisfy a strict scrutiny analysis, that is, it must be narrowly tailored to meet a compelling government interest. With regard to the Banneker program, that compelling government interest was taken to be remedying the proven effects of past discrimination by the state of Maryland.[45] In 1991, the district court found that the evidence that had been provided, including the fact that the Office of Civil Rights had yet to certify that the UMCP was finally in compliance with Title VI of the Civil Rights Act of 1964, sufficed to establish that the university had a compelling interest in remedying the proven effects of its past discrimination. However, the Court of Appeals for the Fourth Circuit in 1991 overruled this decision and remanded the case to the district court, asking it to determine whether further evidence of past discrimination at the UMCP could be found to justify the Banneker Scholarship Program. The court of appeals regarded the evidence so far provided, including the negative evaluations of the OCR, as insufficient to establish that there were current effects of past discriminatory actions by the UMCP.

Responding to this demand for further evidence, the UMCP engaged in an administrative fact-finding process. The university conducted interviews of high school counselors, students, African American parents of college-age children, and those currently involved in recruiting African American students to the UMCP. On the basis of this new evidence, the university identified four current effects of its past discriminatory actions: 1) the university's poor reputation in the African American community, 2) the underrepresentation of African Americans in the UMCP's student body, 3) low retention and graduation rates of African Americans, and 4) the existence of a hostile racial climate at the UMCP. Again, in 1993, the district court agreed with the university, finding that there was sufficient evidence of present effects of past discrimination by the UMCP for which the Banneker Scholarship Program was an appropriate remedy. Yet, here again, in 1994, the Court of Appeals for the Fourth Circuit disagreed. The court of appeals held that the

---

[45]It also should be clear that what are being called effects of past discrimination in this case are often themselves discriminatory actions in their own right. So it is not as though virtually all discrimination is in the past and that now what we are dealing with is just residual effects of past discrimination. Often, the effects of past discrimination are also new and clear instances of present discrimination.

university's poor reputation in the African American community was not a proven effect of past discrimination of the appropriate sort. More specifically, the court argued that

> any poor reputation the University may have in the African American community is tied solely to knowledge of the University's discrimination before it admitted African American students. There is no doubt that many Maryland residents, as well as some citizens of other States, know of the University's past segregation, and that cannot be denied. However, mere knowledge of historical fact is not the kind of present effect that can justify a race-exclusive remedy. If it were otherwise, as long as there are people who have access to history books, there will be programs such as this one.

Despite its rhetorical force, this response of the court was grossly mistaken. Most of the evidence of the university's poor reputation in the African American community was not tied at all to knowledge of the university's discrimination *before* it began admitting African American students. Rather, the evidence was drawn from the time that the university began to slowly and reluctantly integrate its campus, and extended right up to the time of the district court's decision. As one UMCP official involved with recruiting blacks students at the time put it: "the [high school] administrators I spoke to were not telling the students to look to College Park because they believed it was not a good place to go based on their own negative experiences, and based on similar experiences of their former students, whose feedback over the years indicated that life at UMCP for blacks had not significantly changed over time."[46] Notice that the judgments of these administrators also parallel those of the Office of Civil Rights, which had yet to find the university in full compliance with Title VI. At the time, the U.S. Department of Justice reached a similar conclusion in its amicus brief, which argued that the state of Maryland still operated a dual system of higher education, even as it made progress toward eliminating that system.

The court of appeals also went on to reject the district court's decision on the grounds that the racial incidents, which occurred at

---

[46]Quoted in *Podberesky v. Kirwan*, United States District Court for the District of Maryland (1993).

the UMCP with such frequency and regularity that the district court referred to them as a "stream," did "not necessarily implicate past discrimination on the part of the university as opposed to present societal discrimination."

It is important to be clear as to how the term "societal discrimination" is being used here. The term, as first introduced by Justice Powell in *Bakke* (1978), referred to *unproven* discrimination. Later, it was used to refer to discrimination, whether proven or unproven, that is not caused by the agent that is now engaged in remedial affirmative action. In the *Podberesky* case, it is clear that the court of appeals was employing the latter use of the term because, in this case, no one doubted that the issue was the proven effects of past or present discrimination—that stream of racial incidents that occurred on the UMCP campus. Nor was there any doubt that the university had been engaged in discrimination in the past. Rather, what was at issue for the court of appeals was whether the proven effects of past discrimination on the UMCP campus were caused by the past discrimination of the university or by the past or present discrimination of other agents. As the court of appeals saw it, only if the present discriminatory effects on the UMCP campus were caused by the past discriminatory actions of the university would the Banneker Scholarship Program be justified. The court of appeals held this view, however, only because the court employed an unreasonably demanding standard of proof for remedial affirmative action that it derived from *Croson* (1989).

As we noted, the U.S. Supreme Court in *Croson* requires that any institution that seeks to compensate for past discrimination must itself be guilty (or causally responsible) for that very discrimination. Similarly, any institution that seeks to compensate for *the effects* of past discrimination must itself be guilty (or causally responsible) for those same effects, that is, it must be guilty (or causally responsible) for the very same discrimination from which those effects derive.

Yet why should this be a requirement for a justified remedial affirmative action program? If we have proven effects of past or present discrimination, and we have an agent who is willing to engage in remedial affirmative action to correct for those effects, why should we further require that the agent be responsible for the present or past discrimination that has led to those discriminatory effects? This is an unnecessary requirement whose sole effect is to limit our ability to correct for present or past discrimination. Once sufficient evidence of discrimination has been provided, there is no reason to impose the additional requirement that the agent engaged in the remedial affirmative action be implicated in the very discrimination it is seeking to correct.[47]

The Banneker Scholarship Program at UMCP was a remedial affirmative action program that sought to eliminate current effects of past discrimination at the UMCP campus. It attempted to create more of an equal opportunity environment for college-age African Americans by improving the racial environment on campus, changing the university's reputation in the African American community, increasing the representation of African Americans in the UMCP's student body, and the retention and graduation rates of African Americans at the campus. College-age white students, whether considering to attend or actually attending the UMBC campus, did not face comparable restricted opportunities. The Banneker Scholarship Program simply sought to provide college-age African Americans with more of the opportunities that college-age whites possess and often take for granted. Moreover, the program sought to do this without in any way significantly disadvantaging white applicants. As we saw, the program represented only 1 percent of the UMCP's total financial aid budget, and when the program was eliminated, its funding was redirected to other means of recruiting and retaining black students. It did not go into any general scholarship fund from which white students could benefit. So, as an appropriate means for achieving its quite limited goal of creating a more equal opportunity environment for college-age African Americans, the Banneker Scholarship Program was quite successful.

Significantly, the court of appeals did not really question the Banneker program's success in this regard. The court was simply

---

[47]It should also be noted that the Banneker program's being open to non-Maryland residents was not a defect of the program. This is because part of the goal of the program was to compensate for past discrimination to Maryland residents, but another part of the goal was simply to open up the university to African Americans; this can be done by admitting either resident or nonresident African Americans to the program.

concerned with whether the university was causally responsible for those proven effects of discrimination that existed on the UMCP's campus. That issue, which consumed the interest of the courts both here and in *Croson*, I have argued, is beside the point. If an agent is willing and able to do something to help create a more equal opportunity playing field or to compensate for past discrimination, then, other things being equal, we should not require that the agent itself be implicated in the discrimination it is seeking to remedy. It follows that affirmative action scholarship programs such as the Banneker program should be important means for bringing us closer to our ultimate goals of a colorblind (racially just) and gender-free (sexually just) society.[48]

---

[48]In response to the court of appeals decision, UMCP has revised its scholarship programs so that they now include diversity as one of their goals.

8

A Defense of Diversity Affirmative Action

There is another type of affirmative action, however, that is not grounded in the ideal of remedying discrimination, whether that discrimination is present or past. The goal of this type of affirmative action is diversity, which in turn is justified either in terms of its educational benefits or its ability to create a more effective work force in such areas as policing and community relations. The legal roots of this form of affirmative action in the United States are found in *Bakke* (1978).

In *Bakke*, Justice Powell argued that the attainment of a diverse student body was clearly a constitutionally permissible goal for an institution of higher education. According to Powell, in an admissions program that aimed at diversity, "[r]ace or ethnic background may be deemed a 'plus' in a particular applicant's file, yet it does not insulate the individual from comparison with all other candidates for the available seats. . . . The applicant who loses out in the last available seat to another candidate receiving a 'plus' on the basis of ethnic background will not have been foreclosed from all consideration for that seat. . . . It will mean only that his combined qualifications . . . did not outweigh those of the other applicant." Furthermore, an admissions program may "pay some attention to distribution among many types and categories of students," as more than a "token number of blacks" is needed to secure the educational benefits that flow from a racially and ethnically diverse student body.

For almost 20 years, Powell's opinion in *Bakke*, supported by Justices Brennan, Marshall, Blackmun, and White, has been the rationale for the affirmative action used by most American colleges and universities. Even Justice O'Connor, who rejected diversity as a compelling interest for the broadcasting industry in *Metro Broadcasting v. FCC* (1990), has allowed that a state interest in the promotion of diversity has been found sufficiently compelling, at least in the context of higher education.[49]

In 1995, however, the U.S. Court of Appeals for the Fifth Circuit held in *Hopwood v. Texas* that Powell's opinion in *Bakke* is not binding precedent. According to the court, the view that race may be used as a "plus" factor to obtain diversity "garnered only [Powell's] vote and has never represented the view of a majority of the Court in Bakke or any other case." However, it has been generally recognized that the Brennan group (which included Brennan, who wrote the opinion, and Marshall, Blackmun, and White, who endorsed it) did support Powell's view in *Bakke*. In fact, Brennan himself said as much in a subsequent decision. Moreover, the reason why no other case since *Bakke* has supported Powell's view on diversity in education is that no other case since Bakke has dealt with diversity in education.

The *Hopwood* court also ruled that evidence of discrimination in Texas's school system as a whole was not relevant to whether the affirmative action program of the University of Texas law school is justified. Even though, as of May 1994, desegregation suits remained pending against more than 40 Texas school districts, and at the time the *Hopwood* plaintiffs filed suit, the U.S. Office of Civil Rights had not yet determined that the state had desegregated its schools sufficiently to comply with federal civil rights laws, and most of the applicants to the law school had passed through that very same educational system with its alleged inequalities, the *Hopwood* court only allowed the law school at the University of Texas to use evidence of its *own* discrimination to justify engaging in affirmative action.[50]

---

[49]The diversity at issue here is not identical with racial or ethnic diversity, although the latter is an important element in the diversity that is sought. Moreover, as Justice Powell recognized, achieving the educational benefits of a racially and ethnically diverse student body requires a critical mass of underrepresented minority students.

[50]Actually, the University of Texas law school, like most state law schools, does "discriminate" against nonresidents; it reserves 80 percent of its seats for Texas residents.

But, as I have argued earlier, once sufficient evidence of discrimination has been provided, there seems to be no reason to impose the additional requirement that the agent engaged in the affirmative action program must be implicated in the discrimination it is seeking to correct.

Interestingly, the *Hopwood* court supported its overall decision on two contradictory claims about race.[51] First, the court claimed that race does make a difference, that we can't assume there would be proportional participation in the absence of past discrimination. But then the court claimed that race does not make a difference, that race is not a good indicator of diversity. We might try to rescue the court from contradiction here by understanding its first claim to refer to an ideal society, and its second to refer to current U.S society. So understood, the court would be claiming that in an ideal society, race would still make a difference, but in our present society, race does not make a difference. But this would only save the court from a contradiction by committing it to an absurdity. Surely, what we should believe here about actual and ideal societies is exactly the opposite of what the court appears to be claiming. What we should believe about the United States, on the basis of the evidence of past and present discrimination, is that race does make a difference in the kind of life people experience in U.S. society. And what we should believe, or at least hope for, about an ideal society is that in such a society, race will not make a difference because in such a society race will be no more significant than eye color is in most societies. Thus, the *Hopwood* court's decision, based as it is on two contradictory conceptions of race, is deeply flawed.

(1) Recent Michigan Cases

There have also been two recent district court cases in the state of Michigan that, it turns out, have reached diametrically opposed opinions about the legitimacy of using race as a factor to achieve diversity. In *Gratz v. Bollinger* (2000), the District Court for the Eastern

---

[51]For a discussion of this point, see Reva Siegel, "The Racial Rhetorics of Colorblind Constitutionalism: The Case of *Hopwood v. Texas*," in *Race and Representation: Affirmative Action*, Robert Post and Michael Rogin, eds. (New York: Zone Books, 1998), pp. 29–72.

District of Michigan held that under *Bakke*, diversity constitutes a compelling governmental interest that, in the context of education, justifies the use of race as one factor in the admissions process. The court ruled further that the university had provided solid evidence regarding the educational benefits that flow from a racially and ethnically diverse student body.[52] Accordingly, the court found that the university's undergraduate admissions program from 1999 onward satisfies the *Bakke* requirements for a permissible race-conscious affirmative action program. That program uses a 150-point scale and assigns 20 points for membership in one of the identified underrepresented minority categories, as well as points for other factors, such as athletics (20 points) and socioeconomic status (20 points), up to a total of 40 points for such factors. Interestingly, one cannot receive 20 points both for membership in one of the identified underrepresented minority categories and 20 points for socioeconomic disadvantage, but one can receive 20 points for being a nonminority who attended a predominantly minority high school, and one can receive 16 points just for being from the Upper Peninsula of Michigan. At the same time, the court found that an earlier program, which was in place between 1995 and 1998 and which protected a certain number of seats for such groups as athletes, foreign applicants, underrepresented minorities, ROTC candidates, and legacies, did fail the *Bakke* test, but only with respect to its *minority* set-aside. The other set-asides were legally permissible.

By contrast, another judge from the same district court ruled in *Grutter v. Bollinger* (2001) that using race as a factor to achieve diversity was not established as a compelling state interest in *Bakke*; the Brennan group, with its four votes, did not endorse the parts of Powell's opinion that discussed diversity. The court quotes the Brennan group as saying that it "joins Part I and V-C of . . . Powell's opinion." But it goes on to say, "We also agree with Justice Powell that a plan like the 'Harvard' plan is constitutional. . . . " Since the

---

[52]Patricia Gurin, "The Compelling Need for Diversity in Higher Education"; *Gratz v. Bollinger* (2000). For additional evidence, see Thomas Weisskoff, "Consequences of Affirmative Action in U.S. Higher Education: A Review of Recent Empirical Studies," *Economic and Political Weekly*, 22 December 2001.

Harvard plan also sets out the diversity rationale for racial preference, it seems unreasonable to claim that the Brennan group is not also endorsing this aspect of Powell's opinion.[53] As one would expect, however, having denied that Powell's support of diversity in education is a controlling precedent, the court went on to reject the affirmative action program at the law school of the University of Michigan as unconstitutional.[54]

More recently, the *Grutter* district court decision was reversed by the U.S. Court of Appeals for the Sixth Circuit (2002). Earlier, in *Marks v. United States* (1977), the U.S. Supreme Court had

[53]Even if we were to grant that the Brennan group did not even implicitly endorse diversity as an acceptable ground for taking race into account in higher education, preferring instead the ground that it corrects for past discrimination, it would still follow that Powell's opinion is the holding in *Bakke*. This is because, according to the Supreme Court's decision in *Marks v. United States* (1977), "the holding of the Court may be viewed as that position taken by those members who concurred in the judgment on the narrowest grounds." See the argument in the text, which explains how Powell's position is the narrowest grounds.

[54]Recently, in *Johnson v. Board of Regents of the University System of Georgia* (2001), the U.S. Eleventh Circuit Court of Appeals struck down the University of Georgia's affirmative action program on the grounds that its pursuit of diversity was not sufficiently narrowly tailored. The court of appeals allowed that the University of Georgia (UG) had used seven factors to measure diversity in 1999, and had added two more—economic disadvantage and academic disadvantage—in 2000, but the court still argued that this was not enough to be narrowly tailored. According to the court, what the UG needed to do was to include even more factors for achieving diversity and also to read and qualitatively evaluate each applicant's file—something the university did for fewer than 1,000 of its 13,000 or so applicants each year. Typically, the UG admitted 85 percent of its students on the basis of their academic indexes and SAT scores alone. Seemingly, then, the court is proposing that if the UG wishes to use race as a factor in its pursuit of diversity then it would have to do a file by file evaluation each year of all applicants to identify what kind of diversity each person has to offer. Of course, if the university were to just drop race as a factor (or substitute, say, left-handedness), it could go on just as it had been doing, with no objection from the court. It is only because the UG, with 6 percent black students in a state that is almost 30 percent black, sought to maintain or slightly increase its enrollment of minority students that the Court now seeks to impose these more stringent requirements on it, far beyond any requirements that Powell in the *Bakke* decision had envisioned.

argued that "when a fragmented Court decides a case and no single rationale explaining the result enjoys the assent of five Justices, the holding of the Court may be viewed as that position taken by those Members who concurred in the judgments on the narrowest grounds." Applying these instructions from *Marks* to the *Bakke* decision, the Sixth Circuit Court of Appeals found that Powell's opinion represents the holding of the court, arguing that Powell's use of strict scrutiny allows a more limited use of race than Brennan's use of intermediate scrutiny, and so is *Bakke*'s narrowest rationale. The court subsequently ruled that the Michigan law school's affirmative action program met the requirements that Powell set out in his opinion for a justified diversity affirmative action program.

In his dissent to this decision, Judge Boggs argues that Brennan's plurality opinion, rather than Powell's opinion, satisfies the instructions given in *Marks* because Brennan's opinion, not Powell's, would have "invalidated the smaller set of laws." Nevertheless, Boggs does not draw the conclusion that Brennan's plurality opinion is the proper holding for *Bakke*. Instead, he argues that still other interpretations of the instructions given in *Marks* are plausible, and so concludes that *Marks* fails to extract any holding from *Bakke* concerning the constitutionality of diversity affirmative action. Unlike the majority in this case, Boggs refuses to find in Powell's opinion the narrowest possible rationale for justified affirmative action.[55]

Unfortunately, Boggs, as well as the majority in this case, fails to see that there is a straightforward application of *Marks* to *Bakke*. In *Marks*, the majority interpreted its plurality decision in *Memoirs v. Massachusetts* (1966). In that case, three justices wanted to reverse the censorship of a book depicting a prostitute's life on the grounds that while the book was hard-core pornography, the book had *not* been shown to be utterly without redeeming social value. Another justice wanted to reverse the censorship on the grounds that the book

---

[55]Judge Boggs also attached a "Procedural Appendix" in which he took the very unusual step of criticizing the timing and manner in which this case was brought before the Sixth Circuit Court of Appeals. Such public criticism is virtually unheard of with respect to legal decision, and in an earlier case, Judge Boggs himself scathingly attacked a fellow judge for simply revealing a procedural vote count—much less than he himself did in this case.

had not been shown to be hard-core pornography, and two other justices wanted to reverse the censorship on the grounds that they did not think that hard-core pornography should be prohibited. The U.S. Supreme Court in *Marks* determined that the holding in *Memoirs* was the view of the first three justices, because it would reverse the censorship of the book on the narrowest possible grounds.

If we look now to the *Bakke* case, I think we can find a straightforward application of the U.S. Supreme Court's instructions in *Marks*. In *Bakke*, both Powell and the Brennen group hold that race can be used as a factor in admissions programs for educational institutions. Powell thinks that race can be used as a factor when it is a means to achieving diversity in educational institutions, something he takes to be a constitutionally permissible goal. By contrast, the Brennan group thinks that race can be used as a factor in determining admissions for educational institutions on the grounds that it would help remedy the effects of societal discrimination, a goal the group also takes to be constitutionally permissible. According to *Marks*, the holding in *Memoirs* rejects censorship when hard-core pornography can be shown to have some redeeming social value, but allows censorship for the whole range of cases with respect to which the other members of the plurality opposed censorship. Similarly, Powell's opinion as the holding in *Bakke* allows the use of race as a factor when it is a means to achieving diversity in educational institutions, but rejects any more sweeping use of race in educational institutions that the Brennan group might have favored.[56] So we have here what seems to be a fairly straightforward application of the instructions in *Marks* to the *Bakke* case.[57] One hopes that now that

[56]It is true that as the Supreme Court in *Marks* interprets *Memoirs*, there is a rejection of X in one case coupled with an allowance of X in other (broader) cases, whereas in *Bakke*, there is an allowance of X in one case coupled with a rejection of it in other (broader) cases. But this is because *Memoirs* is mainly about rejecting something, while *Bakke* is mainly about allowing something. The inner logic of both cases is still the same, and the holdings with respect to rejecting something in the one case and allowing something else in the other are still "on the narrowest possible grounds."

[57]It might be objected that Powell's justification for using race as a factor in admission programs for educational institutions is not really narrower than the justification of remedying societal discrimination that the Brennan group fa-

the U.S. Supreme Court has chosen to hear together the appeals of the *Grutter* decision from the Sixth Circuit and the *Gratz* decision from the District Court, it will also recognize how its own instructions in *Marks* show that Powell's opinion is the holding in *Bakke*.

One also hopes that the court will be aware of the impact of shutting down affirmative action programs in education resulting from Proposition 209 and various lower court decisions. In 1996, before Proposition 209 took effect in California, there were 89 Hispanic Americans, 43 African Americans, and 10 American Indians enrolled as first-year students at the top three University of California law schools. In 1997, these numbers fell to 59, 16, and 4, respectively. That year saw only one African American enroll in the freshman law class at Berkeley, where there had been 20 enrolled in the first-year class the year before.[58] At the University of Texas at Austin, whose admissions system was challenged in *Hopwood*, the percentage of African American law students entering dropped from 5.8 percent (29 students) in 1996 to 0.9 percent (6 students) in 1997.[59] American Indian enrollment at the law school dropped from 1.2 percent (6 students) in 1996 to 0.2 percent (1 student) in 1997.[60] Hispanic

---

vors. But the justification for using race to achieve diversity in educational institutions that Powell favors would cease once the racial groups at issue were no longer underrepresented minorities in those educational institutions. Once that occured, would the Brennan group still think there was any need to correct for societal discrimination in those institutions? Suppose it would. In that case, Powell's justification would surely be narrower than the Brennan group's justification, as it is usually thought to be. Alternatively, suppose the Brennan group thinks that the need to correct for societal discrimination in educational institutions ceases once the relevant racial groups are no longer underrepresented in those institutions. It would then be even easier to determine the holding in *Bakke*, because under that supposition, the scope for the use of race in educational institutions would be the same under the justification offered by Powell and under the justification offered by the Brennan group.

[58] In 1998, the African American enrollment at Berkeley was 8, in 1999, it fell to 7, in 2000, it remained at 7 and in 2001, it rose to 14.

[59] It then rose to 1.8 percent (9 students) in 1998 and fell to 1.7 percent (9 students) in 1999.

[60] It then increased to 1 percent (5 students) in 1998 but fell to 0.4 percent (2 students) in 1999.

enrollment dropped from 9.2 percent (46 students) in 1996 to 6.7 percent (31 students) in 1997.[61]

What is particularly disturbing about the criteria for admission that are being used once diversity affirmative action has been declared illegal—criteria that have the effect of significantly limiting minority enrollment—is that they are so tenuously related to the sort of graduates these educational institutions ultimately hope to produce. For example, LSAT scores at the University of Pennsylvania law school have only had a 14 percent correlation with students' first-year grades. Moreover, they do not correlate at all with conventional success in the profession, as measured in terms of income, self-reported satisfaction, and service contributions. Moreover, almost all Michigan law school minority graduates who pass a bar exam go on to have careers that are successful by these conventional measures, something that would not have happened for many of them without affirmative action. Interestingly, Harvard University, in a recent study of its graduates over a 30-year period, found only two correlates of its successful graduates, where success was similarly defined in terms of high income, community involvement, and a satisfying career. Those correlates were blue-color background and *low* SAT scores.

In addition, following 9/11, the U.S. Justice Department under John Ashcroft has interviewed more than eight thousand people nationwide—the majority of them Middle Eastern men age 18 to 46 who came to the United States within the last two years on nonimmigrant visas—in search of information on terrorist organizations such as al Qaeda. The Justice Department denies that it is engaging in racial or ethnic profiling. According to Assistant Attorney General Michael Chertoff, "What we are looking to are characteristics like country of issuance of passport. . . . "[62] But as Justice Brennan pointed out in an analogous context, "The line between discrimination based on 'ancestry or ethnic characteristics' and discrimination

---

[61]It then increased to 7.6 percent (37 students) in 1998 and to 8.1 percent (42 students) in 1999.

[62]Michael Chertoff, Testimony Before the Senate Judiciary Committee Hearing on Preserving Freedoms while Defending against Terrorism, Federal News Service, 28 November 2001.

based on 'place or nation of . . . origin' is not a bright one."[63] Thus, if the U.S. government can justify such large-scale uses of "racial and ethnic classifications" for the benefit of the general population, surely it can justify a much more limited use of racial and ethnic classifications to achieve diversity affirmative action in higher education, given the benefits of such programs to their recipients and to the student body as a whole.

In light of these considerations, therefore, the U.S. Supreme Court should reaffirm the *Bakke* decision, which has been guiding educational institutions in the United States for almost 24 years. The case for nonremedial diversity affirmative action is as strong as it ever was; in fact, it is stronger now that we have studies and reports that prove the benefits of racial diversity in education. Accordingly, diversity affirmative action should be regarded as justified when

1. Race is used as a factor to select from the pool of applicants a sufficient number of qualified applicants to secure the educational benefits that flow from a racially and ethnically diverse student body; and
2. Proponents may admit only those candidates whose qualifications are such that when their selection is combined with a suitably designed educational enhancement program, they will normally turn out, within a reasonably short time, to be as qualified as, or even more qualified than, their peers.

But, as I have argued earlier, we could justify affirmative action in higher education on remedial grounds as well. Given that the poorer educational experiences that minorities have in the United States are the result of either present or past discriminatory practices, institutions of higher education should be able to institute affirmative action programs designed to make up for this discrimination. In addition, once the standard of proof for race-based remedial affirmative action programs is suitably lowered to that used for sex-based remedial affirmative action programs, it should be possible to correct for a broad range of present and past discriminatory practices with remedial affirmative action programs in higher education.

---

[63] *St. Francis College v. Al-Khazraji*, 481 U.S. 604 (1987).

9

Objections to Affirmative Action

The types of affirmative action programs I have been defending in this essay have been criticized in various ways. Specifically, critics have claimed that affirmative action is objectionable for the following reasons:

1. It is not required to compensate for unjust institutions in the distant past.
2. It confuses the legitimate goal of eliminating discrimination with the illegitimate one of seeking certain proportionate outcomes.
3. It requires group rights that are not only illegal but immoral.
4. It harms those who receive it.
5. It is directed at the wrong people.
6. It is not directed at all of those who deserve it.
7. It is unfair to the white males against whom it discriminates.
8. Alternative programs are preferable.

The First Objection

In support of the first objection, that the existence of unjust institutions in the distant past, such as American slavery, does not necessitate affirmative action, Christopher Morris argues that compensation for past injustices is owed only to individuals who would have been better off except for those past injustices.[64] With respect to individual African Americans living today, he asserts, it is not true that they would have been better off if there had been no American slavery,

---

[64]Christopher Morris, "Existential Limits to the Rectification of Past Wrongs," *American Philosophical Quarterly* 21 (1984), pp. 175–82.

because, given the contingencies of procreation, most African Americans who are living today would not even have been born if their ancestors had not been forcibly uprooted from Africa, enslaved, and brought to this country. Of course, in the absence of American slavery and the racism it engendered, some Africans would surely have emigrated to the United States, but they would have done so more like other immigrants, and their contemporary descendants would be different individuals from most present-day African Americans who trace their history through the practice of American slavery.

I think the best response to this objection is not to deny that most African Americans today are the product of American slavery and would not have existed without it, but only to point out that the injustices for which present-day African Americans deserve compensation are actually of more recent vintage.[65] For example, there are the injustices of segregated housing, unequal education, job discrimination, and inadequate health and welfare programs, all of which African Americans today would certainly be better off without. Of course, these current injustices do have their origins in the injustices of the past, particularly the institutions of American slavery and the Jim Crow laws that succeeded it, but the grounds that present-day African Americans can claim for compensation need not be the injustices of the distant past, but rather the ongoing injustices that make them worse off as individuals—injustices that other contemporary Americans are responsible for and could do something about, in part by endorsing affirmative action programs.

The Second Objection

In support of the second objection, that affirmative action confuses the legitimate goal of eliminating discrimination with the illegitimate one of seeking certain proportionate outcomes, Carl Cohen, Terry Eastland, Thomas Sowell, and others have distinguished between a "good" form of affirmative action that aims at eliminating racial and sexual discrimination, which they accept, and a "bad" form of

[65]A few African Americans, particularly those who have come or whose ancestors came from the Caribbean, are not the product of American slavery, but almost all African Americans have slavery of some sort in their background.

affirmative action that seeks certain proportionate outcomes based on race or sex, which they reject. The good form is associated with the equal protection clause of the Fourteenth Amendment, the Civil Rights Act of 1964, and certain Supreme Court decisions, and the bad form with certain bureaucratic decisions of the federal government and other Supreme Court decisions that are regarded as objectionable. Thus, Cohen writes: "In its original sense, affirmative action was intended to insure the elimination of racially discriminatory practices—that is the sense in which the phrase is used in the Civil Rights Act of 1964. . . . But if by affirmative action one means (as most Americans now do mean) preferential devices to bring about redistribution of the good things of life to match ethnic proportions in population, affirmative action in this sense must be rejected."[66]

But are these two forms of affirmative action really that distinct? Suppose we want to engage in the first form of affirmative action, that is, suppose we want to eliminate racially and sexually discriminatory practices. How do we go about doing it? Obviously, if we are faced with overt, clearly documented cases of discrimination, our task is comparatively easy. If the law prohibits discrimination, we can, for example, simply remove all "Whites Only" signs. However, at least since the Civil Rights Act of 1964, most discrimination in the United Stated has been covert and not so easy to document. Here, drawing attention to the unusual percentages of minorities or women in certain workplaces or elsewhere can be helpful. For example, in 1973, it was quite helpful to draw attention to the fact that, while half of AT&T's 700,000 employees were women, all of them were either telephone operators or secretaries, and in 1993, it was quite helpful to draw attention to the fact that most of the blacks employed by Shoney's Restaurant chain worked in the kitchen. This is why the Supreme Court has held that

> There is no doubt that where gross statistical disparities can be shown, they alone in a proper case may constitute prima facie proof of a pattern or practice of discrimination.[67]

[66]Carl Cohen, "Should Federal Affirmative Action Programs Continue?" *Congressional Digest,* June-July 1996, p. 185.
[67]*City of Richmond v. J. A. Croson Co.* (1989), p. 501.

However, when we attempt to correct for such disparities because we have determined them to be discriminatory, we are ultimately led to bring about a more reasonable proportionate outcome, with, for example, more women employed in more of the high-paying jobs at AT&T, and more blacks employed outside the kitchen at Shoney's. What this shows is that when we engage in the first form of affirmative action, and attempt to eliminate discrimination, we are led to pay attention to gross statistical disparities effecting minorities or women; when we find that these disparities cannot be justified, we are led to replace them with a reasonable proportionate outcome for the relevant minorities and women. This means that when we engage in the first form of affirmative action, we are led, naturally and justifiably, to engage in the second form of affirmative action; those who endorse the first form of affirmative action, as many do, cannot consistently avoid endorsing the second.

The Third Objection

In support of the third objection, that affirmative action requires group rights that are not only illegal but immoral, Carl Cohen argues: "Moral entitlements are not held by groups. Whites as a group do not have rights; blacks as a group do not have rights. Rights are possessed by persons. And when persons are entitled to be made whole for some injury earlier done to them, the duty owed is not to members of their race or sex or nationality, not to their group, but to them as individuals. The effort to defend preference as group compensation fails because it fundamentally misconceives the relation between wrongs and remedies."[68] But groups can and do have moral entitlements.[69] For example, in most countries, political

---

[68]Carl Cohen, "Should Federal Affirmative Action Programs Continue?" pp. 183, 185.

[69]For the argument that blacks as a group deserve affirmative action, see Paul Taylor, "Reverse Discrimination and Compensatory Justice," *Analysis* 33 (1973), pp. 177–82; Michael Bayles, "Reparations to Wrong Groups," *Analysis* 33 (1973), pp. 182–84; and Albert Mosley and Nicholas Capaldi, *Affirmative Action: Social Justice or Unfair Preference?* (Lantham, MD: Rowman & Littlefield, 1996), chapter 1. For the argument that they don't, see George Sher, *Approximate Justice* (Lantham, MD: Rowman & Littlefield, 1997), chapters 1–8.

parties are morally and legally entitled to use the monetary contributions of their members for various purposes. Moreover, any moral entitlement an individual possesses is always shared by some group or other, that is, it is held in virtue of some feature or other that the individual shares with the members of a particular group. Thus, for example, if a high school student deserves to be admitted to a prestigious college, it is in virtue of excellences the student shares with a group of students who also deserve to be admitted.

Nevertheless, what this objection is really about is when we should compensate for past discrimination. Cohen thinks we should compensate only when we can insure that no one receives compensation who is not the actual victim of proven past discrimination. Since compensation involves benefiting some at the expense of others, Cohen thinks we must be sure that those who benefit truly deserve it. Compensation for past discrimination is regarded as justified only when there has been a specific determination of past discrimination against a specific individual.[70] Accordingly, it would be wrong for a university to employ a remedial affirmative action policy to admit minorities from segregated, underfunded inner-city schools with lower grades and SAT scores without doing a comprehensive evaluation of each minority applicant to determine whether he or she has actually suffered from proven past discrimination. The sort of evaluation Cohen would require is far beyond anything that is currently used by colleges or universities, and few of them would have the resources to carry out such a comprehensive evaluation. So the net effect of imposing such a high standard of proof is that very few cases, if any, will satisfy the standard. Is this the way we should go about compensating for past discrimination?

Let us consider an analogous case. Presumably, prestigious colleges and universities want to ensure that they admit those applicants

---

[70]Cohen also appears to think that to be justified, this determination of past discrimination must be made by a court of equity, and that the institution doing the compensating must also be the institution that did the discriminating. Carl Cohen, *Naked Racial Preference* (Lanham, MD: Madison Books, 1995), pp. 188–89. I have previously argued against this second constraint. The first one is also unnecessarily strong and has been rejected by both the Supreme Court and Congress, which have allowed that the findings of past discrimination can be either "administrative, legislative, or judicial."

who are most qualified to benefit from the educational experience they provide and most likely to make important contributions to the educational development of their peers. Similarly, prestigious professional schools want to ensure that they admit those applicants who will most likely become talented and responsible lawyers, doctors, engineers, accountants, etc. Nevertheless, to implement these goals, U.S. colleges and universities have generally relied on grades and standardized tests. They have done this *not* because they believe this implementation conclusively picks out the most qualified applicants. For example, SAT scores only correlate 18 percent with first-year grades, and they are even less predictive in subsequent years.

Claude Steele illustrates this limitation of standardized tests with a helpful comparison.[71] Suppose you were to select a basketball team based on how many of ten free throws a player makes. The obvious limitation here is that free-throw shooting is only one of many skills needed to play basketball. There are even some great basketball players, like Shaquille O'Neal, who are poor free-throw shooters. Yet the same is true of standardized tests, which measure only a fraction of the skills that comprise a good student—only 18 percent. Another problem arises when we interpret a player's scores. Those players who made ten of ten would be selected for the team, and those who were unable to make any free throws would not be selected; but what about those who made between four and seven throws? Scores such as these could be influenced by many things other than a knack for free-throw shooting or basketball playing, such as the amount of practice or good coaching from which a player has benefited. The same is true for interpreting standardized test scores: Extreme scores (though still not very reliable) might permit some confidence in a student's likelihood of success, but scores in between are far more difficult to interpret. At issue is the degree to which scores are either inflated by middle-class advantages such as private schools and prep courses, or deflated by racial segregation and underfunded schools.

Actually, SAT scores turn out to be more predictive of family income (80 percent) than they are of college grades, and they are not

[71]Claude Steele, "The Compelling Need for Diversity in Higher Education," *Gratz v. Bollinger* (2000).

at all predictive of success after college. Studies have found that LSAT scores are even less predictive of grades. Accordingly, if schools really wanted to ensure that they admitted the most qualified applicants, they would have to maintain an extensive file on each applicant, which included, along with grades and standardized test scores, samples of the applicant's work, reports on the applicant's personal history, family, and friends, reports on interviews with the applicant, etc., that is, a file more like those that are put together when candidates are assessed for appointment to public office.[72]

Obviously, even elite schools of higher education do not have the time or resources to do a comprehensive assessment of each applicant's qualifications. For example, at the University of Texas law school, somewhere between 3,000 and 5,000 applications are received each year. These have to be processed in essentially a one-month period to attain a first-year class of 500 students. There is no way that the admissions committee can do a comprehensive evaluation of each applicant's qualifications. That is why grades and standardized tests are used, even though they are such a relatively poor measure of an applicant's qualifications. So, while prestigious colleges and universities maintain that they should be admitting the most qualified applicants into their programs, they continue to evaluate applicants for admissions in such a way that they end up rejecting a good number of applicants they should accept and accepting a good number of applicants they should reject. For them to do otherwise and really ensure that they admit only the most qualified applicants, they would either have to admit a much smaller number of applicants (whom they were able to determine were really very highly qualified), or expand their admissions staffs many times over, at significant cost to their educational programs, in order to be able to do comprehensive evaluations of still larger numbers of applicants. Obviously, neither of these alternatives is particularly attractive.

Moreover, even if schools began to do more comprehensive evaluations of applicants, they would still be just beginning to approximate the success rate of remedial affirmative action in remedying

---

[72]It turns out that what is most predictive of college graduation—which is probably what we really should be interested in—is the quality of one's high school curriculum in which one has done reasonably well.

past discrimination. Given the widespread racial and sexual discrimination in U.S. society, it is relatively rare for a remedial affirmative action program to go awry and compensate people who do not deserve to be compensated. Unlike the weak correlation between SAT scores and academic excellence, the correlation between being selected as a remedial affirmative action candidate and suffering from the relevant past discrimination must be somewhere around 95 percent. It does seem odd, therefore, to fault remedial affirmative action programs for not being foolproof, when we are willing to tolerate inaccurate school admissions procedures that have far greater negative impact on a just distribution of benefits and burdens in society. If we can tolerate school admissions selection processes that are not very successful at picking out the most qualified applicants for admission to colleges and universities, with all the unfairness in the distribution of benefits and burdens that entails, why should we not be more than tolerant of remedial affirmative action programs that succeed quite well at compensating just those who have suffered from proven past discrimination or the effects thereof, and that thereby contribute to a much fairer distribution of benefits and burdens?

Nor is the defender of affirmative action committed to compensating anyone, for example, because he or she happens to be of a particular race. Even in contexts in which all blacks deserve remedial affirmative action for past discrimination and the effects thereof, they do not deserve it *because* they are black, or because they belong to the group of black individuals, but rather because they have suffered the relevant discrimination or the effects thereof, and, hence, belong to the group of individuals who have suffered from the relevant discrimination.[73] What this shows is that both the

---

[73]While blacks do not deserve compensation because they are black, that is, because they belong to the group of black individuals, it sometimes seems that blacks are discriminated against simply because they are black, that is, simply because they belong to the group of black individuals. But on closer analysis, it would appear that blacks are not discriminated against simply because they are black but because those doing the discriminating unjustifiably believe that blacks are lazy or unclean or something similar. For this and other related points, see James Nickel, "Should Reparations Be to Individuals or Groups?" *Analysis* (1974), pp. 154–60.

defenders of affirmative action and their critics, including Cohen, agree that the only appropriate grounds for claiming that an individual deserves compensation for past discrimination is that the person himself or herself actually suffered discrimination or the effects thereof. Where defenders of affirmative action and their critics disagree, however, is over when we should allow that those grounds are satisfied. Critics of affirmative action want to impose such a high standard of proof that rarely would anyone qualify for compensation. To impose such a high standard would not only deviate radically from other accepted selection procedures (e.g., criteria for college admissions), but it would also allow discriminators and those they privilege to continue to enjoy their ill-gotten gains. On this account, this standard of proof should be rejected in favor of the lower standard of proof I have defended in this essay, a standard that can succeed quite well at compensating just those who have suffered from past discrimination.

It is also important to distinguish between remedial affirmative action that seeks to compensate for past discrimination (which we have just been discussing) and remedial affirmative action that simply attempts to put an end to present discrimination. With regard to this latter form of affirmative action, there is no need to prove that those who benefit from the affirmative action are those who were discriminated against in the past. *Local 28 of the Sheetmetal Workers Union v. EEOC* (1986) provides us with a clear example of this kind of affirmative action.[74] Similarly, we might view the Banneker Scholarship Program at the University of Maryland at College Park (UMCP) as part of an attempt to put an end to the present effects of past discrimination. Through its Banneker Program, what the UMCP was attempting to do, was improve its poor reputation among the African American community and also eliminate the hostile racial climate that existed on its campus, thereby creating, possibility for the first time, an equal educational opportunity environment for prospective African American students at UMCP. If the university had been successful, the main beneficiaries of its remedial affirmative action program would have been African American

---

[74]See the discussion on pp. 208–9

students who were subsequently admitted into the university; most of these beneficiaries would not have previously experienced discrimination from the university. This is just what we would expect, given that the main goal of the university's affirmative action program was to eliminate the current effects of past discrimination. Thus, there is no reason to think that those who would thereby benefit would be limited to persons whom the university had actually harmed in the past. Rather, they would be minorities who now, under conditions of equal opportunity, would be admitted to the university roughly in proportion to the availability of prospective African American students in the state of Maryland and in other areas from which the university draws its students. So it is possible to view the UMCP's Banneker Program as part of an attempt to create an equal opportunity playing field from which African Americans would rightly benefit, even if they hadn't been harmed by the university's past discriminatory practices or their effects. In this case, those who would benefit would be those who had just secured their right to equal educational opportunity at the UMCP.[75]

The Fourth Objection

In support of the fourth objection, Charles Murray claims that affirmative action harms those who receive it by placing women and minorities in positions for which they are not qualified.[76] Murray cites anecdotal evidence of women and minorities who were harmed in this way. In one example, a black woman is hired for a position for which she lacks the qualifications, and, as a result, her responsibilities are reduced, making her job a dead-end position. Yet I have argued that when remedial affirmative action has such an effect, it is not justified. To be justified, it must be directed at candidates

---

[75]A Supreme Court case that is difficult to classify in this regard is *Croson* (1989). Was the City of Richmond here attempting to compensate those who had been discriminated against in the past, or was it attempting to put an end to present discrimination in the construction industry in the Richmond area? I think we can say that it rightly was attempting to do both.

[76]Charles Murray, "Affirmative Racism," in James P. Sterba, ed., *Morality in Practice*, 6th ed. (Belmont, CA: Wadsworth Publishing Co., 2000), pp. 251–57.

whose qualifications are such that when their selection or appointment is combined with a suitably designed educational enhancement program, they will normally turn out, within a reasonably short time, to be as qualified as, or even more qualified than, their peers. So if remedial affirmative action is properly applied and carried out, it will not harm those who receive it.[77]

The Fifth Objection

In support of the fifth objection, that affirmative action benefits the wrong people, James Fishkin claims that affirmative action benefits the most qualified, who are actually the least deserving because they have experienced the least discrimination.[78] Yet the most qualified, who benefit from affirmative action in the U.S, may not have been subjected to less discrimination; they may simply have resisted discrimination more vigorously. And, even supposing that the most qualified were subject to less discrimination, why wouldn't affirmative action be the appropriate response to the degree of discrimination to which they were subjected? If we assume that remedial affirmative action is only provided to those candidates whose qualifications are such that when their selection or appointment is actually combined with a suitably designed educational enhancement program, they will normally turn out, within a reasonably short time, to be as qualified as, or even more qualified than, their peers, then remedial affirmative action does seem to be appropriately directed at the most qualified candidates among those who have suffered from past discrimination. More severe forms of discrimination, whose effects upon a person's qualifications and potential are even more detrimental, may require correctives other than affirmative action, such as remedial education and job-training programs. Moreover, those forms of remedial

---

[77]In the example cited from Murray, the black woman appears to have been so poorly qualified that even "a suitably designed educational enhancement program" would not have resulted in her becoming more qualified than, or even as qualified as, her peers. For that reason, affirmative action was not justified in this case.

[78]James Fishkin, *Justice, Equal Opportunity and the Family* (New Haven: Yale University Press, 1983), pp. 88, 89, 105.

affirmative action that involve opening up relatively unskilled entry-level positions to women and minorities, as in the construction industry, would benefit those who have suffered from the more severe forms of discrimination and who are even more deserving of compensation.

The Sixth Objection

In support of the sixth objection, that affirmative action is not directed at all of those who deserve it, Carl Cohen claims, "Compensatory affirmative action, if undertaken at all, must be undertaken for every person who qualifies on some reasonably objective standard, a standard free of racial (or sexual) orientation."[79]

Robert Simon agrees, maintaining that there are candidates besides women and minorities who have suffered from discrimination and prejudice, or simply from being economically disadvantaged.[80] Cohen mentions Appalachian whites and impoverished Finns from upper Michigan as additional candidates for affirmative action.[81] Why should affirmative action not be directed at these people as well as at women and minorities?

Why not indeed! Surely, if other individuals deserve compensation for other forms of discrimination and prejudice, or for simply being economically disadvantaged, then some remedy would be appropriate. So Cohen and Simon's objection is not an objection to remedial affirmative action per se, but rather an objection to remedial affirmative action as a narrowly conceived rather than a broadly conceived program. So, in fact, Cohen and Simon's analysis

---

[79]Cohen, *Naked Racial Preference*, p. 31.

[80]Robert Simon, "Affirmative Action and Faculty Appointments," in Steven Cahn, ed., *Affirmative Action and the University* (Philadelphia: Temple University Press, 1993), pp. 93–121.

[81]Cohen also suggests, however, that the inclusiveness of such an affirmative action program might lead to its abandonment. He writes: "If the complications grow excessive we may think it well to avoid the artificial inequalities likely to flow from inadequate data, or flaws in the compensatory calculation by refraining altogether from those calculations and again treating all applicants on the same footing." *Naked Racial Preference*, p. 31. But if this is Cohen's view, it would have the effect of simply freezing in place the effects of past injustices.

points to the need for a more broadly conceived affirmative action program.[82]

It should be noted, however, that if remedial affirmative action is to be extended in this way to remedy other injustices in society, it must become a larger program. In the United States, the few positions that have been targeted for affirmative action candidates have been created with the idea of simply remedying injustices suffered by women and/or minorities. If we now wish to remedy other injustices as well, we will need to create many more positions to deal with the increased scope of affirmative action.[83] Properly understood, Cohen and Simon's analysis points to the need for just such an expansion.

Unfortunately, in the United States, no one is offering to pay for such an expanded affirmative action program, with its larger outreach and its suitably designed educational enhancement programs. If we enlarge the scope of affirmative action to benefit a larger class of recipients for, say, $15 billion a year, there is no doubt that defenders of affirmative action would favor it over maintaining and developing current affirmative action programs. But obviously, in the real world in which we live, we do not have the option of having such an expanded affirmative action program. This is simply not a feasible option at present, at least in the U.S. So the question of whether affirmative action is currently justified in the U.S. is the question of whether maintaining and developing current affirmative action programs with their race- and sex-based preferences is justified in

---

[82]Under the eighth objection, I consider the possibility of substituting class-based affirmative action for race-based affirmative action. I take Cohen's and Simon's objection here to be different; it addresses the possibility of broadening affirmative action to include considerations of class as well as race and sex.

[83]Otherwise, socially and economically disadvantaged nonminorities, who tend to be more qualified because they have not suffered from racial discrimination, will fill most of the slots targeted for minorities in the original affirmative action programs. Moreover, if we are forced to choose here, there are good moral grounds for using the law to correct for sexual and racial discrimination rather than for discrimination against, for example, Appalachian whites and impoverished Finns from upper Michigan, given that sexual and racial discrimination are two of the deepest and most pervasive forms of discrimination in our society.

comparison with the other feasible alternatives. Since the alternative of having an expanded affirmative action program is not a currently feasible alternative, its preferability does not count against the justification of maintaining and developing existing affirmative action programs in the U.S. at this point in time.

The Seventh Objection

In support of the seventh objection, Barry Gross claims that affirmative action is unfair to nonminority males because it deprives them of equal opportunity by selecting or appointing women or minority candidates over more qualified nonminority male candidates.[84] To help fix ideas, consider the following two programs. Program A first hires women and minority candidates who are qualified over equally or more qualified nonminority male candidates and then puts them through a six-month training program, after which it lets go any trainees who are not as qualified as, or more qualified than, anyone else in the hiring pool. Program B first admits certain highly qualified women and minority candidates into a six-month training program for which nonminority male candidates are not eligible, and then hires just those women and minority candidates who, after completing the program, are equally qualified as, or more qualified than, anyone else in the hiring pool. I take it that Gross would object to Program A because it involves hiring women and minority candidates who are less qualified, but he need not object to Program B, because he need not object to every attempt to compensate women and minorities for past discrimination, but only to programs (like Program A) that he believes to be unfair because they involve hiring women and minority candidates who are less qualified over more qualified nonminority male candidates.

Bernard Boxill responds to Gross's claim of unfairness by denying that affirmative action is unfair to nonminority males who are passed over for affirmative action candidates.[85] After all, although these nonminority males may not actually have discriminated against

[84]Barry Gross, "The Case against Reverse Discrimination," in Sterba, ed., *Morality in Practice*, 4th ed. pp. 250–60.

[85]Bernard Boxill, "The Case for Affirmative Action," in Sterba, ed., *Morality in Practice*, 4th ed. pp. 260–72.

women and minorities themselves, Boxill argues that they have benefited from the discrimination of others, for example, through unequal educational opportunities.[86] Hence, women and minorities do deserve compensation for this unjust discrimination, and, moreover, affirmative action seems to be an appropriate form of compensation. It also is difficult to understand how the opponent of affirmative action could object to attempts to remedy past discrimination such as Program A while accepting attempts such as Program B, given that they are so similar.[87]

Of course, defenders of affirmative action can be challenged to prove that their candidates for remedial affirmative action have been discriminated against in the past, or that those who have lost out to affirmative action candidates themselves benefited from past discrimination. However, the standard of proof here should not be that of strict scrutiny because, as that standard is understood, only very seldom will the use of racial classifications be justified. Rather, as I have argued, the standard employed here should be the same that the U.S. Supreme Court has employed in cases of sexual discrimination, one that would allow for a variety of remedial affirmative action programs that can better help transform us into a more colorblind (racially just) and gender-free (sexually just) society.

Nevertheless, those who lost out to affirmative action candidates, even when they themselves benefited from past discrimination, might still see themselves as wronged by affirmative action. But how justified is this reaction? Surely, it would have no force against outreach affirmative action or against affirmative action that simply seeks to put an end to existing discrimination, because, while both these types of affirmative action may use race- and sex-based preferences, they only use them to create, possibly for the first time, an

---

[86]Of course, as I noted before, if someone passed over by an affirmative action program could make the case that he or she had not benefited from the discrimination suffered by the relevant affirmative action candidates (something it would be very difficult to do in the U.S. given its level of racial and sexual discrimination) that would have to be taken into account.

[87]I suppose someone could reject both programs on the ground that they both show preferences for women and minorities, although Program B lacks most of those features to which critics of affirmative usually object.

equal opportunity playing field. Surely, those who see themselves as wronged by affirmative action cannot be objecting to an equal opportunity playing field! It is also difficult to see how anyone could justifiably complain against an affirmative action program that aims to compensate for past discrimination or its effects when one has oneself unjustly benefited from that very discrimination. Thus, it would seem that the strongest case for those who claim to be wronged by affirmative action would have to be against diversity affirmative action. The argument would have to be that the benefits of diversity do not sufficiently outweigh the losses imposed on non–affirmative action candidates.[88] To better evaluate this argument, let us consider some other preference programs and practices that are commonly regarded as justified in the United States.

Most relevant to affirmative action in higher education are legacy and athletic preferences. In the United States, legacies constitute about 25 percent of the student body at select colleges and universities, and athletes constitute less than 5 percent of the male student body at a large school such as Michigan but as much as 32 percent at smaller liberal arts colleges. A recent study by the U.S. Office of Civil Rights even found that legacies admitted into Harvard were significantly less qualified than the average admitted nonlegacy. Yet rarely do people object to either of these forms of preference.[89] By contrast, those admitted on the basis of racial preferences make up generally between 5 and 10 percent of the student body at select colleges and universities, and the objectors to this form of preference are legion.

Most relevant to affirmative action in employment are veterans' preferences and nepotism. As part of veterans' preference in the United States, the federal government and most states simply add ten points to the civil service exam scores of disabled veterans or their wives, and five points to the scores of nondisabled veterans.

---

[88]Do the benefits to those who gain from a reliance on standardized tests such as the SAT and the LSAT outweigh the losses to those who lose out from that reliance?

[89]Most public professional schools also significantly favor in-state applicants. For example, the three public medical schools in West Virginia limit out-of-state applicants to 10 percent of their first-year classes.

After bonus points are added, veterans are often preferred over non-veterans with equal scores. Seven states give absolute preference to all veterans who simply pass their civil service exams. Veterans' preference in the United States is also lifelong. Even the Civil Rights Act of 1964 contains the following clause protecting veterans' preference: "Nothing contained . . . shall be construed to repeal or modify . . . special rights or preferences for veterans." It is also noteworthy that the generous veterans' preference enacted after World War II gave the same benefits to those who were drafted as to those who joined up, the same benefits to those who served overseas or saw combat as those who never left the United States.[90] And while it might be claimed that veteran's preference is to some degree earned, nepotism, or preferring one's relatives in employment, is not, yet it is widely practiced in the United States, especially in small businesses. In any case, rarely does anyone object to veterans' preference or nepotism. So if we regard these types of preference as justified, why should we not similarly regard using racial preferences to achieve important educational benefits or a more effective work force as justified? It is also interesting how after the September 11 terrorist attack on the World Trade Center and the Pentagon, the U.S. government has moved to use racial profiling (classifications) in a way that would never withstand strict scrutiny, even while it continues to treat racial classifications to achieve a colorblind (racially just) society quite differently.

But suppose you were against *all* of these forms of preference. In that case, you would need to rank them according to how objectionable each of them happens to be. If you did that, you would surely have to rank athletic and legacy preferences as the most objectionable. Failing to oppose these forms of preference more strongly than racial preference (as most of those who claim to be against all forms of preferences tend to do) would put your whole moral stance into question.

Sometimes it is argued that what is objectionable about racial preference is that "the extension of a right or benefit to a minority [has] the effect of depriving persons who were not members of a minority group of benefits which they would otherwise have enjoyed."[91] Yet transfers of benefits of this sort that have far greater impact on people's lives than affirmative action are often regarded as justified under U.S. law. Consider the following:

1. Open immigration laws benefit businesses by providing them with low-wage labor while decreasing the economic opportunities of the less-skilled residents of our inner cities;
2. keeping the unemployment rate high to fight inflation benefits businesses by restricting the job opportunities of the unemployed; and
3. keeping inheritance taxes relatively low benefits the wealthy at the expense of the poor, who would tend to benefit from greater public revenue.

While these policies, like affirmative action, clearly transfer benefits from some to others, few object to any of these policies. Could the difference be that these policies, unlike affirmative action, generally transfer benefits from the less advantaged to the more advantaged? Surely, that couldn't be an acceptable reason for favoring these policies over affirmative action! In any case, the opponents of affirmative action have to show why such transfers of benefits are justified while affirmative action is not, and it is not clear that they can do so.[92]

Of course, there are nonminority males holding desirable positions in society who have benefited more from past discrimination than have the nonminority males who would lose out to women or minority affirmative action candidates. So, ideally, an affirmative action program should demand sacrifices from these well-positioned nonminority males as well. This could be done by requiring them to retire early, or by reducing their work week to avoid having to lay off affirmative action hires, or by allowing affirmative action considerations to take precedence over seniority rules when actual layoffs become necessary.[93] Maybe we could target, among others,

---

[91]*Bakke* (1978).

[92]And if one thinks that these transfers are also objectionable, why then should they not be the first to be eliminated?

[93]For a discussion of this issue, see Ezorsky 1991. Interestingly, veteran's preference has been understood to trump seniority rules, while racial preference has not.

nonminority male college professors who have taught for more than 20 years. Yet while it would be morally preferable to place the burdens of affirmative action on those who have benefited most from past discrimination, when that is not politically feasible, it would still be morally permissible to place the burden primarily on nonminority males who are competing for jobs and positions with affirmative action candidates, given that they still have benefited from past discrimination, although not as much as others.[94]

The Eighth Objection

In support of the eighth objection to affirmative action, that alternative programs are preferable, Richard Kahlenberg has argued that affirmative action programs should be based on class rather than race, Lani Guinier and Susan Sturm have argued in favor of lottery programs, and others have supported programs like the Texas 10 percent plan or Florida's 20 percent plan. Let us briefly consider these arguments in turn.

Kahlenberg contends that class-based affirmative action is an appropriate substitute for race- and sex-based affirmative action; he wants the benefits that affirmative action provides to go to those who are disadvantaged by the socioeconomic class to which they belong.[95] In his attempt to provide an alternative to race-based affirmative action, Kahlenberg favors a complex measure of social and economic disadvantage, similar to the one that the UCLA law school has recently employed.

The UCLA law school looked at three family factors (an applicant's family income, father's education, and mother's education) and three neighborhood factors (proportion of single-parent households, proportion of families receiving welfare, and proportion of adults who had not graduated from high school). Using this measure

---

[94]In order to distribute the burdens of affirmative action programs more fairly, the government could use public revenues, where appropriate, to defray the costs of whatever educational or training programs are required for implementing such programs.

[95]Richard Kahlenberg, *The Remedy: Class, Race, and Affirmative Action* (New York: Basic Books, 1997); Kahlenberg, "In Search of Fairness: A Better Way," *Washington Post*, June 1998.

of social and economic disadvantage in its class-based affirmative action program, the UCLA law school was more successful than Berkeley's Boalt Hall law school or the University of Texas law school in maintaining some racial diversity in its entering class. Still, as a result of Proposition 209, black enrollment at UCLA law school dropped 72 percent in comparison to recent averages.

However, Kahlenberg favors adding even more factors than the UCLA law school used to measure social and economic disadvantage. For example, he would include net family wealth. He would also accept even lower standardized test scores. Nevertheless, this still will not be enough to capture the socioeconomic disadvantage that minorities, particularly African Americans, experience, such as the unjustified lower expectations of some of their teachers, and the stereotype threat that minorities, particularly African Americans, experience when taking standardized cognitive tests.[96] Of course, in principle, it should be possible to reduce racial disadvantage to a set of factors that do not include the factor of simply belonging to a particular racial group.[97] Nevertheless, if the measure of social and economic disadvantage is to be adequate, it will have to include factors such as "being discriminated against because one is a member of a particular minority group," just as any adequate measure of women's social and economic disadvantage that is due to sexism will have to include factors such as "being discriminated against because one is a woman."[98] Moreover, including such factors in one's measure of social and economic disadvantage should have the result that most middle-class minorities with adequate academic credentials will also qualify for class-based affirmative action. Unfortunately, none of the "class-based" affirmative action programs that have been proposed

---

[96]Claude Steele and Joshua Aronson, "Stereotype Threat and the Intellectual Test Performance of African Americans," *Journal of Personality and Social Psychology* 69 (1995), pp. 797–811.

[97]See my response to the third objection, in which I similarly claim that being a member of a particular racial group is not grounds for receiving remedial affirmative action.

[98]Or more accurately, the factor is being discriminated against because the discriminator unjustifiably believes that all the members of the minority group or all women are inferior for one reason or another, and so treats them in this discriminatory way.

so far include all the relevant factors in their measures of social and economic disadvantage. For that reason, none of them is an acceptable proxy for race-based affirmative action.

Guinier and Sturm's alternative to affirmative action would require schools to establish a minimum test score as acceptable and then hold a lottery for admission among those who meet the minimum standard.[99] Prospective students who offer qualities that are considered especially valuable, like being a Westinghouse Science Finalist, would have their names entered more than once in the lottery to increase their chances of being selected. The use of a lottery does inject an obvious fairness into the selection process, but requiring only a minimum test score will have an undesirable effect on the academic quality of incoming students at selective schools. In any case, at least at selective schools, where the minimum test score is relatively high, there will be disproportionately more whites than minorities in the lottery pool. As a consequence, Guinier and Sturm's lottery system will not function as an acceptable proxy for race-based affirmative action. Thus, for example, the University of Michigan law school has estimated that if it were to first select a pool of applicants with grades above 3.0 and LSAT scores above 150 and then to hold a lottery for admission among those who meet the minimum standard, the number of African Americans who would be enrolled under this system would almost certainly fall below 3 percent, in contrast to the 13 percent that are currently admitted under its existing diversity affirmative action program.

In contrast with Guinier and Sturm's lottery and Kahlenberg's class-based approach, Texas's 10 percent plan and Florida's 20 percent plan seem much more promising. We find that both plans are now successfully admitting minorities into their undergraduate institutions at levels that either match, or, in Florida's case, surpass what they had accomplished with race-based affirmative action programs. This was not accomplished, however, without a substantial increase in scholarship aid for minorities in both states, and without, in the case of Texas, using smaller classes and a variety of

---

[99]See Sturm and Guinier 1996; Lani Guinier, "The Real Bias in Higher Education," *New York Times*, 24 June 1997.

remedial programs.[100] Both plans also rely on at least de facto segregated high schools in their respective states to produce the diversity they have. If the high schools in both states were more integrated, the plans would not be as effective as they are with respect to undergraduate enrollment.

Even so, the plans as they presently exist still have some serious drawbacks. First, the plans do nothing for law schools, medical schools, and other graduate and professional schools where ending affirmative action has been devastating. As we noted before, African American enrollment at the University of Texas law school dropped from 5.8 percent (29 students) in 1996 to 0.9 percent (6 students) in 1997. It then rose to 1.8 percent (9 students) in 1998 and fell to 1.7 percent (9 students) in 1999. Second, the Texas plan has a detrimental effect on the admission of minorities not in the top 10 percent, who, pre-*Hopwood*, might have been admitted. Minority students who are not in the top 10 percent of their high school graduating classes have little hope of admission under the Texas 10 percent plan. These are not satisfactory results. Surely, a race-based affirmative action program can do better.

Nevertheless, if race-based affirmative action is to be justified in the United States, we will need to restrict the beneficiaries of remedial affirmative action that aims at compensating for past discrimination and its effects to those who today still continue to suffer from the effects of historic injustices, that is, to restrict it primarily to African Americans, American Indians, Hispanic Americans and women generally who have suffered from certain forms of discrimination. Other types of affirmative action, however, that aim at outreach, putting an end to existing discrimination, and achieving diversity can be justifiably used more widely to benefit minorities and women generally as they are needed to achieve the ultimate goals of a colorblind (racially just) and a gender-free (sexually just) society.

---

[100]While the Florida plan seems more generous than the Texas plan, appearances are a bit deceiving. The Florida plan does not guarantee admission to the state's two flagship universities, the University of Florida and Florida State University, whereas the Texas plan does guarantee admission to its two flagships, the University of Texas and Texas A&M University.

10

Affirmative Action outside the United States

There are a number of interesting similarities and differences between affirmative action as practiced in the United States and affirmative action as practiced elsewhere in the world. In India, affirmative action, which is called reservation, was endorsed by constitutional convention in 1950–51, following independence, making it the longest continually functioning such effort in the world. The very first amendment to the Indian Constitution empowered the state to make "any special provision for the advancement of any socially and educationally backward class of citizens or the Scheduled Castes and the Scheduled Tribes." The Scheduled Castes are the Hindu untouchables, constituting about 15 percent of the population, and the Scheduled Tribes are geographically isolated groups with aboriginal cultural features, constituting 7.5 percent of the population. The constitutional convention left it to special commissions and the central government to determine who belonged to the socially and educationally backward classes, popularly referred to as Other Backward Classes. Reservation quotas of 15 percent for Scheduled Castes and 7.5 percent for Scheduled Tribes were immediately enacted by the central government for jobs and places at educational institutions under its control. State governments enacted similar reservations. No reservation was originally envisaged for the Other Backward Classes with respect to the central government, but each state government was left free to make such reservations in this regard as it saw fit.[101]

[101]Interestingly, the Indian Supreme Court sees equality as enhanced by reservation. In 1992, the court said, "Equality . . . is secured not only when

Two national commissions in India attempted to specify who should belong to the Other Backward Classes in social and economic terms rather than in terms of caste, but neither was able to do so. The second commission, the Mandal Commission, specified 3,743 castes, making up 52 percent of India's population, as belonging to the Other Backward Classes, and it recommended a 27 percent reservation for those who belonged to those classes. The central government accepted this recommendation in 1991. More recently, an additional preference has been given to those who are most economically disadvantaged within each of these three general caste-based categories of backward classes.

Affirmative action in Malaysia dates from 1969, when Malay natives went on a rampage against ethnic Chinese immigrants in Kuala Lumpur, leaving 196 people dead, three-quarters of them Chinese. Following the riots, the government launched an affirmative action program with two goals: to wipe out poverty, regardless of race, and to restructure society so that no ethnic group could be identified with a specific set of jobs. The results have been impressive. The incidence of poverty has plunged from 74 percent of Malays in 1970 to 6 percent in 1994, and Malays now constitute 64 percent of the students at public universities. The Malay share of national wealth has also soared from about 1.5 percent in 1969 to 19.4 percent in 1998, but the ethnic Chinese share has also increased from 22.8 percent three decades ago to 38.5 percent today. The main losers have been foreigners, whose share has plunged.

In South Africa, progress through affirmative action programs in both the public and the private sectors has been fairly rapid following the rise to power of the African National Congress under the leadership of Nelson Mandela in 1994.[102] So far, more than one million black South Africans have moved from poverty to the middle class,

---

equals are treated equally but also when unequals are treated unequally. . . . To bring about equality between unequals . . . it is necessary to adopt positive measures to abolish inequality." *Inda Sawhney v. Union of India* (1992).

[102]The South African Constitution, like the U.S. Constitution, requires equal protection of the laws, but, unlike the U.S. Constitution, it also expressly permits measures designed to protect or advance persons disadvantaged by unfair competition.

primarily as a result of affirmative action job opportunities. In 1998, the University of Witwatersrand, long known for its promotion of racial diversity, admitted more black than white students for the first time. Nevertheless, women have been ignored in most affirmative action programs in South Africa, where women of all races are still prohibited from opening bank accounts or entering into business contracts without their husbands' permission. While the government did create a Commission on Women's Emancipation to study the problem, it then appointed a man to head the commission.

By contrast, the Court of Justice of the European Union in *Marschall v. Land Nordrein-Westfalen* (1997) has ruled in favor of affirmative action for women where there are fewer women than men in a particular occupational bracket, "unless reasons specific to an individual male candidate tilt the balance in his favor." This decision permits an even stronger preference for women than that allowed by the U.S. Supreme Court in *Johnson v. Transportation Agency of Santa Clara County* (1986). While the *Johnson* decision limits a preference for women to traditionally segregated workplaces, the *Marschall* decision permits affirmative action for women *whenever* there are fewer women than men in a particular occupational bracket.

So we see that affirmative action programs in India, Malaysia, and South Africa are much more extensive than those in the United States, and the European Union now has a broader legal basis for affirmative action for women than the United States does. In addition, the failure in India to find a non-caste-based criterion for reservation is surely relevant to the similar attempt in the United States to find a non-race-based criterion for affirmative action. It suggests that this U.S. attempt will also fail.

11

Conclusion

After the American Civil War, there was a flurry of legal activity during the reconstruction period that attempted to remedy the injustices of slavery. The withdrawal of federal troops from the South in 1877, together with new oppressive state laws and supportive Supreme Court decisions, however, ushered in a period of Jim Crow law, culminating in the Supreme Court's separate-but-equal decision of *Plessy v. Ferguson* (1896). Beginning, however, with the *Brown v. Board of Education* decisions in 1954 and 1955, and continuing through the Civil Rights Acts of 1964 and 1972, including a number of Supreme Court decisions on affirmative action—such as *Gregg* (1971), *Bakke* (1978), *Fullilove* (1980), and *Local 28 of the Sheetmetal Workers Union* (1986)—the United States seemed to be moving toward greater enforcement of racial and sexual justice. Yet recently there has been a shift. Starting especially with the Supreme Court decisions in *Croson* (1989) and *Adarand* (1995), and continuing in the Fifth Circuit decision in *Hopwood* (1996) and California's Proposition 209 (1996), there has been a trend to interpret the equal protection clause of the Fourteenth Amendment in such a way that it now primarily protects the white majority in this country against minority claims to compensation for present and past discrimination. The equal protection clause of the Fourteenth Amendment was enacted to provide special help and protection to blacks against discrimination by state and local governments.[103] Today, it is

---

[103]Eric Schnapper, 1985.

being used primarily to deny most minority claims for compensation because they do not meet an extraordinarily high standard of proof.

Rather than continue in this unfortunate direction, I have argued that we should support the following requirement for *outreach affirmative action*:

> All reasonable steps must be taken to ensure that qualified minority and women candidates have available to them the same educational and job opportunities that are available to nonminority or male candidates.

I have also argued for the following requirements as to when *remedial affirmative action* is justified:

1. The past discrimination that is to be remedied must be proven discrimination, but the institution that is engaging in the affirmative action need not be implicated in that proven discrimination in order for the affirmative action in question to be justified.
2. Although in a colorblind (racially just) society, racial classifications would no longer be presumptively suspect, in the United States, racial classifications must be regarded as presumptively suspect because of 250 years of slavery in the U.S., 100 years of Jim Crow, plus discriminatory practices that continue right up to the present day. However, the standard of proof required to justify the use of racial classifications in remedial affirmative action should not be unreasonably high as it is in the *Croson* case. It should not be easier to correct for sexual discrimination in society than it is to correct for racial discrimination. Accordingly, remedial affirmative action still has a significant role in combating proven past and present discrimination in housing, education, and jobs, unless more broadly conceived and much better funded corrective policies are undertaken.
3. Programs may admit only those candidates whose qualifications are such that when their selection is combined with a suitably designed educational enhancement program, they will normally turn out, within a reasonably short time, to be as qualified as, or even more qualified than, their peers.
4. Those who are passed over by such affirmative action programs would have themselves been found to have benefited from the discrimination suffered by the affirmative action candidates, for example, the

discrimination found in their unequal educational and residential opportunities.[104]

Lastly, I have argued that we should regard *diversity affirmative action* as justified when the following requirements are met:

1. Race is used as a factor to select from the pool of applicants a sufficient number of qualified applicants to secure the educational benefits that flow from a racially and ethnically diverse student body.
2. Only candidates are selected whose qualifications are such that when their selection is combined with a suitably designed educational enhancement program, they will normally turn out, within a reasonably short time, to be as qualified as, or even more qualified than, their peers.

Only by implementing these requirements will we be able to reach that colorblind (racially just) and gender-free (sexually just) society to which both defenders and critics of affirmative action claim to aspire.

---

[104]Of course, if someone passed over by an affirmative action program could make the case that he or she had not benefited from the discrimination suffered by the relevant affirmative action candidates (something it would be very difficult to do in the U.S. given its level of racial and sexual discrimination) that would have to be taken into account.

SECTION THREE

Reply to James Sterba

Carl Cohen

(1) An Overview

Should all those of one race or sex, or of one national origin, be given preference in employment or education or commerce? James Sterba contends that such preference is often right and good; I argue that it is wrong and bad.

Disagreements of this kind cannot be resolved, or even more fully understood, by disputing definitions of affirmative action. The term "affirmative action," originally given to policies designed to *eradicate* all preference by race, is now used also to refer to policies that *employ* race preference rather than eliminating it. The original objective having been very honorable, the words "affirmative action" retain a positive tone. So those who support race preference are pleased to call it "affirmative action"—but under that agreeable rubric they clump policies that are not preferential and not in dispute with outright race preference. This is an understandable strategy, but it badly confuses the issues before us.

Court decisions and public referenda almost invariably avoid using the words "affirmative action" because the meaning of that expression is so badly blurred, so uncertain. It is the use of *race* (or color or national origin) to give *preference* that is the nub of our national controversy, moral and legal. Whether such preference should be given is what this book is about.

How James Sterba defines "affirmative action" is of no consequence in resolving disagreements about preference. Definitions of "affirmative action" are legion, and readers will have no difficulty in formulating definitions of the phrase that would invite its defense, as well as alternative definitions that would insure its rejection. Sterba finds it surprising that "the degree to which people in general are in favor of affirmative action depends in large measure on how that policy is described," but it is not at all surprising that how we judge a policy depends on what we think that policy to be.[1] When the substantive issues in dispute are clear, however, stipulated definitions of loosely used phrases are not helpful.

In this book the questions genuinely in dispute were asked plainly and given straightforward answers in the opening essay:

- Is it *morally right* to give preference by race? I answered that it is not, explaining the immorality of such preference at length in chapter 4.
- Is it *lawful*, or *constitutional*, to give preference by race? I answered that it is not, explaining the unlawfulness of such preference in chapter 5, and the unconstitutionality of such preference in chapter 6.
- Is it *wise*—for minorities and for all Americans—to give preference by race? I answered that it is not, explaining the injuries such preference does to minorities in chapter 7, and the injuries it does to us all in chapters 8 and 9.

I respond here to Sterba's views on these central questions, pertaining to the morality, legality, and wisdom of race preference. I decline the invitation to quarrel about his definition of "affirmative action," or his many dissatisfactions with particular Supreme Court decisions.

Before responding, I note some spheres of agreement. He and I are at one in recognizing that the history of racial oppression in our country is critical in addressing these matters. We both seek racial justice in the light of that history, in our universities and courts and communities as they are, not merely in some ideal world.

Two specific matters, within that larger concern for justice, we also agree upon:

1. Outreach. Some of the disparities in the circumstances and performance of ethnic groups are the result of long-continued

[1]James P. Sterba, "Defending Affirmative Action, Defending Preferences," Chapter 2, p. 199.

racial and national discrimination; some are the result of other historical factors and assorted cultural differences. Whatever the causes have been, where the outcome is reduced participation by ethnic minorities in the professions, or in the universities, or in some spheres of employment and commerce, it is surely right to amend policy so as to encourage the participation of all, and to take great care to see that minorities are not excluded. Public institutions can and should be widely welcoming, reaching out to all. Where barriers to general participation have long stood we ought to act affirmatively to dismantle them. In that egalitarian spirit, James Sterba and I share a commitment to outreach.

2. Race consciousness. We also agree that identifiable wrongs done to persons because of their race or sex or national origin call for remedy, and that such remedy may on occasion require consciousness of race. We both would prefer a world in which the color of skin mattered no more than the color of eye, but we also understand that in contemporary America one cannot be entirely colorblind because attention to skin color is under *some* circumstances (as our courts have noted) a requirement of justice. That far we agree.

However, between the race consciousness that justice may at times require and naked race *preference* (often obscured by calling it affirmative action), there is a profound difference, explained at length in chapter 4. The latter, advantage given to all of a given skin color (or national origin, etc.) simply in virtue of their having that color or origin, cannot be justified either in morals or in law. Sterba does defend such naked race preference, however, and on this matter we are in sharp disagreement. I will respond here to

a. his unwillingness to recognize that race preference is explicitly forbidden, in the United States, by federal law;

b. his misguided complaints about the established constitutional standard of strict scrutiny, by which the permissibility of any racial classification is judged under the equal protection clause of the Fourteenth Amendment; and

c. his defense of group rights and the morality of race preference.

I will conclude by rejoining to his replies—every one of them inadequate—to the eight solid objections to preference that he himself has set forth.

James Sterba is a distinguished professor of philosophy, my colleague and my friend. He is a very good man. Meaning no disrespect, I will for convenience refer to him throughout simply as Sterba.

(2) Sterba on Race Preference and the Law

Sterba does not confront the problem of illegality; he ignores it. But it is no small thing if the policy one supports is a plain violation of law, as race preference indubitably is.

This having been explained in great detail in chapter 5 of my essay, the matter can be dealt with very briefly here. The Civil Rights Act of 1964—a very fine law that we all support and do not seriously think of defying—is unambiguous in stating that it is *unlawful* for employers and institutions receiving federal financial assistance to discriminate against any persons because of their race, color, religion, or national origin. The race preference that Sterba defends does, *must* discriminate against some persons—white persons mainly, but Asians too—because of their race. No one can deny, with a straight face, that this is a violation of that Civil Rights Act.

Sterba does not mention this awkward and inescapable problem. Perhaps he has nothing to say about it, and thinks silence his wisest course. But if he (or any advocate of race preference) were to reply, there appear to be only three options open to him:

1. He might seek to deny that the minority preferences given by universities, employers, and government agencies are the kinds of discrimination the legislature intended to forbid with the Civil Rights Act. In that case, I would ask him to read the debates that took place on the floor of the House and the Senate in 1964, to learn that it was *precisely* preferences of the kind now given that our Congress took themselves to have forbidden. No other construction of the words of that law, examined by legislators in meticulous detail at the time of its passage, can be honestly defended. I think Sterba knows this, but I am not certain that he does.

2. He might seek to deny that preferences on the ground of race and ethnicity are actually given by contemporary institutions. In that case, Sterba, or anyone truly in doubt about current practice, need only read the findings of fact by impartial judges in recent court cases in California, Texas, Maryland, Georgia, and Michigan, and elsewhere. These formal findings plainly confirm what we all know from personal experience: race preferences in America are frequent, significant, and widespread; they are indubitable and they continue as I write. One who denies their reality is not likely to be taken seriously. I believe Sterba knows this well, and this may help to explain his silence about the federal law that forbids them.

3. He might agree unhesitatingly that race preferences are widely given, and agree reluctantly that exactly those race preferences are what the law forbids, but contend that it is a bad law and ought to be repealed or amended to permit the preferences he supports. To this I would respond: a) It isn't going to be repealed or amended, as Sterba knows well; b) obedience to the law, even if one doesn't accept its wisdom, is part of doing justice here and now; and most important c) there is no federal statute of which he and I and all our American readers could be more proud than the Civil Rights Act of 1964. One passage in this law (Section 601, from Title VI) reads:

> No person in the United States shall, on the ground of race, color, or national origin, be excluded from participation in, be denied the benefits of, or be subjected to discrimination under any program receiving Federal financial assistance.

Sterba and his friends have no satisfactory response to the inescapable conclusion that preference by race is flatly unlawful.

(3) Sterba on Race Preference and the Constitution

What is forbidden by the Constitution cannot be authorized by any statute, of course; the Constitution is the highest law of the land. But what is permitted, although not specifically protected, by the Constitution may yet be forbidden by statute—by a law of the United States, or a law of one of the several states. Race preference is certainly not protected by the Constitution, and it is (as explained at length in chapter 5) unambiguously forbidden by federal law. Therefore race preference cannot be defended as lawful by showing that the Constitution permits it. Even if Sterba were correct in believing that discriminating by race is consistent with our Constitution, it nevertheless remains unlawful because it is an indubitable violation of the Civil Rights Act of 1964.

But in fact race preference is *not* consistent with the U.S. Constitution. Anyone who contends that it is must show how such preference can be squared with the forceful words of the Fourteenth Amendment: "nor shall any State . . . deny to any person within its jurisdiction the equal protection of the laws." The amendment in which this rightly famous clause appears was added to our Constitution in 1868 precisely to forbid the use of race or color to discriminate in the application of the laws. The plain words of that clause, as they have been understood and applied over the course of our constitutional history since the Civil War, do not permit deliberate discrimination by race—which is what contemporary race preference admittedly is. This constitutional bar to race preference I recount in detail in chapter 6.

How is Sterba to escape this ineluctable result? He twists and squirms in the effort to convince readers that when the Supreme Court and other appellate courts have thrown out set-asides based on race, and university admissions preferences based on race, and employment preferences based on race, and so on and on, they have been blundering repeatedly because they fail to recognize the reality of race discrimination and thus apply the concept of "equal protection" mistakenly.

But appellate and Supreme Court decisions, rejecting preference by applying the equal protection clause, have been scrupulously fair, and the language with which they have condemned racial discrimination has been emphatic; it is, they repeatedly conclude, *odious* and *intolerable*.

Sterba now defends policies giving deliberate race preference, policies that, by their nature, must discriminate by race. It would surely appear that they violate the equal protection clause. But he and others contend that these are special circumstances under which some ethnic preferences are justified. How ought claims like his be evaluated? What standard should be applied in deciding such controversies? In this—that is, in formulating the test for deciding whether the equal protection clause has been violated—our constitutional history has evolved rationally and fruitfully. The reasoning has been essentially as follows:

Racial classification we know to be insidious and always suspect. We bear in mind the history of the Fourteenth Amendment, adopted in 1868 to incorporate the principle of equal treatment of the races into the Constitution itself. The meaning of the 17 words of the equal protection clause—"nor shall any state . . . deny to any person within its jurisdiction the equal protection of the laws"—construed in the light of that history gives strong reason to conclude that deliberate discrimination on the basis of race or color or national origin is forbidden. We will hear the argument of those who claim, in spite of those plain words, that it is for some reason right to weigh the race of persons differently, but we will hear it skeptically. Two things must be shown if their argument is to succeed. First, they will have to show that their use of race in applying the law responds to a state need that is *compelling*; and second, they will have to show that the use of race they propose very closely serves (is *"narrowly tailored to"*) that compelling state need.

These are the two prongs of the test of *strict scrutiny*. It is a test developed and refined over decades of deliberation, carefully formulated so as to permit the use of race when that use is inescapable, but also to screen out those uses of race that would violate the equal protection clause. Understood in this way, strict scrutiny is not (as Sterba repeatedly suggests) an arbitrary standard of proof imposed to determine the reality of race discrimination. Nor is it an arcane legal technicality. It a reasonable moral criterion with which race preferences, apparently discriminatory but conceivably justifiable, may be justly appraised.

Suppose (for example) a school board gives employment preference to minorities, contending that doing so is consistent with the equal protection of the laws. The preference explicitly provides for different treatment by race, so it would surely seem to be discriminatory. When that preference is defended in a federal court, the first critical question will be: *What is the compelling state need that such race preference is alleged to serve?* Justice Sandra Day O'Connor expressed this demand precisely in pressing an attorney for the Jackson, Michigan, School Board in 1985, as I reported in chapter 6. Said she, losing patience, "Maybe I can't get an answer, but I really would like to know what the compelling state interest is that you are relying on. . . . " If people of different colors are to be treated differently, there must surely be reasons thought to be of great weight, or the board would not come to defend racial discrimination in court. And tell us further, the board will be asked, *how does the racial instrument you use precisely serve that compelling need?* It must have been believed that it does so serve, for if not, that racial instrument would surely not have been used. So speak, says the court, in effect, to the defender of preference: "What is the compelling need you put forward, and how does your race preference address that need?" This is the standard of strict scrutiny.

These questions will not be easy for a school board or a university president (or any other advocate of preference) to answer. But knowing how unjustly race and national origin have been used in our country over the generations, we would not want the test for their just use to be an easy one. Sterba agrees. Recognizing that racial classifications have often been invoked with wrongful and invidious purpose, he joins in finding them suspect. He writes, "in the United States, there are good historical reasons to assume that racial classifications are presumptively suspect."[2] This, he allows, is an entirely "reasonable assumption." Indeed it is. And because that is so, because any use whatever of racial categories by the state is highly *suspect*, every proposed use of race will be obliged to pass that test of strict scrutiny. It is a test applied to the uses of suspect classifications, such as race or nationality, for generations with wholehearted approval. It is, as the judges say, settled law.

There is no serious question about the fairness of this standard. And yet Sterba believes that its requirements are too demanding. He thinks that the elements of strict scrutiny have been recently and arbitrarily imposed by the Supreme Court, *"beginning with the* Bakke *decision in 1978."*[3] He is quite mistaken in this belief. The standard of strict scrutiny has been invoked by the Supreme Court at least as far back as 1886 (in *Yick Wo v. Hopkins*, 118 U.S. 356)

[2]Ibid., Chapter 5, p. 223.
[3]Ibid., Chapter 5, p. 224 my emphasis.

and then reaffirmed by a unanimous Supreme Court in 1943 (*Hirabayashi v. United States*, 320 U.S. 81). It was invoked and emphasized by Justice Hugo Black in 1944 (*Korematsu v. United States*, 323 U.S. 214); invoked and emphasized again by Justice Byron White in 1964 (*McLaughlin v. Florida*, 379 U.S. 184); and then yet again explicitly invoked, using the words "most rigid scrutiny," by Chief Justice Warren in 1967 (*Loving v. Virginia*, 388 U.S. 1). By the time of the *Bakke* decision in 1978, the strict scrutiny standard was deeply and firmly established in our constitutional history; to determine if the preferences given by the University of California were to be acceptable under the equal protection clause, their justification would certainly require both a) the identification of the compelling need they served, and b) the showing that they were narrowly tailored to that compelling need. That standard remains in force, rightly.

This is the reasonable and inescapable demand with which Sterba ought to come to grips. But he does not. What he calls "remedial affirmative action" and "diversity affirmative action" do not satisfy the standard of strict scrutiny; the reasons they do not were given at great length in chapter 6. His defense of those kinds of preference does not confront the strict scrutiny standard forthrightly; he seems not to understand the demands of that standard. He appears to believe that if he (or some state agency defending preference) can pile up enough evidence to show that there really has been racial discrimination in some historical setting, the preferential uses of race would surely be acceptable now, and the test of strict scrutiny would have thus been shown to be unfairly onerous.

"The real worry," Sterba writes, "is that the court has chosen to impose too demanding a standard of proof."[4] But, he continues, in a case (*Croson*) in which a 30 percent racial set-aside by the City of Richmond was held unconstitutional, "the evidence of past discrimination is overwhelming." In his view, if there really and truly has been racial discrimination in the past, the strict scrutiny test rejecting preferences now must be too burdensome. "Given that I have argued that the standard of proof that the court is currently using" he writes, "is too high, it would make sense to lower that

---

[4]Ibid., Chapter 5, p. 216.

standard . . . " [5] But he is missing the moral and legal point. No one is disputing the reality of past discrimination. There *has* been discrimination; of course there has. That is not at issue. The strict scrutiny standard is not invoked to make that determination; the standard is invoked to appraise the acceptability of the race preference presently advanced. About any program Sterba or others now propose, about the racial discrimination being currently defended, we ask: what is the identifiable compelling need *it* seeks to meet? And *does* it meet that need?

The answers—that it is the need for diversity in classrooms, or the need to remedy earlier societal discrimination against blacks and other minorities—have been heard and weighed and rejected by our highest courts again and again—not because there has been no discrimination, but because the programs in question cannot be justified by it. Societal discrimination (whose reality is not in dispute) cannot serve to justify race preferences given now because that discrimination reaches so far back into our history, is so *amorphous*, and has had effects so difficult to measure and specify that permitting it to serve as a justification for remedy now would open the door to unlimited race preferences of unlimited kinds for ethnic groups untold. No, Sterba; societal discrimination, no matter how high one piles the evidence that it was real, cannot satisfy the strict scrutiny test because it does not constitute a compelling state interest that deliberate race preference now can serve.

Even if the quest for historical remedy were thought to be compelling, racial instruments in hiring and firing, or in admitting applicants to college, cannot give the remedy sought. If the historical denial of building contracts to black contractors creates the alleged compelling need, preference given to other black contractors now gives no benefits to parties who were in any way involved in that earlier misconduct and therefore does not meet that need; the benefits of preference now go to those who were not victims, and its burdens now are borne by those who were not perpetrators. If the historical exclusion of black students from a state university, or the inadequacies of public schools, were thought to create a compelling

---

[5] Ibid., Chapter 6, p. 228.

need for redress, preference given to black high school seniors seeking admission now gives no redress whatever to those who had been earlier wronged. If the alleged compelling need is intellectual diversity, as some now argue, it is plainer still that *racial* instruments cannot be tailored to serve it.[6] In neither case can advantage by skin color be a *fitting* response.

Sterba defends "remedial" and "diversity" affirmative action by repeatedly underscoring the cruel reality of discrimination in the past. He flogs a dead horse. His case is not advanced by showing that black students back then really were excluded, that black contractors back then really were discriminated against. They *were*, to be sure. What is at issue is not that history, but whether race preferences now defended can pass the two-pronged test of strict scrutiny.

Because they cannot, Sterba rails against strict scrutiny, suggesting again and again that it is unfairly demanding and excessively strict. He urges that the "standard of proof" be "appropriately lowered." He thinks the courts have been blind to historical discrimination and that his reiteration of the evidence may open their eyes.

---

[6]Justice Powell, in *Bakke*, held that diversity might serve as the requisite compelling need. But no other Supreme Court justice then or since has shared that view. Sterba writes, "it has been generally recognized that the Brennan group (which included Brennan . . . Marshall, Blackmun and White . . .) did support Powell's view in *Bakke*." This is false. It is false that they did support Powell's view, and it is false that they have been generally believed to have done so. The only three segments of Powell's opinion in which diversity is mentioned or discussed are segments that all four of the justices in the Brennan group *specifically refrained from joining*—although they certainly could have joined him without inconsistency. They understood very well Powell's claims about diversity—claims to which they did not wish to sign their names.

Sterba reasons that since both Powell and the Brennan four find the Harvard plan of 1978 constitutional, the Brennan group surely must have endorsed Powell's diversity rationale (p. 67). Not at all! If X implies Z, and Y implies Z, X and Y may yet be very different. If X supports a military buildup with preemptive war in mind, and Y supports the same buildup only to keep the peace, we may not infer that Y would endorse X's rationale for supporting the buildup. That old Harvard plan (i.e., what Harvard then *professed*) was approved by Brennan and by Powell to advance very different objectives. Sterba reasons badly.

But his evidence has been heard repeatedly and in fullest detail; after hearing it, the courts apply to the programs now in question a standard that is rigorous but entirely reasonable. Sterba does not appear to understand the thrust of the constitutional questions confronted: First, is the use of that racial classification by a state government justified by an identifiable need that is compelling now? But we have seen that not one of all the alleged needs advanced by advocates of preference is compelling in the needed sense. Second, has the preference been shown to be "narrowly tailored" to the allegedly compelling need that had been proposed? But we have seen that, even if Sterba had identified a compelling need, no application of preference by race could come close to meeting it; in place of tailors' shears (as one judge has put it) race preference uses a chainsaw.

The scrutiny of proposed uses of suspect categories such as race and national origin *ought* to be strict, very strict. By such scrutiny our highest courts determine whether the equal protection of the laws has been respected. That standard has been reaffirmed countless times over many decades; it will not be relaxed or replaced to permit the preferential uses of race by well-meaning folks. If we apply this standard, race preferences of the sort Sterba defends are not permissible under the U.S. Constitution.[6a]

(4) Sterba on the Morality of Race Preference

Put federal law, and the U.S. Constitution, to one side. What is *morally right* in this controversy? Is it right, as a remedy for injustice, that preference be given (say in employment or in education) to all those applicants who are black because they are black, even if they come from a wealthy family and fine private schools? No; being black is not an injustice deserving special consideration. Moreover, the supposition that the children of all black families are

---

[6a]The forthcoming decision in the Michigan cases *Gratz* and *Grutter* will address the question of what—if anything—the Constitution does permit as a justification for race preference. Sterba pleads that "the U.S. Supreme Court should reaffirm the *Bakke* decision. . . ." (p. 73). The uncertainty to which that outcome alone would lead renders it highly unlikely. But if that were to happen, we would be reminded that the 1978 race preferences of the University of California were struck down in that case; Alan Bakke won.

intellectually or educationally deprived is utterly false—as well as insulting. Special consideration, if ever it is to be given, is deserved only by those who have been wrongfully injured.

Desert is a moral matter; those deserving redress have had their rights infringed. Giving advantage to all of a given skin color, as a remedy, tacitly supposes that the skin color *group* is the possessor of rights that have been earlier infringed. But groups, as I argued in chapter 4, do not have rights, *cannot* have them. Not all Hispanics are the victims of colonialism, although many were. Nor is guilt for the conduct of some members of an ethnic group rightly imputed to the entire group. Not all Hispanics were guilty of atrocities against the indigenous tribes in America, but many were. The holders of rights like the bearers of guilt are persons, individual human beings. Some persons deserve remedy for wrongs done to them and others do not—but whether one has (or does not have) an entitlement to redress cannot be decided simply on the basis of one's skin color group or national origin.

On this point Sterba responds directly. He tells us that groups *do* have rights. His reasoning in support of this claim is extraordinary. Two arguments are given. The first is analogical: that groups have rights is shown, he says, by the fact that political parties are legally entitled to use the monetary contributions of their members for a common purpose. And remember, political parties are groups! The analogy misses the point. Organizations certainly are real; their members contribute to them to advance common purposes, of course. But when the membership in a group is by skin color, the moral issue is entirely different. The political party results from the voluntary activity of its members' joining to achieve some common end; the racial group arises from no joining, no activity, no willing of any kind. The remedy is given to (or the penalty is borne by) every member of a given ethnic group because some members of that group suffered (or committed) an earlier injustice. Inferring that common purpose in the one case (political parties) justifies common redress in the other (racial groups) is simply fallacious.

Moreover, even organizational activity would not justify ascribing some guilt that deserves penalty, or some injury that deserves redress, to every member of the organization in question. Because some Socialist Party candidates have been treated unfairly in past elections, are we to conclude that all Socialist Party candidates are rightly to be given a special advantage in subsequent elections? Electoral misbehaviors by some Democrats or some Republicans in the past have been egregious; should we conclude that such wrongs justify a subsequent electoral burden on all members of the guilty party? Absurd.

There is a *moral* problem in giving race preference that Sterba does not seem to grasp. We can by law assign specific duties or entitlements to formally constituted organizations with membership largely known. But alleged racial entitlements do not flow from established organizations with known objectives and voluntary membership; duties cannot be assigned to all members of an ethnic group; moral claims for (or against) an entire ethnic category cannot be justified.

Behind Sterba's overall view lies an implicit remedial argument—that if members of a minority were repeatedly treated unjustly, members of that minority today are entitled, all of them, to compensatory relief. Many good-hearted folks support race preference in this amiable spirit without careful reflection. Blacks in our country have been given a dreadful deal; so (the reasoning goes) let's now give blacks a somewhat-better-than-even deal. But this remedial response seems plausible only because the indirect object, "blacks," is viewed conceptually as if it were a *unit*, like a person who, having been unjustly deprived before, is now to be made whole by being given extra. And the burdens of that giving are mistakenly supposed to be shared by the subject, the ethnic majority treated as a unit and thought obliged to pay for the better deal to be given—when in fact the burdens of preference are borne not by a mass but by relatively few innocent individuals.

Ethnic groups are not persons, not moral units. That is the point of the frequent and appropriate observation, by judges in our federal courts, that the rights protected by the equal protection clause of our Constitution are *individual* rights. Every one of us, as an individual, is guaranteed equal treatment before the law. The fact that members of our ethnic group, whatever it may be, behaved very badly in the past cannot justify imposing a penalty upon us. The fact that members of our ethnic group, whatever it may be, were dealt with cruelly and unjustly does not entitle all in our group to recompense. It is we, as individuals, not our ethnic groups, who are the holders of moral rights and moral duties.

If ever a group were treated with cruel injustice, the Jews who suffered in Nazi Germany were—and they are, indeed, entitled to compensatory relief. But the "they" in this sentence refers to the persons and families who were so deeply wronged. I, who write this, am as fully Jewish as any one of them, and I am entitled, because of their great injury, to nothing. Compensation to Jews around the world as payment for the great hurt done to their fellow religionists has no moral justification whatever. Those Jews in Germany were wronged because they were Jews, to be sure; the Nazis were avowed racists and anti-Semites. But their atrocities were inflicted on *persons*; it is not the ethnic group but the *persons* and families having suffered those horrors who are entitled to redress.

Many well-meaning folks like Sterba think habitually of ethnic groups as units, and seek to deal with them, and give to them, as if they were unitary. But good will, as a consequence of this habit, is misdirected; benefits are mistakenly awarded, burdens are unfairly assigned. Sterba's second reason for concluding that groups have rights illuminates this misdirection. Moral entitlements are payable to groups, he asserts, because those entitlements are "held in virtue of some feature or other that the individual shares with the members of a particular group."[7] He takes the sharing to be the key. But a shared entitlement for redress, if there is one, can arise only from a shared injury, a shared deprivation; it does not arise from *any* feature of those persons that they may share. It is not the *sharing* that yields the entitlement, but the *injury*. I am Jewish, and I share much with other Jews. But if other Jews are tortured and their worldly goods confiscated, I am not entitled to relief on their behalf because I share their religious convictions or their heritage. Again and again, Sterba makes the same blunder, treating people as group members above all else, rather than as the individuals to whom redress may indeed be owed.

This is the deep root of the entire matter, and the heart of the disagreement between Sterba and me. The assumption of group rights gives rise to misunderstandings that now tear our national fabric. At bottom it is not merely the Constitution (which commands equal treatment for all persons) or federal law (which forbids

[7]Chapter 9, p. 255.

discrimination by race against any person) but, underlying them, morality itself that is offended by ethnic preference. It is wrong to deal with people as though they are but tokens of a group. It is wrong to impose handicaps upon people because of their color or origins, just as it is wrong to give them special favor for those same reasons. Preference by race, by sex, by national origin—even when motivated by a spirit of generosity, as in Sterba's case—is morally corrupt. It violates the most fundamental principles of personal entitlement and responsibility, and it inevitably corrupts the society in which it is given.

(5) Objections, Replies, and Rejoinders

Eight objections to race preference are listed in the penultimate section of Sterba's essay, each followed by his answering defense. In truth, every one of those objections, fully understood, is sound. Some of them Sterba does not appear to understand fully; some he understands but presents inadequately; in every case his answers are shallow. I conclude my reply to him by addressing each of these eight concerns in turn.

First objection: Race preference is not required to compensate for unjust institutions of the distant past.

Indeed it is not. This objection is really only part of a larger concern about the suitability of preference as remedy. Preferential schemes are commonly viewed as a way of making up for oppression in the distant past. But with the passage of time and the maturation of new generations, Sterba agrees, race preference today cannot be justified as redress for ancient cruelties. So he must put forward a different set of injuries for which the preferences he defends are to be seen as remedies. The lapse of time between injury and remedy is not a serious objection to race preference, he argues, because the real injuries for which race preference is to compensate are ongoing injustices suffered by present-day African Americans that "other contemporary Americans are responsible for."

The reasoning here is crude. Ethnic preference he now puts forward as remedy for a host of social problems that it does not even touch upon, and some of which are not injuries inflicted by anyone.

"Segregated housing" has many causes and is not to be blamed simplistically on any racial group. "Job discrimination" is an injury for which specific legal remedies, targeting those who discriminate, already exist. And even those who share Sterba's political convictions about welfare and housing will find it difficult to explain how "inadequate welfare programs"[8] are to be remedied by race preference in law school admissions, or by preference in fire department promotions. To escape the problem of time lapse, Sterba offers a list of current social problems, conceived by him as blameworthy injuries, without even a hint as to why preference is an appropriate "remedy" for them.

But to think of it as a remedy, one must *suppose* that the instrument is appropriate in view of the alleged injury suffered. Anyone who makes that supposition must confront those many difficulties, discussed at length in chapter 4, in deciding who was hurt, how badly hurt, how the hurt might be remedied, and who ought properly bear the cost of the remedy if any remedy is possible. Sterba finds it convenient to bypass all of this, simply asserting, without any rational support, that the race preferences he defends give proper recompense for inequities imposed by an uncaring majority.

But preference to *all* members of a minority cannot be just compensation for injuries to some of them, ancient or recent. Preferences fail as compensatory devices not only because of the time lapse that Sterba acknowledges, but also for the deeper reason that because they are given on the basis of color or national origin, they cannot be a genuine response to injury. Sterba defends *naked* preferences, preferences awarded to all the members of certain ethnic groups, merely in virtue of their membership. Ward Connerly, regent of the University of California, observes: "When we give a preference to a Latino applicant over an Asian to compensate for what a white student's ancestor did to a black student's ancestor, your head starts to spin." And Toni Morrison, Nobel Laureate in literature and profound student of American life, sums up the matter with eloquent concision: "When you know somebody's race, what do you know? Virtually nothing."

---

[8]Ibid., Chapter 9, p. 252.

Second objection: Race preference confuses the legitimate goal of eliminating discrimination with the illegitimate goal of proportionate ethnic outcomes.

Indeed it often does. Sterba replies to the objection by suggesting that there *is* no real difference between eliminating discrimination and achieving proportionality—thus providing a vivid illustration of the moral mistake he takes himself to be answering.

Discriminatory practices often have ethnically disparate outcomes—a fact not in dispute. From this fact, Sterba infers that efforts to undo disproportionate outcomes, to "replace them with a reasonable proportionate outcome for the relevant minorities and women," are no more than attacks on discrimination itself. But this is simply false; he makes an embarrassing logical blunder.[9] From the fact that racial discrimination may result in racial disparities, it certainly does not follow that the racial disparities we encounter generally are to be understood as everywhere the *consequence* of racial discrimination. Not at all. In schools and colleges, for example, racial disparities have stubbornly persisted in spite of prolonged, vigorous, and deeply committed efforts by schools and communities to overcome them. Racial clustering in residence, and racial patterns in employment and in recreation, are largely the results of unforced choices.

So there is indeed a huge difference—a difference of great moral consequence—between ethnically disparate outcomes that may have many causes, on one hand, and deliberate race discrimination, on the other hand. It is indeed a mistake, therefore, to suppose that to overcome unjust discrimination we must eliminate the ethnic disproportions that pervade social life. The pursuit of ethnic proportionality, which Sterba warmly supports, is certainly *not* to be identified with efforts to extirpate discriminatory practices. The latter is affirmative action in its honorable and original sense; the former, the idealization of group proportionality, is unjustifiable social engineering with a racial twist.

[9]Ibid., Chapter 9, p. 254.

Third objection: Race preference "requires"—that is, it supposes—that groups have rights.

Indeed it does. In the preceding section of this response, on the morality of race preference, I explain the assumption of group rights that race preference entails, and the deep mistake embodied in that assumption. Sterba's wholly inadequate replies—the first relying upon the analogy of political parties, and the second upon the sharing of entitlements by members of a group—are dealt with at length in that section.

But in replying to this third objection, Sterba makes an admission very damaging to the case for preference; he allows expressly that, in truth, "the only appropriate grounds for claiming that an individual deserves compensation for past discrimination is that the person himself or herself actually suffered that discrimination or the effects thereof."[10] In this, he thinks his critics correct—but the problem with their argument, he says, is that *their standard of proof is too high!* Now, what is this unreasonable standard we critics insist upon? We ask what compelling state interest is being served by the race preference proposed, and we ask whether the proposed preference is properly devised to meet that allegedly compelling need. Our critical standard is only the standard long established and applied by the U.S. Supreme Court: the standard of *strict scrutiny.* Sterba would reject it "in favor of the lower standard of proof I have defended in this essay."[11] Sterba's lower standard of proof, it turns out, yields the result that race preference is justified where disparate ethnic outcomes can be shown; entitlement to that preference is established by proving certain national origins or exhibiting certain skin colors.

Fourth objection: Race preference harms those who receive it.

Indeed it does. The damage done to minorities by preference is cruel, long lasting, and manifold. The many injuries done to minorities by giving preference—all ignored by Sterba with only one

---

[10]Ibid., Chapter 9, p. 259.
[11]Ibid.

exception—are explained at length in chapter 7. I recap them here: Preference obscures the real problem of why many minority members are not academically competitive; preference obliges a social choice of some minorities to be preferred over other minorities; preference compels a determination of how much blood is needed to establish race membership; preference removes incentives for academic excellence; preference encourages separatism by minorities, divides the society, and seriously injures race relations over the long haul. But worst of all, race preference undermines the credentials of all the members of a minority, reinforcing stereotypes of inferiority, humiliating and stigmatizing minority members who cannot respond or cleanse themselves of the imputed weakness. All things considered, race preference (although it does directly benefit a few minority members) is a dreadful and penetrating burden for the minorities preferred.

About all of this Sterba has nothing whatever to say. Injury to minorities he does list as the "fourth objection," but his very brief reply to it addresses only the mismatch of minorities and academic institutions that some critics find to have damaged those who were given preference. Sterba's entire response to all the injuries preference imposes on minorities is given in three sentences, and amounts only to saying that we must be careful to avoid that mismatch of capacity and role, and that if preference be given only to qualified minority candidates the mismatch won't arise, so any concern about injury to minorities may be put aside. In truth, it is probable that color preference will result, as it has resulted, in the inappropriate admission or appointment of marginally qualified persons. But that is only one, and not the worst, of many injuries.

The major harms done to minorities by preference, which are of quite another sort, Sterba does not seem even to have considered. The *subversion* of all members of a minority by the preferences only some of them receive, the *stigmatization* of minorities, the *humiliation* of minority scholars and professionals who have no need of charity but are presumed to need it, the *reinforcement of stereotypes* and the creation of links between minorities and the inferior performance produced by corrupt admissions and appointments—all of these deeply destructive injuries, discussed in detail in chapter 7, Sterba leaves wholly unattended.

In fairness, it should be emphasized that some minority members derive real advantage from preference; in exchange for admission to an Ivy League college, for example, many persons will find some stigma to be a tolerable price. But those benefits reaped by a few among the minority are vastly outweighed by the long-term injuries done to the minority as a whole. Preference by race is no service to the races preferred; it is in fact (as I earlier explained at great length) a source of profound and long-lasting hurt. And these are only some of the reasons that preference is bad as well as wrong.

Fifth objection: Race preference benefits the wrong people.

It does indeed. The real objection here has many layers, but Sterba replies (in one paragraph) only to the complaint that the beneficiaries of preference are likely to be the persons least harmed by discrimination. That isn't a serious problem, he says, because those minority members who do get the preference are likely to perform better than those minority members who (although they really were discriminated against) do not get it. It doesn't trouble him that the products of fine schools, reared in fine homes, who yet receive preference because they are black or Hispanic may truly deserve no preference at all. Why should skin color yield entitlement? Those (of any color) who can plausibly apply to a fine law school or medical school are sure to have received an upbringing and an education superior to that of the vast majority of whites and persons of all other colors.

But if there are those, Hispanic or black or white, who have been left so far behind that such an application for advanced study cannot be seriously considered, they will garner absolutely no benefit from the preference. That is indeed a pity, says Sterba—those who really have been hurt by discrimination "may require correctives other than affirmative action."[12] This leaves entirely unanswered the very reasonable objection that the benefits bestowed by race preference are indeed most likely to be received by those least likely to deserve it.

[12]Ibid., Chapter 9, p. 261.

Race preference bestows rewards unjustly; this objection has far greater reach than Sterba appears to recognize. The difficulty is not merely distortion in the light of relative desert. Group preference rewards *all* those in a given group, and within that group many will deserve no preference whatever. Preferences for women in universities sometimes yield special advantages to persons who have no justifiable claim to them. At many colleges, the number of undergraduate females is so great that admission preference has been given (at the University of Georgia, for example) to males. Preference by national origin is also generally undeserved. "Spanish descendancy" does not merit special treatment. All ethnic preferences are *over*inclusive because they presume some deprivation or some injury suffered by all of those who have a given origin or a given color of skin.

The objection that race preference is "directed at the wrong people" is entirely sound. A just compensatory response to injury requires a finding that those to be compensated have been injured. Race preference bypasses the most essential elements of fairness.

Sixth objection: Race preference is not directed at all those who deserve it.

This objection we may reformulate by saying that race preference is *under*inclusive as well as overinclusive. Indeed it is. Who might in truth "deserve it" is unclear—but if all those who suffered an injury or deprivation of a given kind deserve some compensatory relief, any preferential system that awards relief only to a racial subset of those deserving it is indeed despicable. To reward, from among all worthy claims, only the claims of minority members is plainly unfair. That unfairness is a common feature of preferences now widely given. Some minorities are favored; others—Asian Americans and many other cultural and national minorities, as well as impoverished whites—get no consideration whatever.

Sterba refers correctly to a passage that appears in an earlier book of mine.[13] I wrote:

> Some past injuries may be thought so cruel and damaging as to justify special consideration for professional school admission. But whether a

---

[13]Ibid., Chapter 9, p. 262.

particular person has been so injured is a question of fact, to be answered in each case separately. If special consideration is in order for
those whose early lives were cramped by extreme poverty, the penuri-
ous Appalachian white, the oppressed Asian American from a Western
state, the impoverished Finn from upper Michigan—these and all others similarly oppressed are equally entitled to consideration.[14]

Surely this demand of justice may not be flouted. If compensation
for injury is the operative principle, we cannot justly say: "You, X,
get relief because you are black, but you, Y, although your injury is
no different, get no relief because you are white."

Sterba, a generous soul, has a charming response. Make the preferences more widely available! No skinflint he; let everyone share
the spoils! Sterba explicitly supports preferences for categories of
persons without limit. This may not be feasible at present, he allows,
but "such an expanded affirmative action program with its larger outreach" does meet with his enthusiastic approval.[15] Since we cannot
have that, he concludes with regret, let us at least go on giving preferences as we do.

But what is viewed as redress for injury cannot be justly reserved
for those of certain favored ethnicities; this widespread unfairness
of racially restricted benefactions Sterba cannot rationally defend;
he does not even attempt to defend it.

Seventh objection: Race preference is unfair to the white males against whom it discriminates.

Indeed it is. The unfairness of preference is obvious when one asks
what our response would be if white skins were systematically preferred. We would be outraged. Our outrage would be justifiable, and
it would be caused not merely by the fact that whites were long preferred in fact. We would say, emphatically, that *no* preference by
skin color is acceptable under *any* circumstances. Race preference
in college admissions is commonly defended by calling attention to
the fact that race is "only one of many factors" considered. But this

---

[14]Carl Cohen, *Naked Racial Preference* (New York: Madison Books, 1995), pp.
30–31.
[15]Sterba, "Defending Affirmative Action. . . .": Chapter 9.

is no defense at all! If now it were proposed to give preference to whites once again, do we think that obvious injustice mitigated by the fact that their whiteness would be only one of many factors, and that academic considerations would also be weighed? Of course not.

And when race preference is awarded by agencies of the state, such as public schools or state universities, we would say that such discrimination becomes utterly intolerable. When Thurgood Marshall, as executive director of the Legal Defense Fund of the NAACP, presented to the U.S. Supreme Court his constitutional argument against racial segregation in the public schools, he wrote:

> Distinctions by race are so evil, so arbitrary and invidious that a state, bound to defend the equal protection of the laws, must not invoke them in any public sphere.[16]

The integrity and force of that moral conviction resonate still.

But preference cannot be unfair to white males, Sterba says in his reply, because women and minorities have been discriminated against in the past, and hence preference for them now does no more than create "an equal opportunity playing field"—and how could white males be wronged by that?[17]

Groupthink gets the better of him once again. For Sterba, if women were discriminated against, women deserve compensation, and if men did the discriminating, men deserve to pay the penalty. That the women and the men in the one case are not the women and the men in the other does not much trouble him. Most of the women and minorities against whom white males now compete were not discriminated against, and most of the white males in this competition had no role in any injury that may have been done to the forbears of minority applicants. That white males are now commonly discriminated against, in applications for employment, for professional school admission, and the like, is plain fact. Sterba may think the sins of the fathers are rightly visited upon their sons, but he cannot seriously contend that a white male now applying, for example, to the law school at the University of Michigan finds himself on an

---

[16]Brief of the Legal Defense Fund, in *Brown v. Board of Education* (1954).
[17]Sterba, "Defending Affirmative Action, . . ." Chapter 9, p. 266.

"equal opportunity playing field." Sterba may be unworried if white males get a nasty taste of what was long dished out to black females; he may even be secretly pleased at the reversal. But he will not persuade us that when preference is explicitly given to certain minorities, those in the majority suffer no racial discrimination.

Eighth objection: Alternative programs are better than race preference.

Indeed they are. Programs that do not discriminate by race are preferable to those that do. The objection Sterba has chiefly in mind here is one that would replace preference by race with preference based on socioeconomic class, or by a weighted lottery or some other nonpreferential scheme. These cannot suffice, he thinks, because they will not yield the ethnic proportionality that he takes to be the true measure of racial justice. On the other hand, replacing race preference in university admissions with a system that guarantees admission to a specified proportion of the graduating classes of high schools—the 10 percent plan in Texas and the 20 percent plan in Florida—he finds more agreeable. These programs are grafted onto systems of public education that are de facto segregated, and thus yield enrollment outcomes much closer to his ideal of proportionality.

That ideal of ethnic proportionality—sometimes explicit, more often tacit—is the vision that underlies the arguments of most of those who defend race preference. In the earlier chapters of the book, I sought to explain why this ideal is profoundly mistaken. It is a standard for judgment that arises from the conviction that if only discrimination could be eliminated, society would become somehow homogenized, that a society without discrimination would be a society in which ethnic clustering—in employment and schooling and recreation—would wither away. Convinced of this, the advocates of preference conclude that any continuation of such clustering must be evidence of continuing discrimination.

The egalitarian spirit that underlies such thinking is admirable. The cultural universalism implicit in the ideal is surely disputable. But the beliefs on which it is grounded are simply false. For those who prize cultural variety and the vigor possible only if voluntary ethnic clustering is protected, the ideal of ethnic proportionality is downright unwholesome, neither fitting nor feasible for the American body politic. The tacit application of that ideal is therefore misguided; we cannot fairly judge alternative programs by estimating the degree to which they will advance ethnic proportionality.

Which social programs are thought most "preferable" will depend upon one's larger aims, of course, and our aims will differ widely. But whatever our aims may be, I submit, they and the means employed to advance them ought to be wholly free of racial discrimination. The preferences that are the focus of this book are, in their essence, racially discriminatory—deeply wrong and very bad.

SECTION FOUR

Reply to Carl Cohen

James P. Sterba

There is much to admire in Carl Cohen's essay, as well as in his previous work on this topic. Cohen has been at the forefront of the discussion of affirmative action/racial preference for many years, even before the publication of his book *Naked Racial Preference*. In 1995, Cohen used the Freedom of Information Act to require the University of Michigan to reveal its own records on the affirmative action/race preference given to applicants for admission; his action gave rise to two lawsuits that now have been reviewed by the U.S. Supreme Court in the spring of 2003. He testified before the House Judiciary Subcommittee on the Constitution in 1997 and was an expert witness for the plaintiff in *Podberesky v. Kirwan*, Fourth Circuit, U.S. Court of Appeals (1994). What is most distinctive and impressive about his writings on affirmative action/racial preference is that, unlike most philosophers writing on this topic, Cohen strikes an admirable balance between attending to moral and political issues and to the legal and constitutional issues. This makes his work not only philosophically interesting but also extremely relevant to the current moral and legal issues we face in this area. Since I, too, want my work to be relevant to those same moral and legal issues, I am very pleased to have the opportunity to offer a critical response to Cohen's view.

It should come as no surprise that Cohen presents himself as an opponent of racial preference. Unfortunately, in so doing, Cohen is being a bit deceptive, because he does not oppose all uses of race or racial classifications, but only some. To quote Cohen, "The equal protection of the laws does not forbid *every* racial classification."[1] Those uses he opposes he refers to as "racial preferences." He could have made the same point, less deceptively, by referring to justified and unjustified uses of racial classifications/preferences, but he does not. Cohen's deceptive terminology here connects with the fact that he provides no general definition of affirmative action. While he recognizes a bad form of affirmative action which aims at racial preference and a good form that does not, he does not allow that the two of them share anything in common in virtue of which they are both "affirmative action," except for the fact that the bad form has historically tended to replace the good form. However, he could have done more. He could have allowed that both forms of affirmative action employ racial (or sexual) classifications, or racial (or sexual) preferences (used in a neutral sense), and that one form does it correctly while the other form does not.[2] But Cohen doesn't do any of this. Instead, he employs a terminology that has the net effect of making him appear more opposed to the use of racial classifications/preferences than he really is.

Once this deception is revealed, however, it becomes clear that Cohen agrees, at least in theory, with defenders of affirmative action who regard just some uses of racial classifications/preferences as morally justified, or just some uses of affirmative action as morally justified. Thus, my real debate with Carl Cohen has to be over which forms of racial (and sexual) classifications/preferences, or which forms of affirmative action (defined in terms of racial (and sexual) preferences are justified and which are not.

---

[1]See Carl Cohen, "Why Race Preference is Wrong and Bad," chapter 6, p. 74.

[2]One might think that defining affirmative action in terms of racial or sexual preference is an undesirable feature of affirmative action because someone might argue some forms of affirmative action, e.g., outreach, do not use racial or sexual preferences. As I define it, however, outreach affirmative action has the goal of searching out qualified women and minority candidates who would otherwise not know about or apply for the available positions, but then hire or accept only those who are actually the most qualified. It does, therefore, involve a preference for women and minorities; it involves doing something for them, preferring them, in a way that will create a real equal opportunity among the entire pool of candidates.

Cohen claims to oppose affirmative action on four grounds. First, he thinks it is *immoral*. Second, he thinks it is *illegal* because it is in violation of the Civil Rights Act of 1964. Third, he thinks it is *unconstitutional* as interpreted by recent Supreme Court decisions. Fourth, he thinks it *harms* just about everybody. I will examine each of these charges in turn.

First Charge: Affirmative Action/Racial Preference Is Immoral

Cohen thinks that certain racial classification/preferences are immoral because they aim at racial proportionality and to provide benefits to the members of a racial group simply because they happen to be of a member of that group. Actually, Cohen's objection here depends upon an interesting philosophical thesis. It is the thesis made famous by the Scottish philosopher David Hume, namely, that you cannot derive an "ought" from an "is." In this context, Hume's thesis implies that the conclusion that so-and-so *ought* to receive affirmative action cannot be derived simply from *is* statements, such as that so doing would result in racial proportionality, or that so-and-so is a member of a certain racial group.

Fortunately, a defense of affirmative action/racial preference does not need to violate Hume's thesis, as Cohen claims; it does *not* require a move from "is" to "ought." Rather, just as Cohen attempts to do with respect to those uses of racial classifications/preferences he regards as justified, a defense of affirmative action/racial preference can attempt to derive its "oughts" from other "oughts."

To see how this can be done, recall the Supreme Court decision in *Local 28 of the Sheetmetal Workers Union v. EEOC* (1986) discussed in my essay. In that case, the virtually all-white Local 28 had been found to be in contempt of every legal order to admit minorities between 1964 and 1986. To put a stop to that discrimination, the Supreme Court imposed a racial proportionality. It required the New York City–based union to increase its minority membership by admitting into its training program one minority apprentice for each nonminority apprentice until it reached a 29 percent minority membership. The goal of 29 percent was based on the number of minorities in the relevant labor pool in New York at the time. The argument of the court can be expressed as follows:

1. The racial discrimination of Local 28 *ought* to be stopped.
2. The proposed racial proportionality is an appropriate means for stopping that discrimination.
3. Hence, an affirmative action program employing the proposed racial proportionality *ought* to be implemented.

Clearly, this argument moves from an "ought" to an "ought," and so it does not violate Hume's thesis, although we may still choose to criticize the argument on other grounds.

An argument with a similar structure can also be used to support the settlement in the Shoney's Restaurant chain case reached in 1993, discussed in my essay. In that case, to put an end to discrimination and to compensate for past discrimination, the court awarded minority employees a financial settlement and moved them out of the kitchen and into the dining area in order to more accord with the percentage of the Shoney's work force they constituted.[3]

Of course, Cohen could have directed his critique at just some uses of racial proportionality rather than at all uses, and he could have criticized them for reasons other than that they violate Hume's thesis. Then our attention could have focused on whether particular uses of racial proportionality are justified. Unfortunately, Cohen chose to illegitimately target all forms of racial proportionality simply for attempting to derive an "ought" from an "is."

Cohen also goes on to identify all diversity affirmative action with the pursuit of racial proportionality and to condemn it on those grounds.[4] But this hardly does justice to diversity affirmative action. Racial proportionality has its applications in the context of remedial affirmative action. By contrast, diversity affirmative action is a non-remedial form of affirmative action; it claims to be justified on the basis of the future benefits that diversity provides, not as a remedy

---

[3]This argument can be expressed as follows:
  1. The discrimination practiced in the Shoney's Restaurant chain ought to be stopped and compensation paid.
  2. The proposed financial settlement and reassignments are an appropriate means for stopping and compensating for that discrimination.
  3. Hence, an affirmative action program employing just those means ought to be implemented.
[4]Cohen, chapter 4, pp. 37–39.

for past discrimination.[5] Diversity affirmative action aims to achieve a critical mass of underrepresented minority students in order to attain the benefits of racial diversity in various academic settings. That critical mass is determined not by the percentage of underrepresented minority students graduating from the relevant high school populations, as would have to be the case if racial proportionality were the goal. Rather, the number of students admitted is designed to be "sufficient to enable under-represented minority students to contribute to classroom dialogue without feeling isolated."[6] For example, at the University of Georgia, that number turned out to be about 6 percent of the student body, while the percentage of high school graduates in the state that are underrepresented minorities is 37 percent.[7] In my teaching experience, the critical mass sufficient to enable under-represented minority students to contribute to classroom dialogue without feeling isolated for a class of 30 is 4 or 5 students. To achieve that ratio in comparable classes throughout a college or university would then presumably require 13 to 17 percent minority enrollment.

As I noted earlier, Cohen also thinks that affirmative action/racial preference is immoral because it aims to provide benefits to the members of a racial group simply because they happen to be members of that group. But no defender of affirmative action need hold

[5]Of course, one could argue in such contexts that the same affirmative action that is justified on diversity grounds could also be justified on remedial grounds. Although I would want to make such an argument, many defenders of diversity affirmative action, aware of the current U.S. Supreme Court's hostility to remedial affirmative action, do not advance such an argument. See, for example, Ronald Dworkin, "Race and the Uses of Law," *New York Times*, 13 April 2001. In any case, it should be recognized that there are two separate arguments here for affirmative action.

[6]*Grutter v. Bollinger*, Sixth Circuit Court of Appeals (2002).

[7]The estimate for a critical mass at the University of Georgia was extremely conservative. For undergraduate admissions at the University of Michigan, that number was set at about 13.6 percent of the student body, when the proportion of underrepresented minorities in the relevant high school population is about 17 percent. In neither university does the percentage of underrepresented minorities approximate the proportion of those minorities that graduate from high schools in their respective states. See *Knocking at the College Door: Projections of High School Graduates by State and Race/Ethnicity 1996–2012.* (Western Interstate Commission on Higher Education, 1998).

such a view. Rather than argue that affirmative action is justified because it provides benefits to the members of a racial group *simply* because they happen to be members of that group, defenders of affirmative action can argue that it is justified for other reasons, for example, because it provides diversity or compensates those who actually have suffered discrimination. In this way, the racial predicate (being a member of a particular racial group) is linked to a nonracial predicate (e.g., providing diversity or having actually been discriminated against), with the goal of identifying an "ought" premise from which an affirmative action "ought" conclusion can then be derived.[8] Of course, we can always debate whether particular instances of this form of argument are justified.[9] Yet what is perfectly clear is that defenders of affirmative action need not be attempting to derive an "ought" from an "is," as Cohen claims.

Cohen further maintains that affirmative action/racial preference is unfair to those who lose out to affirmative action candidates. According to Cohen, this is because affirmative action both aims at racial proportionality and attempts to provide benefits to the members of a racial group simply because they happen to be members of that group. I have just countered both of these arguments. So is there any other reason for thinking that affirmative action/racial preference is unfair to those who lose out to affirmative action candidates?

[8]The arguments in these examples can be expressed as follows:
  1. A student body ought to have the educational benefits of diversity.
  2. Underrepresented minorities can provide that diversity.
  3. Hence, an affirmative action program that favors underrepresented minorities to achieve diversity ought to be implemented.

  1. Those who have suffered from past discrimination ought to receive compensation.
  2. Each member of a particular racial group in a particular context has suffered from past discrimination.
  3. Hence, an affirmative action program that compensates the members of that racial group ought to be implemented.
[9]For example, we might envision someone arguing in support of affirmative action starting from the premise that people *ought* to be compensated simply because they belong to a group many of whose members have suffered from discrimination. But while Cohen would surely reject such a premise, so would most defenders of affirmative action/racial preference.

Cohen thinks there is. It is that those who lose out to affirmative action candidates have not benefited from racial discrimination. Or, as he puts it, "racial instruments invariably impose penalties upon those who deserve no penalty at all."[10] Of course, this reason for thinking affirmative action/racial preference is unfair makes most sense in the context of remedial affirmative action, which attempts to compensate for present or past discrimination. It makes less sense in the context of diversity affirmative action since that form of affirmative action does not attempt to compensate for present or past discrimination. But even in remedial contexts, where this reason for thinking affirmative action/racial preference makes most sense, it is nothing more than the empirical claim that, in such contexts, those who would lose out to affirmative action candidates have not themselves benefited from present or past discrimination. Surprisingly, Cohen provides no evidence in support of this empirical claim. This is surely a place where an empirical premise plays a crucial role in Cohen's argument against affirmative action/racial preference, and where he simply leaves that premise unsupported.

In this context, Cohen also makes a number of related empirical claims:

1. "Those favored invariably include many who have been earlier deprived of nothing, and were never injured because of their race.[11]
2. "Many who are minority members deserve no remedy.[12]
3. "[M]any of Hispanic ancestry now enjoy here, and have long enjoyed circumstances as decent and as well protected as Americans of all other ethnicities. The same is true of African Americans. . . . "[13]
4. Even if those receiving race preference now had been injured earlier because of their race (a very dubious supposition). . . . "[14]

[10]Cohen, chapter 4, p. 33.
[11]Ibid.
[12]Ibid.
[13]Ibid., chapter 4, p. 27.
[14]Ibid., chapter 4, p. 33. The parenthetical material "(a very dubious supposition)" appeared in the penultimate draft and was removed from the final draft, presumably for stylistic reasons.

Surprisingly, Cohen leaves all these empirical claims unsupported, although he does offer considerable evidence to support other claims that he makes.[15]

Of course, if Cohen could have shown that these general empirical claims were true, he could then have profitably used them to provide a wholesale critique of particular remedial arguments that have been offered for affirmative action/racial preference in various contexts. Unfortunately, he simply does not provide *any* evidence at all for these claims, and so he cannot justifiably use them to support his critique.[16]

In my own essay, I cite considerable evidence showing that minorities and women are still subject to discrimination and to the effects of past discrimination. Even so, I never advanced any general overall argument for remedial affirmative action, but rather claimed that remedial affirmative action had to be defended on a case-by-case basis. For example, I defended the City of Richmond's minority set-aside program that was described in *Croson* (1989). I also argued that the poorer educational and residential experiences of

---

[15]For example, his case against Michigan's affirmative action programs is based on a detailed discussion of the specifics of the Michigan programs. Nevertheless, Cohen does tend consistently to *not* support the general *empirical* claims that he makes.

[16]In an addition made to the final version of his essay, Cohen cites (in a footnote) a case, *Worth v. Martinez*, that has recently been brought by the Center for Individual Rights against the U.S. Department of Housing and Urban Development (HUD) suggesting that "the passion to remedy the underrepresention of minorities is not matched by a concern for the underrepresentation of the white majority." But the idea that we should be as concerned about the underrepresentation of the white majority as we are about the underrepresentation of minorities is ridiculous. The United States has a long history of discrimination against certain minorities, but no comparable history of discrimination against its white majority! In fact, any prestigious area where minorities, particularly African Americans, are disproportionately represented, as in the NBA, always seems to attract considerable attention, but virtually no one suggests that whites are being discriminated against in such areas. So the idea that we should be equally concerned to search out and locate areas of both white and minority underrepresentation to check them out for possible discrimination flies in the face of U.S. past history and present reality. This is not to say that some attempts to discover areas where minorities are underrepresented and correct for them have not been unjustified. HUD may have engaged in some unjustified affirmative

minorities in the United States, experiences that are traceable to present and past discriminatory practices, justify remedial affirmative action. So we have here a contrast between Cohen's sweeping objection to remedial affirmative action based on unsupported general empirical claims and the case-by-case defense of remedial affirmative action that I favor, which is based upon considerable evidence relevant to each case. Surely, the contrast in argumentation could hardly be more striking.

As it turns out, however, failure to support empirical claims upon which his moral critique of affirmative action/racial preference rests is not Cohen's only failing here. He also attempts to use his unsupported empirical claims to attack diversity affirmative action programs in higher education, wrongly treating such programs as if they were remedial affirmative action programs when they clearly are not. For example, Cohen claims that "a daughter of a black physician who graduates from a fine college has been done no injury entitling her to preferential consideration in competitive admissions."[17] But even if this were true (and again Cohen offers no evidence to show that even middle-class blacks in the United States do not suffer from white privilege[18]), the claim is simply irrelevant as a critique of

---

action as is claimed in *Worth v. Martinez*. However, when minorities are underrepresented in a certain area, we are not required to prove that they have been discriminated against before we can demand a corrective; it suffices if the relevant employers cannot show the underrepresentation is due to business necessity. Moreover, when women or minorities are well represented in some general category of employment, it can still be reasonable to check out how they are doing in the more prestigious and better paying sub-categories of employment within the general category. This is because as women and minorities in greater numbers move into more and more categories of employment, some sub-categories of employment within those categories may become the last bastions of discrimination. Before any corrective can be required, however, employers must be given a chance to show that the underrepresentation in those sub-categories of employment is due to business necessity.

[17]Ibid, chapter 4, pp. 30–31.

[18]White privilege is an unearned privilege that all whites have but rarely notice that puts nonwhites at a disadvantage. Some examples of privilege are the following:

1. Whites can go shopping alone most of the time, pretty sure that they will not be followed or harassed.

diversity affirmative action. Diversity affirmative action does not purport to be justified on the backward-looking grounds that its recipients have suffered from present or past discrimination. Rather, it purports to be justified on the forward-looking grounds that its recipients can provide diversity, and this is surely something that even middle-class blacks who graduate from fine colleges can succeed in doing.

Of course, the ability of affirmative action candidates to provide diversity is not unconnected to present and past discrimination. Usually, it is because underrepresented minorities have experienced the effects of present or past discrimination themselves that enables them to bring diversity into educational contexts, and this is true even of middle-class minorities.[19] Still, the justification for diversity affirmative is not any compensation that its recipients might receive

---

2. Whites can use checks, credit cards, or cash, and can feel confident that their skin color will not work against the appearance of financial reliability.
3. Whites can arrange to protect their children most of the time from people who do not like them.
4. Whites can do well in a challenging situation without being called a credit to their race.
5. Whites are never asked to speak for all the members of their racial group.
6. If a traffic cop pulls them over or if the IRS audits their tax returns, whites can be sure they haven't been singled out because of their race.
7. Whites can be fairly confident that if they ask to talk to the "person in charge," they will be facing a person of their race.

Many more examples can be found in Peggy McIntosh, "White Privilege: Unpacking the Invisible Knapsack," http://seamonkey.ed.asu.edu/~mcisaac/emc598ge/Unpacking.html.

As one commentator has put it, "the only real disadvantage to being white is that it so often prevents people from understanding racial issues." See also Sylvia Law, "White Privilege and Affirmative Action," *Akron Law Review* 32 (1999), pp. 603–27.

[19]Patricia Gurin gives the following example of how middle-class blacks can aid the understanding of minority perspectives in a classroom setting. She reports:

In one class session, a white woman student who had grown up in a homogeneously white town in Michigan expressed, with considerable emotion, that she was tired of being categorized as white. "I'm just an individual.

for present or past discrimination, but rather to promote the diversity from which all can benefit. In sum, Cohen's attack on affirmative action here not only rests on unsupported empirical claims, it also inappropriately uses those claims to raise (unsupported) remedial objections to nonremedial affirmative action programs.

Nevertheless, later in this section of his essay, Cohen does raise an appropriate objection to nonremedial affirmative action programs that seek to provide diversity. He challenges such programs for failing to treat people as equals. The benefits of diversity, Cohen claims, cannot override our obligation to treat people as equals. To support his claim, Cohen asks us to suppose that segregated classrooms significantly improved learning and teaching. If we think that such educational benefits cannot justify the inequalities of segregated

---

No one knows if I hold similar beliefs to those of other white students just by looking at me. I hate being seen just as white." She ended in tears. An African-American male student who had grown up in a virtually all white city in Connecticut replied as he walked toward her across the classroom, "I just want to be an individual also. But every day as I walk across this campus—just as I am walking across this room right now—I am categorized. No one knows what my thoughts are, or if my thoughts align with other African-American students. They just see me as a black male. And at night, they often change their pace to stay away from me. The point is— groups do matter. They matter in my life and" (as he approached the other student whose hand he then took) "they matter in your life." There was silence in the room.

Gurin further comments, "The students learned about the meaning of groups and the meaning of individuals in a way that they won't soon forget." See Patricia Gurin, Response to the Critique by the National Association of Scholars of the Expert Witness Report of Patricia Gurin in *Gratz v. Bollinger* and *Grutter v. Bollinger*, http://umich.edu/admissions/new/gurin/html.

Similarly, in *Grutter v. Bollinger*, Sixth Circuit Court of Appeals (2002), Justice Clay maintains, "Notwithstanding the fact that the black applicant may be similarly situated financially to the affluent white candidates, this black candidate may very well bring to the student body experiences rich in the African-American traditions emulating the struggle the black race has endured in order for the black applicant even to have the opportunities and privileges to learn." Justice Clay also notes, "A well dressed black woman of wealthy means shopping at Neiman Marcus or in an affluent shopping center may very well be treated with the same suspect eye and bigotry as the poorly dressed black women of limited means shopping at Target."

classrooms, Cohen argues, then we should also think that the educational benefits of diversity cannot justify departing from our obligation to treat people as equals.

But while Cohen's comparison between segregated classrooms and diverse ones is appropriate here, his argument fails. This is because the problem with racially segregated classrooms is that they do not significantly improve learning and teaching for all students. Separate but equal simply does not work for all students. And, if for some inexplicable reason *everyone* happened to do just fine under a segregated, equal educational system (a claim that is sometimes made in support of sex-segregated schools), then there would no longer be any objection it. Thus, the argument against segregation is, in fact, based on its bad effects, particularly for those who are less advantaged. We reject racial segregation because of its bad effects, and we endorse diversity in education because of its good effects.[20] So while Cohen's comparison between segregated and diverse classrooms is surely appropriate here, the differences in their effects require that we evaluate them differently.

Moreover, if using racial preference for the sake of diversity violates our obligation to treat everyone as equals, then so would the use of athletic, veterans', and legacy preferences, and so would the many laws in the United States that favor the rich and the middle class over the poor. But Cohen says nothing explicitly about these other "preferences," except to claim that racial preferences "have most corrupted admissions in recent years," which could imply that they are much more morally objectionable than either legacy or athletic preferences.[21] In any case, Cohen provides no argument for this assertion.

In my essay, I claimed that we need an argument that compares racial preferences with these other forms of preference. I pointed out that about 25 percent of the student body at select colleges and universities receive legacy preferences and as much as 32 percent of the student body at smaller liberal arts colleges receive athletic preferences, while only 5 to 10 percent of the student body at

---

[20]On this point, see Bernard Boxill, *Blacks and Social Justice*, rev. ed. (Lanham, MD: Rowman and Littlefield, 1992), chapters 4–6, especially p. 146.

[21]Cohen, chapter 8, p. 139.

select colleges and universities receive racial preferences. Clearly, these other forms of preference have a far greater impact on college admissions, and are arguably far less justified, than are racial preferences, and the same holds true for many legally established preferences that favor the rich and the middle class over the poor, such as anti-inflation fiscal policies and low inheritance taxes. So if we seek to treat everyone as equals, we would certainly have to focus our critique on legacy, athletic, and other legally established preferences that favor the rich and the middle class over the poor, rather than focus, as Cohen does, on critiquing racial preferences.

In sum, in arguing that affirmative action/racial preference is immoral, Cohen makes a number of fundamental mistakes. First, he misinterprets his opponents, mistakenly thinking that they are attempting to argue from "is" to "ought" in violation of Hume's thesis, and that they are necessarily aiming to provide benefits to the members of a racial group simply because they happen to be members of that group. Second, he relies on unsupported empirical claims. Third, he misidentifies diversity affirmative action with remedial affirmative action, criticizing it for being something it is not. Fourth, he fails to comparatively assess racial preferences and other forms of preference, a necessary requirement for any adequate moral assessment of racial preferences. All of these mistakes, taken together, clearly add up to a fatally flawed moral critique of affirmative action/racial preference.

Second Charge: Affirmative Action/Racial Preference Is Illegal

Cohen rejects affirmative action/racial preference not only because he mistakenly thinks it is *immoral* but also because he also thinks it is *illegal*, in virtue of being in violation of the Civil Rights Act of 1964. According to the act,

> No person in the United States shall, on the grounds of race, color, or national origin, be excluded from participation in, be denied the benefits of, or be subjected to discrimination under any program or activity receiving Federal financial assistance.

Clearly, the Civil Rights Act does prohibit racial preferences that exclude or discriminate, but it should not be taken to prohibit all forms of racial preferences, because that would mean that it would prohibit the very preferences that are needed to correct for violations of the Act itself, thus making its enforcement impossible. So despite what Cohen claims, affirmative action/racial preference is not *illegal* in virtue of being in violation of the Civil Rights Act of 1964.

Think of a law that prohibits the use of coercion in a certain context. Surely, that law should not be taken to prohibit whatever coercion is necessary to correct for violations of the law itself. If it did that, then the law's prohibition of coercion would be unenforceable. Just as sometimes we need to use coercion to correct for the violations of laws that prohibit the use of coercion, so sometimes we need to use racial preferences/classifications to enforce or correct for violations of laws, such as the Civil Rights Act, which prohibits the use of racial preferences/classifications. Furthermore, the prohibition of the use of racial preferences/classifications in some contexts should not preclude their use in other, e.g., as a means for providing diversity in an educational context. Even racial proportionality can be used in a legitimate remedial affirmative action program, as we saw in *Local 28 of the Sheetmetal Workers Union v. EEOC* (1986). Here again, the Supreme Court does not see racial proportionality as being in violation of the Civil Rights Act of 1964.

Cohen himself recognizes the need to use racial classifications (in some contexts) to correct for violations of laws that prohibit the use of racial classifications (in other contexts). Where Cohen and defenders of affirmative action differ, therefore, is not over whether racial classifications can be legitimately used (we all agree that they can be legitimately used), but rather over how extensive that use should be.

Nevertheless, Cohen argues that defenders of affirmative action support their (broader) use of racial preferences by *subterfuge* and *unsound* argument. The *subterfuge* to which Cohen refers involves the use of terms such as "disadvantaged business enterprises" when what is clearly meant is "disadvantaged *minority* business enterprises." Here I agree with Cohen that we should have truth in labeling. Unlike Cohen, however, I think that after we employ the correct labeling, the argument for affirmative action/racial preference will still go through, whereas Cohen thinks it will not. As I see it, the Supreme Court's decision in *Bakke* is just such a case in which truth in labeling was introduced by the court and still a decision in favor of diversity affirmative action/racial preference emerged.[22]

The one argument in support of affirmative action/racial preference that Cohen attacks as legally *unsound* is the six-to-two decision written by Justice Brennan in *United Steelworkers v. Weber* (1979). The facts of this case are as follows. Blacks represented 39 percent of the local population in Gramercy, Louisiana, but only 2 percent of the craftworkers and 15 percent of the unskilled workers at the plant, up from 10 percent in 1969, when the company began to hire unskilled workers at the gate on a "one white, one black" basis. However, the company continued the practice of hiring skilled craft workers from virtually all-white craft unions outside the Gramercy area, an activity that accounted for the small percentage of minorities in craft positions at the plant. Under pressure from the federal government, Kaiser Aluminum and the unions agreed to jointly manage a craft apprenticeship program that would accept one minority worker and one white worker from two different seniority lists until the percentage of minority workers approximated the percentage of minorities in the Gramercy area. In this case, Justice Brennan, writing for the majority, distinguished between what the Civil Rights Act of 1964 forbids and what it permits. What the act forbids, Brennan argued, is imposed racial preferences in certain contexts; what it permits are voluntary preferences, such as those found in the "voluntary" agreement between Kaiser Aluminum and the unions.

Now, I admit that the Supreme Court's decision in *United Steelworkers v. Weber* (1979) represents a strained interpretation of the Civil Rights Act of 1964. Here again, Cohen and I are in agreement. I would just point out that the court's decision was affected by the way that the case had been brought before it. Neither Kaiser Aluminum nor the unions nor Weber, who brought suit against the apprenticeship program, was interested in justifying the program as a means for putting an end to discrimination at the Gramercy plant.

---

[22]One might ask for an explanation of this inaccurate labeling. One possible explanation is that it results from a concern to do what is morally right in a context in which one is not sure that the law permits it; one thus looks for a description of what one is doing that clearly passes legal muster.

As a consequence, the case was argued and decided on other grounds. But it could have been argued and decided on remedial grounds in the same way that *Contractors Association of Eastern Pennsylvania v. the Secretary of Labor* (1973), dealing with the Philadelphia Program, was argued. In that case, the federal court was concerned with a five-county Philadelphia area where minorities were 30 percent of all construction workers but only 1 percent of the workers in six craft unions. The federal government's Philadelphia Program conditioned the granting of federal construction money upon accepting a set of goals and timetables for improving minority apprenticeship or membership with respect to these unions. In this case, the federal court found the Philadelphia Program to be an acceptable way of increasing equal opportunity for minorities in the Philadelphia area. Since in *United Steelworkers v. Weber* (1979), the factual situation is quite similar, it could have been argued and decided on similar remedial grounds, and thus Justice Brennan's strained interpretation of the Civil Rights Act could have been avoided altogether.

In brief, with regard to the second charge, that affirmative action/racial preference is illegal, Cohen cannot mean, and should not mean, exactly what he says here—that all affirmative action/racial preference is in violation of the Civil Rights Act of 1964—since he too recognizes the legitimate use of racial classifications/preference under certain circumstances. Thus, the real disagreement between Cohen and defenders of affirmative action has to concern, not whether, but when, racial preferences can be justified.

Nevertheless, Cohen is right in criticizing certain affirmative action programs for resorting to subterfuge and others for less-than-persuasive arguments. However, in the cases he discusses, when the subterfuge is removed by using truth in labeling and when the less-than-persuasive arguments are replaced with the sound and convincing ones that are available, the legal case for affirmative action/racial preference can be shown to be as cogent as ever.

Third Charge: Affirmative Action/Racial Preference Is Unconstitutional

In addition to mistakenly thinking that affirmative action/racial preference is *illegal* in violation of the Civil Rights Act of 1964, Cohen thinks that it is also *unconstitutional* in light of recent Supreme Court decisions. Part of Cohen's critique here depends upon the same mis-construal of the argument for affirmative action that undermined his moral challenge to affirmative action/racial preference. In that ear-lier challenge, Cohen misinterprets defenders of affirmative action to be defending group rights (that is, to be aiming to provide ben-efits to the members of a racial group *simply* because they happen to be members of that group). Here, he charges that such group rights are not protected by the U.S. Constitution, particularly the equal protection clause of the Fourteenth Amendment, which ap-plies to every single person individually, not as a member of a group. However, in my essay and earlier in this response, I argued that de-fenders of affirmative action need not base their defense on group rights. They are not committed to compensating anyone, for exam-ple, simply because he or she happens to belong to a particular racial group. Even in contexts in which all blacks deserve remedial affir-mative action for past discrimination and the effects thereof, they do not deserve it because they are black, or because they are part of the group, but rather because they have suffered the relevant dis-crimination or the effects thereof, and, hence, belong to the group of individuals each of whom has suffered from the relevant discrim-ination.[23] What this shows is that both the defenders of affirmative action and their critics agree that the only appropriate grounds for claiming that an individual deserves compensation for past discrimi-nation is that the person himself or herself actually suffered that dis-crimination or the effects thereof. So here too, as before, Cohen's group rights objection to affirmative action/racial preference fails.

In addition to interpreting equal protection as applying to individ-uals only, the Supreme Court, as Cohen notes, has also required that

---

[23]While blacks do not deserve compensation because they are black, that is, be-cause they belong to the group of black individuals, it sometimes seems that blacks are discriminated against simply because they are black, that is, sim-ply because they belong to the group of black individuals. But on closer anal-ysis, it would appear that blacks are not discriminated against simply because they are black but because those doing the discriminating unjustifiably be-lieve that blacks are lazy or unclean or something similar. For this and other related points, see James Nickel, "Should Reparations Be to Individuals or Groups?" *Analysis* vol. 41 (1974), pp. 154–60.

remedial affirmative action be based on proven discrimination specified by a judicial, legislative, or administrative finding of constitutional
violations. Here, too, defenders of affirmative action should have no
problem limiting remedial affirmative action to proven discrimination,
even though they would quibble a bit about who is capable of making an appropriate finding of past discrimination. However, no one is
really interested in compensating for "societal discrimination," understood here to mean unproven discrimination.

Cohen cites the Supreme Court's decision in *Wygant v. Jackson
Board of Education* (1986) to show that the pursuit of racial balance
or racial proportionality is unconstitutional. But while the court
rejected the Jackson Board of Education's pursuit of racial balance/
proportionality in its layoff policy, it did not do so unconditionally.
The court held that if sufficient evidence of past discrimination in
teacher hiring had been provided, a racially balanced layoff policy
would have been justified. Accordingly, Justice Marshall, writing for
the dissenters, wanted the case sent back to the district court so that
evidence of past discrimination in the Jackson School District could
be assessed. The majority disagreed, going so far as to chastise Marshall for even mentioning some of the relevant evidence that the district court never considered in arriving at its decision. So here too,
Cohen and I should be able to agree that racial balance or racial
proportionality is only justified when there is sufficient evidence of
past discrimination.

Next Cohen turns to a constitutional assessment of diversity affirmative action. Downplaying the importance of the *Bakke* decision's support for diversity affirmative action, Cohen notes that five
of the current sitting Supreme Court justices seem poised to reject
the use of diversity affirmative action in educational institutions. Cohen not only rejects diversity affirmative action as racial discrimination; he also claims that efforts to show ethnic diversity in educational
institutions has important benefits have failed to do so. He cites the
National Association of Scholars critique of Patricia Gurin's Expert
Report in *Gratz v. Bollinger*; authors of the former claim that Gurin's
own data disconfirms that campus racial diversity is correlated with
educational excellence. But here, unfortunately, Cohen neither sets
out Gurin's argument nor considers her response to the critique of
her work by the National Association of Scholars (NAS).

Gurin had argued that the racial and ethnic composition of the student body is positively correlated to classroom diversity and to having informal discussions of race and building friendships across race, which in turn are positively correlated with positive learning and democracy outcomes (e.g., more active thinking processes and citizen engagement). In their critique, the authors of the NAS study speculated that if Gurin's data were subject to a regressive analysis that controlled for taking diversity courses and having informal discussions of race or close friends of a different race, it would yield no correlation at all between the racial and ethnic composition of student bodies and positive learning and democracy outcomes. In her response, Gurin claims that this speculation is absolutely correct, but that it in no way adversely affects her argument.[24] If we were to do a regressive analysis that controlled for taking diversity courses and for having informal discussions of race or close friends of a different race, there should be no correlation at all between the racial and ethnic composition of student bodies and certain learning and democracy outcomes just as, if we were to do a regressive analysis that *controlled* for damage to lung tissue in a study of smoking and lung cancer, we should expect that there would be no correlation at all between smoking and lung cancer. In the smoking/lung cancer case, the effect that is controlled for (i.e., damage to lung tissue) is the very mechanism by which smoking has its cancerous effect. Likewise, in Gurin's study, taking diversity courses and having informal discussions of race or close friends of a different race are the very mechanisms by which diversity has its positive learning and democracy outcomes.[25] Hence, this failed critique by the NAS

---

[24]Gurin.

[25]Gurin provides one student's report of how taking a diversity course affected her:

> The most helpful aspect of the course was reading the articles from so many different perspectives and then discussing them with so many different kinds of students in the class. Living through the heated discussions in class and being asked to participate actually rocked my world. I realize that my past pattern of not talking in class and being invisible was a way of avoiding having to think about or engage in difficult and complex issues. Now that I have engaged and even disagreed with others, it seems like

provides no support at all for Cohen's constitutional attack on diversity affirmative action.[26]

Cohen also quotes from the abstract of study that sought to establish that diversity does *not* improve university education.[27] Unfortunately, Cohen does not tell us how the authors got to their conclusion; he just appeals to their authority. Beyond raising doubt about the wording of questions asked in previous studies, what the authors of this report did was to use data from a random sample to determine whether the satisfaction of college students was positively correlated with the level of diversity at the college they attended. The authors found that it was not. In fact, they found that, to some degree, it was negatively correlated.

As it turns out, the authors of this study make the same mistake at a practical level that the NAS authors made at the theoretical level. The latter had speculated that if Gurin's data were subject to a regressive analysis that controlled for taking diversity courses and having informal discussions of race or close friends of a different race, it would yield no correlation at all between the racial and ethnic composition of student bodies and positive learning and democracy outcomes. Gurin in her response to their critique had agreed

---

there is no turning back. I'm ready now to wrestle with ideas and multiple perspectives. This change has spilled over into other areas of my life also. I actually am doing much better in my other classes because I am not afraid to think, speak, and be challenged intellectually. The racial and ethnic diversity in this class did this for me. This finally feels like what college is supposed to be about.

See Supplemental Expert Report of Patricia Gurin, *Grutter v. Bollinger*, 11 January 2001.

[26]Cohen also mentions another study (Robert Lerner and Althea Nagai, "A Critique of the Expert Report of Patricia Gurin" [Washington, D.C.: Center for Equal Opportunity, 2001]), which was critical of the Gurin report. Cohen, however, does not mention Gurin's response, which is that the study fails in much the same way as the National Association of Scholars's study fails: it expects racial and ethnic diversity to produce positive educational outcomes directly and not indirectly, by way of diversity courses and having informal discussions of race or close friends of a different race.

[27]Stanley Rothman, Seymour Martin Lipset, and Neil Nevitte, "Does Enrollment Diversity Improve University Education?" *International Journal of Opinion Research* (forthcoming).

with the speculation of the authors of the NAS's study that if we were to do such a regressive analysis, there should be no correlation at all between the racial and ethnic composition of student bodies and certain learning and democracy outcomes, just as if we were to do a regressive analysis that controlled for damage to lung tissue in a study of smoking and lung cancer, there should be no correlation at all between smoking and lung cancer. Nevertheless, as Gurin argues, in neither case would this show that there was no correlation. In the smoking/lung cancer case, the effect that is controlled for (i.e., damage to lung tissue) is the very mechanism by which smoking has its cancerous effect. In Gurin's own study, taking diversity courses and having informal discussions of race or close friends of a different race are the very mechanisms by which racial and ethnic composition of student bodies has its positive learning and democracy outcomes. Accordingly, the lack of correlation that the authors of the NAS's study speculate would obtain is just what is predicted by Gurin's study.

Significantly, this new study does not simply *speculate* what would be the result of controlling for the mechanisms by which the racial and ethnic composition of student bodies has positive educational outcomes. It goes further and *actually* carries out a study that controls for these mechanisms by ignoring them and just comparing the racial and ethnic diversity with positive educational outcomes. Not surprisingly, the study shows that racial and ethnic diversity and certain positive educational outcomes are not correlated. To get a positive correlation, according to Gurin, colleges and universities need to have in place the diversity courses and informal discussions of race that serve to translate racial and ethnic diversity into positive educational outcomes. Thus the new study in no way supports Cohen's constitutional attack on diversity affirmative action, and Cohen himself develops no other argument against this form of affirmative action.[28]

---

[28]It is interesting to note that just a few years ago, Cohen defended Justice Powell's opinion in *Bakke* (1979) on the constitutional permissibility of diversity affirmative action. See Cohen's *Naked Racial Preference* (Boston: Madison Books, 1995), chapter 3. Nor has Cohen simply been misled by what we now see is the

It is worth pointing out that in *Gratz v. Bollinger* (2001), both sides had agreed to a summary judgment acknowledging that there was no disagreement of fact, only one of law. Specifically, during the course of the trial, the counsel for the plaintiffs conceded that diversity at the University of Michigan was "good, important and valuable." It was only after the plaintiffs lost the case at the district court level that their counsel introduced the NAS critique as an amicus brief to challenge Gurin's report. We have seen that this study and two related ones are fundamentally flawed.[29] Additionally, introducing the study at this point in the legal proceedings is objectionable because it attempts to supplement the factual record on appeal and sidestep the rigors of cross-examination that assure the integrity of facts found at the district court level.

As Cohen goes on to note, the role model justification for affirmative action/racial preference has not fared well in Supreme Court decisions. Justice Powell in *Wygant* (1986) seems particularly concerned that a role model justification, unlike a remedial justification, has "no logical stopping point." Yet the diversity justification that Powell supported in *Bakke* (1978) is similar to a role model justification in this respect; it, too, might be thought to have no logical stopping point. That would make it difficult to consistently accept the one justification while rejecting the other. In fact, however, both the diversity and role model have the logical stopping point that Powell desired. It is the point where regular admissions or regular hiring practices provide the needed diversity or role modeling in the absence of affirmative action. Role modeling also provides benefits to both minority and nonminority members in the workplace that are quite similar to the benefits that diversity provides in the edu-

---

failed attack of the National Association of Scholars on Patricia Gurin's empirical defense of diversity affirmative action. Rather, his current view is that diversity affirmative action would not be justified *even if* it produced beneficial results because it fails to treat all citizens as equals in the way that the U.S. Constitution requires. (See Cohen, "Why Racial Preference . . . ," chapter 6, pp. 93–94 and note 126.) But here again, Cohen ignores the comparative question of how we can oppose this form of "preference" and still justify other forms of preference, most of which are far more sweeping in their effects on people's lives.

[29]One of these two related studies is discussed in the text, the other in note 26.

cational arena. In fact, it is hard not to see role modeling as a kind of diversity—a diversity in the workplace that is quite similar to the diversity sought in the educational arena.[30] Thus, recognizing the constitutional acceptability of a diversity justification for affirmative action/racial preference should open the door to recognizing the constitutional acceptability of a role model justification as well.

Beyond endorsing the Supreme Court's unfortunate rejection of a role model justification for affirmative action, Cohen also endorses the Court's similarly unfortunate rejection of the use of affirmative action/racial preference to "insure better professional services for minorities." In *Bakke* (1978), Justice Powell argued that the desirable goal of insuring better professional services for minorities could be effectively secured by nonracial criteria. But clearly this is an empirical question that cannot be answered simply by recourse to the U.S. Constitution. Moreover, judging from UCLA law school's analogous attempt to use nonracial criteria to achieve diversity, I think that the answer to this empirical question has to be "No." As I discussed in my essay, the UCLA law school looked at three family factors (an applicant's family income, father's education, and mother's education) and three neighborhood factors (proportion of single-parent households, proportion of families receiving welfare, and proportion of adults who had not graduated from high school). Using these measures of social and economic disadvantage in its class-based affirmative action program, the UCLA law school was more successful than Berkeley and the University of Texas in maintaining racial diversity in its entering class. Still, when UCLA used only nonracial criteria, black enrollment at the law school dropped 72 percent in comparison to pre–Proposition 209 averages.

Even if we add other factors to measure social and economic disadvantage, such as net family wealth, and we accept even lower SAT scores, we still will not be able to capture the socioeconomic advantage that minorities, particularly African Americans, experience, such as teachers' lower expectations for minority students, and the stereotype threat that minorities, particularly African Americans, ex-

---

[30]I think that one can interpret many of the 100 or so briefs filed in favor of the University of Michigan's affirmative action programs as also favoring role-model affirmative action.

perience when taking standardized cognitive tests.[31] Of course, in principle, it should be possible to reduce racial disadvantage to a set of factors that do not include the factor of simply belonging to a particular racial group.[32] Nevertheless, if the measure of social and economic disadvantage is to be adequate, it will have to include factors like "being discriminated against because one is a member of a particular minority group," just as any adequate measure of women's social and economic disadvantage that is due to sexism will have to include factors like "being discriminated against because one is a woman."[33]

Unfortunately, none of the non-race-based affirmative action programs that have been proposed so far include all the relevant factors in their measures of social and economic disadvantage. For similar reasons, it would seem that no non-race-based criteria could be effectively designed to "insure better professional services for minorities." If someone thinks that there are such criteria, we simply need to put his or her offerings to the test. If none of these criteria effectively work to achieve our legitimate goal of insuring better professional services for minorities, then we are surely justified using a race-based affirmative action to ensure this goal. Moreover, we now have considerable empirical evidence showing that race-based affirmative action is an effective way of insuring better professional services for minorities.[34]

Cohen goes on to endorse Justice Powell's attempt to distinguish the race preference used in school desegregation cases from the race preference used by the Davis medical school in *Bakke* (1978). According to Powell, the key difference is that Bakke was harmed in a way that whites under school desegregation plans were not. Under

---

[31]Claude Steele and Joshua Aronson, "Stereotype Threat and the Intellectual Text Performance of African Americans," *Journal of Personality and Social Psychology* 69 (1995), pp. 797–811.

[32]See my response to the third objection, in which I similarly claim that being a member of a particular racial group is not grounds for receiving remedial affirmative action.

[33]Or more accurately, the factor is being discriminated against because the discriminator unjustifiably believes that all the members of the minority group or all women are inferior for some reason or other, and so treats them in this discriminatory way.

[34]See Lois Choi, "Affirmative Action in Medical School Admissions," *The Pharos* (autumn 2000), pp. 4–9.

school desegregation plans, Powell claims, white children were bused to comparable school in other neighborhoods, whereas under Davis's affirmative action program, no arrangement was made for Bakke to attend a comparable medical school elsewhere. As Cohen puts it, the difference is that in desegregation cases, equal treatment is required for all, whereas in Davis's affirmative action plan, Bakke would clearly have lost out.

Actually, the difference between school desegregation plans and Davis's affirmative action plan is much less stark than Powell and Cohen make it out to be. Whites who were bused to achieve school desegregation did not always receive educational facilities equal to the ones they enjoyed before in their segregated schools. Frequently, white students lost out so minority students could gain access to benefits traditionally denied them.[35] In many cases, white families pulled their children out of public schools and put them into private schools in order to avoid what they clearly regarded as a loss. In many other cases, white families moved to new or wealthier neighborhoods in search of less integrated/desegregated schools. Thus, school desegregation was surely not widely perceived to be the win-win situation that Powell and Cohen describe.[36]

Nor would the loss that would have been suffered by Bakke and others have been that great if the constitutionality of Davis's program had been upheld. Bakke was a high-paid engineer working for NASA who wanted to make a career change.[37] He applied twice to Davis's medical school because Davis at the time was a third-tier school, having just opened its doors, and his chance of gaining admittance there was high.[38] Being turned down by Davis hardly seems like a great loss for Bakke. School desegregation plans have surely

[35]This is particularly true for whites in majority-black schools. See Gary Orfield, *Must We Bus?* (Washington, D.C.: The Brookings Institution, 1978). As Justice Thurgood Marshall pointed out in his dissent in *Board of Education v. Dowell* (1991), all African American schools "continue to suffer from high student-faculty ratios, lower quality teachers, inferior facilities and physical conditions, and lower quality of course offerings and extracurricular programs."

[36]Thomas Cottle, *Busing* (Boston: Beacon Press, 1976); Tom Wicker, *Tragic Failure* (New York: William Morrow and Co, 1996), pp. 93–96.

[37]Howard Ball, *The Bakke Case* (Lawrence: University of Kansas, 2000), pp. 46–47.

[38]Michael Selmi, "The Life of Bakke: An Affirmative Action Retrospective," *The Georgetown Law Journal* 87, pp. 984–85.

had greater adverse effect on white children and their families than
any loss Bakke would have suffered. So Powell and Cohen are simply mistaken that school desegregation plans have an advantage over
compensatory affirmative action programs with respect to the harm
they cause to those disadvantaged by them.

In his final section of this chapter, Cohen denies the constitutionality of using affirmative action/race preference to achieve integration. Here he cites the Supreme Court's decision in *Board of
Education v. Dowell* (1991), in which the court imposed a time limit
on a school desegregation plan in Oklahoma City. Surely, a Supreme
Court that is backing away from enforcing school desegregation plans
is not likely to sanction affirmative action programs designed to promote either desegregation or integration. In addition, the Supreme
Court's reliance on an artificially contrived distinction between de
facto and de jure segregation has brought us to the point where our
schools are now more segregated than they were in the 1960s—
surely a state of affairs that we should hardly be proud of.[39]

But there is much we can do to improve the situation. First, we
must attack the widespread discrimination in housing that significantly contributes to school segregation. Second, the Supreme Court
should reverse its five-to-four decision in *Milliken v. Bradley* (1974),
denying the state of Michigan (and thereby other states similarly situated) the authority to promote desegregation and to equalize funding across school district lines. In the absence of such improvements,
there is surely a moral case for compensatory affirmative action, and
there is a constitutional case as well, as many have argued, if we take
the equal protection clause of the Fourteenth Amendment as requiring substantial equality between citizens.[40]

In attempting to establish the unconstitutionality of affirmative action/racial preference, Cohen sought out Supreme Court

---

[39]The distinction between de facto and de jure segregation is artificially contrived, I claim, because it ignores the effect that discrimination in housing has
in creating "de facto" segregated school districts. See Orfield 1978, p. 35. On
the way in which school segregation is itself a cause of housing discrimination, see Marshall's dissent in *Dowell* (1991).

[40]See, for example, Andrew Kuppleman, *Antidiscrimination Law and Social
Equality* (New Haven: Yale University Press, 1996).

decisions, or parts of them, that support his anti–affirmative action stance, while rejecting other decisions, or parts of them, that oppose his stance. In so doing, Cohen sometimes misinterprets his opponents (e.g., mistakenly thinking they must endorse group rights), sometimes agrees with them (e.g., in the need for proven discrimination in remedial affirmative action cases), and sometimes misinterprets the Supreme Court's own view (e.g., when he interprets the court to be unconditionally against racial balance in *Wygant* [1986]). Yet even when Cohen's interpretations are correct, it is still possible to argue that both Cohen and the court are mistaken. This is what I have argued with respect to their rejection of a role model justification for affirmative action (which I have said is analogous to diversity affirmative action, of which the court approves), and with respect to their rejection of a better professional services for minorities justification for affirmative action (which I have argued can be empirically substantiated). I have also argued that the use of race preference in both desegregation and affirmative action cases is not as dissimilar as Cohen and the court have claimed. Finally, since the ultimate test of constitutionality in this context is the equal protection clause of the Fourteenth Amendment, it is certainly possible to give good arguments for affirmative action that oppose Supreme Court decisions, or at least parts of them, as long as those arguments can be shown to be in accord with the substantial equality required by that amendment.

Fourth Charge: Affirmative Action/Racial Preference Harms just about Everybody

Cohen claims that "racial preference is bad for everyone." Yet "its worse consequences," he claims, "are the injuries it inflicts upon the racial minorities who are preferred."[41] But this cannot be exactly what he thinks, because he also claims that it is reasonable for every minority to believe he or she will probably benefit from racial preference/affirmative action, which couldn't be the case if race preference were bad for everyone, and especially bad for the racial

---

[41]Cohen, "Why Race Preference . . . ," chapter 7, p. 110.

minorities who receive it.[42] What Cohen must really think, then, is
that some, very talented minorities will be harmed by affirmative action because they would have done even better for themselves if people did not think of them as affirmative action recipients, and so better
off if there were no affirmative action. Cohen gives the example of
his former student, identified as MKF, who was admitted to the
Michigan Law Review simply on his merits, just before it launched
a diversity affirmative action program. Cohen also quotes at length
from Stephen Carter's *Losing the Race*. Carter claims that he and
other very talented minorities are harmed by affirmative action. But
the argument that Cohen raises against affirmative action/racial preference here could also be raised against other forms of preference.
It could, for example, be raised against veterans' preference. Surely,
the success of some veterans, e.g., after World War II, would have
been greater if people did not think of them as veterans' preference
recipients, and so those individuals would have been better off if there
had been no veterans' preference.[43] No one, however, should think
that this undercuts the case for veterans' preference.

Similarly, when people have been treated unfairly, the fact that
some would be better off than others if there were no attempt to
correct for the unfairness does not undercut the case for pursuing
the general corrective. So the fact that individuals, such an MKF or

---

[42]Ibid., chapter 7, pp. 121–2. Paradoxically, Cohen also holds that affirmative
action is harmful to minorities as a group! Ibid., chapter 7, pp. 110 and 121.
But how could affirmative action be harmful to minorities as a group if each
individual minority can expect to benefit from affirmative action, and only
some will lose out because of it? Is it that the gains to the larger number of
individuals are outweighed by the losses to a smaller number of individuals
who are harmed? But Cohen provides no evidence at all that would support
this kind of assessment. It is also odd that Cohen is here resorting to the notion of group harm to support his argument against affirmative action/racial
preference when he has attacked defenders of affirmative action/racial preference (mistakenly, as I have argued—see pp. 254–260, 309–70) for basing
their defense of affirmative action on what happens to groups, not individuals.

[43]It is important to remember that the generous veterans' preference enacted
after World War II gave the same benefits to those who were drafted and
those who joined up, the same benefits to those who served overseas or saw
combat and those who never left the United States. See John Skrentny, *The
Ironies of Affirmative Action* (Chicago: University of Chicago, 1996).

Stephen Carter would be better off without affirmative action does not undercut the case for affirmative action programs which compensate for past discrimination or achieve the benefits of diversity that would thereby benefit a much larger number of people.

There is also considerable evidence that minorities have benefited significantly from affirmative action. In *The Shape of the River*, William Bowen and Derek Bok did a study of 60,000 current and former students at 28 selective universities from 1970 to 1996.[44] In the study, all minority graduates reported high incomes (averaging $105,000 in 1996 dollars), 75 percent of them reported that they were satisfied with their careers, and 60 percent reported that they engaged in unremunerated service to their communities (compared to a reported 50 percent for white students).[45] According to another study, undergraduate grade point averages and LSAT scores have no positive relationship to achievement after law school, whether that achievement is measured in terms of earnings, career satisfaction, or unremunerated community service.[46] The only correlation that was found in this regard is, in fact, a negative one—students with higher admission scores tended to provide less community service.[47] In any case, what is clear is that there is plenty of empirical evidence to show that minorities, despite their lower grade point averages and SAT and LSAT scores, do benefit from affirmative action/racial preference. Cohen offers no evidence that minorities do not benefit except for a few anecdotes, but by his own admission, making inferences from anecdotes is "a silly mistake."[48]

---

[44]William Bowen and Derek Bok, *The Shape of the River: Long-Term Consequences of Considering Race in College and University Admissions* (Princeton: Princeton University Press, 1998).

[45]Ibid., pp. 385–86. In a 1999 survey of 1,800 law students at Harvard University and the University of Michigan, 9 out of 10 said racial and ethnic diversity made a positive impact on their education, and 8 out of 10 said discussion with students of other races had affected their views of the criminal justice system. See "Debating the Benefits of Affirmative Action," *The Chronicle of Higher Education*, 18 May 2001.

[46]Richard Lempert, David Chambers, and Terry Adams, "Doing Well and Doing Good," University of Michigan Law School, http://www.law.umich.edu/newsandinfo/lawsuit/survey.htm.

[47]Ibid.

[48]Cohen, "Why Race Preference is Wrong and Bad," chapter 8, p. 138.

Moreover, in the affirmative action/racial preference I defend, only candidates are selected whose qualifications are such that when their selection is combined with a suitably designed educational enhancement program, they will normally turn out, within a reasonably short time, to be as qualified as, or even more qualified than, their peers. Viewing affirmative action/racial preference this way definitely undercuts the relevance of Cohen's fanciful tale of a preference program for short people. While discrimination in society based on height is clearly a minor form of discrimination—too minor, in fact, to justify any kind of a coercive corrective program—if we were to correct for this form of discrimination, presumably we would look for fully qualified short people to fill jobs and positions in roughly the same proportion as their percentage in the relevant market. And, given that height discrimination is only a minor form of discrimination, it should not be that difficult to come up with a sufficient number of fully qualified "short" people who are as qualified or more qualified than any "non-short" candidates we have for the relevant jobs and positions. However, if perchance some short people were qualified, but not as qualified as the non-short candidates due to discrimination that they suffered from in the past, we might still select those people as long as when their selection is combined with a suitably designed educational enhancement program, they would normally turn out, within a reasonably short time, to be as qualified as, or even more qualified than, their peers. Accordingly, if affirmative action for shorts were implemented in just this way in Cohen's example, there would be no reasonable basis for anyone to stigmatize shorts. Likewise, there would be no reasonable basis for anyone to stigmatize women or minorities in real-life cases if affirmative action programs are similarly implemented, as I have argued they should be.[49]

There is also no way that Cohen's even more fanciful example of affirmative action for white athletes in the National Basketball Association could ever be justified. Surely, no one could argue that

---

[49]I am not denying that affirmative action programs are sometimes not implemented in this morally defensible way. Like Cohen, I hold that sometimes affirmative action is morally justified and sometimes it is not. Where we differ is in the range and number of affirmative action programs we find justifiable.

white athletes have been discriminated against by the NBA in the past and so now deserve remedial affirmative action. Nor could it be argued that white athletes would provide some needed diversity that would enrich the game. Nor could these less qualified white athletes meet the requirement that I have imposed on such programs, if they are to be justified. To meet the requirement, these white athletes, within a reasonably short time, would have to show themselves to be as qualified as, or even more qualified than, their peers. And this they cannot do.

Near the end of his chapter on why affirmative action harms those who receive, Cohen quotes approvingly his former student MKF, who claims that "An affirmative action policy that was truly aimed at developing minority students would involve . . . sessions in which writing techniques can be taught and feedback given on writing samples, but most of all, expecting of minority students the same excellence that the *Law Review* expects of others."[50] This, of course, is just what a morally defensible affirmative action program aims to do on my account. The suitably designed education enhancement program which I have incorporated into a morally defensible affirmative action aims to normally turn out, within a reasonably short time, beneficiaries of affirmative action who are as qualified as, or even more qualified than, their peers. So if Cohen agrees with MKF here, as he seems to do, he should agree with me as well.

Unfortunately, Cohen not only claims that affirmative action/racial preference is bad for racial minorities, he also claims that it is bad for colleges and universities. His argument is that it leads them to lower their standards. Of course, those who are admitted to a college or university on the basis of affirmative action are only a small percentage of the total admitted. So even if one thought that affirmative action led to a lowering of standards, one could argue that other forms of preference, such as athletic and legacy preferences, have a much greater impact on lowering standards. Legacy preferences are given to as much as 25 percent of the student body at select colleges and universities, and athletic preferences to as much as 32 percent of small liberal arts colleges, compared to about 5 to 10

[50]Ibid., chapter 7, p. 127. Part of this quote from MFK was cut from the penultimate draft of Cohen's essay.

percent for affirmative action. So clearly these other forms of preference should be the main target, if, that is, one is really concerned
about the lowering of standards at colleges and universities. Yet let
us assume that Cohen grants this point.[51] Let us assume that Cohen
grants that if we are concerned with the lowering of standards at colleges and universities, then we should be primarily concerned about
athletic and legacy preferences and not about affirmative action/
racial preferences.

Having granted this, is there anything to the claim that affirmative action/racial preference harms colleges and universities by leading them to lower their standards? Of course, if we take the standards
of a college or university to be an index of grade point averages and
SAT or LSAT or MCAT scores, then there is a clear sense in which
affirmative action, like athletic preferences and legacy preferences,
involves a lowering of standards, because they all depart from these
standards to some extent.[52] Yet that leads us to question why we
think of university and college standards in these terms.

As an alternative, we might think of such standards as determined
by the goals of colleges or universities. If we suppose that the main
goal of colleges and universities should be to produce graduates who
go on to successful careers measured in terms of income, self-
reported satisfaction, and community service, then we would know that
grade point averages and standardized test scores do not correlate at

---

[51]Although I do not think that Cohen would actually grant this point. During
our debate on this topic at Notre Dame, I pressed him with the comparison
to other forms of preference, and he refused to take a stand on whether other
forms of preference are far more objectionable and worthy of criticism than
affirmative action. He simply wants to go on record as being against affirmative action/racial preference, and he is silent with respect to the merits or de-
merits of other forms of preference. This hardly helps if one's goal is to sketch
out what should be our social policy in this area.

[52]Since Cohen tends to identify the appropriate standards for colleges and universities with SAT scores, it is interesting to note that the average SAT score
of black matriculants of these schools surveyed in 1989 was higher than the
average for all matriculants in 1951. (See Harry Holzer and David Neumark,
"Assessing Affirmative Action" *Journal of Economic Literature* 37 (2000), p.
512). So much, then, for Cohen's claim about there having been a long-term
decline in college and university standards (even judged in his preferred terms)
since the '40s and '50s. See Cohen, "Why Race Preference . . . ," chapter 8.

all with success as measured in terms of reaching this goal. Accordingly, if producing graduates who go on to have successful careers is the main goal of colleges and universities, then clearly their standards should not be limited to grade point averages and standardized test scores, which do not correlate with that goal. We also know that scores on tests such as SAT and LSAT correlate only 16 to 18 percent with first-year grades and even less with grades in subsequent years. So even if having their students achieve high grades were a secondary goal of colleges and universities, basing admissions on standardized tests would not be a very effective way to achieve it. Moreover, if we recognized certain learning and democracy outcomes (e.g., more active thinking processes and citizen engagement) to be among the goals we had for graduates of colleges and universities, then Patricia Gurin's study, as we noted earlier, empirically substantiates that affirmative action/racial preference positively correlates with achieving these goals. And if we had the further goal of rectifying for proven past discrimination, I have argued that affirmative action/racial preference also positively correlates with achieving that goal as well. So if we think that colleges and universities should produce graduates who go on to successful careers measured in terms of income, self-reported satisfaction, and community service; should achieve the learning and democracy outcomes that Gurin identifies in her study; and should rectify for proven past discrimination, then implementing affirmative action programs should accord well with our highest standards for colleges and universities.

In passing, Cohen notes the educational problems that City College of New York has had with its open enrollment policy, a policy that necessitated adding a considerable number of remedial classes. Unfortunately, Cohen's solution to these educational problems does not include paying for the extensive remedial programs at the grade school and high school levels so as to significantly reduce the need for remedial courses at the college level. Nor did Cohen note how CCNY has been so successful with its educational programs that more of its graduates go on to obtain graduate degrees than is true for some who attend the more academically prominent private universities.[53]

---

[53]See Susan Sturm and Lani Guiner, "The Future of Affirmative Action," *California Law Review* 84 (1996), p. 953.

Having thus failed to show that affirmative action/racial preference is bad for the minorities who receive it or bad for colleges and universities who implement it, Cohen in the last chapter in this section of his essay makes a half-hearted effort to show that affirmative action/racial preference is bad for society as a whole. Yet beyond recounting a few incidents of racial conflict—including one at the University of Michigan over the appropriateness of "black lounges,"—Cohen offers no evidence at all that affirmative action is bad for society as a whole. Cohen does speculate that affirmative action breeds racial resentment. But this speculation is undercut by the evidence we have from Bowen and Bok's study of 60,000 current and former students at 28 selective universities which shows that almost 80 percent of white graduates favored either retaining the current emphasis on enrolling a diverse class or emphasizing it more, and that their minority classmates supported these same policies even more strongly.[54] In addition, as I reported in my essay, if you ask people about affirmative action programs at their workplaces, 80 percent of Euro-American workers strongly support the programs they know about and that directly affect them. Where, then, is the empirical evidence that society as a whole is being harmed by affirmative action/racial preference? Cohen has done nothing here to make his case.

Nevertheless, Cohen does point to what are some real difficulties in determining who should receive affirmative action/racial preference in the United States. In my essay, I claimed that if affirmative action is to be justified, we will need to restrict the beneficiaries of remedial affirmative action that aims to compensate for past discrimination and its effects to those who still suffer the effects of historic injustices, that is, African Americans, American Indians, Hispanic Americans, and women generally who have suffered from certain forms of discrimination. I further argued that other types of affirmative action that aim at outreach, putting an end to existing discrimination and achieving diversity, can be justifiably used more widely to benefit minorities and women generally, as they are needed to achieve the ultimate goals of a colorblind (racially just) and a gender-free (sexually just) society. In the case of remedial affirmative action, the argument must be made case by case, on the basis of

[54]Bowen and Bok (1998).

proven past or present discrimination or the effects of that discrimination. In the case of outreach or diversity affirmative action, with respect to minorities, the argument must also be made case by case with respect to the relevant underrepresented minorities in question. If these particular arguments for remedial and diversity affirmative action can be made, however, it does not matter how mixed the ancestry of affirmative action recipients happens to be.

In any case, there is no basis for comparing today's affirmative action programs to Germany's Nuremberg Laws, which took away citizenship from Jews in Nazi Germany. The Nuremberg Laws instituted a severe form of racial discrimination that was explicitly modeled after Jim Crow laws in the United States. By contrast, affirmative action is designed to correct for past discrimination that stemmed in part from those same Jim Crow laws. Thus, an appropriate comparison to affirmative action is clearly not the Nuremberg Laws, but rather the large compensations that the West German government paid to individual Jews and to the newly created state of Israel after World War II, or to the affirmative action programs that are now beginning to be put in place in Germany to deal with discrimination against long-term resident immigrants.[55]

In sum, Cohen's fourth reason for opposing affirmative action/racial preference, that it harms just about everyone, is by far the most poorly defended. Beyond a few anecdotes and hypothetical examples, Cohen offers no evidence that affirmative action/racial preference harms those who receive it, and he instead ignores the considerable contrary evidence that has been presented to show that affirmative action/racial preference does benefit those who receive it. Nor is Cohen's case that affirmative action/racial preference harms college and universities by requiring them to lower their standards any better. Here Cohen fails to critically examine what should be the appropriate goals and standards for colleges and universities and how affirmative action might serve to promote those goals and implement those standards. Lastly, Cohen's case that affirmative action harms society as a whole is simply a wild gesture. Here again, Cohen offers almost no evidence at all. He also fails to assess the

[55]See William Barbieri, *Ethics of Citizenship: Immigration and Group Rights in Germany* (Durham: Duke University Press, 1998).

evidence that others have provided, and he ends this chapter with an offensive and inappropriate comparison of affirmative action programs to the Nuremberg Laws.

Epilogue: *Gratz, Gutter,* and the Future of Affirmative Action/Racial Preference

In an epilogue added after the U.S. Supreme Court had agreed to hear together both *Gratz v. Bollinger* and *Grutter v. Bollinger*, Cohen reviews the legal history of these two cases. Surprisingly, he makes no mention of the United States Supreme Court's *Bakke* decision, as if the two sides in these cases were not in fundamental disagreement over the holding in *Bakke*, and how that holding applies at the University of Michigan. Cohen also misstates Judge Duggan's decision in *Gratz*. Duggan did not hold "that the newer point system (used in Michigan's undergraduate admissions) crosses the 'thin line' of permissibility." Rather, he held that an earlier undergraduate admissions program, from 1995 to 1998, which protected a certain number of seats for such groups as athletes, foreign applicants, underrepresented minorities, ROTC candidates, and legacies, did "cross the line from the permissible to the impermissible," but only with respect to its *minority* set-aside. What Duggan found objectionable about the earlier program was not the number of minorities that were admitted through it, but the way the minorities who were admitted were not in direct competition with nonminorities for all the available seats. More importantly, Duggan's main holding in *Gratz v. Bollinger* was that the university's undergraduate admissions program from 1999 to the present satisfies the *Bakke* requirements for a permissible race-conscious affirmative action program.

Cohen's principal objection to affirmative action at the University of Michigan is over the higher proportion of nonminorities to minorities who are rejected with the same SAT or LSAT and grade point averages. Presumably, Cohen favors an admission system that relies heavily on test scores and GPAs, even when it is known that standardized test scores correlate very poorly with first year grades, and even less with grades in subsequent years, and not at all with success after graduation. Moreover, an admission system that does not rely exclusively on standardized test and grade point scores actually benefits nonminorities more than it does minorities. According to one study, 20 percent of nonminorities admitted at selective schools would not have been admitted if those schools had relied exclusively on standardized test and grade point scores.[56]

Rather than rely exclusively on standardized test and grade scores which are such poor predictors of success both in school and not at all after graduation, the University of Michigan has introduced a number of other factors for determining admissions. With respect to undergraduate admissions, traditional academic factors can count for up to 110 points of the 100 to 110 points that are typically needed for admission. Up to 80 points are available for an academic GPA from the eleventh and twelfth grades, up to 12 points for standardized test scores, and up to 10 points for the academic strength of one's high school; 4 points can be subtracted for taking a weaker curriculum when a stronger one was available, and up to 8 points can be added for an applicant who selects more challenging courses. However, the university also gives up to 40 points for factors that indicate an applicant's potential contribution to the university. Accordingly, applicants may receive 20 points for one of the following: having membership in an underrepresented minority group, being an athlete, experience socioeconomic disadvantage, or attending a predominantly minority high school. The 20 points may also be awarded at the Provost's discretion. In addition, applicants can receive 10 points for just being a resident of Michigan, 6 more points for being a resident in one of Michigan's underrepresented counties, 2 points for having residency in an underrepresented state, as many as 4 points for being a legacy, up to 3 points for writing a good personal essay, up to 5 points for demonstrating leadership and service, and up to 5 points for showing other personal achievement.

So to which of these point assignments does Cohen object, other than the 20 given for membership in an underrepresented minority group? Does he object to the 16 points given to residents of the Upper Peninsula of Michigan, the 20 points for athletes, the 4 points for legacies, or the 20 points that can be given at the Provost's discretion (probably to the sons and daughters of wealthy donors)? Cohen gives no indication that he objects to any of these other forms

[56]Linda F. Wightman, "The Threat to Diversity in Legal Education," *New York University Law Review* vol. 72 (1997), p. 53.

of preference. It is only the 20 points that are given for membership in an underrepresented minority group that appears to bother him.

And why is that? Is it that only racial preferences are objectionable, and that nonracial preferences for college admissions are never objectionable? Surely, we could imagine increasing Michigan's preference for legacies to, say, 50 points, and then surely virtually everyone would object. So nonracial preferences in admissions can be objectionable. We therefore need an explanation of why a nonracial preference of 20 or 16 points is acceptable but a racial preference of 20 points for reasons of diversity is not. Cohen never gives us the required explanation.

Sometimes Cohen writes as though any degree of racial preference in college or university admissions is unacceptable. Race, he says, cannot be the basis for preference, presumably not even when it serves the goal of diversity.[57] But that would mean that he wants the University of Michigan minority enrollment to drop from 13.6 percent in the undergraduate college and 10 to 12 percent in the law school to about 3 percent at each institution, as has been projected to happen if using race as a factor in admissions is abandoned at the University of Michigan. This would reduce underrepresented minorities to a token presence at the university, and it would virtually put an end to the university's attempt to provide the educational benefits of racial diversity on its campus.

In my years of teaching, I have noted that where there is just one minority student in a class of about 30, that student will usually find the situation too intimidating to speak out on race-related issues in class discussions.[58] In such classes, and in classes where there are no minority students, race-related issues cannot get adequately explored. There is a real absence of learning and understanding. In Michigan's law school, it is estimated that the odds of having at least three African American students and three Hispanic students in each first-year section of 85 would fall from nearly 100 percent at present to 27 percent under a race-blind process. The odds of having

---

[57]Cohen, "Why Race Preference . . . ," chapter 4, p. 24.

[58]Although I have found that such students often have very insightful things to say on such topics to me, one to one, after class.

such minimal racial diversity in each half-section would fall from 76 percent to 4 percent. And the odds of having it in each residential dormitory section would fall from 34 percent to 1 percent. That would result in a loss of learning and understanding with regard to race-related issues.

It may be the case that Cohen and other critics of affirmative action are not objecting to just any degree of racial preference, but rather to the particular degree of racial preference that is given by the University of Michigan. Possibly Cohen could live with a 5 to 7 percent enrollment of underrepresented minorities, but not one of 13.6 percent, as in the undergraduate college, or the 10 to 12 percent, as in the law school. However, these percentages of underrepresented minorities at the University of Michigan do not result from simply picking a number out of a hat. Rather, they are based on what numbers of underrepresented minorities are needed for a critical mass of students in classroom discussions. It is the number of students "sufficient to enable under-represented minority students to contribute to classroom dialogue without feeling isolated."[59] In my own teaching experience, that number for a class of 30 is 4 or 5 students. To achieve that ratio in comparable classes throughout a college or university would then presumably require 13 to 17 percent minority enrollment.

Still, Cohen might object that the degree of racial preference that is really needed to secure the benefits of racial diversity is just too large. Yet look at it this way: It is no larger than the athletic preference and almost as large as the preference for residents of the Upper Peninsula of Michigan. In 2000, the median college GPA of admitted students was 3.68 for white students and 3.4 for African American students, or slightly less than the difference between an A and a B+. For Michigan's law school, using the plaintiff's own grids for 2000, it turns out that 71 white applicants were admitted with grade and test scores the same or worse than minority applicants who were rejected. And if "other Hispanic" applicants, which were strategically excluded from the plaintiff's own grid, are reintegrated into the data, the number of white students admitted in preference to rejected minorities with equal or better grade and test

---

[59]*Grutter v. Bollinger*, Sixth Circuit Court of Appeals (2002).

scores jumps to 223 of an entering class of about 350. Again, in 2000, Michigan's law school offered admission to 38 percent of Caucasian applicants, 35 percent of African American applicants, 38 percent of Native American applicants, 32 percent of Latino applicants, 30 percent of Asian American applicants, and 43 percent of unknown race/ethnicity applicants. In the year that Jennifer Gratz applied to Michigan's undergraduate program, over 1,400 non-underrepresented minorities with lower GPAs or standardized test scores than hers were admitted, while 2000 non-underrepresented minorities with higher GPA or standardized test scores were rejected. What these comparisons indicate is that for many applicants, particularly those who are neither at the top nor at the bottom with respect to their GPAs or standardized test scores, a wide range of other factors determine whether or not they are admitted. So we cannot very well be against the use of racial preferences in admissions without doing a comparative evaluation of the other preferences that are used in admission. Moreover, if the preferences that are appropriate to use are justified in terms of their beneficial consequences, then, as discussed earlier, the beneficial consequences that flow from using racial preferences to achieve diversity should put them near the top of the list. For example, in a survey of law students at the University of Michigan and Harvard University, 9 out of 10 said racial and ethnic diversity made a positive impact on their education, 8 out of 10 said discussion with students of other races had affected their views of the criminal justice system.[60]

Yet granted that there are substantial benefits from securing racial diversity in educational institutions, if diversity is the ultimate goal, aren't there other forms of diversity that should be pursued as well? Surely there are, but there is also considerable evidence that they are being taken into account. Thus, we find that the University of Michigan's law school admitted several applicants—none of whom were members of historically underrepresented minorities—for whom the Law School's concern for diversity played a role in the decision to offer them admission. One applicant had a LSAT score around the 50th percentile and a 2.67 GPA from Harvard but was

---

[60]See "Debating the Benefits of Affirmative Action," *The Chronicle of Higher Education*, 18 May 2001.

born in Bangladesh, received outstanding references from his professors, and had an exceptional record of extracurricular activity. Another applicant was a single mother from Argentina who also had a lower LSAT score than most admitted applicants, but who had graduated summa cum laude from the University of Cincinnati and was fluent in four languages. Nevertheless, while the University of Michigan should continue to take into account applicants who can contribute such extraordinary diversity, if the university is to realize its legitimate commitment to achieve the educational benefits of racial diversity by enrolling applicants from historically underrepresented minorities in the United States, it will need to continue to enroll a critical mass of such students to effectively achieve those benefits.[61]

Yet even granting that racial diversity should be taken into account by enrolling a critical mass of underrepresented minorities to achieve the educational benefits of racial diversity, are there not racially neutral ways to achieve that same result? What about Texas's 10 percent plan and Florida's 20 percent plan, and what about Judge Boggs's suggestion that the University of Michigan assemble a class that is racially and ethnically diverse as the qualified applicant pool itself by conducting a lottery for all students above certain threshold figures for their GPAs and standardized tests? Actually, all of these and one other alternative to using racial preferences to achieve desired diversity in educational institutions were discussed in my

[61]Beyond the extraordinary forms of diversity, there are also other forms of diversity—such as being a registered Republican or a registered Democrat or (if underage) being from a family of Republican or Democratic registered voters, or being conservative or liberal in one's political views—that some might argue should be taken into account to achieve diversity in admissions. But how are such political differences supposed to be taken into account at state schools where voters are heavily Democratic or Republican or predominantly conservative or liberal in their political views? Moreover, these political differences are easily altered or faked, as people change their party affiliations or their expressed political views. In contrast, the differences associated with underrepresented minorities are more persistent and will continue to provide the basis for extremely beneficial educational exchanges, at least until those minorities are no longer underrepresented in college and university admissions.

essay.[62] Judge Boggs's proposed alternative is identical to one proposed by Lani Guinier and Susan Sturm in 1996 that has been discussed extensively in the literature.[63] I will not rehearse here the particular reasons that I gave in my essay showing why these alternatives cannot be effectively used to achieve the same desired educational benefits that come from using racial preferences to achieve diversity. There is, however, still another reason that may trump the ones I have given. It is that despite their claims to be race-neutral, these alternatives are really all race-based themselves. They are all means that are chosen explicitly because they are thought to produce a desirable degree of racial diversity.[64] In this regard, they are no different from the poll-taxes that were used in the segregated South, which were purportedly race-neutral means, but were clearly designed to produce, in that case, an objectionable racial result—to keep blacks from voting. Accordingly, if we are going to end up using a race-based selection procedure to get the educational benefits of diversity, we might as well use one that most effectively produces that desired result, and that is a selection procedure that explicitly employs race as a factor in admissions. Furthermore, my earlier argument—that achieving racial diversity is a legitimate means for pursuing the benefits of diversity in educational institutions—and my current argument—that using an explicitly racial selection procedure is the most effective means for achieving that result—when combined, should suffice to meet the U.S. Supreme Court's requirement of strict scrutiny. This is because together they establish that a *Bakke*-styled procedure is narrowly tailored to meet the compelling governmental interest of achieving the benefits of diversity in educational institutions.

Yet is this the sort of decision we can expect from the U.S. Supreme Court when it hears both *Gratz v. Bollinger* and *Grutter*

---

[62]These are all discussed in my reply to the eighth objection, which claimed that such alternative programs were preferable.

[63]Unfortunately, Judge Boggs seems to have been unaware of their proposal or the discussion that it received.

[64]The percentage plans actually produce a degree of racial diversity, although as I argued, in my essay not the right kind or amount. The lottery suggestion of Guinier and Sturm, and now Boggs, will not produce any more diversity than we get from not using any racial preference at all.

v. Bollinger in the spring of 2003? Certainly, this is not the decision that Cohen expects from the Supreme Court, and here his expectations may be justified. In recent years, the court has become generally hostile to affirmative action, as seen in such decisions as *City of Richmond v. Croson* (1989), *Wards Cove v. Antonio* (1989) and *Adarand v. Pena* (1995). As I have argued in my essay, the fact that both the constitutional and moral arguments favor the earlier Supreme Court decisions in this area has not stopped the Court, with its new conservative activist members, from striking down earlier decisions, even one unanimous decision (*Griggs v. Duke Power* [1971]), with five-to-four votes. So I wouldn't want to bet against a similar decision from the court with regard to the Michigan cases.

On the other hand, the U.S. Supreme Court has not heard a case regarding the use of affirmative action for admissions in educational institutions since the *Bakke* decision in 1978. Up to this point, all the Supreme Court's anti–affirmative action decisions have pertained to affirmative action in employment, where the goal of the affirmative action programs that were struck down was, at least in part, to compensate for past discrimination or the effects of that discrimination. The Michigan cases are different. The expressed goal of the University of Michigan's affirmative action program is to achieve the educational benefits of diversity; it is not justified at all as a compensation for past discrimination or the effects of that discrimination.[65] So it is possible that the current Supreme Court will decide these cases differently. The court may choose not to overturn *Bakke*'s long-standing precedent, thus permitting diversity affirmative action to continue in U.S. educational institutions.

Justice O'Connor will most likely be the key person in any decision the court makes. Although she has been part of the majorities in all of the court's anti–affirmative action decisions, in her opinion in *Metro Broadcasting v. FCC* (1990), she did describe the Supreme Court's decision in *Bakke* as recognizing that a diverse body contributing to a robust exchange of ideas is a constitutionally

---

[65]Of course, the Intervenors (another party to the case) have taken up this compensatory line of argument, and although I have much sympathy with their stance, holding a similar one myself, I do not think it will succeed with the Supreme Court.

permissible goal on which a race-conscious university program may be predicated. More recently, in *Easley v. Cromartie* (2001), Justice O'Connor, who had been a key player in striking down earlier race-based redistricting cases in North Carolina, deserted her fellow conservative activists and accepted a race-based redistricting plan. So it is possible that Justice O'Connor might desert them again and join a five-to-four decision in favor of diversity affirmative action programs.

In conclusion, I have tried not to leave a stone unturned in my reply to Carl Cohen's critique of affirmative action/racial preference. I have faced head-on virtually every argument he has raised against affirmative action and have responded, either in the text proper or in footnotes. Throughout my essay and in this response, I have stressed our common ground. It is clear that Cohen and I agree that racial classifications can be legitimately used in affirmative action programs. But this agreement, as we have seen, turns out to be more theoretical than practical. While Cohen theoretically grants that there can be justified uses of racial classification in affirmative action, as a practical matter, no affirmative action program seems to pass muster for him. Thus, in his writings, Cohen cites *no* actual example of a justified affirmative action program.[66] Moreover, it is no accident that this is the case. Although Cohen does not want to be described as an opponent of affirmative action (but rather an opponent of racial preference), the standards he favors for evaluating affirmative action programs are so demanding that virtually no program could satisfy them. So it is difficult to see how any opponent of affirmative action could be more opposed to affirmative action than Cohen is, at least in practice. At the end of the day, therefore, the choice between my own view and Cohen's really comes down to the stark one between being in favor of affirmative action and being opposed to it. For the reasons I have given in my

---

[66]Unless you count his earlier endorsement of the *Bakke* decision, which he now recants.

essay and in this response, I hope we, along with the U.S. Supreme Court, will make the right choice.[67]

[67]As I finish this response on December 15, 2002. Trent Lott, a senator from Mississippi with a segregationist past, is struggling to undo yet another of his lapses into endorsing segregation so that he can resume majority leadership of the Senate; meanwhile, in the Supreme Court, a rare emotional outburst from Justice Clarence Thomas was apparently needed to help some of his conservative colleagues on the Court see the difference between burning an American flag in protest and burning a cross to terrorize African Americans. To my mind, events such as these should make it clear that we in the United States are still far removed from that ideal colorblind society where we would no longer need to take race into account.

SECTION FIVE

Comments on the Supreme Court Decision

Carl Cohen and James P. Sterba

Cohen's Conclusion

Within my statement I quote some of the words of the justices in the two cases. Since the formal report of the two cases in *U.S. Reports* has not yet been printed, I must use the pagination of the slip opinions, which have a number, each given in the covering paragraph below. For each footnote, after each quotation, I provide the name of the author, the decision referred to (*Grutter* or *Gratz*—since most of the justices wrote separately in both) and the page number within that opinion. Thus, for example, my very first paragraph contains words quoted from Justice O'Connor's opinion in *Grutter,* and the footnote is: O'Connor, *Grutter,* p. 15); in the second paragraph are words quoted from Justice Rehnquist's opinion in *Gratz,* and they are referenced as: Rehnquist, *Gratz,* p. 27.

Gratz-Grutter Epilogue

Two cases, involving race preference in admission to the University of Michigan, were decided by the Supreme Court of the United States on June 23, 2003, as this book goes to press. Those two cases are *Grutter v. Bollinger* (No. 02-241), in which the race preferences employed by the law school of the university were upheld, and *Gratz v. Bollinger* (No. 02-516), in which the race preferences employed by the undergraduate college of the University of Michigan were struck down. Brief commentary on these two cases and their impact here follow.

The Supreme Court of the United States held (in *Grutter v. Bollinger*) that "the educational benefits that flow from a diverse student body" are, in the context of higher education, a compelling state interest.[1] Deliberate racial discrimination as practiced by the law school of the University of Michigan was thus found to be consistent with the constitutional guarantee of the equal protection of the laws. That is now the law of the land.

The court also held (in *Gratz v. Bollinger*) that a numerical admission system used by Michigan's undergraduate college, in which a given number of points was awarded to all applicants in certain ethnic categories, violates the equal protection clause of the Fourteenth Amendment, as well as the Civil Rights Act of 1964.[2]

The controversies explored in this book are intensified by these two decisions. Some probable consequences of them are noted below.

The court's well-established standard of *strict scrutiny* review requires that when a state gives preference by race, that preference must be shown to serve a compelling state interest. Intellectual diversity is a good thing, reasonably sought by universities; but in any normal sense of the word "compelling," diversity of skin color in university admissions is not a *compelling* interest of the state.

Four justices dissented from the *Grutter* decision, writing separately as well as jointly. Justice Clarence Thomas pointed out that even the very maintenance of a law school by the state of Michigan, which is surely a good thing, is not a compelling need: many states thrive without one. Justice Antonin Scalia pointed out that Michigan's interest in maintaining a "prestige" law school whose normal admission standards disproportionately exclude blacks and other minorities is certainly not compelling. "If that is a compelling state interest," Justice Scalia writes, "everything is."[3]

---

[1]O'Connor, *Grutter,* p. 15.
[2]Rehnquist, *Gratz,* p. 27.
[3]Scalia, *Grutter,* p. 1.

Where racial classifications by an arm of the state are to be defended, the question confronted is not whether there is a rational relation between the objective sought and the racial instrument used, but whether there is a truly *compelling state need* being served by that racial instrument. Such a need, as the dissenters point out irrefutably, was never shown.

The standard of strict scrutiny also requires that any racial instrument be *narrowly tailored* to the achievement of the alleged end. That demand is also not satisfied by the law school, as the university's own figures demonstrate. The educational benefits of race preferences are alleged to have been achieved in the law school by the artful selection of a "critical mass" of students in each of three minority groups. Whatever the actual number of students a critical mass would entail, it plainly must entail the same number for each minority to be a critical mass. But for years the numbers of students admitted in the three minority categories have been very different, in each case closely tracking the differing number of applicants from that group. "The Law School's disparate admissions practices with respect to these minority groups [writes Justice Rehnquist for the four dissenters] demonstrate that its alleged goal of 'critical mass' is simply a sham." Go beneath the sham and the law school's real objective emerges: "The tight correlation between the percentage of applicants and admittees of a given race . . . must result from careful race based planning." The law school, in truth, is engaged in "a carefully managed program designed to ensure proportionate representation of applicants from selected minority groups."[4] That was the real goal, the *balancing of the races;* but of course it could not be honestly confessed because such racial balancing, as the majority itself makes very clear, is to be condemned as "patently unconstitutional."[5]

So the race preferences of the law school should plainly fail the test of strict scrutiny honestly applied—*both* because the objective is not a *compelling need of the state,* and because the instrument is not narrowly tailored to achieve the need alleged. In *Grutter,* strict scrutiny is called for, all agree, but it is never given.

---

[4]Rehnquist, *Grutter,* pp. 8-9.
[5]O'Connor, *Grutter,* p. 17.

That student body diversity is a compelling state need is asserted by the *Grutter* majority baldly; race preference is then said to serve this end under the law school's system in view of the individualization with which ethnicity is supposedly considered: allegedly as no more than a "plus factor" in the files of "particular applicants," all the attributes of each applicant having been "holistically" appraised, and "all pertinent elements of diversity considered in light of the particular qualifications of each applicant."[6] The fact that, of two law school applicants with identical academic credentials, the black applicant's chances of admission are *hundreds* of times greater than those of the white applicant is, one must suppose on this account, no more than a coincidence. Odds ratios of this magnitude demonstrate that whenever race enters as a substantial factor, it serves to trump all other factors.

In undergraduate admissions, however, Michigan's uses of race were neither hidden nor holistic, and were found flatly unconstitutional. The practical consequence of the two findings is obvious: Michigan (like many other universities) will henceforth formulate its undergraduate preferential schemes with comforting phrases that echo the language of the law school program. The words that appear to have talismanic powers in the court are now known. We can be quite certain that, beginning in the fall of 2003, these words and phrases—"individualized review," "holistic," "critical mass," "plus factor," "a particular applicant's file," etc.—will appear ubiquitously in the description of admission systems used by universities from coast to coast.

But it will be far easier to profess the adoption of such highly individualized review than to realize it in truth. The law school enrolls some 350 new students each year; of several thousand who apply, a good number can be speedily disqualified. Many applicants for admission are interviewed in person, and the complete file of every admitted applicant is examined by one person, the assistant dean for admissions. The requisite individualization, as described by the law school and approved by the court, may be feasible in that context, if with some strain. Our undergraduate college, on the other hand, receives *more than 25,000 applications for admission each year.* It

[6]Ibid., p. 25.

is utterly impossible for the University of Michigan—not to speak of universities in Minnesota and Ohio and other states where undergraduate colleges are substantially larger than ours—to review all the particular qualifications of each applicant, weighing race as but one plus factor, *without using some numerical calculus. Any future claim that such individualized evaluation is being achieved without using a numerical weighting of race of the sort rejected in* Gratz is almost sure to be—to put it gently—deceptive. It will not be the first time, in this arena, that universities have deceived.

Picture a gymnasium in which are stacked 25,000+ fat application files. They are to be evaluated comparatively, race and many other factors given varying and appropriate weights in the *individualized* assessment of each candidate, but without any system of numerical values assigned. Suppose they are in piles six feet high. Some 350 piles, or more, will pretty nearly stuff that gymnasium. How, in the name of reason, might one even imagine that this nonquantitative, holistic comparison of 25,000 applications will be carried out? Even for an army of admissions officers the needed individualized cross-comparisons would be out of the question.

In its written argument defending the mechanical award of points for race, the University of Michigan admitted candidly that "[t]he volume of applications and the presentation of applicant information make it impractical for [the undergraduate college] to use the . . . admissions system" of the law school,[7] upheld in *Grutter*. Of course. But then, says the university in effect, since the racial results sought can only be achieved (in view of the great mass of applications) using a system in which numerical weights are assigned to race, it must be permissible to use such a system, since the aim of diversity has been approved, and there is no other way to achieve it.

No! responds the court. The use of race is permitted in some ways, but not urged, and you are certainly not entitled to do whatever you think using race requires. The limitations imposed by *Grutter* are not to be bypassed: "[T]he fact that the implementation of a program providing individualized consideration might present administrative challenges does not render constitutional an otherwise problematic system." A university may not "employ whatever means

---

[7]Rehnquist, *Gratz,* p. 26.

it desires to achieve the stated goal of diversity without regard to the limits imposed by our strict scrutiny analysis."[8]

Since the university is forbidden (under *Gratz*) to do what it asserts it must do in order to achieve the racial objective it asserts it must pursue (and which has now been found "compelling" under *Grutter*), the pull of the two decisions against one another can only result in continued, and ever more pervasive, obfuscation and hypocrisy when dealing with race. Justice Ginsburg, in her *Gratz* dissent (supporting the now unlawful point system), frankly acknowledges that universities are deceitful and sly in this arena. She writes, "One can reasonably anticipate, therefore, that colleges and universities will seek to maintain their minority enrolment . . . whether or not they can do so in full candor." She goes on to explain, at length and accurately, how colleges "resort to camouflage" by encouraging applicants, and their supporters, to convey their minority identification deviously and underhandedly. Justice Ginsburg then concludes: "If honesty is the best policy, surely Michigan's accurately described, fully disclosed College affirmative action program is preferable to achieving similar numbers through winks, nods, and disguises."[9] A nonindividualized program, assigning a fixed number of points for skin color, is urged by Justice Ginsburg on the ground that if we don't permit that, the result will be widespread cheating. She is certainly right about the cheating.

But the winks, nods, and disguises are made (for those who would give preference) a practical necessity by *Grutter*, which approves only those uses of race that are particularized and unsystematic. In a footnote to the majority opinion striking down the point system Justice Rehnquist answers sharply: "These observations [by Justice Ginsburg] are remarkable for two reasons. First, they suggest that universities—to whose academic judgment we are told in *Grutter* we should defer—will pursue their affirmative action programs whether or not they violate the United States Constitution. Second, they recommend that these violations should be dealt with, not by requiring the universities to obey the Constitution, but by changing the Constitution so that it conforms to the conduct of the universities."[10]

[8]Ibid., p. 27.
[9]Ginsburg, *Gratz*, p. 8.
[10]Rehnquist, *Gratz*, p. 27.

This footnote, destined to become famous, goes to the heart of the two Michigan admissions cases. What is plainly wrong and ugly when confronted openly is condoned by our universities and five members of the court if buried and well hidden. In the context of university admissions race preference has been found, by one vote, to be constitutional when adequately obscured. But then, even the judges who thus find it tolerable reluctantly acknowledge that "there are serious problems of justice connected with the idea of preference itself."[11] These problems of racial justice may, by this profoundly regrettable decision, saddle our universities for years to come.

How many years? The court accepts the university's assurance that the racial discrimination it now condones must someday end; the firmly expressed expectation of the court is that it will end within 25 years.[12] Justice Thomas, after calling attention to the humiliation and damage that race preference imposes on the minorities themselves, points out gently that the principle of equality ought not have to wait a quarter of a century to be vindicated.[13] The race preference that will be morally and legally wrong in three hundred months is morally and legally wrong now.

Sterba's Conclusion

On June 23, 2003, responding to the Supreme Court decisions in *Grutter v. Bollinger* and *Gratz v. Bollinger* handed down earlier that day, Jeffrey Lehman, the dean of the University of Michigan Law School, said: "By upholding the University of Michigan's Law School's admissions policy, the Court has approved a model for how to enroll a student body that is both academically excellent and racially integrated. The question is no longer whether affirmative action is legal; it is how to hasten the day when affirmative action is no longer needed." By contrast, that same day, Clint Bolick, vice president of the Institute for Justice, a private legal advocacy group, claimed that the Supreme Court's failure to answer "no" to the question of whether the government may discriminate on the basis of race in educational opportunities "means that Americans will con-

[11]O'Connor, *Grutter,* p. 29.
[12]Ibid., p. 31.
[13]Thomas, *Grutter,* p. 31.

tinue to be racially divided by their government, perpetuating more than two centuries of racial discrimination." Given these quite different reactions to these two U.S. Supreme Court's decisions, the controversy surrounding affirmative action and racial preference in the United States is sure to continue for some time to come.

In both decisions, there was a majority that held that it is constitutionally permissible to use racial preferences to achieve the educational benefits of diversity. In *Grutter,* the majority further approved the University of Michigan Law School's way of achieving those benefits. In Gratz, the majority rejected the university's way of achieving those benefits for its undergraduate program.

Yet without a doubt, the most important finding of the court was the constitutional permissibility of using of racial preferences to achieve the educational benefits of diversity. That, of course, had been the opinion of Justice Powell in *Bakke* (1978). But, as we have noted, there has been considerable debate about whether Powell's opinion represents the holding of the court in *Bakke,* and whether the Supreme Court's instructions in *Marks* (1977) could be applied to *Bakke* to help determine that holding. In *Grutter,* Justice Sandra Day O'Connor, writing for the majority, cut short that discussion by simply adopting the opinion of Powell in *Bakke* as the opinion of the majority in *Grutter.* "Today, we hold that the Law School has a compelling interest in attaining a diverse student body." In doing this, the court also deferred to "the Law School's educational judgment that such diversity is essential to its educational mission." The grounds for this deference is the First Amendment's protection of educational autonomy, which secures the right of a university "to select those students who will contribute to the "robust exchange of ideas" (quoting Powell). At the same time, the court is moved by evidence of the educational benefits of diversity provided by the law school and by briefs of the amici curiae (friends of the court):

> American businesses have made clear that the skills needed in today's increasingly global marketplace can only be developed through exposure to widely diverse people, cultures, ideas, and viewpoints.
>
> What is more, high-ranking retired officers and civilian leaders of the United States military assert that "[b]ased on [their] decades of experience," a "highly qualified, racially diverse officer corps . . . is es-

sential to the military's ability to fulfill its principle mission to provide national security."

Yet while affirming the constitutional permissibility of using racial preferences to achieve the educational benefits of diversity, the Supreme Court in *Grutter* accepted the law school's affirmative action admissions program at the same time that the court in Gratz rejected the undergraduate school's program.

The difference between the two programs, according to the majority in *Grutter,* is that the undergraduate program, by automatically assigning 20 points on the basis of race or ethnicity, operated in a too-mechanical, nonindividualized manner. If race or ethnicity is to be a factor in admissions, the majority contends, there needs to be "individualized consideration of each and every applicant." The law school, seeking to admit 350 students from 3,500 applicants, had used a more individualized admissions process that the court has now endorsed. The College of Literature, Science, and the Arts, facing the task of admitting 5,000 of 25,000 applicants, had chosen a more mechanical admissions process, still believing that it was sufficiently individualized to meet the court's requirement of strict scrutiny. Now the court has ruled that its requirement of strict scrutiny, which demands that any use of race or ethnicity in admissions be narrowly tailored to achieve the educational benefits of diversity, cannot be met unless each and every applicant's qualifications are individually considered. Accordingly, the University of Michigan will presumably have to significantly increase its undergraduate admissions personnel in order to provide this individualized consideration of each and every applicant.

Of course, colleges and universities are only required to adopt this individualized approach if they seek to use race as a factor in admissions. If a college or university only takes nonracial factors into account in its admissions process, it is free to use virtually any mechanical, nonindividualized admissions procedure it wants. For example, it can give 20 or 30 points (with, say, 100 points needed for admission) to sons and daughters of those who donate a certain amount of money to the school or to sons and daughters of alumni. It is only when race is taken into account (usually to the benefit of underrepresented minorities) that the court has imposed a significant constitutional hurtle. So although the Supreme Court decision in *Grutter* is surely welcomed for permitting the individualized use of racial preferences to achieve the educational benefits of diversity, the court's decision actually does little to achieve *real equality* of educational opportunity in higher education, which would require, among other things, significantly limiting the role of donor and legacy preferences in admissions (legacies presently constitute about 25 percent of the student body at select colleges and universities in the United States), and providing sufficient need-based support.

Objections to the *Grutter* Decision

One objection to the majority decision in *Grutter,* most forcefully stated by Chief Justice Rehnquist, was that the law school admitted African American applicants in roughly the same proportion to their number in the applicant pool as Hispanic and American Indian applicants, even though some African American applicants had grade and test scores that were lower than some of the Hispanic applicants who were rejected. Given that the law school was looking for a critical mass of each underrepresented group, Rehnquist finds the rejection of these Hispanic applicants hard to explain, particularly since the law school admits twice as many African Americans as Hispanics, and only one-sixth as many American Indians. How could the law school be admitting a critical mass of each group?

The law school, however, never claimed to be admitting a critical mass of each group. It was only aiming at that goal, and clearly it was far from reaching it with respect to American Indians. In addition, there surely are other relevant factors, such as the quality of essays and of letters of recommendation, that could explain why some African Americans with lower grade and test scores were admitted while some Hispanic applicants with higher grade and test scores were rejected. The objection that Rehnquist raises here had not been raised before. Nor was it raised in the oral argument before the Supreme Court. So it is not clear exactly how the law school would respond. Still, responses of the sort I have sketched here appear to support the law school's admissions process in this regard.

Justice Thomas, in his dissent, suggested that the court's reliance on social science literature showing the benefits of diversity at Michigan might require a similar reliance on social science literature showing that black students experience superior cognitive development at historically black colleges (HBCs) and that a substantial diversity moderates the cognitive effects of attending an HBC. Yet it is surely possible for HBCs to undertake supportive measures in light of such social science literature without violating the major recent ruling of the court with regard to HBCs. That ruling, which Thomas himself cites, holds that "a State cannot maintain . . . traditions by closing particular institutions, historically white or historically black to particular racial groups."[1] Thus, there is really no conflict with the *Grutter* majority here.

Thomas also questions how the court in *Grutter* can defer to Michigan Law School's educational judgment that diversity is essential to its educational mission when it did not defer to the Virginia Military Institute's (VMI) judgment that the changes in its "adversative" method of education required for admitting women into its educational program would be too great. Thomas suggests that the reason for the difference is that Michigan Law School belongs to the elite establishment whereas VMI does not.

But there are other explanations available. At the time of the VMI case, the U.S. military academies, as well as ROTC programs around the country, had for many years been admitting women into their programs, with the major effect being that the U.S. military now has much smarter military personnel, as judged by grades, test scores, and academic honors, than it would otherwise have had.[2] So while VMI cannot draw any support from comparable institutions and programs, Michigan Law School has the overwhelming support of educational institutions across the entire country, as the briefs of the amici curiae attest. Surely this justifies a difference in deference.

Justice Scalia's main objection to the *Grutter* decision, which Justice Thomas more expansively develops, is that Michigan does not have a compelling state interest in maintaining a law school that is both elite and diverse. If it wants to have a diverse student body, it

---

[1]*United States v. Fordice* (1992).

[2]Linda Bird Franke, *Ground Zero: The Gender Wars in the Military.* (New York: Simon & Shuster, 1997). Pp.16, 198.

can simply lower its standards and achieve the desired diversity without using affirmative action.[3] Thomas adds to this argument by noting that while Michigan Law School accounts for nearly 30 percent of all law students graduating in Michigan, only 6 percent of its graduates take the bar exam in the state, although about 16 percent elect to stay in the state. By contrast, Wayne State University Law School is said to send "88% of its graduates on to serve the people of Michigan." Thomas concludes that Michigan does not even have a compelling state interest in having a law school, let alone in having one that is both elite and diverse.

Of course, percentages don't tell the whole story here, and Thomas neglects to assess how well placed and influential that 6 or 16 percent of Michigan Law School graduates who stay or practice law in the state turn out to be. Moreover, the suggestion that Michigan could not have a compelling state interest in doing something that primarily benefits the rest of the country is extremely odd. It is like saying that Michigan could not have a compelling state interest in controlling the sulfur emissions of its power plants that cause, let's suppose, much of the acid rain that negatively affects New England states.

In response to *Grutter*, conservatives are now talking about using the affirmative action issue as a litmus test for future Supreme Court nominees, hoping thereby to overturn *Grutter*'s 5-to-4 majority when Justice O'Connor retires. In addition, there is talk of using referendums, like Proposition 209, that can frame the issue in terms of racial preferences rather than affirmative action and the benefits of diversity, as yet another way of undercutting the decision.

In the end, conservatives on this issue seem to be in the grips of an odd notion of racial equality. They seem unconcerned with the kind of evidence Justice Ruth Ginsberg cites in her dissenting opinion in *Gratz*, showing widespread discrimination against minorities in the workplace and the housing market. They do not call for increasing the meager efforts of the federal government to prosecute this sort of discrimination. Nor are they interested in overturning the more recent Supreme Court decisions that make it very difficult

---

[3]Actually, the desired diversity is not thereby guaranteed, as my discussion of the lottery alternative in my main essay and response shows.

to prove or correct for discrimination against minorities. Nor are they generally in favor of the large increases in spending that are needed to provide all students in the United States with at least a K-through-12 quality education. Rather, they are simply focused on eliminating diversity affirmative action, which benefits underrepresented minorities by way of benefiting the student body as a whole. But this selective concern with just eliminating certain benefits to minorities is far too narrow and inadequate an idea of racial equality. We should be very pleased, therefore, that at this moment in our history, the Supreme Court has opted for a broader and far more adequate ideal of racial equality. Still, much more remains to be done if we are to achieve that colorblind (racially just) and gender-free (sexually just) society in which affirmative action will no longer be needed.

BIBLIOGRAPHY

Badgett, M. V. Lee. *Economic Perspectives on Affirmative Action* (Washington, D.C.: Joint Center for Political and Economic Studies, 1995).

Bayles, Michael. "Reparations to Wrong Groups," *Analysis* 33 (1975).

Beauchamp, Tom L. "In Defense of Affirmative Action," *The Journal of Ethics* 2 (1998), pp. 143–58.

Bergmann, Barbara. *In Defense of Affirmative Action* (New York: Basic, 1996).

Bowen, William, and Derek Bok. *The Shape of the River: Long-Term Consequences of Considering Race in College and University Admissions* (Princeton: Princeton University Press, 1998).

Boxill, Bernard. *Blacks and Social Justice,* rev. ed. (Lanham, MD.: Rowan & Littlefield, 1992).

———. "The Case for Affirmative Action," in James P. Sterba, *Morality in Practice*, 4th ed. (Belmont, CA: Wadsworth Publishing, 1994), pp. 260–72.

Cahn, Steven, ed. *Affirmative Action and the University* (Philadelphia: Temple University Press, 1993).

Clayton, Susan, and Faye Crosby. *Justice, Gender, and Affirmative Action* (Ann Arbor: University of Michigan Press, 1992).

Cohen, Carl. "About Personal Consequences in the Academy when a Professor Opposes Racial Preferences." *Journal of Blacks in Higher Education,* no. 34 (Winter, 2002).

———. *Naked Racial Preference* (Boston: Madison, 1995).

———. "Preference by Race is Neither Just nor Wise," *Philosophic Exchange* (SUNY Brockport, 1998).

————. "Preference by Race in University Admissions and the Quest for Diversity," *Journal of Urban and Contemporary Law* 54 (1998), pp. 43–72.

————. "Race Preference and the Universities—A Final Reckoning," *Commentary*, 112/2 (September 2001).

————. "Should Federal Affirmative Action Programs Continue?" *Congressional Digest* (June–July 1996).

————. "The Uses of Race in Admission under *Regents v. Bakke*," *The Journal of Law in Society* (Winter, 1999).

Curry, George, ed. *The Affirmative Action Debate* (Reading, MA: Perseus, 1996).

De Zwart, Frank. "The Logic of Affirmative Action: Caste, Class and Quotas in India," *Acta Sociologica* 43 (2000), pp. 235–49.

D'Souza, Dinesh. *The End of Racism* (New York: The Free Press, 1995).

Dyer, Holly. "Gender-Based Affirmative Action: Where Does It Fit in the Tiered Scheme of Equal Protection Scrutiny? *University of Kansas Law Review* 41 (1993), pp. 591–613.

Eastland, Terry. *Ending Affirmative Action: The Case for Colorblind Justice* (New York: Basic, 1996).

Epstein, Cynthia. "Affirmative Action," *Dissent* (Fall 1995), pp. 463–65.

Epstein, Richard. *Forbidden Grounds: The Case against Employment Discrimination Laws* (Cambridge, MA: Harvard University Press, 1992).

Ezorsky, Gertrude. *Racism and Justice: The Case for Affirmative Action* (Ithaca, NY: Cornell University Press, 1991).

Fish, Stanley. "Reverse Racism, or How the Pot Got to Call the Kettle Black," *The Atlantic* (November 1993).

Fishkin, James. *Justice, Equal Opportunity and the Family* (New Haven: Yale University Press, 1983), pp. 88, 89, 105.

Forbath, William and Gerald Torres. "The Talented Tenth," *The Nation*, 15 December 1997.

Furman, Todd Michael. "A Dialogue Concerning Claim Jumping and Compensatory Justice," *Teaching Philosophy* 21 (1998), pp. 131–51.

Grapes, Bryan, ed. *Affirmative Action* (San Diego: Greenhaven Press, 2000).

Gross, Barry. "The Case against Reverse Discrimination," in James P. Sterba, ed., *Morality in Practice*, 4th ed. (Belmont, CA: Wadsworth, 1994), pp. 255–60.

Guinier, Lani. "The Real Bias in Higher Education," *New York Times*, 24 June 1997.

Gurin, Patricia. "The Compelling Need for Diversity in Higher Education." *Gratz v. Bollinger* (2000).

Gutmann, Amy, and Anthone Appiah. *Color Conscious: The Political Morality of Race* (Princeton: Princeton University Press, 1996).

Hacker, Andrew. *Two Nations* (New York: Ballantine, 1992).

Harwood, Sterling. "Affirmative Action Is Justified: A Reply to Newton," *Contemporary Philosophy* (1990), pp. 14–17.

Hettinger, Edwin. "What Is Wrong with Reverse Discrimination?" *Business & Professional Ethics Journal* 6 (1987), pp. 39–55.

Hiebert, Murray, and S. Jayasankaran. "May 13, 1969: Formative Years," *Far Eastern Economic Review*, 20 May 1999.

Kahlenberg, Richard. "Class, not Race," *New Republic*, 3 April 1995, pp. 21–26.

———. *The Remedy: Class, Race, and Affirmative Action* (New York: Basic, 1997).

———. "In Search of Fairness: A Better Way," *Washington Post*, June 1998.

Loury, Glenn. "How to Mend Affirmative Action," *The Public Interest* (Spring 1997).

Malamud, Deborah. "Affirmative Action, Diversity, and the Black Middle Class," *University of Colorado Law Review* 68 (1997), pp. 939–99.

———. "Assessing Class-Based Affirmative Action," *Journal of Legal Education* 47 (1997), pp. 452–71.

Massey, Douglas, and Nancy Denton. *American Apartheid* (Cambridge: Harvard University Press, 1993).

McGary, Howard Jr. "Justice and Reparations," *Philosophical Forum* 9 (1977–78), pp. 250–63.

Merritt, Deborah Jones. "The Future of *Bakke*: Will Social Science Matter?" *Ohio State Law Journal* 59 (1998), pp. 1054–67.

Morris, Christopher. "Existential Limits to the Rectification of Past Wrongs," *American Philosophical Quarterly* 21 (1984), pp. 175–82.

Moskos, Charles. "Success Story: Blacks in the Military," *The Atlantic*, May 1986.

Mosley, Albert, and Nicholas Capaldi. *Affirmative Action: Social Justice or Unfair Preference* (Lanham, MD: Rowan & Littlefield, 1996).

Murray, Charles. "Affirmative Racism," in James P. Sterba, *Morality in Practice*, 6th ed. (Belmont, CA: Wadsworth Publishing, 2000), pp. 251–57.

Neckerman, Kathryn M., and Joleen Kirschenman. "Hiring Strategies, Racial Bias and Inner-City Workers," *Social Problems* 38 (1991), pp. 433, 437–41.

Needlham, Amie. "Leveling the Playing Field—Affirmative Action in the European Union," *New York Law School Journal of International and Comparative Law* 19 (2000), pp. 479–97.

Newton, Lisa. "Reverse Discrimination is Unjustified," *Ethics* 83 (1973), pp. 308–12.

Nickel, James. "Should Reparations Be to Individuals or Groups?" *Analysis* 41 (1974), pp. 154–60.

Orfield, Gary, and John Yun. "Resegregation in American Schools," *The Civil Rights Project,* Harvard University (1999).

Orfield, Gary. "The Resegregation of Our Nation's School," *Civil Rights Journal* (Fall 1999).

Paul, Ellen Frankel. "Set-Asides, Reparations, and Compensatory Justice," in John Chapman, ed. *Compensatory Justice* (New York: New York University Press, 1991), pp. 97–142.

Pojman, Louis. "Straw Man or Straw Theory: A Reply to Mosley," *International Journal of Applied Philosophy* 17 (1998), pp. 169–80.

———. "The Case against Affirmative Action," in James P. Sterba, ed., *Morality in Practice*, 6th. ed. (Belmont, CA: Wadsworth, 2000).

Post, Robert, and Michael Rogin, eds. *Race and Representation: Affirmative Action* (New York: Zone, 1998).

Purdy, Laura. "In Defense of Hiring Apparently Less Qualified Women," *Journal of Social Philosophy* 15 (1984), pp. 26–33.

Roberts, Albert. *Helping Battered Women* (New York: Oxford University Press, 1996).

Rosen, Jeffrey. "Is Affirmative Action Doomed?" *The New Republic*, 17 October 1994.

Rosenfeld, Michael. *Affirmative Action and Justice* (New Haven: Yale University Press, 1991).

Russell, Diana. *The Secret Trauma* (New York: Basic, 1986).

Schnapper, Eric. "Affirmative Action and the Legislative History of the Fourteenth Amendment," *Virginia Law Review* 71 (1985), pp. 753–98.

Sher, George. *Approximate Justice* (Lantham, MD: Rowan & Littlefield, 1997).

Simon, Robert. "Affirmative Action and Faculty Appointments," in Steven Cahn, ed., *Affirmative Action and the University* (Philadelphia: Temple University Press, 1993), pp. 93–121.

Siegel, Reva. "The Racial Rhetorics of Colorblind Constitutionalism: The Case of *Hopwood v. Texas*," in Robert Post and Michael Rogin, eds., *Race and Representation: Affirmative Action* (New York: Zone, 1998), pp. 29–72.

Skrentny, John. *The Ironies of Affirmative Action* (Chicago: University of Chicago Press, 1996).

Sowell, Thomas. *Affirmative Action Reconsidered* (Washington, D.C.: The American Enterprise Institute for Public Policy Research, 1975).

———. *Civil Rights: Rhetoric or Reality?* (New York: William Morrow, 1984).

———. *Preferential Policies: An International Perspective* (New York: William Morrow, 1990).

———. *Race and Culture* (New York: Basic, 1994).

Steele, Claude, and Joshua Aronson. "Stereotype Threat and the Intellectual Text Performance of African Americans," *Journal of Personality and Social Psychology* 69 (1995), pp. 797–811.

Steele, Claude. "The Compelling Need for Diversity in Higher Education," *Gratz v. Bollinger* (2000).

Steinberg, Stephen. *Turning Back: The Retreat from Racial Justice in American Thought and Policy* (Boston: Beacon Press, 1995).

Sterba, James P. *Justice for Here and Now* (New York: Cambridge University Press, 1998).

———. *Three Challenges to Ethics* (New York: Oxford University Press, 2001).

Sturm, Susan, and Lani Guinier. "The Future of Affirmative Action: Reclaiming the Innovative Ideal," *California Law Review* 84 (1996).

Sunstein, Cass. "Why Markets Don't Stop Discrimination," in *Free Markets and Social Justice* (Oxford: Oxford University Press, 1997), pp. 151–66.

Taylor, Bron. *Affirmative Action at Work: Law, Politics, and Ethics* (Pittsburgh: University of Pittsburgh Press, 1991).

Taylor, Paul. "Reverse Discrimination and Compensatory Justice," *Analysis* 33 (1973), pp. 177–82.

Tummala, Krishua. "Policy of Preference: Lessons from India, the United States and South Africa," *Public Administration Review* 59 (1999), pp. 495–508.

Wasserstrom, Richard. "Racism, Sexism and Preferential Treatment," *UCLA Law Review* 24 (1977) pp. 581–622.

Watkins, Steve. *The Black O: Racism and Redemption in an American Corporate Empire* (Athens: University of Georgia Press, 1997).

Weiss, Robert J. *We Want Jobs* (New York: Garland, 1997).

Weisskoff, Thomas. "Consequences of Affirmative Action in U.S. Higher Education: A Review of Recent Empirical Studies," *Economic and Political Weekly*, 22 December 2001.

Woo, Deborah. *Glass Ceilings and Asian Americans* (Lanham, MD: Rowan & Littlefield, 2000).

INDEX

academic standards: admissions criteria and, 134–35, 138–39, 163, 336–37; curriculum corruption and, 157–58, 163; diversity and, 92, 113, 323; eased requirements and, 157–58; incentives for excellence and, 109, 127–28, 297; lowering of, 113, 131, 132–46, 155–57, 159–63, 298, 335–36, 339; open admissions and, 144–45, 337; performance standards and, 125, 136; potential and, 138; race and ethnicity relationship, 131–32, 139; race-differentiated, 136, 137n.185, 154–55, 162–63; race-preference inferiority stereotype and, 110, 121, 163, 298; SAT/high school grades and, 112, 141–42; shortage of qualified minority applicants, 155–56; student intellectual profile and, 138
ACT, 139
Adamany, David, 120
Adarand Constructors, Inc. v. Pena (1995), 51n.49, 77n.99, 197, 224, 276, 347; on strict scrutiny, 223
Adarand Constructors v. Mineta (2001), 77n.100
admissions systems, 134–58, 163; alternatives to affirmative action, 269–72; athletes/ legacies preferences, 266, 267, 316–17, 335–36, 341, 342, 343;

candidate's potential and, 232–33, 277, 278, 341; comprehensive assessment and, 257–58; disguised inequities in, 149–51; diversity and, 90n.118, 91, 93, 244, 246, 326, 344–45, 347–48; high school top percentile, 41–42, 198, 269, 271–72, 303, 345; individualization and, 142–43; manipulations of, 154–55; minority critical mass goal, 309, 309n.7, 343, 345; "odds ratios," 150–51, 156n.213; percentage plans, 41–42, 198, 269, 271–72, 345; qualifications basis, 255–58, 277; qualifications definitions, 135; qualifications vs. universal equality in, 17–18; remedial affirmative action and, 232–33, 250; standards and, 134–45, 163, 336–37; three measures in, 138–39. *See also* grade point averages; standardized tests; University of Michigan; University of Michigan law school
affirmative action: alternative programs, 269–72, 303–4, 327–28, 345–46; arguments against, ix, 3–188, 251–72, 279–304, 306, 331–36, 338–40; benefits from, 333; benign vs. invidious distinction, 223–24; as bureaucratic industry, 146–48; Civil Rights Acts and,